Government and British Civil aerospace

Keith Hayward

GOVERNMENT AND BRITISH CIVIL AEROSPACE

A CASE STUDY IN
POST-WAR TECHNOLOGY POLICY

Manchester University Press

Published by
Manchester University Press
Oxford Road, Manchester M13 9PL
and
51 Washington Street, Dover,
New Hampshire 03820, USA

British Library cataloguing in publication data

Hayward, Keith
  Government and British civil aerospace.
  1. Aerospace industries – Great Britain
  2. Great Britain – Politics and government –
  1945 –
  I. Title
  338.4'8'62910941   HDw711.5

Library of Congress Cataloging in Publication Data

Hayward, Keith.
  Government and British civil aerospace.
  1. Aircraft industry–Government policy–Great
Britain. I. Title.
  HD9711.G72H39   1983   338.4'56291333'0941   82–20857

ISBN 0–7190–0877–8

Photoset in Plantin
by Northern Phototypesetting Co., Bolton
Printed in Great Britain
by Redwood Burn Ltd, Trowbridge, Wiltshire

Contents

Preface   vii

Chronology of major events 1943–81   ix

Abbreviations used in the text   xiii

Introduction   1

1 Establishing the Partnership, 1945–59   12

2 Confirming the Partnership, 1960–4   38

3 Subsonic Politics, 1964–70   69

4 Government, Rolls-Royce and the RB211, 1962–71   99

5 Controlling Concorde, 1962–81   124

6 Government and Civil Aerospace in the 1970s   153

7 From Private to Public Enterprise, the Monitoring and Control of Civil Aerospace, 1970–81   187

8 Conclusions   210

Notes   236

Appendices   257

Index   262

To my family

Preface

I first became interested in the relationship between the British civil aircraft industry and Government as a result of an article I wrote on the European Airbus. This was followed by an examination of the EEC's policy towards aerospace undertaken with colleagues from the Universities of Manchester and Lancaster. In the course of this latter study, I first came into contact with officials and industrialists. Talking to them, I discovered just how fascinating the whole post-war period had been in terms of civil aerospace policy-making. The result is this 'archaeology' of a civil technology, heavily and historically dependent on the state for financial assistance, and deeply affected by Government actions and political interests. Generally speaking, academic studies of British policy-making have tended to neglect industrial and technological subjects. The position is far better now than it was when I began work on this book, which I hope will contribute to our broader understanding of the interaction between Government and technological development in Britain.

My research was greatly helped by a number of interviews with industrialists, officials and ex-Ministers responsible for civil aviation and aerospace. Since many expressed a wish to remain anonymous, I would like to thank them all for their time and assistance. I would also like to thank my colleagues in the Department of International Relations and Politics at the North Staffordshire Polytechnic. They have been forced to listen, often at some length, to stories about aeroplanes, but have nevertheless helped me to refine my arguments and ideas. I owe a special debt to Dr Trevor Taylor, who, in the middle of his own sabbatical leave, took the time to read and to advise upon my manuscript. Thanks must also go to Mrs Sheila Berrisford and to Mrs Sue Goulborn for typing the manuscript, and to my father-in-law, Mr Laurence Corbett, for applying his headmasterly eye to my spelling and syntax. I would also like to express my gratitude to the Directorate and Governing Body of the Polytechnic for granting me sabbatical leave, during which most of my interview data were gathered. However, the deepest thanks of all must go to Martin Edmonds and to Professor Roger Williams who first stimulated my interest in technology policy, and who later encouraged me to research this area of governmental activity. The final responsibility for this book, and for any misjudgements, errors and omissions it may contain, remains my own.

Chronology of major events 1943–1981

1943 Brabazon Committee formed.

1945 Ministry of Aircraft Production absorbed into Ministry of Supply. Elaboration of the three-staged programme for civil aircraft development. Civil Aviation Act reiterates 'buy British' principle.

1946 Formation of Ministry of Civil Aviation.

1948 Avro Tudor crash; Court of Inquiry criticises system of centralised nationalised airline procurement. Hanbury-Williams investigation and report suggests reforms.

1948 and 1949 Civil Aviation Acts establish nationalised airline procurement on commercial basis; Minister authorised to direct purchases if considered to be 'in the national interest'. Legislative authority for continued Government sponsorship of civil aircraft and engine development.

1949 First flight of De Haviland Comet, world's first jet airliner.

1951 Conservative Government elected, committed to reducing state's role in industry. Private venture policy for civil aircraft development.

1952 PanAm orders Comet Three's. Boeing launches development of 707. Vickers V1000 launched for RAF transport requirement.

1953 Douglas launches DC8.

1954 Comet disasters; Comet One withdrawn from service. RAF orders V1000.

1955 Government rescues De Haviland aircraft company. PanAm order Boeing 707 and DC8. RAF cancels V1000, BOAC refuses civil version, prefers to rely on turbo-props for long-range routes. First flights of French Sud Caravelle, medium-range jet airliner.

1956 BOAC buys Boeing 707s for long-range services. BOAC investigates 'Empire route' jet airliner. Supersonic Transport Aircraft Committee formed. First flight of Vickers Vanguard, medium-range turbo-prop.

1957 Defence Review indicates substantial reduction in demand for military aircraft. Government announces that it intends to encourage the rationalisation of the aircraft industry through the direction of remaining contracts. BEA selects De Haviland 121 (Trident) as new jet airliner. Government delays permission as De Haviland unwilling to form part of larger group.

1958 BOAC orders Vickers VC10 for 'Empire routes'. De Haviland announces formation of Airco consortium to build DH121. BEA order DH121. Government policy statement declares private-venture/rationalisation strategy to be success.

1959 BEA requests major design change to DH121. Boeing launches 727. Ministry of Aviation formed, incorporating aircraft responsibilities of MoS and Ministry of Civil Aviation. Duncan Sandys becomes Minister, initiates acceleration of industrial rationalisation. STAC report. First opening to French on SST cooperation. SST feasibility studies let to industry.

1960 Formation of British Aircraft Corporation (BAC), Hawker Siddeley Aviation (HSA) and Bristol Siddeley Engines (BSE). Announcement of new procedures for launch aid. Vickers reveals crisis in VC10 development; BOAC orders Super VC10. BAC awarded SST design-study contract.

1961 Britain announces decision to seek membership of EEC. Anglo-American talks on SST cooperation break down. Cabinet authorises discussions with French on SST cooperation. BSE and SNECMA conclude agreement to develop civil supersonic engine (Olympus). Rolls Royce begins work on large fan engine. BAC 1–11 launched.

1962 Interdepartmental review of SST. BAC and Sud Aviation present SST outline. Anglo-French agreement to develop SST (Concorde).

1963 Corbett Inquiry into BOAC financial crisis; resignation of Chairman and Managing Director (Sir Matthew Slatterly and Sir Basil Smallpiece). Sir Giles Guthie appointed Chairman and Managing Director.

1964 Guthie plan for BOAC entails cancellation of VC10 orders. Government agrees to financial reconstruction in return for reduction in VC10 orders. Labour win General Election, Roy Jenkins appointed Minister of Aviation. Lord Plowden to chair Committee of Inquiry into Aircraft Industry.

1965 Cancellation of major military projects, including TSR-2. Publication of Plowden Report. BAC proposes 'Superb' for BOAC's high-capacity requirement. Anglo-French talks on civil and military aerospace collaboration. Anglo-French industrial proposals for 'Airbus'-type airliner. Official talks begin on Airbus. Rolls-Royce obtains launch aid for RB178 large-fan demonstrator. French reject British request to cancel Concorde.

1966 Ministry of Aviation absorbed by Ministry of Technology. Board of Trade takes over responsibilities for civil aviation. BAC refused launched aid for 'Superb'. BEA requests Boeing 727, 737 aircraft. Ordered to 'buy British'. A300 details announced, HSA British airframe contributor. Rolls-Royce makes successful bid for BSE. BAC–HSA nationalisation – merger talks announced. BAC announces BAC 2–11; BEA requests permission to order 2–11.

1967 Failure of BAC–HSA nationalisation merger negotiations. Tony Benn becomes Minister of Technology. Rolls-Royce large-fan (RB207) named engine for A300. Memorandum of Understanding signed launching A300. BAC 2-11 refused launch aid. BEA directed to buy Trident 3. Rolls-Royce launches RB211 for consideration by Lockheed and McDonnell-Douglas. Government agrees to give launch aid for RB207/211 'Dual Programme'. Review of Concorde programme.

1968 Rolls-Royce signs contract with Lockheed for RB211. A300 design team announces smaller, less costly version, the A300B. RB207 cancelled. BAC reveals BAC 3-11. Anglo-French Concorde production finance agreements.

1969 British Government withdraws from Airbus. HSA signs private-venture contract to design and build A300B wings. IRC loan for Rolls-Royce. Concorde first flight. Elstub Report.

1970 Conservatives win General Election. Government refuses both launch aid for BAC 3-11 and opportunity to rejoin Airbus programme. Ministry of Aviation Supply takes over aerospace responsibilities. Government banks' rescue package for Rolls-Royce.

1971 Collapse and nationalisation of Rolls-Royce. Renegotiation of Lockheed contract. CPRS Review of Concorde. Department of Trade and Industry takes over responsibility for aerospace and civil aviation. Rayner Report leads to establishment of Ministry of Defence (Procurement Executive) responsible for all aerospace contracts and programme monitoring (Concorde as sole exception). Cast and Europlane design consortia formed.

1972 Marshall Report (internal inquiry into state of aircraft industry). Sir Kenneth Keith appointed Chairman of Rolls-Royce (1971) Ltd.

1973 Government gives launch aid for HS 146. Yom Kippur War leads to large increase in fuel costs. Slump in airline market.

Concorde options collapse. Rolls and P&W begin negotiations on joint engine development.

1974 Labour win General Election. Tony Benn appointed Secretary of State for Industry. Anglo-French agreement to limit Concorde production. HS146 'suspended'. Formation of EURAC (Group of Six). Nationalisation of HSA and BAC announced. NEB established, and given responsibility for Rolls-Royce (1971) Ltd.

1975 Lord Beswick appointed Chairman-designate of British Aerospace (BAe). Publication of EEC Action Programme on European Aerospace (the Spinelli Report). Eric Varley replaces Tony Benn. Aircraft and Shipbuilding Industries Bill introduced.

1976 Aerospatiale signs letter of intent with Boeing. Dassault announces cooperative venture with McDonnell-Douglas. Boeing offers collaborative proposal to BAe. Aircraft and Shipbuilding Industries Bill reintroduced.

1977 BAe formally established. Formation of Joint European Transport (JET) consortium. Rolls–P&W link breaks down.

1978 Formal offer from Boeing to BAe to join in Boeing 757 programme with RB211-535 as launch engine. British Airways requests permission to order Boeing 757. Airbus Industrie announces formal launch of A310. JET development effectively terminated. UK Government decides to rejoin Airbus programme, and to finance RB211-535 for use on Boeing 757. BA allowed to order Boeing 757. HS146 relaunched.

1979 Conservatives win General Election. Government announces intention of selling up to half of BAe. UK Government write off BA's Concorde procurement costs. Clash between Sir Kenneth Keith and Chairman of NEB, Sir Leslie Murphy. Rolls-Royce taken out of hands of NEB. NEB Board resigns.

1980 Sir Kenneth Keith retires, succeeded by Sir Frank McFadzean. BAe 'privatised'. Rolls-Royce announces the Anglo-Japanese RJ500 engine.

1981 Rolls-Royce loses important Boeing 757 order to General Electric. Industrial launch of A320 (150-seat airliner). Lockheed announces intention to close L1011 production.

Abbreviations used in the text

AI Airbus Industrie
BA British Airways
BAe British Aerospace
BAC British Aircraft Corporation
BEA British European Airways
BOAC British Overseas Airways Corporation
BoT Board of Trade
BSE Bristol Siddeley Engines
CPRS Central Policy Review Staff
DH De Haviland
DoI Department of Industry
DoT Department of Trade
DTI Department of Trade and Industry
FAA Federal Aviation Authority (USA)
GE General Electric
HSA (or HS) Hawker Siddeley Aviation
ICAO International Civil Aviation Organisation
IRC Industrial Reorganisation Corporation
JET Joint European Transport
MoA Ministry of Aviation
MAP Ministry of Aircraft Production
MoD Ministry of Defence
MoD (PE) Ministry of Defence (Procurement Executive)
MTCA Ministry of Transport and Civil Aviation
MoS Ministry of Supply
NEB National Enterprise Board
PAC Public Accounts Committee
PanAm Pan American Airlines
P&W Pratt and Whitney
RAE Royal Aircraft Establishment (Farnborough)
RR (or Rolls) Rolls-Royce
SBAC Society of British Aerospace (formerly Aircraft) Constructors
SST Supersonic Transport
STAC Supersonic Transport Aircraft Committee

Sud   Sud Aviation
TARC   Transport Aircraft Requirements Committee.

Introduction

The second world war was a watershed in the history of civil aviation. The logistical demands of global war confirmed the feasibility of regular, long-range transportation by air of goods and personnel. Moreover, through the stimulus of military requirements, dramatic improvements were made in the design of aircraft, aero-engines and ancillary equipment. The most significant of these was the pioneering, especially by the British, of the jet engine. Although the jet has not had as radical an effect on the economics or the design of the airliner as the aerodynamic and structural innovations of the interwar years had, it nevertheless caused a second revolution in the development of civil aircraft. The jet was far more powerful than the piston engine, and while initially it was less efficient, eventually, by allowing the construction of much larger and heavier air frames, it reduced substantially the costs of airline operation.[1] The jet airliner therefore both responded to, and helped to create, an explosive demand for air travel in the post-war years. The market for civil aircraft grew commensurately, and by the late 1950s civil development was beginning to assume a substantial proportion of the aircraft industry's business.

However, post-war changes in the scale of civil production were not without their costs or problems. Most significantly, the financial outlay involved in launching a civil type became increasingly burdensome. For example, in developing its first jet airliner, the DC8, Douglas lost $109 million between 1959 and 1960 and had to write off $298 million spent on development and production losses up to 1960. The development of larger, more complicated aircraft and engines required a longer lead time between gestation, production and revenue earning. This not only increased the cash-flow needs of the manufacturer, but also put a premium on accurate technical and commercial judgements. With longer replacement cycles, the price of market failure rose; it became more difficult, and certainly more expensive, for a firm missing out on one generation of aircraft to challenge for success in the next. In short, although the rewards of civil aerospace increased in the post-war years, so did its costs and risks.

Internationally, civil aerospace has always been subsidised to some extent by the state. Technical and commercial initiatives may have come from industry (publicly or privately owned) but money for the launch of new projects has often come from public sources. The civil sector has benefited hugely from military expenditures, and from technological advances stemming from defence programmes. Profits earned from defence contracting have similarly helped firms to finance civil production. Governments have also extended direct assistance for civil development by giving repayable loans on favourable terms, by influencing domestic airline procurement, by the imposition of direct or indirect protection against imported equipment, or by financing the export of civil aerospace products.[2] With variations from country to country, either regularly or periodically, the hand of government has reached out to encourage and to protect civil aerospace. Under these conditions, the development of civil aircraft and engines can hardly be regarded as a wholly commercial business, with investment decisions dependent entirely on the judgement of a free market.

In Britain, the dependence on government has been especially marked. As a deliberate act of policy, the post-war Labour Government financed a programme of civil prototype development in order to facilitate the recovery of civil production after a wartime hiatus. Even during the 1950s, when the Conservatives stressed private venture development, direct aid was still provided for some advanced projects and a 'buy British' doctrine was maintained as a basis for public sector procurement. Since the 1960s, when launch aid was reintroduced for suitable aircraft and engines, no major project has been developed without some measure of Government help.

Between 1945 and 1974, £1504 million (1974 input prices) was spent directly on civil aerospace, two-thirds being allocated after 1960. Equally notable was the fact that between 1962 and 1970, the proportion of public to private capitalisation changed from 10 per cent to over 75 per cent.[3] Since nationalisation in the 1970s, most launch capital has been provided by public sector borrowing or by private capital backed by Government guarantee. Most of the industry's basic research has been supported by work done by the various Government Research Establishments, particularly at the Royal Aircraft Establishment (Farnborough) and the National Gas Turbine Establishment. Additionally (although this has diminished in significance lately), by requiring the public sector airlines to purchase the products of the indigenous industry, regardless of additional operating costs, the Government has helped to ensure the existence of a publicly financed base market for British aircraft or engines.

The significance of civil production to the British aircraft industry has also grown steadily. In 1960, civil aerospace represented one-eighth of expenditure on military research and development; by 1967 it was a quarter and rising. In 1977, civil business accounted for a third of the industry's annual turnover. The sales of civil aircraft alone, especially in terms of exports, matched those of military types. Moreover, the Department of Industry calculated that between 1945 and 1971, either through exports or by saving on imports, the civil aircraft sector had contributed over £8000 million to the balance of payments.[4]

Individual projects have also been associated with political controversy. Most spectacularly, the Concorde Supersonic airliner, built in collaboration with the French, has cost the UK taxpayer, depending on how the figures are calculated, between £800 and £2000 million.[5] It has been one of the worst examples of escalating development costs and an utter commercial failure. Equally dramatically, the development of the RB211 aero-engine caused the bankruptcy of Rolls-Royce, perhaps one of Britain's most prestigious 'blue chip' companies. Other projects have, from time to time, been the centre of major political disputes, often related to the directed purchase by a nationalised airline of a British aircraft and, in later years, have been the focus of intense diplomatic activity. In short, civil aviation has often had a high political salience and technological decision-making in this sector has consequently become heavily politicised.

To a large degree, of course, the British aerospace industry as a whole has depended on Government. Few other industries can (or would want to) claim a comparable depth and variety of experience of Government involvement in their affairs. The liaison has grown and expanded since the early days of aviation, when military interest first precipitated the relationship, to include all phases of manufacturing and virtually every aspect of aerospace technology. Governments have been concerned not only with setting overall strategic objectives for the industry, but also with the minutiae of design, development and production. If military demands still provide a significant motivation for maintaining the connection, wider issues of national technological competence, the perceived value of the industry to the economy and, latterly, an international collaborative context, have drawn industry and government even closer together.

The importance of Government in the functioning, indeed to the existence, of the industry, was clearly and unequivocally stated by the Plowden Report of 1965;

> The aircraft industry differs from most other industries in that it depends on the Government for its very existence. An examination of the proper role of, say, the motor car or machine tool or chemical industries might lead to suggestions of ways in which Government could help the industry to change its size or structure or efficiency. But any Government act would be marginal. On the other hand, a decision to buy all future defence equipment from abroad would kill the aircraft industry. Thus the basic question is whether the Government should continue to act so as to keep an aircraft industry in existence.[6]

Although there are other industries with similar characteristics, and although the general trend is still toward more rather than fewer industries having ties with the state, aerospace is, to reiterate, significant as being one of the first to establish close links and notable for the depth and variety of the association.

Relations between the two parties have seldom been easy. Indeed, as Reed puts it, the story of the British aircraft industry since the war has been 'marred by a series of shuddering starts and stops stemming from its tumultuous, abrasive and largely unhappy relationship with successive governments'.[7] On many occasions each has been bitterly resentful of the demands and thoughtlessness of the other. Conflicts have raged over decisions affecting projects and their costs, as well as over the future of industrial development. Naturally enough, some of the tension has been a direct result of private industry being so dependent on public money and of private enterprise being so close a servant of the interests of the state. Governments have been criticised for the privileges apparently extended to the aircraft industry, the extravagance with which public money has been invested in unsuccessful projects, the weak control exercised over costs, revelations of excessive profits on defence contracts, and the absence of an immediately evident return to the economy. Indeed, the dependent condition of firms led to calls for the outright public ownership of the industry.

Since the early 1970s, with varying degrees of enthusiasm on the part of the Government of the day, the industry has been nationalised. Yet the fact of public or private ownership has not seriously affected the nature of the relationship between the Government and the industry. During the 1920s and 1930s, once having rejected public ownership of the industry following the first world war, the Government agreed to limit its orders to a 'magic circle' of established manufacturers. Military contracts were closely supervised by Air Ministry and Admiralty officials. There was even one case of officially inspired competition between 'private' and 'public' enterprise in the development of the R100/R101 Airships. The second world war naturally brought strict controls over development and production in private industry. Even the post-war Labour Government, while set on nationalising other industries heavily dependent on public money or vital to the economy, asserted that it was unnecessary in the case of aviation because 'private enterprise does not exist in the aircraft industry'.[8] In the 1950s, non-interventionist Conservatives imposed a fundamental reorganisation of privately owned companies, using the Government's power over the allocation of contracts and the promise of money for civil development, to bring about a much needed degree of rationalisation to a fragmented industry.*

The significance of a growing reliance on public money and

* See Appendix 4, for details of structural changes in the British aircraft industry.

Government policy on the part of a private sector industry struck Plowden as worthy of special mention, and the Report uniquely singled out one piece of oral evidence for quotation:

> In the aircraft industry, many new factors have accumulated in recent years, the combined effect of which has been to dilute the classical advantages of private enterprise. The industry is dependent to an increasing extent upon Government policy, Government decision-making, and Government money: as a consequence one must accept participation of Government agencies in many domestic issues normally a concern to a Company's management only. It stands as an island of commercial activity surrounded by public authorities and is dominated by issues of public policy outside of its control.[9]

In the 1960s, the Labour Government attempted, unsuccessfully, to acquire a controlling interest in the airframe sector; nevertheless, the Government continued to play a vital role in the industry's civil and military business. In 1971, in the aftermath of the Rolls bankruptcy, the Conservatives nationalised the firm 'in the national interest'. They too, even though at the time endeavouring to 'disengage' from industry generally, believed that aerospace was a special case requiring state aid.

When, in 1976, Labour introduced legislation which led to the nationalisation of the airframe industry, the dependence on public money and Government policy was offered as a major reason for public ownership. It would, Ministers suggested, end the 'confusion of roles' which existed in the relationship between state and industry. Similarly, it would obviate the need for close Government monitoring of industrial activities essential when public money was spent in the private sector. Naturally, however, public ownership would not affect the Government's participation in 'corporate or strategic level' decision-making.[10] Since then, the Conservatives, led by Margaret Thatcher, have enacted measures designed to reintroduce a degree of 'privatisation' in the industry. However, it remains to be seen whether private capital will now be more willing than it has been in the past to invest in the aircraft industry. Certainly, one cannot readily envisage a diminution of Government interest in and concern for the industry's affairs.

It seems unlikely that the question of ownership, certainly in recent years, has ever made much difference to the substantive relationship between Government and the aerospace industry and their partnership in development. Whether the industry has been nationalised or privately owned, Government has been directly or indirectly involved in the launch of most major programmes; the management and control of development, especially of costs, has been a continually troublesome issue; and there have always been strong institutional links between the two parties. The advent of international cooperation requiring the Government to negotiate technical and commercial agreements with other countries, to participate in transitional management structures and to defend national industrial interests in a cooperative context, has increased still further its role in corporate policy making.

Governmental involvement in civil aerospace, however, has been an area of particular controversy. To a significant extent, the military sector has possessed an element of self-justification on the ground that the state's concern to maintain independent production is consistent with national security. On the other hand, the launch and development of civil aircraft and engines has associated the state with technical, commercial and managerial decisions which many have argued are simply not the province, or within the competence, of government. In any case, the British civil aircraft industry has rarely been able, by dint of its own profitability, to establish an independence from the state which companies in the United States have been able to claim.

The need for public assistance in the financing of a civil technology is generally explained by the inadequacies of the private capital market in undertaking large-scale, advanced technological enterprise. It is said that investment is deterred by the sheer scale of the commitments involved, the long period of gestation before profits can be earned, the problems of technological uncertainty, with the attendant difficulties of accurate cost estimation, the effects of inflation over this timescale, the cash-flow problems resulting from all of these factors, and the uncertainty of markets and indeed of ultimate profitability.[11] It has also been suggested that aid is essential because Britain's main competitors receive it, and because the rate of return on defence contracting has been insufficient to allow the build up of the necessary financial reserves for private venture development.[12] Similarly, because British firms have been smaller than many of their foreign counterparts, they have been undercapitalised and have had limited R&D and production capacity.

However, the strongest deterrent to private investment surely must be the industry's poor record of profitability. Despite a string of fine, technically sound projects, commercial success has eluded all but a few British aircraft. Table 1 gives some indication of the scale of the problem. Although it does not do proper justice to the more successful engine sector, it shows nevertheless the relative production figures for most American, British and European turbine-powered civil aircraft developed since the war. Another measure of the lack of return is that the Government received less than £150 million (1974 input prices) from the levy on sales applied to all launch-aided projects up to 1974.[13]

Although Sir Frederick Handley Page once asserted that the role of the state was to 'provide facilities for fattening the goose which will lay the golden eggs', successful projects have been in short supply.[14] Without Government aid, it is clear that the survival and growth of the British civil aircraft industry since the war would have been doubtful. Sir Arnold Hall, Chairman of Hawker Siddeley Aviation, summarised in 1970 the importance of public support in maintaining the health of a British civil aerospace industry:

Table 1 Civil aircraft production 1956–79

Type	Country of origin	No. built or on order	Class
Boeing 707	US	941 [a]	Long-range jet
DC8	US	556	
VC10	UK	34	
CV990	US	37	
Comet One	UK	11	Medium-range jet
Boeing 720	US	154	
Boeing 727	US	1,720 [b]	
Boeing 757	US	40 [a, c]	
Trident	UK	117	
Comet 4/4C	UK	56	
Caravelle	France	280 [a]	
Comet 4B	UK	18	
Boeing 737	US	742 [b]	Short-range jet
DC9	US	1,034 [b]	
BAC 1-11	UK	230	
Mecure 100	France	10 [b]	
Electra	US	170	Turbo-prop airliners
Viscount	UK	440	
Vanguard	UK	44	
Britannia	UK	83	
748	UK	347 [b]	
Concorde	Anglo-French	16	Supersonic transport
Boeing 747	US	507 [a, b]	Long-range, wide-bodied
DC10	US	360 [b]	
L1011	US	216 [a]	
Airbus (A300)	European (inc. UK)	189 [b]	Medium-range, wide-bodied
Airbus (A310)	European (inc. UK)	62 [c]	
Boeing 767	US	148 [c]	
Boeing 757	US	150 [a, c]	

Notes
[a] British engined, or versions available with British engines.
[b] Still in production.
[c] New projects launched 1978/9.
Source Flight annual surveys of civil airliners and B. Gunston, *Early Jetliners*, London, 1980.

I have no hesitation in saying that if this country wishes to maintain a civil aircraft industry then it must also contemplate government as a lender of last resort making money available.[15]

As a proportion of public expenditure, civil aerospace has not absorbed anything like as much as the military sector, nor the amount of money which has been devoted since the war to civil nuclear energy. But equally, being a 'lender of last resort' has involved successive governments in the outlay of far from trivial sums.

The crux of the matter lies in the rate of return which the state has obtained, or apparently failed to obtain, from its financial involvement in a civil, commercially orientated technology. Successive Governments have frequently declared that the primary objective of supporting civil aircraft and engines has been to obtain a commercial return on public investment. However, the justification for continuing to finance development despite a generally poor sales record has embraced a wider range of goals. These have included employment, foreign policy interests and the improvement of Britain's balance of payments position. Moreover, civil aerospace has held an important place in the widespread and (as a general proposition) valid belief that public support for advanced technology is a significant factor in the promotion of economic growth. The relevance of civil aerospace as an example of public support for civil technology relates both to the duration of the policy, now over forty years, without establishing a clearly viable sector, and the lessons it reveals for any association by the state with comparable managerial and commercial choices. We have, on the one hand, a broadly continuous theme of 'strategic' involvement in development; decisions as to whether or not to support key projects; pressure applied to the public sector airlines to buy British aircraft; the effects of government policy towards industrial structure and ownership; and, in recent years, an international dimension as civil aerospace has become a factor in UK techno-diplomacy.

On the other hand, the expenditure of public money, quite apart from the obvious political concern these projects often generate, has required Government to monitor and to supervise civil development. This 'tactical' involvement in civil aerospace has not been easy; indeed, on occasion it has become extremely troublesome. Since the end of the second world war, but especially since 1960, this aspect of policy has almost invariably illustrated a classic dilemma of public policy. This dilemma can be summarised as the 'independence–control' dichotomy. While Government is clearly obliged to oversee and to be accountable for a particular programme, it is usually felt to be desirable, even necessary, in order to secure successful outcomes, that the executive agency should be responsible for managerial control over day-to-day progress and over technical or commercial decision-making. Although, therefore, the Government as paymaster and a politically interested partner, should exercise some control over the executive of publicly sponsored activity,

... some measure of genuine independence is vitally important to effective performance. The contractor cannot perform its task effectively and cannot contribute creatively to the end sought unless it has enough freedom and the right kinds of freedom.[16]

The problem, of course, is to find the optimum balance between control and independence; one which provides Government with adequate supervision and sufficient information to monitor and review progress without superseding, undermining or obstructing the authority and judgement of the executive agent.

Governmental involvement in, and responsibility for, British civil aerospace development has frequently given cause for concern, either because of its impact on 'strategic' questions, or because of a failure to strike an effective balance between control and independence. This issue has, of course, not been confined to civil aerospace. Military developments have been the scene of many conflicts and disputes between state and industry. Similarly, virtually every area of publicly supported technology has suffered from at least one case of major cost escalation. However, because of its ostensibly commercial orientation, some of these problems have been felt in particularly acute forms in the development of civil aircraft and engines. Moreover, while the relationship between the aircraft industry and Government has frequently been difficult, industrialists have been especially unhappy with their dependence on the state and the impact of Government on civil projects. Sir Arnold Hall, giving evidence in 1971 to a House of Commons Select Committee, cited the then recent case of Britain's official withdrawal from a European civil project. As Chairman of Hawker Siddeley Aviation, he said that his company had been on the receiving end of changing government policy. He raised it as an example of the vicissitudes of publicly financed civil technology;

> One of the difficulties which we have . . . got to face . . . is that moods change because ministers change, but these projects do not change. They are governed by the laws of nature . . . They also take a long time, normally longer than the lifetime of governments and, in my opinion, decisions are made more pragmatically than those who suggest a high analysis would contend, because they are at the time subject to the moods, pressures and influences of the time . . . [T]hese changes going on underneath are quite inevitably disruptive. There will be those who say . . . that this is the price of democracy. All right the price must be paid, but it is not good for doing good engineering.[17]

Clearly tension does exist between the timescale of technological activity and that accepted as normal by politicians and officials. The temptation to mould projects to short-term policy needs is bound to be present.

There is a corollary to the vulnerability of programmes to changes in political interest and commitment. Once established, commitments to technically complex, large-scale, long-lead-time projects may serve to limit the Government's real freedom to control events. Advanced technologies generate powerful, technically fluent and articulate lobbies within Government and industry, shaping both the specialist and policy advice offered to Ministers. With projects spanning many ministerial careers, requiring the acquisition of a high level of knowledge to form an independent judgment, and with, perhaps, politically sensitive issues like unemployment dependent on decisions, the tendency is often to rely on the specialist or to postpone any decision which would fundamentally alter the course of development. Similarly, the emergence of a major commitment may be incremental, with no obvious point for a single, definitive decision. Ministers wake up suddenly to a large, perhaps irrevocable demand for further resources. Responsibility becomes attenuated over the years, and momentum rather than choice determines events.

Problems of control and policy coherence in civil aerospace have been further exacerbated by the adoption of international collaboration as a means of reducing the costs of development and widening the base market for aerospace products. Ostensibly, British participation in civil joint ventures has been for commercial reasons. However, political motives have frequently entered into key decisions, and Britain's position in turn has been affected by the political interests of other states. Collaboration has inevitably added to the difficulties of domestic control; parties to an international agreement insist on rights to involve themselves in the design, development and production of projects; specifications have to be concerted, usually necessitating some compromising of national requirements; design and production responsibilities will be shared, increasing the total cost over a comparable nationally produced aircraft; binding commitments, with or without satisfactory release provisions, may have to be accepted, constraining future freedom to take unilateral action; finally, and conversely, a project vital to one state depends on the continued interest of others. In Britain's case, the Government has also had to contend with diverging views and interests within the domestic industry about the value and direction of collaboration. No collaborative scheme has yet satisfactorily resolved the conflicting demands of national interests, differing national motivation, cross-national technical/cost monitoring, an equitable sharing of development, and industrial efficiency.

In his book on British nuclear weapons policy, Pierre suggests that the easiest way to explain a complex of technological and political events is to adopt a broadly historical approach. As technology is basically developmental, an underlying descriptive narrative tends to make better sense of an often bewildering array of projects, both actual and proposed.[18] Simple description is, of course, not enough; our objectives are to analyse the expanding scope of Government involvement in civil aerospace and to identify and evaluate the implications and problems associated with this expansion. Taken as a whole, therefore, the book progresses steadily from approximately the end of the second world war to the first few years of the Thatcher Government. However, the material is organised so as to focus on specific issues which tend to congregate around discussions of various, often interrelated aircraft and engines. Chapter 1 is an extended prologue, recounting both the post-war recovery programme instituted by Labour to re-establish civil production after a wartime hiatus and the limitations of Conservative attempts during the 1950s to base development on private venture financing. 1960 was the watershed: from this point the cost of Government involvement rose substantially and the problems of control and accountability steadily became more difficult to resolve. Chapter 2, therefore, examines the rationale and principles of launch aid; the acceptance by Government that it has to assume full responsibility for a 'support-through-the-market' policy; and, using the Anglo-French Concorde agreement as a focus, we establish the international theme.

Chapters 3, 4 and 5 analyse three major civil programmes which dominated the mid to late 1960s, which, indeed, continued to affect policy well into the 1970s and beyond. The first of these describes the launch of, and British participation in, a European medium-range wide-bodied airline, the A300 Airbus, and the relationship between this project and Rolls-Royce's decision to go for an American contract for its RB211 turbo-fan engine. This established a conflict of interest which shaped British civil aerospace policy for over ten years. Chapters 4 and 5, however, focus primarily on 'tactical issues'; the control and independence dichotomy. Chapter 4 concentrates on the relationship between Rolls and the Government over the RB211 programme and analyses the events leading to Rolls's bankruptcy in 1971. This was a clear case of a breakdown in launch-aid policy assumptions and built-in provisions for control over public money in the private sector. Chapter 5 has a similar story to tell, but here the Government nominally had a much more direct responsibility for development. It is essentially an examination of British management of the Concorde programme, but naturally some reference is made to the effects of collaboration on the maintenance of control. Overall, these three chapters describe conditions and events between Government and a largely privately owned industry.

In the course of the 1970s, these conditions changed. Rolls was nationalised following its bankruptcy; the airframe industry followed it into public ownership in 1977. However, the strategic and tactical issues facing Government did not become any easier. Chapter 6 analyses the interaction between the various domestic problems and interests and differing internationally orientated industrial strategies. Chapter 7 again looks to contemporary 'tactical' questions related to the control of civil projects within a nationalised aircraft and aero-engine industry. Finally, Chapter 8 summarises the narrative and analytical arguments and an assessment is made of the specific and general lessons of forty years of Government involvement in a civil, commercially orientated technology.

1

ESTABLISHING THE PARTNERSHIP, 1945–59

The post-war recovery programme

During the 1930s aircraft manufacturers had competed to build a truly economic airliner. This race was dominated and eventually won by the Americans and, by the end of the decade, British firms were lagging behind. This sufficiently worried the Cadman Committee, which in 1938 reviewed British Air Policy for the Chamberlain Government, to recommend the encouragement of comparable British civil designs. However, the more urgent demands of the pre-war rearmament programme led to the deferment of new civil projects.[1] In the spring of 1940, the Government finally stopped all civil production in order to concentrate on bombers and fighters. Transport aircraft were to be bought from or supplied by the United States.

The Americans, of course, capitalised on the expansion of military aircraft and continued the development of types which readily converted into civil airliners at the end of hostilities. Consequently, American companies were able to exploit the rapid growth of air travel which occurred after 1945. It was evident that the British aircraft industry would find it difficult to re-establish a civil capability against competition from technically far superior American airliners. This prospect was anticipated by the British Government, and from 1943 to the end of the war, preparations were made to help industry overcome this disadvantage.

The Brabazon Proposals

A focus for post-war reconstruction was provided by the Committee chaired by Lord Brabazon of Tara, remitted by the Cabinet to plan a programme of designs to be the basis for civil production at the end of the war. The Brabazon Committee began work in 1943 and by November 1945 it had detailed nine outline specifications (the 'Brabazon Types') to be sponsored and, where necessary, financed by the Government. The Committee, and especially its Chairman, also played an active role in encouraging and promoting interesting proposals from individual firms. In this way, the Committee acted as a useful intermediary between the industry, its potential domestic customers (the airlines and the military), and the Ministry of Aircraft Production (MAP).

The Committee had to work under very difficult conditions. Quite apart from the obvious fact that the war effort took priority over any civil work, the war itself was creating new opportunities, technical and commercial, for civil air transport. Naturally, many of the Committee's assumptions and much of its evidence were derived from pre-war notions about air travel. Accurate information about future trends, especially about developments in the United States, was hard to obtain and the exigencies of war ruled out elaborate surveys and design studies. The Committee did appreciate, however, the opportunity afforded by Britain's substantial lead in the field of jet engine design to leap-frog American superiority in conventional, piston-engined airliners. Indeed, four of the Brabazon Types called for either prop or turbo-jet engines.[2] In short, the Brabazon programme was a creditable, if not always accurate, prediction of future civil requirements. In spite of its limitations, it formed the backbone of Government policy towards post-war civil aircraft production.

As the war drew to a close, the MAP realised that the Brabazon programme had to be supplemented by projects which would be available earlier than the Brabazon Types. The MAP directed the conversion of bombers into civil transports and sponsored the construction of airliners based on bomber designs, the so called 'interim designs'. These would enable industry to get some kind of civil production underway as soon as possible. Even if this would not result in particularly advanced aircraft, firms would have something to sell and British airlines a domestic product to buy, while the more ambitious Brabazon Types were being developed. In effect, the MAP established a three-stage programme which the Labour Government inherited in the spring of 1945.

The new Government accepted the programme virtually unchanged, as well it might, for the approach adopted by the MAP was wholly consistent with Labour's general commitment to a planned, centrally directed industrial and economic recovery. More specifically, civil research, development and production could be integrated into the Government's overall approach to aircraft construction. The civil programme complemented the policy of maintaining a 'strategic reserve' of industrial capacity which would be available in time of war. Moreover, the sponsorship of civil production helped to ease the problems caused by the Government's decision to limit the procurement of new military types.[3] The Government also believed that its sponsorship of civil aircraft would lead to commercially successful projects. During the war, aircraft manufacturing had become one of the nation's most important industries and civil production would naturally help to maintain employment in and, hopefully, the profitability of a strategically and economically vital sector. The Government was also well aware of the value of civil development in protecting and improving the balance of payments during a particularly difficult period of sterling crises. Finally, there was considerable institutional pressure from the Ministry of Supply (which absorbed the MAP's functions in October 1945) to 'get on with the programme'.Officials were acutely conscious of the lead built up by the Americans and in their opinion, unless the programme was rapidly and comprehensively implemented, the gap would grow even wider.

By accepting a responsibility towards the British civil aircraft industry, the Government was naturally involving itself in the commercial activities of private firms. In the event of a project selling well, the Government's investment would be repaid through the R&D levy on each sale. Where an aircraft or engine failed to break even, or, worse, was cancelled, both parties would lose whatever they had invested in the enterprise. Even so, in this case the private company would still have had the experience of developing the aircraft which, presumably, would be of value in subsequent projects. Not every civil aircraft developed in this period was financed either wholly or in part by the state.[4] Similarly, the actual level of public expenditure involved some £78·7 million, compared with, for example, the £1,800 million (current prices) spent on military aircraft up to 1955.[5] The distinction between public and private investment, however, does not appear to have unduly worried the Government; indeed, Ministers tended to view the aircraft industry as a *de facto* public enterprise.[6] This was, therefore, one of the first British cases of Governmental involvement in civil, technology-based industry and an early example of fusion between public and private interests characteristic of much post-war economic activity.

Government involvement extended beyond simply providing finance for individual projects. The MoS acted as a central administrative agency for the aircraft built under its sponsorship. It was responsible for issuing the contracts for prototypes and for monitoring development through the old MAP wartime system of industrial overseers located in aircraft factories. The MoS also 'bought in' most of the ancillary items of equipment needed for development and supplied them as 'embodiment loan' to private industry. This was a cumbersome arrangement; for example, there were many outstanding but now irrelevant wartime contracts for embodiment loans to be sorted out and there was often considerable delay before vital equipment could be transferred to the civil programme. Still more contentiously, the MoS acted as the procurement agency for the nationalised airlines as well as dealing with all orders from private customers. Increasingly, the MoS system was criticised for its delays and the barriers it erected between the industry and its market.

The Government defended centralised control on the grounds of both efficiency and equity. On the one hand, it allowed the Government to incorporate civil RD&P into an overall strategy for the aircraft industry. This led to greater efficiency because the MoS was able to effect 'vast economies by ensuring that the common interest in development leads to the best results for all concerned'. On the other hand, as all the interested parties in aircraft development and production were consulted in decision making, the MoS could ensure that no one element dictated the pattern of future development and obtained too great a share of available resources. In short, the MoS was seen as a referee in the struggle between civil and military requirements, ensuring that everyone got 'fair play'.[7]

The Air Corporations, BEA and BOAC, were not convinced that their interests were, in fact, being protected by these procedures. The Government had made it quite clear that they would have to 'buy British' aircraft and that, in effect, meant taking what the MoS and the recovery programme provided. The airlines were able to negotiate modifications to any aircraft ordered on their behalf, and where there was a choice between two comparable British types, an airline would usually be able to select the one best suited to its requirements. Of course, the Government was aware that the early products of the recovery programme were not as good as equivalent American aircraft, but the attendant difficulties had to be borne as an 'honourable legacy of the war'. Ministers were confident that by the end of the decade, once the Brabazon Types were available, British airliners would be 'second to none'. The air corporations, however, would just have to wait for better British equipment.[8]

Both BOAC and BEA, with varying degrees of enthusiasm, accepted that they would face some constraint on their freedom to buy aircraft outside of the United Kingdom, but they did object to what seemed like a permanent subordination of their commercial interests to those of the aircraft industry. Despite the MoS's claims to the contrary, it was clear that industrial needs had an overriding priority. The MoS did not have a direct responsibility for the airlines, that was the function of the newly formed and more junior Ministry of Civil Aviation. Tension between the two ministries did not help the airlines' case, and increasingly they felt that the MoS was an unnecessary intermediary between them and their suppliers. If they were going to buy British, they believed that they had some right directly to determine the type of aircraft they would order as well as the source of supply.

Relations between the airlines and the various aircraft manufacturers were, on the whole, quite good. BEA and Vickers worked together to produce the Viking 'interim design' and, in spite of an initial setback, did so again to develop the highly successful turbo-prop Viscount. Similarly, BOAC and De Haviland shared the credit of developing the world's first jet airliner, the Comet. However, because they were not directly responsible for the cost of development and for the price charged for each aircraft, there was a tendency for the airlines to insist on a steady stream of expensive modifications. More worrying for all concerned, most of the interim designs were disappointing and only a few of the Brabazon Types looked like being much better.

The Hanbury-Williams Report
The Government remained optimistic about the future for both the airlines and the aircraft industry, but both the system and its products faced mounting criticism from the air corporations and the Conservative Opposition. Some form of help to the aircraft industry might be desirable, at least in the short term, but as matters stood, neither industry nor its customers were benefiting from close Governmental supervision and control. It was time, perhaps, to adopt a more commercial system. The Government's confidence in its approach was severely shaken by the 1948 Court of Inquiry report into the crash of the Avro Tudor, an interim design developed for BOAC. The report concluded that many of the problems in design which had dogged its construction had been caused by the MoS-centred system of procurement. Early in 1948, George Strauss, the Minister of Supply, admitted that the Government was itself not 'fully satisfied with the procedures' for developing and procuring civil aircraft. He announced that steps were being taken to find ways of improving matters and Sir John Hanbury-Williams, the Chairman of Courtaulds, had been asked to lead an internal inquiry.[9]

Hanbury-Williams's recommendations were based on the logical assumption that the customer was likely to be the best judge of what it wanted from an airliner. From this premise, it was suggested that the most promising route to commercial success in civil aircraft development lay in allowing direct and unhindered collaboration between the manufacturers and airlines. In short, the main conclusion of the inquiry was that the Government should abandon its centrally directed, programmatic approach to civil aircraft development. The nationalised airlines should be allowed to negotiate directly with industry and if Government help in the launch of new aircraft was needed, it should come after, and not in advance of, orders from a major airline.[10]

In defence of the programme, it did lead to three outstanding projects, including the world's first turbo-prop and prop jet airliners, the Vickers Viscount and the De Haviland Comet. The third, the De Haviland Dove feeder-liner, was privately financed, but as a Brabazon Type, it could accurately be credited to the recovery programme. The Viscount, ultimately the most successful British civil aircraft produced since the war, survived an initial decision by BEA in favour of its piston-engined competitor, the Airspeed (De Haviland) Ambassador, partly because Vickers continued to pay its share of development costs, but equally because the MoS maintained its support for the project.[11]

The Comet would have been the technological crown of the recovery programme; it was certainly regarded as Britain's best opportunity to beat the Americans. Originally conceived by the Brabazon Committee as a transatlantic mail-carrier, De Haviland convinced BOAC and the MoS that a fully fledged airliner was both feasible and commercially a better use of resources. Although many aspects of its design were conventional, the Comet was a gamble. Decisions to use readily available engines also adversely affected the Comet One's operating economics. But the promise of greater speed led BOAC to accept its limitations; as an official BOAC report put it 'the aircraft represents a great improvement over any existing or proposed aircraft'.[12] Prototype development was financed by the MoS, but De Haviland carried the greater part of subsequent development on the basis of a BOAC order placed in January 1947. The Comet's first flight in July 1949 seemed to symbolise both the aircraft industry's and the nation's recovery from the rigours of war. Technically and commercially, the Comet One would only hint at the revolutionary impact that the jet would ultimately have on civil aviation, but for the British civil aircraft industry, as much as for De Haviland, it still represented a lead over the Americans of nearly three years.[13] This bold venture exemplified the partnership between private industry, a nationalised airline and the state, which the Government had hoped to achieve on a much broader front for civil aircraft development generally. In this instance it was a partnership much envied by American manufacturers who were unable or unwilling to take similar risks unaided.[14]

Sadly, most of the others in the programme were disappointing and some were quite disastrous, commercially and technically. The piston-engined Bristol Brabazon, Type One of the Brabazon series, was both over-sophisticated and some three years behind economically superior American piston-engined types. Built at a total cost of £13 million, it never entered airline service. Development continued into the early 1950s, when it was finally cancelled.[15] The recovery programme probably contained too many projects but, even more seriously, the MoS was insufficiently selective and ruthless in its approach to either contract allocation or the cancellation of ailing projects. Some firms unquestionably exploited the system to acquire a capability in civil development when it might have been better if assistance had been confined to firms with some past experience of building civil aircraft. The wide distribution of contracts also helped to encourage industrial fragmentation where rationalisation might have been more advantageous. Similarly, the MoS and the Government may have been too ready to oppose licensed construction of American aircraft. This would have been an equally quick way to rebuild a basic civil industry, with proven designs and one which would not have obstructed the development of the technically more advanced jet-engined projects. Various proposals were turned down, usually because of foreign exchange costs and because the MoS felt that the Americans would deny British firms access to data which would help them in subsequent independent development.[16] However, it was also true that both industry and the MoS simply underestimated the problems of re-entering the market during a period of rapid commercial and technological changes and following such a long hiatus in civil development.

The Government accepted the basic recommendations of the Hanbury-Williams Committee, and the Civil Aviation Acts of 1948 and 1949 reflected some of its conclusions. This legislation stated that the Government retained an authority to use public money to support the 'design, manufacture and maintenance' of civil aircraft and engines. The air corporations, however, were given the freedom to choose aircraft which, in their opinion, best suited their commercial needs. This was not an unqualified victory for the airlines: for not only was the responsible Minister enabled to issue 'general directives in the national interest' affecting airline policy, but the Government would also be able to exert considerable influence over airline procurement through its control over airline borrowing. In practice, the nationalised airlines would still be expected to 'buy British' but at least they would be able to negotiate direct with the manufacturers and would not have to accept a programme of development defined and directed by the MoS. These changes represented a move towards a more commercial approach to civil development without removing the notion that Government could and should stand as the lender of last resort. Government also still retained considerable scope to involve itself directly and indirectly in the civil aircraft industry, if it so wished. In 1951, the Conservatives returned to power determined progressively to reduce still further overt support for civil projects. After six years of Government support, the new administration believed that the aircraft industry was strong enough to finance its civil projects as private ventures. The power to intervene, directly or indirectly, in civil development would, however, remain in the hands of any Government; a power which the Conservatives, despite their liberal economic doctrines, would use during the 1950s.

Private venture policy

Conservative policy towards civil aircraft production did not appear as a grand statement of principles and intentions. Until 1958, policy, in fact, consisted of a series of separate decisions on individual projects. There were, however, two related themes underlying the Conservative approach: a general feeling that the fusion of public and private interests which had emerged under Labour should cease and, consequently, that private industry should, in all but the most exceptional circumstances, finance its own civil, commercially orientated development. This was again consistent with a general policy towards industry; the new Government was set on dismantling the last vestiges of wartime planning and central control over industry and applying liberal economic doctrines in relation to state intervention. Although in certain respects the aircraft industry escaped a stringent application of liberal philosophy, the private venture approach to civil production did have a significant effect on development. The manufacturers would have to accept the burdens and disciplines inherent in private venture activity. There would be no more speculative development financed by the state. The Government would not entirely abandon its obligation to help the civil sector, but this would have to be confined largely to retaining the 'buy British' principle for the air corporations. The Government believed that a private venture policy would also lead to less overt interference and involvement in the selection and development of individual projects.

The Comet failure

The aircraft industry certainly seemed to be in a healthy enough state and the time was therefore ripe for a change in policy. The Viscount was going to sell well, and there was every hope of repeating this success with the larger turbo-prop airliners. Indeed, the Bristol Britannia, a long-range turbo-prop ordered for BOAC in 1947, was the last aircraft to be sponsored as part of the recovery programme. The Comet, of course, promised the most. It entered service with BOAC in May 1952 and, although it was not as economic to operate as piston-engined aircraft, it quickly demonstrated the passenger appeal of jet travel. With its monopoly on jet operations, BOAC was able to fly the aircraft at a profit.[17] The prospect of larger and genuinely economic Comets excited the world's airlines. In 1952, Pan American placed an order for three Comet Threes, with an option on seven more. This appeared to be the vital breakthrough, even if PanAm's order was probably aimed at getting American firms to launch jet airliners.[18]

The Government certainly recognised the importance of the Comet and the lead it represented over the Americans. Speaking in the House of Lords in July 1952, the Minister for Materials, Lord Swinton, described how Britain had got such a lead in civil jet aviation that 'we may not only get orders which airlines all over the world may want to place, but we may have collared the market for a generation'. It was, in fact, he said, 'one of the greatest chances we have ever had'.[19] Along with the buoyant state of the military sector, a result of the Korean War rearmament programme and American-sponsored exports of British equipment, there was no reason to suppose that industry would not be able to sustain its own civil activities. The Treasury was happy to see the end of what it regarded as a wasteful and unnecessary use of public money and even industry was not entirely disappointed to see the back of MoS sponsorship. Significantly, the steep rise in R&D costs precipitated by the jet airliner had yet to take full effect so morale was high within the industry and the future for British civil aircraft development, with or without state aid, seemed to be relatively cloudless.

Then, early in 1954, following two fatal crashes, BOAC suspended its Comet operations and the aircraft's Certificate of Airworthiness was withdrawn. After an intensive and pioneering exercise of technical detective work, the cause was eventually revealed to have been structural failure due to cracking of the aircraft's outer skin. While the experience led to new standards of testing and safety for the next generation of aircraft, the material costs to De Haviland and BOAC were high and the event came as an appalling shock to morale in the British aircraft industry as a whole. In the short term the problem was solved by strengthening the areas where the failure had been shown. Eventually, the later Comets were effectively redesigned, incorporating the latest fail-safe techniques up to the new standards laid down by the Air Registration Board.[20] The Comet 4 did beat the 707 into service across the Atlantic, but it never fulfilled the high commercial hopes of the early 1950s. The last Comet in airline service was withdrawn in 1981, but the airframe still soldiers on as the basis for the Nimrod strike/reconnaissance/airborne early-warning aircraft.

The wider impact of the Comet failure on British civil development was profound. For a short, but crucial period, BOAC turned against the idea of jet operation; some elements within the airline even went so far as to suggest that it was time to stop pioneering on behalf of the British aircraft industry and to seek the best aircraft available, regardless of their country of origin. Whitney Straight, BOAC's Chairman and an enthusiatic advocate of the Comet, was able to save it from outright cancellation, and in May 1955 BOAC ordered nineteen Comet Fours for its 'Empire' services to Africa and the Far East. However, BOAC decided that the turbo-prop was the 'right formula' for its important, long-range services, pre-eminently those across the North Atlantic.[21] BOAC's judgement in this respect was vital, for it effectively determined what type of long-range aircraft British industry could launch. Without BOAC's positive support, firms would not take on alone the financial burden and risk of development and the Government was certainly not going to provide money for new aircraft.

In the short term, the Government could not ignore the financial consequences of the Comet failure for De Haviland. The company was left with £15 millions worth of unsaleable aircraft, useless jigs and tools; the loss threatened a major military and civil producer with bankruptcy. The Treasury was prepared to let De Haviland sink, but the Government decided that in the national interest it had to mount a salvage operation designed to 'safeguard the public interest in the Comet and other projects'. In March 1955, the MoS ordered eighteen suitably modified Comet Twos for the RAF and advanced money for further development. Later, the Government provided £6·5 million in direct assistance to ease a cash-flow crisis. Government aid to De Haviland eventually totalled £10 million in loans and procurement contracts.[22] Not unnaturally, the MoS insisted on delivery of the RAF's Comets before De Haviland could return to developing the Comet for airline use. Although the Government's intervention undoubtedly saved De Haviland, the priority given to the military Comets also prevented any immediate attempts to salvage the technical and commercial lead generated by the Comet One.[23] The Americans were not deterred by the Comet failure. Boeing and Douglas especially had been considering jet designs since the late 1940s, but had considered it unwise to launch a jet airliner which was not optimised for economic operation across the Atlantic. The incentive to innovate, particularly for the market leaders, Douglas and Lockheed, was also constrained by their unwillingness to abandon known and profitable technology until forced to do so. The Comet One had come as a shock to American firms, and PanAm's order even more so. By 1952, however, more powerful and efficient engines were available, and the launch of American jet airliners was imminent. There was still considerable commercial uncertainty surrounding long-range jet operation and clearly development costs were going to strain corporate finances.[24] Boeing's decision in 1952 to launch a jet transport was therefore a bold gamble. In the first instance, Boeing's private venture 367–80 was aimed at the USAF's requirement for a long-range tanker–transport aircraft. Obviously, winning this contract provided Boeing with a financial cushion on which to launch the civil 707. However, the 707 differed quite substantially from the military KC-135 and Boeing had to support a very costly development programme. Beginning a year behind Boeing, and without the direct help of Pentagon money, Douglas launched the DC8, but with its reputation for producing fine airliners, this proved to be no real disadvantage. The 707 and the DC8 triggered a 'rush to jets'; within four months of PanAm's first order for both aircraft in October 1955, their sales totalled 221.[25] The British aircraft industry simply had nothing to offer, although the Comet Four did beat the Americans to the first North Atlantic jet service. By the end of 1956, the technical and commercial initiative in long-range airliners had passed once again to the United States.

The rapid spread of large, long-range jets effectively eclipsed turbo-props like the Britannia. Beset by technical problems, the Britannia entered service barely a year before the big jets and few airlines were prepared to buy what was a virtually obsolete technology. The turbo-prop lasted a little longer on short- and medium-haul routes, where the turbo-prop offered distinct economic advantages over the jet and where the jet's superior speed appeared to have little value. Vickers and BEA certainly felt that there was room for a larger successor to the Viscount. The Vanguard was duly launched in 1955 as a private venture on the back of a BEA order. At the same time, the French started development of a medium-range jet, the Sud Caravelle. Sponsored and financed by the French Government as part of its plan to rebuild the French aircraft industry, the Caravelle used British engines and many other items of British manufacture.[26] In the event, the Caravelle beat the Vanguard into service and BEA was faced with the prospect of jet competition. BEA had anticipated some of the problems that this would cause by ordering Comet 4Bs as an interim type while a new jet was built to its specification. Neither Vickers nor BEA expected the jet to sweep the turbo-prop from all major routes, but the passenger appeal of the jet proved to be overwhelming. By the end of the decade, all hopes for the large turbo-prop were virtually extinct, with disastrous consequences for Vickers and Bristol.[27]

We are, however, getting a little in advance of events. The first impact of foreign jets on the British aircraft industry was in the long-range sector of the market. Indeed, as we shall discuss, there was still a good chance of matching the French and leading the Americans in short- and medium-range types. The prospects were not so good for British long-range development. The failure to produce larger Comets after the Comet One's initial breakdown was one of the main factors in Britain's lost opportunity. Admittedly, the De Haviland rescue package amounted to a substantial modification in the Government's general attitude to the civil aircraft industry. However, there were other interests besides the Comet at stake and this exceptional act did not imply that the Government would return to a policy of sponsoring civil prototypes. Moreover, with BOAC set against buying big jets, the Government had no reason to suppose that the delay caused by its order for Comet Twos would injure the long-term commercial interests of the Comet. Having paid for a number of military aircraft, the Government would have been under pressure if it had not insisted on its order taking priority. To have delayed their construction in favour of the civil Comet, an aircraft only hesitantly supported by BOAC, would have threatened the credibility of the private venture policy before it had even been fully established.

V1000 and VC10

The combination of no public support for speculative development and BOAC's commitment to the turbo-prop effectively undermined an opportunity to stay in touch with the Americans. This was provided by the Vickers V1000, a long-range jet transport designed to an RAF requirement and started in the same year that Boeing launched the 367–80. In June 1954, Vickers was awarded a production contract for six aircraft to be powered by the new Rolls-Royce Conway engine. Vickers had earlier approached BOAC with a proposal for a civil version, the VC7, but the airline, fully committed to the Comet series and the Britannia, turned Vickers down. The military programme proceeded uneventfully, although it did prove to be more protracted and more expensive than either Vickers or the MoS expected. In the summer of 1955, under pressure to cut expenditure, the RAF had second thoughts about its need for a costly, custom-built transport. Preferring to protect its front-line aircraft programme, the RAF decided to buy Britannias instead of the V1000. The V1000 was cancelled in an advanced stage of development at an estimated cost of £4 million.[28]

At this point, Vickers again canvassed the possibility of launching the VC7. BOAC's reaction was extremely cool. In spite of the claims being made by Boeing and Douglas, BOAC was still convinced of the superiority of the turbo-prop. The airline accepted that a big jet would eventually supersede the Britannia, but that this would not occur until the early 1960s. The civil V1000 had the support of some officials at the MoS and, reportedly, that of the Minister, Reginald Maudling. The Treasury naturally opposed giving Vickers any aid for a civil aircraft, especially when the firm was prepared to launch the Vanguard with its own capital. In any event, even if he was personally sympathetic, Maudling was not going to support a large-scale project without a major order. The crux of the matter remained BOAC's disinclination to buy the V1000. The Canadian airline, CP, was interested, but no other customer emerged to provide Vickers with a sufficiently large basis for development. Without the support of either BOAC, or an equally important airline, or the state, Vickers was not willing or, perhaps, able to carry the risk alone. In November 1955, just as the 'rush to jets' began, the V1000/VC7 was finally cancelled.[29]

Announcing his decision to the House of Commons, Maudling defended it by referring to BOAC's judgement that the turbo-prop would be viable well into the next decade. The lack of a long-range jet, he said, would not 'seriously damage' the British civil aircraft industry. 'All that we have not got', he explained dismissively, 'is a pure jet aircraft capable of crossing the Atlantic non-stop in the early 1960s.' Others, however, expressed amazement that the Government had allowed BOAC to reject the V1000 when many other airlines were flocking to buy 707s and DC8s. One Conservative backbencher called it 'one of the most disgraceful, most disheartening and most unfortunate' decisions ever taken by a Minister responsible for aviation. It was confidently predicted that BOAC would soon be asking for Government permission to buy an American aeroplane.[30]

This was precisely what happened; early in 1956, forced by the actions of other airlines to reconsider its views on jets, BOAC began to look for a comparable British design. Now that the V1000 production line had been torn up, it found that 'in the time available nothing of the sort could be done'. Consequently, in the summer of 1956, BOAC requested authorisation to buy eighteen Boeings.[31] In October, the Minister of Civil Aviation, Harold Watkinson, announced that BOAC would be buying fifteen 707s, but that they would be powered by the Rolls-Royce Conway. He fully admitted that it had been a mistake to rely exclusively on the turbo-prop Britannia, but all concerned had been caught out by the unexpectedly rapid success of the big jets. BOAC would be allowed its Boeings, however, on the clear understanding that the remainder of its requirement for long-haul jets would be provided by a British manufacturer. Similarly, the fact that BOAC's 707s would be powered by British engines was seen as a 'sensible and not unsatisfactory compromise' between commercial necessity and the desirability of 'buying British'. The order was regarded simply as an 'exceptional measure to bridge the gap until a new British type is produced'.[32]

BOAC had already begun to consider a jet aircraft to replace its Comets on the 'Empire' services and in 1956 the airline had held a series of talks with Vickers. An outline specification produced by the airline's planning staff called for a design optimised for operation out of 'hot and high' airfields with limited facilities and inadequate runways. This tended to emphasise take-off and landing capability at the expense of outright flying performance. Similarly, because of the low traffic densities of these routes, BOAC was interested in an aeroplane with 'a smaller carrying capacity than either of the American jets'. This, according to BOAC's planners, would 'best serve the needs of the Corporation'.[33] In spite of the disagreement over the V1000, the negotiations between BOAC and Vickers proceeded amicably. By the autumn of 1956, they were all well advanced towards a detailed specification. The panic over the 'rush to jets' then intervened and in line with the Government's 'buy British' directive, BOAC had to re-evaluate its procurement policy.

The specification BOAC and Vickers were working on was certainly consistent with Watkinson's view that it would be commercially inadvisable to produce a copy of the 707 or the DC8.[34] The 'Empire' route specification emphasised design characteristics not possessed by either American aircraft. However, the Government wanted BOAC to consider buying a De Haviland aircraft, the DH118, effectively a Comet Five. Negotiations between Vickers and BOAC were suspended. Publicly, Watkinson defended the Government's intervention by referring to De Haviland's unrivalled experience as a manufacturer of jet airliners. The inference was, of course, that BOAC would get a better aircraft if it chose the DH118. There was another, probably more important, motive: the Government had invested quite handsomely in De Haviland, but its financial position was still far from healthy. Vickers, on the other hand, not only had the profitable Viscount, but had equally high hopes of the Vanguard. Clearly, the Government hoped to distribute major orders within the industry and to protect an important design centre. As Sir Gerald d'Erlanger, BOAC's new Chairman told his Board, the Government had intervened in BOAC's choice in order to 'preserve the overall balance and welfare of the aircraft industry'.[36] This was hardly the action of an economically liberal Government, and it showed that there were already limits to the Government's disengagement from civil development.

The private venture policy was still the primary element in the Government's approach to the civil aircraft industry, and in spite of its preference for De Haviland, the company would nevertheless have to find its own money for the DH118. BOAC was also told that it need not accept a minimum order. In the event, De Haviland wanted both Government assistance and stipulated a launch order of fifty aircraft as the only basis on which it would begin development. De Haviland was not happy with the specification, arguing that it would lead to an aircraft with only a limited sales potential. In December, negotiations had stalled, the Government refused De Haviland's request for aid, and neither the manufacturer nor the airline was prepared to budge on the minimum order. Finally, BOAC was allowed to consider other design submissions and, from six, Vickers again emerged as the only realistic option.[37]

The crucial factor in BOAC's choice of Vickers' VC10 design besides the fact that it was 'tailored' to the airline's requirement, was that only Vickers was prepared to launch its design as a private venture. Government policy and the economics of airliner development conspired to limit severely BOAC's real as opposed to theoretical freedom to buy the aircraft which best suited its needs as an airline. This was neatly described by Sir Matthew Slattery, BOAC's Chairman from 1961 to 1963:

> There was only one company . . . prepared to embark upon such an aeroplane and that was Vickers . . . we now get to the stage where you could have any colour so long as it is black. You have got to have a British aircraft, and there is only one possible aircraft.

Slattery added ironically, 'I am quite sure that the Corporation were quite free to make any choice they liked.'[38] A colleague was equally forthright, 'It was a question of the VC10 or nothing.'[39]

Later, BOAC executives claimed that they had really wanted a British copy of the 707, which in fact had been opposed on commercial and political grounds. Certainly, Watkinson wrote to D'Erlanger suggesting that a mere copy of the 707 would be of little use to BOAC and that it 'would not sell in world markets'.[40] However, in April 1957 BOAC's Aircraft Requirements Committee concluded that the VC10 'appears to be the most promising conception of which we have had details and . . . as attractive an aircraft we can hope to obtain for our Eastern Hemisphere operations in 1963–4'. In reply to Watkinson, d'Erlanger stated that the VC10 was 'tailored to our requirement of up-to-date design and conceived for delivery in the mid-sixties when we want it'. At the time, according to ministry officials, BOAC 'really seemed pleased with it'.[41]

For the manufacturers, Sir George Edwards said that BOAC had always wanted a specialised design for its 'Empire' routes. The VC10 was deliberately optimised for those services. Consequently, when compared with the American jets on other routes, it was inevitably less economic to operate. If Vickers had been required to build a British 707, it would have been designed along the lines of the recently cancelled V1000.[42] At a late stage in the contract negotiations, both parties did express some doubts about the initial specification. It had become evident that the DC8 and the 707 would be able to operate throughout the Far East and Africa and the Boeing was about to launch the 720, a smaller version of the 707, which would be a major competitor to the VC10 on lower density routes.[43] Vickers and BOAC agreed that the original specification was too narrow and so it was adjusted to give the VC10 a better overall performance. At this juncture, BOAC's Engineering Department mounted a late challenge to the whole VC10 concept. This opposition was overruled by the BOAC Board, and in January 1958, an order for thirty-five aircraft worth £68 million was placed with Vickers. This was then the most expensive single order for a British civil aircraft.[44]

This was an unusually large initial order, and it is clear that BOAC would have preferred a smaller one, buying more as demand grew. However, Vickers had made it clear that thirty-five was the minimum order on which it could safely launch the programme as a private venture. The airline was put in a difficult position. Its most optimistic market forecasts seemed to justify an order of this size, but it was risky and commercially undesirable to have so much capital tied to such a large fleet. Outsiders certainly felt that BOAC was gambling on winning a large share of a market which might not materialise. Even officials later conceded that thirty-five may have been a 'bit high'. However, BOAC needed a new jet and the Board was all too conscious of the pressure to 'buy British'. The Government leaned on BOAC to accept Vicker's conditions, which it should be recalled, De Haviland had failed to achieve. The Ministers of Supply and Civil Aviation were present during some of the negotiations on the minimum order and would have been aware of BOAC's concern. Certainly, by setting a sole supplier against a monopsonist, the Government had engineered a situation in which both had 'little room for manoeuvre'.[45] The VC10 was an important contract for the British civil aircraft industry; it was, perhaps, the last opportunity to capture a share of the long-haul market. But it also had to be presented as a private venture, as it would be an important precedent in future civil projects. The obvious solution was to intervene in the domestic market, where the 'hidden hand' could be supplemented by discreet but firm nudges from the Government. In this fashion, responsibility for launch and development appeared to remain fully in the hands of the customer and the manufacturer, but with the Government still prepared to defend a key industry, even if at one remove.

The VC10 had an uphill struggle competing against the DC8 and the two Boeing aircraft. It was a late entrant to a market heavily penetrated by the big American jets. Worse still, its specialised design features were of marginal value on its main routes and a distinct disadvantage on others.[46] The American firm Convair experienced similar difficulties with its 880/990 design; both companies suffered heavy losses as a result. For that matter, Boeing and Douglas were also hard-pressed by the demands of launching their aircraft, and severe price-cutting helped neither their position nor that of the late entrants.[47]

In retrospect, Sir George Edwards believes that the cancellation of the V1000 was responsible for Vickers' later problems and was a watershed in the history of British post-war civil aviation. It was a grave error of judgement on the part of BOAC and the Government from which the British civil industry never fully recovered;

> I think that had we got on with the V1000 and with developments of it, we might very well have carved ourselves out a place in the long-range subsonic business that was as good as we had carved . . . in the short-range subsonic business. From the moment that project was taken away, we were behind all the time.

This view is shared by Sir Arnold Hall, Chairman of Hawker Siddeley;

> I see as a major turning point . . . the decision not to go ahead with the Vickers V1000 airliner . . . The nation turned from long-range jet aviation, cancelling the V1000, at precisely the moment when it was about to grow and we were ahead of everybody.[48]

On the other hand, Millar and Sawyer argue convincingly that the V1000 would have been inferior to its American competitors. It might have been bought by BOAC instead of the 707, 'but the most likely outcome of its development would have been that this airline would have found itself operating a less efficient airplane than its competitors'. Had Vickers been so sure of the V1000, it should have been launched as a private venture.[49]

Vickers was not willing to accept that degree of risk without the cushion of Government aid or a launch order from BOAC. For its part, the Government was not prepared to overrule BOAC's commercial judgement. Even in the case of the VC10, the Ministers concerned do not appear to have influenced radically BOAC's technical–commercial view of what type of aircraft it required. There, pressure was applied to ensure the application of the 'buy British' doctrine and to ease, but not to relieve, Vickers' financial risk. It may have represented a fine distinction between non-interference and overt interventionism, but it was nevertheless more or less consistent with the Government's private venture policy, whereas overt support for the V1000 was not. The Government felt it neither wise nor desirable to return to the previous administration's programmatic approach to civil development nor to sponsor speculative prototypes. Unfortunately, therefore, ill fortune, bad judgement and the intrinsic weakness of its manufacturers, combined to undermine Britain's chances of securing a commercially significant share of an important market, and the Government would eventually have to face up to the consequences.

Private venture and industrial rationalisation

The successful launch of the VC10 as a private venture was seen as a bench-mark for future development. The Government's stand on private venture had a gratifying affect on attitudes within the industry. According to MoS officials, the general outcome of the policy was that if one firm offered a private venture in response to an air corporation requirement, it stimulated others; 'They want to raise the finance because of the fear that the private venture chap has a lead over them.'[50] Vickers, of course, was financially strong enough to sustain the cost of developing the VC10; profits from the Viscount were growing and the company had high hopes for the Vanguard. However, by the mid-1950s there was growing concern that the majority of British firms lacked the financial strength to carry the cost of private ventures or to survive a period of general increase in R&D costs and declining demand for military aircraft.

The post-war policy of maintaining a 'strategic reserve' in the aircraft industry through small, competing companies had been steadily undermined by changing military and economic conditions. The rapidly increasing cost and risk of R&D, the growing use of guided weapons in place of manned aircraft and the realisation that, in a nuclear context, industrial mobilisation would no longer be possible, implied that the United Kingdom neither could afford nor required a fragmented aircraft industry. In 1956, there were still over a dozen separate airframe and aero-engine companies in Britain, as many, in fact, as in the United States. As it became obvious that the British Government was planning to reduce substantially its need for military aircraft, there were many in the industry who were very pessimistic about the future.[51]

It was clear to realists like Lord Hives of Rolls-Royce that rationalisation was both desirable and, perhaps, long overdue.[52] Officials at the MoS openly advocated the need for stronger technical units, and in 1956 told a Commons Select Committee that they had already identified 'candidates for relegation' in the industry.[53] The 1957 Defence Review provided both the catalyst and the means of forcing rationalisation. The Review baldly stated that there would be only one more major military requirement, the Canberra replacement (OR339) and that other projects were to be cancelled. On the one hand, the Government believed that the reduction in demand that these decisions entailed would be matched by a greater emphasis on civil and export-orientated work.[54] On the other hand, 'some consolidation of resources' was inevitable.[55] The Government did not intend to dictate or to direct the rationalisation process. Firms would have to merge 'naturally', but the Government would encourage mergers through the 'selective allocation of contracts'.[56] OR339 was particularly significant here; by manipulating the various submissions and by insisting on joint ventures, the MoS was able to establish the outline of two central groups of companies, one of which was awarded the contract.

The Trident

The Government also intended to use BEA's requirement for a new medium-range jet in the same way; in Harold Watkinson's words, 'This will be the last major order for a while. Therefore an opportunity is provided for a concentration of resources which will be of great importance to the future of the industry.'[57] BEA had already begun its search for a new aircraft, and early in 1957 decided on the De Haviland DA121. BEA's specification was tightly drawn and set a number of tough technical objectives. De Haviland was already supplying Comet 4Bs to BEA and was willing to accept BEA's stringent requirements. In August, BEA asked the Minister of Civil Aviation for permission to start contract negotiations. De Haviland said the 121 would be privately financed but the Government, advised by the MoS, doubted the firm's ability to carry the risk alone. The MoS preferred the Bristol 200, a design sponsored jointly by Bristol and Hawker Siddeley. Not only was this regarded as a better commercial proposition, it was also consistent with the Government's rationalisation drive.[58] Consequently, BEA's request was deferred for further consideration.

The Ministry's main objection to De Haviland was the company's dogged refusal to join with another until it had been awarded the contract for the DH121. De Haviland did not object in principle to rationalisation, but its Board was determined to dictate the terms of any joint programme. Preliminary investigations of possible combinations had suggested that De Haviland would have to modify the 121 design and to accept a much smaller share of development than the Board thought desirable. Critically, BEA supported both De Haviland and the 121 with an unwavering determination. Lord Douglas of Kirtleside, BEA's formidable Chairman, lobbied vigorously on behalf of the 121. He was totally unimpressed by the view that BEA should consider the wider sales prospects of an aircraft it ordered from a British manufacturer. 'It is surely not suggested', he said, 'that BEA should leave the choice of their new jet aircraft to a foreign airline or airlines?'[59] BEA even challenged the MoS's assessment of De Haviland's financial strength; by commissioning an independent audit, BEA appeared to rebut the MoS's claim that De Haviland would not be able to launch the 121 as a private venture.[60]

Lord Douglas eventually convinced Watkinson, but Aubrey Jones, the Minister of Supply, and his officials remained sceptical. Tension between the two Ministers grew and eventually broke into open conflict over the issue. The debate spilled over into the public arena with suggestions that the Bristol 200 was technically inferior to the DH121. Hawker Siddeley was sufficiently aroused to issue an official statement:

Let there be an end . . . to this ill-informed gossip that the product we are offering is technically inferior to that of our competitors, and that we at

Hawker Siddeley are engaged in some form of plot with the connivance of Ministers of the Crown to force an inferior product on a reluctant customer.[61]

The dispute was increasingly embarrassing to the Government, and the MoS came under pressure to settle the matter.

On 30 January 1958, De Haviland announced that it had formed a production consortium with Fairey and Hunting, two much smaller aircraft companies. This was to be called Airco with De Haviland holding two-thirds of its shares and the other two the balance. The MoS was not entirely happy with this, since Airco still only had a total capitalisation of less than £100 million which the MoS considered to be inadequate. With BEA demanding a speedy decision and the Cabinet looking for a quick solution, the MoS withdrew its objections. In August, BEA signed a contract for twenty-five aircraft, now called the Trident, worth £39 million. The delay caused by the Government's intervention was not regarded as being significant and De Haviland expected the Trident would win a large share of a market then estimated at over 550 aircraft.[62]

The Trident was another victory for the private venture policy and the formation of Airco a partial one for rationalisation. Jones conceded that some people had found it hard to adjust to these new demands, but he was sure that the industry 'should not be seen to be too dependent on Government.'[63] Similarly, rationalisation would create a stronger base for private venture development: 'The Government consider that, providing the necessary rationalisation is carried out, the industry in general should be able increasingly to finance the development of new civil projects without Government assistance.'[64] Jones went on to summarise the role of Government in the rationalisation process. The proper course, he said, was 'something intermediate between full government authority and complete *laissez faire*. What we need is a combination of impulse from above compelling the assumption of responsibility on the part of industry inself.'[65]

Significantly, Jones did not rule out the possibility of giving aid for really advanced civil designs. Here he singled out the supersonic transport (SST) project in which the Government had already taken the lead over private enterprise.[66] The Government realised that there was, perhaps, a limit to what industry could do without some direct assistance in civil R&D. As long as industry assumed the burden of launching conventional types, the Government would consider investing in the more advanced project 'on the merits of the case'. For the rest, though, the only aid which would be forthcoming would be through the nationalised airlines, and even here, Jones was careful to note that he could not compel them to support the domestic industry. In short, the Government intended to 'nudge or edge the industry to a greater degree of self-reliance without, however, ... refraining from extending aid where it is genuinely needed.'[67] In the three years between the V1000 cancellation and the Trident, without modifying its basic theme, Government policy had acquired a degree of subtlety. It was certainly now a more coherent doctrine related to a wider strategy for industrial change. The difficulty was, however, that the whole notion of a self-reliant industry, with a commercially viable civil sector, was becoming increasingly problematic. Launch costs were rising rapidly and, more insidious in its effects, the limitations of a small and parochial domestic market were beginning to appear. Rationalisation would undoubtedly help, but it was too little and too late.

Buying British and Design Parochialism

Although the Conservative Government eschewed giving direct assistance to the civil aircraft industry, it should be obvious from the above that it still imposed a 'buy British' policy on the air corporations. There were, of course, exceptions but, as Aubrey Jones put it, the nationalised airlines had 'voluntary' but nevertheless 'special responsibilities' towards the aircraft industry. In fact, they carried a 'far greater responsibility than the customers of any other industry and it is upon them that depends whether we ultimately make or mar this industry'.[68] The 1949 Civil Aviation Act had ostensibly left the nationalised airlines free to choose airliners best suited to their commercial requirement. The Treasury certainly argued that this principle should prevail, even if it ran counter to the 'convenience of some broader manufacturing programme'.[69] In practice, the airlines were nevertheless expected to give priority to British-built equipment, even if this meant 'leaning a little backwards' in favour of domestic manufacturers.[70]

The Government had considerable, if often informal and ambiguous, power to influence airline decisions. General directives could be issued, but as we have seen, pressure was usually more subtle. A strong and confident Chairman was also better placed to resist such pressure, but throughout the 1950s both airlines were largely led by men who conceived it as their duty to help the British aircraft industry. Lord Douglas of Kirtleside, for example, recognised that 'one of the most important of BEA's special obligations is to assist development of British transport aircraft'.[71] Similarly, Sir Gerald d'Erlanger was also reported to have said that he never believed that it was the Corporation's job to make profits, 'the Corporation was there to support the British aircraft industry, to develop routes around the world, and so on'.[72] There was, however, a considerable difference in the degree to which each was forced to compromise his airline's commercial interests in order to assist the aircraft industry.

'Buying British' was an expensive business. BOAC and BEA had to

bear the costs of 'proving' new aircraft once in service; technical
problems, delays in development, could lead to lost revenue. As one BEA
executive put it, 'The costs of an airline for being part producer of a new
type are enormous.' The nationalised airlines had to make substantial
progress payments to British manufacturers, which could be as high as 90
per cent of the total value of the order. A minimum launch order, as in the
case of the VC10, might also be stipulated, committing the airline to a
massive capital investment with interest charges to pay, well in advance
of demand. BOAC in particular believed that it was disadvantaged
competitively by always being the 'first' (and perhaps the only) customer
of a new aircraft. The Comet failure cost BOAC £7·8 million and the late
delivery and subsequent technical problems with the Britannia cost
£22·4 million (largely as a result of having to make stop-gap purchases of
American piston-engined aircraft). Ordering aircraft 'off-the-peg' from
an American firm was cheaper and likely to be free of technical snags. It
would also require smaller progress payments.[73] The Select Committee
on Nationalised Industries sympathised with the airlines' plight: 'Your
Committee emphasise that the cost of developing new aircraft at present
appears to fall too heavily on the Air Corporations, and places them at a
disadvantage compared with their foreign competitors who use American
aircraft.'[74] During the 1950s both airlines appealed frequently to the
Government for help. Ministers were unmoved, and equally consistently
refused to subsidise the 'buy British' policy, yet in effect the airlines were
doing precisely that on behalf of the aircraft industry.

Needless to say, there were some commercial advantages to be derived
from being the first with a new type. Passengers were attracted by novelty
and if the aircraft was a significant advance on previous equipment, the
airline might gain a temporary advantage over its competitors. However,
the most important feature of 'buying British' so far as BEA and BOAC
were concerned was the opportunity to have their 'special needs'
safeguarded.[75] Given the possible costs of buying a new British aircraft,
the airlines jealously guarded their privilege of 'tailoring' designs. Sir
Anthony Millward, Lord Douglas's successor at BEA, made this quite
clear: 'If you buy an aircraft for your own use, it must be to your own
requirements.'[76]

'Tailoring' the VC10 and Trident

Both the VC10 and the Trident were so 'tailored', and neither benefited
commercially from the experience. In the first instance, the VC10's
specification was directed at BOAC's 'Empire' routes and reflected the
current feeling that the more conventionally designed American jets
would not be able to operate out of primitive airports. In the event, these
were rapidly improved with the advent of jet services.[77] From the
discussion above, it should be clear that Vickers and BOAC did reconsider
the specification and doubts were expressed about the design. The Select

Committee on Nationalised Industries had no doubt that BOAC itself
should have reopened the question of 'buying British' for a specialised
task when it was increasingly evident that the 'Empire' route assumptions
were of doubtful validity. However, the BOAC Board was heavily
influenced by the 'buy British' doctrine, both BOAC and Vickers were
committed to the VC10 more or less as originally specified. In this case, as
Millar and Sawyer put it, 'neither side seems to have shown much
judgement of its commercial needs'.[78] The result was a technically
satisfactory aeroplane, which proved to be very popular with passengers,
but which did not have any particular design edge over the already
established American long-range jets. It might be argued that the VC10
should not have been built at all, and that Britain should have then opted
out of the long-range subsonic market. In any case, developing the VC10
on an unnecessarily restrictive specification only compounded the
problems faced by a late entrant to the market.

In the longer term, the Trident was a much more telling example of
'tailoring', for here the design concept was well in advance of any
potential competition. Yet in spite of this lead, and evident commercial
promise, the Trident was commercially eclipsed by Boeing's 727. The
primary reason for this was again the restrictive nature of the Trident
specification, or more accurately, the changes to it insisted upon by BEA
after the contract was signed with Airco. The airline was quite honest in
stating that the Trident was 'built to BEA's operational requirement' and
that the initial specification went into great detail 'about what we want'.
The possible danger of limiting the wider sales of such an aircraft
influenced the MoS's preference for the Bristol 200, and others also
pointed out the pitfall of designing 'exclusively for one customer an
aeroplane that has potentially a much wider scope'.[79] However, BEA was
hopeful that 'other airlines will find that it suits their pattern of routes as
it does ours'.[80]

There is no evidence to suggest that De Haviland protested about the
initial specification. In any case, De Haviland desperately needed the
contract. The company had turned down BOAC's requirement and it was
inconceivable it could reject a second big order without jeopardising its
entire civil operation. Consequently, it accepted a contract 'more onerous
than anything De Haviland has previously undertaken'.[81] There was
some resistance from the design team to some of the more sophisticated
requirements, but the original design had plenty of scope for
development. It was certainly of roughly the right size, up to 111 seats,
with the proposed big Rolls RB141-3 Medway providing plenty of
'stretch' potential.

Early in 1959, BEA's Commercial Division predicted a sharp drop in
demand leading to over-capacity in the planned fleet of Tridents and
Vanguards. BEA asked De Haviland to reduce the range and size of the
Trident, limiting it, in fact, to a maximum of eighty-seven seats. More

importantly, this meant rejecting the 14,000lb-thrust Rolls RB141 in
favour of a new smaller engine, the 9,800lb RB163 (Spey). This limited
the 'stretch' available for further development. BEA paid De Haviland
£333,000 in compensation for the alterations, but at a stroke the
attractiveness of the Trident to other airlines was severely affected and
six months were lost on the programme. There was opposition to these
changes from within De Haviland, but the Managing Director vetoed
discussions with other airlines until the changes were made.

In 1959 Boeing launched the 727, a similar tri-jet aircraft.
Significantly, Boeing was influenced by the De Haviland design, but from
the outset built the 727 with a larger (up to 131 passengers) capacity.
Boeing also optimised the 727's airfield performance, whereas the
Trident was designed to reflect BEA's insistence on a higher cruising
speed than the Caravelle. The 727 also had plenty of 'stretch' and it
entered service before the Trident.[82] The American aircraft ran away
with the market, selling over 2000 copies to the Trident's 115. Its
capacity, performance, delivery were all better than the Trident's, but
above all the 727 was of a size more suited to most airline requirements.
BEA's pessimistic forecasts about the market proved false, and the airline
continually sought larger versions of the Trident. Eventually, BEA even
wanted to buy the 189 seat 727-200.[83]

The 1959 design change was, if not by itself fatal to the Trident's
commercial prospects, seriously damaging to its wider market
penetration. Harlow, for example, suggests that the original DH121 was
already structurally limited and would have been unattractive to
American customers.[84] BEA certainly felt that De Haviland's market
research was inadequate and denied that it had any responsibility for De
Haviland's mistake. The specification was there and De Haviland had
every opportunity to reject it. De Haviland's limited production facilities
did not help delivery times, and Boeing's superior productivity enabled it
to come from behind and beat the Trident into service. But clearly, BEA's
tight control over the specification, the reduction in size and De
Haviland's timid acceptance of its prime customer's *diktat*, had a highly
detrimental effect on the Trident's commercial future.

Tailoring was a blight on British civil aircraft design during the 1950s,
and was retrospectively condemned by many official and unofficial
analyses. Later, it was generally agreed that an airliner should not be
launched on the basis of a single customer's special requirements.[85] As
Harlow again suggests, the interests of the British aircraft industry in the
1950s might have been better served by opening up the domestic market
to foreign products, so that 'when a British project was chosen it would
stand comparison with all the alternatives'.[86]

The private venture policy: an assessment
Clearly, this was as much a structural and attitudinal problem as a

direct consequence of Government policy. However, the *ad hoc* nature of Government involvement in decision-making had paradoxical effects. Firstly, Government insistence on the VC10, or at least a British long-range jet, helped to constrain BOAC's choices and to encourage Vickers' design submission. But secondly, despite the MoS's grave doubts about the Trident, once some movement had been made towards rationalisation, the Government allowed BEA and De Haviland to go their own way. The private-venture, self-reliant policy certainly aimed to limit Governmental involvement in civil development. Machinery for consultation and the harmonisation of requirements was theoretically provided by the Transport Aircraft Requirements Committee (TARC), which had replaced an Interdepartmental Committee on transport aircraft in the early 1950s. Membership of TARC was drawn from the Ministries of Supply and Civil Aviation, the Services and the Research Establishments, as well as all the major domestic airlines. A small part-time secretariat was provided by the MoS. Because the merits of individual projects could be the subject of meetings, the aircraft manufacturers were only invited to technical sub-committees and special *ad hoc* bodies. TARC was intended to provide a forum for the consideration of future transport aircraft development, with a special emphasis on the harmonisation of civil and military requirements. It had no executiive function, and although important matters of current debate were submitted to TARC for consideration (these included the V1000 decision, BOAC's 707 order and the Trident) its impact on actual events was slight.

Later, following the publication of the 1957 Defence White Paper, there were signs that TARC's scope might have been broadened. TARC was required to draw up a long-term plan for civil research and development to fill any deficiencies made by the decline in military-orientated research which would be vital to civil programmes. TARC was also remitted to consider the possibility of developing a civil supersonic airliner, and a sub-committee, the Supersonic Transport Aircraft Committee (STAC) was formed to examine the problem. However, as far as key policy decisions were concerned, TARC remained a consultative body, meeting spasmodically and unable to influence in any discernible way the specifications and requirements of the nationalised airlines. On the formation of the Ministry of Aviation in 1959, TARC's already limited functions tended to diminish still further.[87] The MoS itself had little expertise to evaluate commercial data, most of which in any case came from the nationalised airlines or through commercial attachés in British embassies abroad. The MoS had a responsibility to ensure that the Government would not be called upon to bail out a company if it got into difficulties, but it had no authority and little competence to intervene systematically in the affairs of a private company, ostensibly financing its own civil programmes.

That, of course, was the crux of the matter: the Government did not provide direct assistance to the civil aircraft industry, but indirectly, through the nationalised airlines, public money was still the vital life-support system for civil development. Responsibility for project choice, monitoring and control was left in limbo between a full, free market private enterprise system and state interventionism. Moreover, the market at which British aircraft were almost invariably directed initially was at the same time parochial and too easy. The commercial failings of the VC10 and the Trident were not caused by Government, but the prevailing policy left little in the way of alternative industrial strategies.

Unlike their American counterparts, British firms did not have the help of a large and generally buoyant defence sector to provide additional money for civil development. British manufacturers and air corporation Chairmen certainly believed that firms in the United States derived an enormous advantage from defence contracts for transport aircraft and the cash flow generated by military work.[88] This advantage should not be overstated, for even Boeing with its KC-135 contract, had to raise a lot of private capital for the 707. Vickers also based its civil V1000 on an RAF contract for a military transport. The Government was conscious of the possibilities of harmonising civil and military requirements. That after all, was one of TARC's main functions, but in practice, the scope for harmonisation was very limited indeed.

Although there were few technical or operational problems in the harmonisation of long-range transport designs, as defence budgets became tighter and the spread of British military interests overseas diminished it became far cheaper for the RAF to buy a civil product virtually 'off the shelf'. Extensive use was also made of trooping contracts with domestic airlines. In the case of short- and medium-range transports, there were real and important operational and technical problems in arriving at a common specification. Harmonisation was in fact most successful in the field of engine and equipment development. Orders by the RAF for civil aircraft were important, and played a significant role in more than one rescue operation of an ailing or endangered civil project. Generally speaking, military orders were limited in numbers and often placed spasmodically.[89] For example, the RAF's order of six V1000s, with the possibility of a few more, was hardly the equivalent of the production finance generated by the USAF's huge purchases of KC135 tanker–transports from Boeing.

The Government's own defence policies did not help the industry to make the transition to independent, self-financing civil programmes. As a result of Korean War rearmament, the British aircraft industry in mid-decade was in a financially healthy state. A number of civil projects were undoubtedly launched with the profits and money generated by the military sector. Even then, however, manufacturers complained that the Government failed to allow a level of profitability which would have facilitated the accumulation of a usable liquid capital reserve. Once the Government began to review its defence requirements, the industry had fewer military projects and experienced a sharp decline in the value of its defence business. The absence of suitable new projects also began to erode its share of export business. In short, the British civil aircraft industry could not rely on orders from the RAF or profits earned from defence work to provide any additional capital for private ventures.

Rationalisation was bound to help, but even that, in the first instance at least, was to be encouraged, prodded, but not hurried by Government action. It was, as Frank Beswick, Labour spokesman on aviation suggested, a case of 'leading from the rear'. Indeed, he and other critics felt that the Government's whole approach to aerospace, and to civil production in particular, 'smacked of the Treasury'.[90] In reducing defence expenditure, the Government had failed to recognise a crucial link between military production, defence-related R&D and the ability of firms to carry the cost of civil development. By the same token, it was persisting with the private venture policy for civil aircraft when launch costs were increasing significantly. There was considerable doubt, in fact, whether even a rationalised industry would find sufficient risk capital for civil projects.[91] Equally, the Government was also accused of being somewhat sanguine about the commercial future of current types: 'In official circles many think that the civil market is a golden apple only waiting to be plucked from the tree, when it is a very tough competitive market.'[92]

Technically, the British civil aircraft industry in 1959 bore no comparison with the sorry state of affairs in 1946. In most areas, design capability was second to none and in some respects, most notably in engines, British firms were amongst the most advanced in the world. Commercially, the picture, though not entirely bleak, was not so satisfactory. The Comet failure and the hiatus in jet development had been a grievous blow. The eclipse of the turbo-prop was already affecting the financial health of two of the most important civil producers, Vickers and Bristol. Finally, while both the VC10 and the Trident had yet to prove themselves, even there, the prognosis was not unequivocally optimistic. Developing these would be expensive and was bound to increase the strain on companies struggling to make up for a much reduced defence sector and, at the same time reorganise themselves. The Government had stuck to its private venture policy, but had both reinforced the 'buy-British' doctrine and, towards the end of the decade, had hinted that it would help in the development of technically advanced concepts. However, this qualified 'free market' approach had to bend to the reality of launching increasingly expensive civil projects on the basis of a limited and often parochial domestic market. If the United Kingdom was to remain a major centre of civil aircraft manufacturing, there was ultimately little alternative to some form of systematic support policy.

2

CONFIRMING THE PARTNERSHIP, 1960–4

The period between 1959 and 1964 was an important one in the relationship between Government and the civil aircraft industry. Under increasing pressure from firms struggling to finance civil projects, the Government was forced to concede the need for launch aid. Similarly, BOAC's financial problems led the Government to accept full responsibility for the nationalised airlines buying British. At the same time, the likely costs of developing a supersonic transport as well as the presence of wider political advantages stimulated interest in international collaboration. By 1964, the Government had again become directly involved with civil aerospace and was embarked upon a course of action which, by the end of the decade, left the state as the primary source of capital for the industry's civil activities.

The reintroduction of launch aid

During 1959, the combined impact of the 1957 Defence Review, the poor sales of the larger, second-generation turbo-prop airliners, and the costs of developing the new jets for BEA and BOAC, began to have an adverse effect on the financial stability of many British companies. Bristol was seriously affected by the limited sales of the Britannia and although it participated in the early stages of the supersonic transport project, the company had no money for future civil ventures. As had been feared by the MoS, De Haviland, although part of Airco, found it difficult to finance the Trident. The Hawker Siddeley Group, without a large civil sector to compensate for falling military demand, was severely hit by the Government's changing defence requirements. Even Rolls-Royce, despite the fact that engine sales were not directly linked to the success of indigenous airframes, was finding private venture development increasingly hard to sustain.

Vickers' position was similarly grave but, because of the company's earlier confidence in launching two large airliners as private ventures, especially significant for the future of civil production in the United Kingdom. Its problems had appeared rapidly; in 1956, Vickers reported a trading profit of £3·1 million and two more equally successful years followed; but by the end of 1959, Vickers was facing a substantial loss on its aircraft operations. The Vanguard was severely straining company cash flow without showing much evidence of generating additional revenue over the original BEA order. Vickers was well placed to win a share of OR339 (the Canbera replacement) in collaboration with English Electric, but the VC10 would be another major commitment in advance of sufficient sales to cover the costs of launch. Matters were not helped by an error in estimating the VC10's costs; according to Sir George Edwards, while over-optimism was common to all aircraft cost-estimating, in this case the estimates 'proved to be wrong by quite a bit'. A vicious cycle of price cutting, started by Boeing and Douglas, exacerbated Vickers' problems which, combined with the launch of the smaller Boeing 720 and the Convair 880/990, increased competitive pressure and further threatened VC10 earnings.[1]

In June 1959 Vickers' Chairman, Lord Knollys, predicted a gloomy outlook for the firm unless the Government changed its policy on launch aid for civil aircraft. Speaking at Vickers' AGM, Lord Knollys told shareholders that the Government had to appreciate and ease

> ... the great and disproportionate financial burden borne by Vickers and other companies in private ventures such as the Vanguard and the VC10. Without firm and early support by the Government, through RAF orders and otherwise, to back up the initiative of private enterprise in maintaining design and production facilities and in forward planning, this country is more likely, sooner than some people might expect, to find itself without a real aircraft industry at all ... All we ask is for the same kind of practical far-seeing support which the United States Government affords to its private enterprise aircraft industry.[2]

Similar views were expressed by the Society of British Aircraft (later Aerospace) Constructors, who, on behalf of industry as a whole, presented a memorandum to the Government on the state and future of aircraft manufacturing in Britain. As far as civil production was concerned, the SBAC claimed that the Government assumed a 'progressive readiness in private sources of capital to invest at risk in a market where the magnitude of risk is progressively growing for technological reasons, while the character of the risk is progressively being determined by political and strategic considerations'. Such a policy, the report concluded, simply 'cannot succeed'.[3]

In the summer of 1959, Vickers approached De Haviland with a proposal that they put a joint submission to the Government for help in launching a new airliner. Vickers hoped that this might form the basis for merger negotiations and, in return, persuade the Government to relax its private venture policy. Unfortunately, although initially welcoming Vickers' suggestion, De Haviland still fought shy of comprehensive steps towards rationalisation. In any case, at the MoS, Aubrey Jones was unimpressed by Vickers' request. Indeed, his only response was to

commission an independent survey of Vickers' financial problems which
criticised the company's management for exhibiting 'a lack of awareness
of market economics'. Jones rejected the proposal and suggested that
Vickers would be best advised to accelerate its entry into a larger group.
Jones also turned down similar requests for aid from Hawker Siddeley
and Handley Page.[4]

However, Jones's stringent view on civil development was increasingly
at variance with that of the Cabinet as a whole. With a General Election
looming, the Government was becoming sensitive to criticism that it was
not supporting civil technology adequately and was worried that
unemployment in the aircraft industry might directly affect its electoral
position. Paradoxically, Jones was, generally speaking, an advocate of
increasing state support for advanced technology. On the other hand, he
felt that there were some aspects of commercially orientated technology,
and civil aerospace was largely in this area, which were better left to
private enterprise and the judgement of a more or less free market.
However, his own support for the SST illustrated a basic problem in
distinguishing between civil technology which should rightly deserve
state support and that which should and could be left to the private sector.
As R&D costs grew in all fields, it was ever more difficult to distinguish
clearly between 'advanced' and 'conventional' projects. At some point,
the launch costs for even a modest civil aircraft would be beyond the
capacity of British firms. The question then would be not whether a
particular project was commercially viable but whether the United
Kingdom would remain in the first rank of aircraft manufacturers.
Industry already felt that this point had been reached, and that survival
hung upon Government realising that fact.

Duncan Sandys and the reintroduction of launch aid

Once the General Election was safely won, the Conservative
Government began to take steps which would increase the institutional
importance of aerospace generally and which would also lead to
conditions favouring the reintroduction of launch aid for civil aircraft. In
October, the MoS was dismantled and all aviation responsibilities,
military and civil, passed into the hands of a single ministry, the Ministry
of Aviation. The Prime Minister, Harold Macmillan, had long been
concerned at the apparent lack of coordination between the Ministries of
Supply and Civil Aviation, which during the Trident affair had led to an
embarrassingly public fight between the two Ministers. It was hoped that
the new Ministry of Aviation (MoA) would be better able to establish a
coherent policy for civil aviation. Similarly, by establishing a separate
specialised Ministry, the Government aimed to improve the efficiency and
effectiveness of military procurement.

Apart from the addition of civil aviation staff, there was little change
made in the administration of civil aircraft development. There was some

tension between the newcomers and the old MoS personnel, but even this eased in time. The merger certainly enhanced the Ministry's capability to assess the market for civil aircraft; but on the other hand, the enlarged ministry resisted any suggestion that, for example, through enhancing the range and scope of the Transport Aircraft Requirements Committee, it should surrender to outside agents any of its functions related to civil development.[5] In general, the establishment of a Ministry of Aviation increased the institutional commitment to aerospace as well as reinforcing the political salience of all aviation matters. The MoA was a formidable, sectionally orientated department, staffed by experts and technological enthusiasts, willing and able to promote the interests of aerospace, the industry and its products. Although the political prominence of individual Ministers of Aviation would vary, the MoA rapidly acquired an enviable reputation for taking on and beating the Treasury.

The most immediate problem for the MoA and its first Minister, the energetic and politically well-connected Duncan Sandys, was to complete the rationalisation process and to attend to the growing financial crisis in the industry. Sandys quickly made it known that any measures designed to ameliorate the latter would be conditional on industry rapidly achieving the former. In November 1959 Sandys met senior industrialists to discuss his plans for rationalisation. Unlike his predecessor, Sandys was determined to play an active role in expediting the reorganisation of industry. He told the various companies that he thought that there was room only for two airframe and two engine groups and that they had better sort themselves out as soon as possible. He promised to act as an intermediary (or marriage bureau as he termed it) helping firms to overcome their natural reluctance to surrender their separate identities. Sandys also said that not only would he reintroduce launch aid once rationalisation was complete, but all future orders would be concentrated on the new groups.

By using this carrot-and-stick technique, Sandys got his way. Between November 1959 and January 1960 there was a flurry of merger negotiations and take-overs. Hawker Siddeley was particularly aggressive, successfully bidding for a number of smaller firms. Its most important acquisition was De Haviland; although Hawkers knew De Haviland was financially weak and that the contract with BEA to build the Trident was a distinct liability, the latter's civil design capability was seen as a vital complement to Hawker's military work. The resulting group took the name of Hawker Siddeley Aviation (HSA). A second group, the British Aircraft Corporation (BAC), was based on the design consortium which had been selected by the Government to build an aircraft to the OR339 specification. This emerged as the TSR-2. The original consortium of Vickers and English Electric was completed by Bristol and the smaller firm of Hunting, which had been a member of

Airco. Vickers, English Electric and Bristol formed the major shareholders of what was in effect a holding company of the three firms' aviation interests. Bristol had taken the plunge once it became clear that unless it merged it would lose any chance of being part of the SST programme. The BAC organisation would be financially responsible for new projects, but all existing commitments remained the separate concern of the individual shareholders. This might have hurt Vickers with its large and burdensome investment in the VC10, but, as we shall see, the Government specifically helped Vickers in order to overcome any residual obstacles to the creation of BAC. Bristol's engine interests were hived off, and with Armstrong Siddeley, became part of Bristol Siddeley engines. Rolls-Royce, however, were virtually unaffected by the changes and alone formed the second of Sandys' two engine groups.[6]

Although many associated with the British aircraft industry regretted the passing of some of the most famous names in aviation, there were few who doubted the ultimate wisdom of rationalisation.[7] Reorganisation on this scale was a long overdue response to radical changes in the nature and context of aerospace development. It was a necessary precondition for civil and military programmes in the 1960s which would necessarily be more complex and certainly more expensive to design and produce.

For his part, Sandys fulfilled his side of the bargain by announcing changes in Government policy towards civil aircraft launch aid and aerospace procurement. On 15 February 1960, he told the House of Commons that henceforward all Government orders, and those subject to Governmental approval, would be concentrated on the new groups. He also stated that the Government intended to reintroduce direct financial assistance for civil aircraft and engines.

Of course, the Government hoped to obtain a return on its investment, and as such, launch aid would again be subject to a levy on the sale of successful aircraft. He also made it clear that any agreement between the Government and a private company would be a risk-sharing arrangement with a limit placed on the amount of public money which would be made available for any one project.[8] This announcement officially re-established the Government as a full partner in civil aerospace and confirmed that industry could again expect the state to participate directly in the financing of civil development.

Launch aid: principles and procedure
It should be emphasised that the reintroduction of launch aid was no more than a political decision to use the provisions long present in the 1949 Civil Aviation Act. However, the procedures adopted as a result of this decision, while following the pattern of aid-with-levy associated with the 1940s, were to be more formal and systematic than they had been in the past. The underlying principle of 1960 launch aid was that the state would provide money for civil aircraft production but, equally, it should

not entirely remove the element of commercial risk inherent in private venture development. Launch aid was officially defined as an '. . . interest-free financial contribution to the launching costs of a civil aircraft or aero-engine project, repayable as a levy on sales and licences to the extent that these are achieved'.[9] Such costs comprised the cost of design and development, production jigs and tools, and learner costs (higher labour charges and so forth) incurred in the early stages of production. According to the 1960 procedures, the Government's contribution would be fixed as an agreed proportion of the manufacturer's estimated costs negotiated at the outset of development. This would be limited to 50 per cent of the total, and the company concerned should not generally expect additional help if those estimates were exceeded.[10] This was designed to provide that crucial element of commercial displine in launch aid agreements, and theoretically placed a limit on the Government's risk in any one project. If the contractor encountered unforeseen problems requiring greater than expected expenditure, or had been too optimistic at the outset, 'the whole cost is left with the company'.[11]

Naturally enough, the Ministry of Aviation (and later the Ministry of Technology) was concerned to ensure that firms did not take unnecessary risks or attempt to mislead them about the true estimates of launching a particular aircraft or engine. Every proposal was, therefore, examined by officials. Although they were interested in the technical and commercial aspects of a design, they were concerned to verify the manufacturer's estimates of cost. The intention was to ensure that an inflated estimate was not used as the basis for assessing the level of aid, thereby weakening the commercial discipline imposed on the firm. The assumption was that, once this initial examination had been made, technical and commercial decision-making was best left to private industry. Certainly, officials readily conceded that the Ministry did not have any real expertise to assess either the market or the commercial rationale for civil projects. In this respect, they had to rely on information supplied by private industry, supplemented by information obtained from commercial attachés in the various British embassies. TARC again provided a forum for some useful discussion of commercial requirements, but this was largely confined to domestic matters. The Ministry of Aviation, with direct access to the skills and experience of both the old MoS and Ministry of Civil Aviation, was better placed to assess new projects, but in general, there were serious limitations in its ability to evaluate civil programmes.[12] During the 1960s some improvement would be made in this area; in 1965 a small team was formed in the MoA to assess future markets and to evaluate launch aid submissions for the basis of both commercial and technical criteria. Officials saw their function as acting as restraint on the natural optimism of companies seeking assistance; but with only limited facilities, they were only able really to spot the 'big holes' in an industrial presentation. Of course, both then and in 1960 this was not regarded as an important or potentially damaging weakness. The self-policing nature of launch aid provided the ultimate check on private enterprise and some guarantee against industrial inefficiency.

The Government's investment would, it was hoped, be repaid with some profit through the R&D levy attached to every sale. In the 1940s, the levy had been based on a fixed rate of return and was much criticised for favouring the Government over the private contractor. In 1960 a new formula was introduced, which was more flexible and, in fact, tended to favour the manufacturer, although this did not prevent some industrialists from later criticising the principle of a sales levy on exports.[13] The system was based on the principle that the manufacturer should have a chance of getting its money back before the Government. Where launch costs were divided equally, for instance, the Government only took 25 per cent of any revenue until the firm had recovered its costs. The proportions were then reversed until the Government was repaid with some profit. At this point, the rate of recovery reverted to the initial arrangement until the end of production. The Government would, of course, receive a similar return on the sale of spares.[14]

The system of varying rates of recovery was one reason why the Government insisted on monitoring development. Not only had the Ministry to render the normal degree of accountability in public expenditure, but it had to know at what point any readjustment in the rate of return should legitimately be made. The control and monitoring of launch aided projects was not as detailed or extensive as in the case of fully funded programmes, either military or civil. Firms were expected to give regular progress reports and, as aid was given in instalments, a full review was undertaken at the beginning of each major stage. Companies were expected to provide extensive documentation and, of course, to give detailed estimates in their initial submissions to the Ministry. BAC, for example, established a Programme Control Department to handle these requirements. On the other hand, the Ministry's Resident Technical Officers, placed in firms to monitor military projects, were not directly concerned with launch aided aircraft or engines. They were expected to give some early warning of major technical problems, but were not in any systematic fashion to monitor civil development. In short, a company in receipt of launch aid could take its own technical and commercial decisions with a minimum of Government intervention.[15]

This was the central premise of the launch aid system: as the manufacturer would carry the greater part of any risk and obtained launch aid in the clear knowledge that the Government's commitment was not open-ended or subject to upward revision, an elaborate and close system of monitoring was simply not needed. For the same reason, an extensive review of a project's commercial prospects was felt to be unnecessary, as was any overall assessment of a firm's ability to finance its share of development. The knowledge that Government aid was limited, according to officials, meant that companies would have to assess realistically the risks involved in launching a new project; 'As it is their money primarily which is being put at risk, so their hope is qualified by the loss to which they stand subject.'[16]

A fixed limit to the Government's contribution was also viewed as the most effective supervisory instrument available to the Ministry. In order to keep their prices down and to avoid losses which they would have to bear, companies would have to monitor and control progress efficiently. The private firm, therefore, had the freedom to manage its business, but the Government could be assured that it had a satisfactory check on expenditure and would avoid large-scale and open-ended claims on the Exchequer. It appeared, in fact, that the 1960 policy had struck a successful balance between control and autonomy. Unlike earlier approaches to the sponsorship of civil aerospace, it did not undermine the independence of private industry or leave the state vulnerable to costly, ill-judged projects. As one Ministry spokesman confidently asserted, 'Risk and the possibility of profit thus remain with the manufacturer and provide a commercial incentive and a spur to exercise commercial judgement.'[17]

The Treasury was largely happy with the new arrangements. Officials were pleased with the limits launch aid placed on the amount of public money likely to be at risk in any one project. This, according to one, gave the Ministry a 'critical element of control' and the wish was expressed that similar methods might be employed in defence contracting.[18] However, the Treasury was concerned that the initial grants of launch aid were made to projects with scant prospects of commercial success and which would clearly give the Government little opportunity of recovering its investment. These, as the Ministry of Aviation conceded, had been made as an 'act of deliberate policy by the Government . . . to encourage manufacturers to embark on projects which otherwise they might not have embarked upon'.[19]

Critics of launch aid have seized upon this observation as indicating the basic weakness of launch aid; namely, that by reducing the costs of civil aircraft manufacture, firms were able to accept greater risks than they might otherwise have done. Consequently, the state was permanently involved in a high-risk commercial business which it ought to have left to the mercies of the private capital market. The provision of direct financial assistance had the effect, according to this view, of cushioning the British civil aircraft industry from the salutary consequences of commercial misjudgement.[20]

It should be noted, however, that these criticisms were made in the context of Concorde's cost escalation and the problems associated with the Rolls RB211 aero-engine. At the time, and in a number of later instances, the Government had every hope of encouraging commercially viable production. Undoubtedly, the first grants of launch aid were used to ease the aircraft industry's financial problems and to encourage rationalisation. HSA received £5·1 million for the Trident 1E and BAC obtained £9·75 million for the BAC 1-11, a new short-haul jet airliner. Vickers' difficulties were helped by the £9·4 million given to improve the basic VC10 and to launch a 'stretched' Super VC10. As we shall see, MoA also pressed BOAC to provide additional support for the Super VC10 programme.[21] Officials at the MoA accepted then that much of this and especially that granted to the Trident and VC10 would not be recovered. But once the Groups had settled down, launch aid would only be granted to commercially viable projects. Naturally, given the industry's past record, this required a degree of optimism; as one official said, 'one can only live in hope' that new projects would be successful.[22]

Obviously, the Government hoped to receive a return on its investment, both recovering its share of development costs and earning some profit. However, other benefits, for example the contribution civil aerospace made to the balance of payments, were expected to mitigate some of the losses incurred by an individual project. Launch aid was not seen as a substitute for private capital, merely as a supplement improving company cash flow and cushioning the large outflow of funds necessary before profits could be generated by a new aeroplane. It was still hoped that firms would eventually be able to undertake projects without any Government assistance, but by making money available for commercially attractive designs, the Government was helping to maintain the welfare of a strategically and economically important industry. Launch aid would be given in order to facilitate the production of aircraft and engines which would 'make some contribution to the whole economy, that it is in the national interest to have developed but which the manufacturer, without some form of aid of this kind, would not in fact develop'.[23]

Although the Government's investment in the Trident and the VC10 had to be written off, a fair number of early launch aided projects were more successful.[24] Crucially, however, the largest and most important project launched in the 1960s and ostensibly subject to all the constraints and controls outlined above, the RB211 aero-engine, demonstrated that the policy had, in fact, many limitations. Most significantly of all, it exposed the inadequacy of a system of control and monitoring based on self-policing procedures. Indeed, largely as a result of this experience, the utility of launch aid, as originally conceived in 1960, for all but the most modest civil project would be seriously questioned. However, for the rest of the decade the 1960 procedures were generally regarded as a satisfactory basis for state aid to private industry, containing as they did a nice balance between governmental control and managerial independence.

The Super VC10: subsidising the 'buy British' doctrine

The reintroduction of launch aid was gratefully received by the aircraft industry. There were a few grumbles; some overheads, especially those associated with marketing and commercial support generally, were not included in the MoA's assessment of launch costs, nor could they be set against the Government's levy. A launch aid policy, however, was far better than none, and most industrialists agreed that the taxpayer was entitled to a return on his investment. There was no relief on the other hand for the air corporations. The vexed question of proving costs and other financial burdens of buying British were not settled by Sandys' policy. The MoA felt it was more advantageous to concentrate financial aid on manufacturing and the Treasury opposed giving a procurement subsidy to any nationalised industry. Lord Douglas wryly noted that though there were words of sympathy for the airlines there was 'no hard cash'.[25]

BOAC in particular faced further pressure to compromise its own commercial interests in order to support the aircraft industry. The issue arose out of Vickers' deteriorating financial position and the increasing strain of developing the VC10. In January 1960 BOAC was told that the entire VC10 programme was in danger of cancellation. Even though Vickers was about to become part of BAC, the company still had to carry the cost of the VC10. To ease Vickers' cash-flow difficulties, BOAC was asked to confirm its option on ten more aircraft. BOAC had its own problems; its re-equipment programme was already a heavy commitment, and new airlines in the emerging nations of the Third World were competing on routes where BOAC once had a virtual monopoly. Traffic generally was slack. Similarly, BOAC, like other airlines, found that the second-hand value of its non-jet aircraft had plummeted. BOAC was therefore, a little reluctant to increase its order for VC10s.[26] During negotiations with Vickers, BOAC was asked to reconsider an earlier proposal made by Vickers to order a stretched version of the VC10, the Super VC10. Vickers had suggested this in 1959 with a view to improving the aircraft's operating economics on longer-range, higher-density routes. BOAC had then felt that a larger aircraft would lack the flexibility of the standard VC10 and in any case BOAC planned to use only 707s on its North Atlantic services.[27] Vickers' announcement radically altered the situation; BOAC had to reconsider its VC10 order and accept the possibility of buying the Super VC10. Either alternative was undoubtedly going to cost BOAC a great deal more than the original contract at a time when its own financial position was being strained. Vickers certainly stood to gain by renegotiating the VC10 order, but the benefit to BOAC was more doubtful. Admittedly, the loss of the VC10 would have been awkward, but no doubt some in BOAC would have gratefully turned to Boeing. However, the BOAC Board accepted as a basic duty that it should help the British aircraft industry. More important still, the Government, through the Minister of Aviation, intervened in support of Vickers' request.

Sandys told BOAC that he was equally concerned about the financial health and welfare of both the airline and the aircraft industries, but in this instance a larger order for the VC10 would help secure the formation of BAC.[28] Obviously, it would hardly be an auspicious start for the new group if a major part of it was in deep financial trouble and one of the industry's most important civil projects on the verge of cancellation. Sandys and his officials made it clear that any decision would have to be commercially sound for BOAC, but as the Select Committee on Nationalised Industries reported, '. . . BOAC's confidential documents show that the rehabilitation of Vickers and their merger with other companies to form what became the British Aircraft Corporation was constantly in the minds of BOAC's Board, and particularly of their Chairman, Sir Gerald d'Erlanger, in the discussion that followed.'[29] Consequently, in June 1960, BOAC placed a revised order for thirty Super and fifteen Standard VC10s. At the time, *Flight* thought it odd that BOAC was taking on such a large additional increase in capacity when traffic was falling, and even Sir Basil Smallpiece, BOAC's Managing Director, admitted that it was indeed 'a bit of a gamble'.[30] BOAC's new Chairman, Sir Matthew Slattery, who succeeded Sir Gerald d'Erlanger in the autumn of 1960, effected some changes in the order and specification. He had no doubt that the decision was not in BOAC's best interests and that it was definitely commercially unsound.

He immediately tried to get a clear statement from the Government about his duties and obligations as Chairman of BOAC. On his appointment, he recalled, he had been given no terms of reference save for a 'chance remark by Mr. Duncan Sandys that I was to make the Corporation pay'.[31] Clearly, the VC10 order would make this more difficult than ever. In August 1962, he tried to obtain a formal summary of the criteria on which he was to base airline policy. Writing to the Minister of Aviation, now Julian Amery, he noted that even though there was no statutory obligation so to do, over the years BOAC had often accepted the need to 'buy British'. In this, and other non-commercial decisions, it had often been 'actively encouraged by Ministers'.[32] Various Chairmen had held 'elastic' views on what was in BOAC's best interests commercially; now it was time to clarify matters. 'A policy decision', he wrote 'on this point is most urgently required as many of the Corporation's problems and the solutions thereto derive from the absence at present of a clear definition of purpose.' This, however, was not forthcoming and Slattery said that the Minister did not even reply to his letter.[33]

The 1963 White Paper

By the summer of 1962 BOAC's financial position had deteriorated sharply; the account for 1962 showed a deficit of £50 million. BOAC's earlier problems had worsened and their full effects were being felt. On top of these pressures, the re-equipment programme was straining BOAC's borrowing requirement and would be a burden well into the 1960s. Publication of the deficit led to a bitter and acrimonious exchange between Slattery and Amery. The Government commissioned an independent inquiry into the causes of BOAC's losses. The results of this inquiry – the Corbett Report – were not published. However, the Government did issue a White Paper based on its findings, blaming BOAC's Board and management for the deficit.[34] Slattery and Smallpiece resigned, amidst a welter of newspaper commentary, much of which condemned the Government's refusal to shoulder any of the responsibility for BOAC's plight.[35]

The VC10 order figured prominently in the debate on BOAC's problems. The Government hotly denied that any pressure had been put on BOAC to take decisions detrimental to its commercial interests. Officials and Ministers claimed that the Super VC10 had been presented to Sandys as a completely commercial action. Indeed, Sandys was said to have delayed authorising the necessary increase in BOAC's borrowing requirement until he had been convinced that the order was fully justified. The Government's view of the decision was summarised by Amery, 'if there have been errors, they have been entirely those of the Corporation; the Ministry could find no evidence that the Government were responsible for it'.[36]

However, in the light of information revealed by the Select Committee on Nationalised Industries, the Government's denials were scarcely credible. John Cronin, Labour's aviation spokesman, felt that '. . . this rather scandalous crisis . . . has been the direct responsibiliy of the Government. I think that the Minister is playing a shabby part in denying all responsibility'.[37] Even if, as the Select Committee report concluded, the Corporation had allowed itself to be 'deflected from its purposes by other influences', the Government had at least condoned the actions of its management and had provided the most powerful of those influences.[38]

Of course, d'Erlanger and his Board should have requested a directive and not anticipated the Government's interests in promoting the welfare of the aircraft industry by placing the orders for the Super VC10. MoA officials, however, admitted that not only was this usually discouraged because of the potentially damaging affect a directed purchase might have on the sales prospects of the aircraft concerned, but there was some doubt of the legality of such a specific request. In theory directives could only be given on matters of general policy. It was agreed that as a rule, some Chairmen were loath to press their case against a well-known and clearly expressed Government policy. In this case, one Ministry witness imagined that the Corporation, 'faced with a pretty clear and pretty firm view from the Government, might have come to the conclusion that they should not exclusively rely on their commercial judgement on the matter'.[39]

Much depended on the personalities involved. The statutory relationship between Minister and Chairmen was only a rough guide to reality. 'The actual relationship which exists', explained an official, 'is really a matter of complete goodwill between the Minister and the Chairmen . . . one might say that it goes on in spite of the rules there are in the Act than because of them'.[40] Compared with, for example, Lord Douglas of Kirtleside, Sir Gerald d'Erlanger lacked the confidence and experience to stand up to the Minister, especially one as forceful as Duncan Sandys. To be fair, Sir Gerald, like Lord Douglas, accepted as a matter of duty an obligation to further the national interest, including the necessity of buying British whenever possible. But in this case, as a senior civil servant in the MoA at the time recalled, 'we bullied d'Erlanger' on the VC10 order.

Commenting the performance of BOAC and BEA during the late 1950s and early 1960s, Robson suggests that their Chairmen acquiesced too readily in the demands of Government. 'Both Corporations seem always to have accepted, usually without protest, the Minister's interference with their commercial judgement even when he was acting without legal authority.'[41] Corbett, on the other hand, argues that the creation of the Ministry of Aviation was as much to blame, contrasting the Minister's power to influence the manufacturers with what he could wield over the airlines.

> The Ministry's real power over the airlines is direct, substantial and comprehensive; but when the Ministry deals with the aircraft manufacturers it must use persuasion, inducements, the promise of orders or subsidies or the threat of withdrawal. The Minister may find it easier, and less likely to cause political trouble, if it sacrifices the interests of the airlines to those of the manufacturers simply because the airlines are easier to deal with.[42]

This judgement is over-simplistic. The creation of the Ministry of Aviation did not cause the problems faced by the air corporations when faced with the 'buy British' policy or their other obligations to help the aircraft industry. These had been present long before the formation of the Ministry of Aviation, and persisted after its dissolution. Nevertheless, the 'buy British' doctrine, or more accurately the Government's refusal to underwrite the economic consequences of marginal decisions made 'in the national interest' to support the aircraft industry, was at the heart of BOAC's problems. The VC10 affair showed quite graphically that Government would have to assume not only the financial and political responsibility for measures designed to support British aircraft directly through launch aid, but also a similar responsibility that extended indirectly through the domestic market for civil airliners.

The Government's White Paper on BOAC reaffirmed that any air corporation must operate as a commercial undertaking. Accordingly, if the national interest should appear 'whether to the Corporation or the Government to require some departure from commercial practice, this should only be done with the agreement or at the insistence of the Minister of Aviation'. BOAC's new Chairman and Managing Director, Sir Giles Guthrie, also secured a formal statement of his duties and obligations as well as receiving assurances from the Government that he would have complete freedom to plan BOAC's commercial recovery. Guthrie was a hard-headed business man, and brooked no interference from the Minister. He also had a clear idea of BOAC's basic requirements. He worked to a very simple principle; it was, he said, 'BOAC's business to take care of its own commercial interests, not to look after anybody else's'. In particular, subsidising British aircraft development was a Ministerial problem, and not one for BOAC to worry about.[43]

The Guthrie plan

Early in 1964, Guthrie revealed his plan for BOAC's revival; and its central point was a dramatic reduction in the number of VC10s BOAC would buy. In his opinion, the airline had bought twenty-three too many Super VC10s and he proposed to cancel the entire outstanding order and replace them with seven additional Boeing 707s.[44] This would have been a death blow to the VC10 programme, and was bitterly resented by the manufacturers, already smarting from an earlier exchange with BOAC over problems with the aircraft's performance. The Government was caught between the pledge it had given to Guthrie and the disastrous effect that terminating production of the VC10 would have on Vickers, BAC and the British civil aircraft industry as a whole. Understandably, the Government took some time to consider its decision. In the meantime the Cabinet came under considerable pressure from its own supporters to protect the aircraft industry and, with an election pending, the Opposition made considerable capital out of their discomfiture.[45] Attempts were made to get Guthrie to modify his proposals, but, according to one participant, like a good trade union official negotiating a pay claim he stuck to his position.

On July 20, Amery announced that Guthrie would be allowed to run BOAC as a fully commercial operation. However, with considerable understatement, he noted that outright cancellation of the VC10 would 'damage its commercial prospects'.[46] BOAC would, therefore, be required to take seventeen of its original order, the RAF would have three, and the remainder would be 'suspended without prejudice' until their future could be studied at leisure. In return, BOAC would receive a full capital reconstruction. The Government admitted that there had been a clear choice between the interests of a British airline and those of the aircraft industry. 'Both of these interests should be the concern of the Government and we believe that the solution put forward is in the best interests of both.'[47]

Guthrie was satisfied with the outcome, arguing that buying the VC10 was not a subsidy to BOAC but a 'payment through us to the British aircraft manufacturing industry so as to ensure a "fly British" policy'.[48] BAC made the best it could of the decision. The company hoped to minimise the disruption in VC10 production schedules caused by the cancellation and, more importantly, to overcome the damage to sales which such an open dispute with a major customer inevitably caused. BAC executives later saw this setback as the final blow to the VC10's chances to sell in a market dominated by the Americans. Despite its apparently poor operating economics, the VC10 had considerable passenger appeal and those who built it feel that BOAC never gave the aeroplane sufficient credit for its success. The ten suspended orders were cancelled in 1966, and like the Trident, only a few VC10s were sold other than those bought by BOAC and the RAF.

The VC10 affair finally clarified the relationship between Government and the air corporations. It forced the former to recognise the potential conflict which could exist between a nationalised airline's commercial interest and the 'buy British' doctrine. More importantly, it established a precedent for resolving that conflict, namely that a nationalised airline could expect to be compensated for any uncommercial action caused by Government policy or forced upon it by Ministerial decision. As one civil servant admitted, 'We cannot some years later pillory them for losing money when in fact they have not been able to exercise their commercial judgement.' Or, in Julian Amery's words, the Government would have to 'indemnify the Corporation for the consequences of carrying out those Government requests'.[49] In the long run, financial compensation was in itself an unsatisfactory way to run an airline efficiently, whether publicly or privately owned, and expect it at the same time to act as a closed market for British aircraft. Paying a reluctant customer to fly a particular airliner was not the best advertisement for the product. The problem was, however, that while the United Kingdom could be a major air transport nation without an indigenous aircraft industry, it was 'highly unlikely that we could continue to be a major producer of civil aircraft unless this activity were supported by British airline operators'.[50] Decisions by BEA and BOAC to buy one aircraft rather than another were politically significant, were important to the aircraft industry as a source of launch orders and represented a way of keeping a production line open. Insofar as the Government retained an interest in the health of the domestic aircraft industry, BEA and BOAC could never wholly disengage their procurement policies from the 'buy British' doctrine. The lesson provided by the VC10 was that buying British, if opposed by the airline concerned, would have to be admitted as a deliberate act of policy in support of aircraft manufacturing, or for the advancement of some other Government objective.

Concorde and the internationalisation of civil aerospace development

The reintroduction of launch aid and the Government's recognition of its political and financial responsibility for the 'buy British' doctrine, was a major element in the state becoming, on a permanent basis, the lender of last resort for British civil aircraft development. The formation of larger groups undoubtedly helped to improve the industrial efficiency and enlarged the financial base of private companies, but rationalisation and reorganisation were in themselves insufficient to limit industry's claim on public expenditure. R&D costs continued to rise, and as we shall see, this was especially marked in the aero-engine sector; the level of profitability which private investors could expect from civil production did not improve, certainly not to the degree which might have justified accepting a greater than ever risk. Under the circumstances it was inevitable that the Government should come under pressure to relax its self-imposed limit of 50 per cent of a firm's estimated costs. Even under the terms of launch aid, the Government would still have to finance a growing proportion of industry's costs simply in line with increasing expenditure on R&D. By the early 1960s, therefore, the Government was more than willing to consider new ways of reducing the net cost of aerospace (military as well as civil) to the Exchequer.

The supersonic transport, better known as Concorde, exemplified the problem of financing large-scale, high-risk and highly expensive civil projects and, in due course, suggested a possible solution. From the outset, the Government accepted that development of an SST would be beyond the capabilities of private enterprise. If such a project was desirable, even necessary for the health of the aircraft industry, the state would have to sponsor its construction. In the event, the Government insisted, and industry had to concede, that this project was best produced, for political and economic reasons, in conjunction with another country. The interaction between domestic and international politics and the important role played by a technological lobby within Whitehall in the decision to build Concorde, has been well covered elsewhere.[51] However, it was such an important event in post-war civil aerospace policy, both in respect of the project's domestic origins as well as being one of the first collaborative projects, that many of these issues need to be re-examined.

The RAE and the Supersonic Transport Aircraft Committee

Let us first consider the origins of the SST in Britain. British work on the SST began in the early 1950s, largely as a result of initiatives taken by the Royal Aircraft Establishment (RAE), Farnborough. In 1954, the RAE's Deputy Director, Morian (later Sir Morian) Morgan was concerned that Farnborough's activities were primarily directed at military research. Morgan, perhaps anticipating the drift towards guided weapons in British defence policy, wanted to expand the RAE's civil interests. Attention was focused on the possibilities of civil supersonic flight; a logical step given the fact that each new generation of civil aircraft had tended to increase the speed of airline operation. Given the high subsonic speed of the new jet transports under development, it was only a matter of time before the 'classic curve of speed' would demand commercial supersonic aircraft.[52]

Morgan saw in civil supersonic flight precisely the opportunity he needed to diversify Farnborough's research. Sooner rather than later, he felt, private industry and the Government would need to discuss with the RAE the chances of building a supersonic transport in the United Kingdom. 'It would be desirable', he told his colleagues, 'for the RAE to have given some thought to it in the meanwhile, with a view to seeing if the requirements of a civil supersonic aircraft give any different guidance to research.'[53] Later, following the Comet disaster, the RAE was also concerned to ensure that Britain did not lose a similar technological lead by neglecting long-term development work, and the SST again looked like the most obvious trend for civil aviation to follow in the mid- and late 1960s. In the event, Farnborough's preliminary studies were discouraging; it seemed as though a commercial SST was beyond the state-of-the-art. However, a watching brief was maintained as an offshoot of work being done in support of the RAF's supersonic strategic bomber. This paid off when, in 1956, an RAE scientist made a number of vital theoretical advances in the aerodynamics of supersonic wings. Morgan and the new Director of the RAE, Gerald Gardner, felt that the time was now ripe for an extensive, official review of civil supersonics and the possibilities of organising a full-scale research effort.[54]

The RAE was convinced that Britain should build an SST, and supporters of the concept were prepared to lobby hard within the official machinery for such a project. Morgan and Gardner pressed the MoS to mount an official investigation, and in November their efforts were rewarded with the establishment of the Supersonic Transport Aircraft Committee (STAC). The STAC was remitted to examine the '. . . state of knowledge of all aspects of the problem and also to undertake a programme of research into specific subjects which need to be studied as a background before a design project could be started'. The STAC comprised representatives from the Ministries of Supply and Civil Aviation, other research establishments and the aircraft industry; Morgan himself took the chair. The Treasury made £700,000 available to pay for a number of industrial research contracts.[55] The SST also attracted the general support of the Minister of Supply, Aubrey Jones, who singled it out as an example of the kind of civil project the Government was prepared to support even if conventional aircraft had to be privately financed.[56]

Jones received a final report from the STAC in March 1959. It recommended the launch of two supersonic projects, a medium- and a long-range design, but it was generally recognised that the latter was the more important and commercially the more promising. The STAC estimated that the long-range version would cost between £78 and £98 million, but that this would be justified by a large, if unquantified market. Some mention was made of the potential environmental problems of civil supersonic operation, but these, including that of the sonic boom, were felt to be fairly minor issues and would, no doubt, be resolved during development.[56] Despite the STAC's confidence in the SST concept, there were a number of important areas of uncertainty. Theoretically, a commercial SST seemed feasible, but this would have to be confirmed by a long and extensive research programme. On the basis of past experience, this almost inevitably would be more protracted and costly than expected. The STAC's estimates already suggested that the SST would be more than twice as expensive to develop as the VC10, then Britain's most ambitious civil programme. There was certainly no guarantee that the SST would not be far more expensive than predicted. Similarly, although in the past airlines had tended to buy speed, without a more elaborate investigation of the market sales potential had to remain a matter for optimistic conjecture. Given the likely length of SST development, naturally it would be vulnerable to changes in the pattern of civil aviation demand. However, with American manufacturers known to be interested in an SST, it was not unreasonable to assume that there would always be a lucrative market for a faster aircraft than the last generation of airliners.

Nevertheless, the question of cost loomed large in Jones's thoughts as he considered the STAC report. He was intuitively suspicious of the STAC's figures, which, in fact had been the subject of a heated debate within the MoS. Gardner had originally suggested that the long-range SST would cost £60 million, whereas another senior official thought it would probably be nearer £100 million. The final, official figure represented a compromise between these two guesses. Outside the MoS, the ICAO estimated that a long-range commercial SST could cost between £100 and £300 million; Sir Arnold Hall of HSA, never an SST enthusiast, felt that £300 million should always have been regarded as a minimum.[58] The official estimate contained an alement of rational calculation, but equally, it also contained more than an element of 'bid pitching', presenting a reasonable and credible figure for consideration, which, at the same time, would not frighten the politicians or attract early and fatal opposition from the Treasury. Jones himself mentally doubled the estimates presented by the STAC. But in truth, at that stage, nobody could have accurately predicted the likely costs of such a complex piece of technology. In any event, the decision to launch Concorde was not taken as a result of long and intensive cost-effectiveness calculations; it was essentially a politically inspired choice based on subjective evaluation and the interplay of official, scientific and political groups within the Government. Indeed, even the aircraft industry tended to be more affected by (rather than participants in) the decision-making process or the initial lobbying associated with the launch of SST research and development.

The political debate

The political, or at any rate, the wider industrial case for developing an SST almost regardless of any cost, was first put by Morgan himself. In a covering letter to the MoS attached to the STAC report, he stressed the consequences of not launching such an aeroplane,

> We must emphasise that a decision not to start detailed work fairly soon on the transatlantic aircraft would be in effect a decision to opt altogether out of the long-range supersonic transport field. Since we would never regain a competitive position, this could have a profound effect on the pattern of our aircraft industry and on our position as a leading aeronautical power.[59]

This became an oft-repeated theme. In the summer of 1961, when Duncan Sandys sought Cabinet permission to begin negotiations with the French about a collaboration on an SST, he told his colleagues that '. . . if we do not go in for the next generation of civil aircraft we might as well pack up the British industry'. He added bluntly, 'We have to go on or opt out.'[60] In November 1962, during the Cabinet's only full-scale examination of the project, and before he was allowed to sign the Anglo-French treaty committing the United Kingdom to the SST, Julian Amery also argued that the British aircraft industry would not recover from a negative decision. Indeed, the implications might have been even more disastrous; without the SST, he told the House of Commons, 'our industry would slip back from the front rank of aircraft constructors and that would have a serious effect on the economy of this country'.[61]

In his superb analysis of the Concorde decision, Henderson notes that on no occasion did the Government consider what might have been a reasonable price to pay for either the sheer prestige of developing an SST, or for its wider value to the aircraft industry and to the economy as a whole.[62] The Treasury did mount, in effect, a guerrilla campaign against the SST which periodically errupted into open field warfare. Certainly, once the more attractive option of collaborating with the Americans collapsed, the Treasury was increasingly worried about the unquantifiable nature of the SST programme. But the MoA, and especially the tightly knit group of officials responsible for the SST, made it very difficult for the Treasury to discover much detail of the project.

Moreover, the MoA organisation as a whole constituted a pretty formidable team of experts when it came to discussing complicated technical matters. However, helped by a general deterioration in Britain's economic outlook which inevitably put pressure on the Government to cut public expenditure, in the summer of 1962, the Treasury forced an interdepartmental review of the SST.

This took the form of a Cabinet sub-committee investigation headed by Macmillan's trouble shooter, Lord Mills. The MoA produced, in the words of one participant, a 'massive presentation' of the data in favour of developing an SST. This included a very impressive performance from Sir George Edwards representing the airframe contractor, BAC. The Mills Committee was evidently told that the two versions proposed by the STAC would cost in the region of £170 million, which would be recovered on less than 200 sales. (As far as I am able to judge, evidence presented to the House of Commons Select Committee on Estimates in 1964 reflected the case put by each side. This has been supplemented, and to some extent confirmed, by interviewing some of the participants.) The estimated cost of development represented little change from the STAC's original figure, and the MoA admitted that this was 'rather speculative'. The MoA nevertheless felt that it was a reasonably cautious estimate, and the French even believed it to be unduly pessimistic.[63] The MoA also referred to the promises Sandys had made to the aircraft industry in 1960 to help civil aircraft production and stressed the effects which failure to develop an SST would have on the commercial and employment prospects in the industry.

The Treasury, on the other hand, pointed to the speculative nature of the proposal and the impossibility of forecasting confidently the ultimate cost of development. On the basis of past experience with large-scale military projects, it was almost inevitable that the SST would encouter technical problems which would invariably force up costs and delay production. It was, as one official told a Select Committee, 'idle to pretend that the estimates we have been working on . . . will necessarily stand up over a period of time'.[64] The Treasury's case was strong enough to prevent Mills from giving the SST his full approval and recommending a positive decision to the Cabinet. However, he was impressed by the MoA's arguments and suggested that every consideration be given to starting a programme. Although this was not a clear-cut victory for the SST and its supporters, it was enough that the project had survived virtually the only full-dress examination of its relative costs and merits.

In spite of the uncertainties surrounding its potential cost, the SST was accepted as being necessary and, indeed, vital to the long-term future of British aerospace. This was unreservedly the view of the RAE scientists who promoted the SST vigorously throughout its early stages; it was an argument which was readily accepted by the MoS and MoA officials most closely associated with aircraft production; and most important of all, it was the one which captured the political imagination. As Henderson succinctly observes, it was the kind of presentation which reduced 'a complex set of problems to simple terms', providing a clear and 'unambiguous guidance to busy men, in a rather complicated situation where there were conflicting arguments and judgements'.[65] The Treasury continued to fight it to the last, but increasingly, the SST acquired an inexorable political momentum as domestic issues were reinforced by the exigencies of foreign policy.

International cooperation and the SST

The internationalisation of the SST came to be seen as part of a wider and logical response to the problem of rising costs and limited domestic markets for European advanced technology projects. At the time, the decision to launch Concorde as a collaborative venture was both a matter of political judgement and a response to economic and industrial realities. International collaboration, certainly in aerospace, was conceived and evolved within a higher political environment; a truism perhaps, which the later development of British civil aerospace policy would repeatedly confirm. The underlying philosphy of European technological cooperation itself contained a strong element of emotion and fear; a growing perception that, individually, European states were being surpassed economically and industrially by technologically superior American enterprise. In the mid-1960s, this would be articulated as the 'American challenge' based upon a perception that a number of 'technology gaps' in key sectors, such as aerospace, nuclear energy and computers had opened up between European countries and the United States. Whether real or not, many political figures came to believe in the danger of losing the ability to control one's own national or regional destiny to power centres across the Atlantic.[66] One option was to strengthen national technological capability; for Government increasingly to support advanced projects; to sponsor coherent and deliberate national strategies for science and technology; to take steps to broaden and improve the industrial base, encourage mergers, aid private and public enterprise and control the domestic market for advanced technological products. Alternatively, though by no means mutually exclusive of a domestic policy to improve capability, the relatively small R&D activities of the separate European states could be joined together to recreate the conditions believed to be the reason for American successes in these fields, namely substantial economies of scale in development, production and marketing.

American aerospace firms were much bigger than their European counterparts and were able to call upon larger production and financial resources. Moreover, the sheer size of their domestic market, both for military and civil equipment, reinforced by explicit and implicit protective barriers, enabled far longer production runs, substantially reducing the unit costs of American aircraft and engines. This, and the unquestioned efficiency and greater productivity of American companies, gave the United States an enormous competitive edge over Europe. Collaboration, restated, aimed to create some of those conditions and advantages by pooling national resources, sharing costs and by broadening initial markets for aerospace products. It was known from an early stage that the logistics of joint development and production would involve delicate political questions related to industrial and technological sovereignty. Accurately enough, as it turned out, it was also realised that collaboration would inevitably increase the cost of individual programmes, even if the overall cost to each participating state would be lower. Optimistically, these difficulties were dismissed as 'growing pains', for, in Julian Amery's words, although cooperation would indeed bring 'marginal additions to come costs', these would be 'outweighed by the major economies which followed from the elimination of duplicated national effort'.[67]

International cooperation necessarily increased the political salience of the technology concerned because it emphasised the role of Government in negotiating and administering a joint programme. Involvement in a joint venture would also require the Government to defend and promote national technological and industrial interests, the importance of which would be directly proportional to the size, complexity and cost of the project concerned. There was expertise to be gained, and competitive advantages over past and possibly future rivals to be lost; factors which would colour both industrial and Governmental attitudes in respect of both the general principle and the detail of collaborative proposals. Individual market requirements might also have to be compromised; consequently domestic customers, whether airforces or airlines, could be expected to buy aircraft which did not entirely suit their own needs but which instead satisfied the lowest common denominator of design amongst the participating countries. Financial support and industrial activity would have to be organised and monitored trans-nationally, adding, of course, to the accountability problems inevitable in any large-scale public programme. Governments would also have to face, and make due allowance for, fundamentally different motives and attitudes about collaboration; a country wanting and prepared to 'buy a capability' could easily have diametrically opposed views about a project and its viability compared with one more concerned simply to reduce the cost of aerospace production and to improve the commercial return on development. Finally, collaborative ventures could hardly be free from wider political considerations. The general diplomatic relations between states would inevitably affect their functional relationships; a collaborative project could become both an instrument of foreign policy and, conversely, a source of friction between governments. Either way, technological collaboration would be affected by, and have an influence on, an often problematic international political context.

Before Concorde, British attitudes in the 1950s towards the various collaborative and co-production schemes undertaken by European firms had been somewhat dismissive. For example, the French felt that BEA should have bought the Caravelle instead of the Trident. The Caravelle contained many British components supplied directly or built under licence in France. In the eyes of some French industrialists, this made the Caravelle a 'European' airliner which could easily have been the foundation for a more ambitious Anglo-French civil programme capable of successfully challenging the Americans in the market for short- and medium-haul aircraft. At the time neither BEA nor the British aircraft industry saw much advantage in collaborating. A few firms had some links with continental producers, but the majority, confident of their own industrial and technical prowess, were uninterested in collaboration. In any case, British firms were too preoccupied with the problems of domestic rationalisation to bother about the additional complication of international alignments. For its part, the Government was also more concerned with domestic reorganisation, and had yet to discover or consciously apply the political uses of international collaboration to a wider policy towards Europe.

Almost inevitably, therefore, an early proposal to build the SST in conjunction with the French received a lukewarm response in the United Kingdom. In the summer of 1959, while he was still considering the STAC report, Aubrey Jones visited the Paris airshow. Concerned as he was about the likely cost of producing the SST, besides being an early convert to Europe, Jones discussed with his French opposite number the possibility of launching a joint programme. The French, though then in some respects technologically inferior to the British, had also been considering a supersonic airliner and Jones's proposal was warmly welcomed. But on his return to Britain, to use his own words, the idea was 'laughed to scorn'. The MoS was not enthusiastic about internationalising the British SST, and industry believed that there was nothing to be gained from cooperating with what were generally regarded as technically less advanced companies. In fact, the one large hole in French capabilities was in the field of civil engine development; her airframe industry, if not then the equal of the best in Britain, was rapidly becoming so. More important, however, the Cabinet politically saw no reason for departing from a purely indigenous programme.

Between the summer of 1959 and the autumn of 1961, Britain's policy towards Europe, and particularly membership of the EEC, underwent a radical change. Following the General Election victory of October 1959, Macmillan's new administration contained a larger number of 'Europeans' and, in the light of changing economic and political circumstances, began seriously to consider applying for membership of the Common Market. In July 1961, Macmillan announced that the

Government intended to open negotiations with the Six. The prospect of dealing with the French Government, deeply suspicious of the sincerity and seriousness of Britain's newly discovered Europeanism, added greatly to the significance of any avenue for broadening and demonstrating a commitment to the continent. In this context, a joint programme to develop the SST was especially promising.

Duncan Sandys and his Parliamentary Secretary, Geoffrey Rippon, who chaired the MoA's SST committee, were themselves ardent Europeans. They were also strongly in favour of building the SST. Sandys urged the adoption of a collaborative approach and in the Summer of 1961, he obtained Cabinet approval to begin negotiations with the French.[68] Officials associated with the programme had, in some cases reluctantly, to accept that for political and economic reasons some form of joint venture was necessary. It was also quickly appreciated that by successfully identifying the SST with the Government's European ambitions, they would strengthen their case against the project's Whitehall enemies.

The MoA was keeping its collaborative options open, however; at the same time as talks were being held with the French, MoA officials were in contact with the Americans. An Anglo-American SST programme had the attraction of linking British industry with technically and certainly commercially stronger companies, and would make penetration of the vital American market that much easier. The prospect of transatlantic cooperation also helped to mollify the Treasury's growing concern about the costs of producing an SST; officials there felt that the Americans would be more likely to insist on tight financial control over development and to emphasise commercial reality over technological enthusiasm.[69] Indeed, until November 1961, the MoA was confident than an agreement could be reached. At the last minute, the Americans backed off. Evidently the FAA's Chief Technical Advisor cast doubts over British preference for a Mach 2.2 design using conventional materials and structures. In return, the British delegation were opposed to a more advanced and more expensive Mach 3.0 proposal from the Americans. This left the French as the only possible partners.

With the benefit of hindsight, the Anglo-American project was not a credible proposition. The British clearly needed the Americans more than the Americans needed them. Similarly, for all the emerging differences between the British and the French over the SST's basic design, they were always much closer on general principles than the British were with the Americans. The most telling issue was undoubtedly Britain's application to join the EEC. For the United Kingdom to have decided in favour of the Anglo-American project could have torpedoed its application even before serious negotiations had begun. The French were already unhappy with Britain's deep involvement with the United States as far as military technology was concerned.[70] A transatlantic SST would have been final confirmation of Britain's role as America's 'Trojan Horse' within Europe.

Negotiating the Anglo-French agreement

Once the American option disappeared, the MoA pursued the French connection even more vigorously. Amongst the politicians and officials, substantial progress towards a draft agreement was reported. The most serious problem was getting their respective industries to accept collaboration and to produce a common design. Admittedly, relations between the engine companies were very cordial. In the domestic competition to choose a suitable engine for the British SST, BSE had beaten Rolls-Royce. BSE had had the advantage of offering a relatively cheap conversion programme based on the Olympus supersonic engine under development for the TSR2 and had already established links with the French engine company SNECMA. With a large supersonic engine already in an advanced stage of design and as SNECMA was clearly the technical inferior to BSE, the French were happy to concede leadership on the engine programme to the British. Indeed, collaboration on an equal status with the British was an ideal opportunity for SNECMA to build up its own expertise. As early as November 1961, the two companies were able to announce that they were ready to agree on a joint programme to develop the Olympus as a civil supersonic engine.[71]

The main cause of industrial tension and conflict, however, was the relationship between the designated airframe contractors, BAC and Sud Aviation. BAC, or rather its Bristol component, had been closely involved in the SST from its early stages. Eventually, BAC (Bristol) was awarded the more favoured long-range design feasibility study and in the summer of 1960, the MoA awarded it a full design study contract. Interestingly enough, in view of his later advocacy of the Concorde, Sir George Edwards, the Vickers' Chief Civil Designer, on becoming Managing Director of BAC, was not particularly in favour of developing the SST, especially if it took money away from subsonic types. However, the Bristol team, led by the redoubtable Archibald Russell, was heavily committed to the SST and BAC was not about to waste this asset or to reject Government money for an important project. By the end of 1961, Russell's team had outlined the Mach 2.2 BAC 223, capable of carrying 100 passengers non-stop between London and New York, and Edwards had become a strong SST advocate.[72]

As a condition of the earlier feasibility study contract, BAC had been instructed to consider collaboration. Considering it and practising it, however, were two very different matters. BAC and Sud differed over design and development strategy. BAC was convinced that the long-range SST, though likely to take a considerable time to develop, was commercially the only viable option. Sud wanted to press on more quickly with a less advanced medium-range type and then build up to a transatlantic type. Mutual antagonism between senior managers exacerbated the technical problems, and the combination of personal and corporate rivalry made progress towards a common programme very slow indeed. In short, neither firm was prepared to concede any aspect of design or industrial leadership to the other.

From the British side, this was an extension of the 1950s sense of superiority. To the French, it was misplaced arrogance, with Sud resenting the implication, in the light of the Caravelle, that it was technically any less able than BAC. Considerable emphasis was placed on the question of leadership; rightly, perhaps, because of commercial and industrial advantages which could accrue from leading a joint programme. But excessive preoccupation with design leadership bedevilled this, and nearly all the early collaborative programmes. As Sir George Dowty, President of the SBAC, put it at the time, '. . . there cannot be two queen bees in any hive. Is one country going to knuckle down to another? This is the root difficulty of an international effort, for one company must always be the leader.'[73] In the event, the two governments simply had to knock heads together and force an agreement, or at least get an acceptable compromise out of the warring airframe contractors.

Given the complexity of the problems facing the designers, this, in retrospect, was a mistake. Under intense pressure from the two Governments, BAC and Sud simply agreed to differ. In October 1962, BAC and Sud presented an outline consisting of two designs using the same engine and many other shared components. But essentially, they were different aircraft reflecting each one's preference for a long- or medium-range airliner. This solution did little to resolve the underlying tension between the two companies and ensured that two years would pass before the French finally conceded the wisdom of going for the most lucrative market and concentrating all effort on one basic design. The final treaty also left many issues, often highly complicated administrative and managerial points, to be worked out in practice. Certainly, in its rush to sign the agreement, the British Government may well have been too prepared to sacrifice a strong negotiating position. The French needed the British to provide the necessary engine expertise. This advantage might have been better used, if not to win airframe design leadership, perhaps to force the French to accept the principle of one long-range design.

This, of course, was the crux of the matter; the British SST lobby wanted the programme launched, the Government wanted a spectacular assertion of Britain's 'Europeanism' at a crucial stage in the EEC negotiations. Consequently in his final presentation to the Cabinet on 28 and 29 November 1962, Amery stressed both the domestic and international political aspects of the SST. Urged on by the Foreign Office, Amery raised the spectre of France going it alone on the SST, an unlikely but not wholly incredible threat, which would have untold consequences for British industry and certainly undermine Britain's chances of gaining

entry to the Common Market. Put in these terms, and despite some
opposition from the Treasury Ministers, the Cabinet agreed to the Treaty
as presented. Set against these broadly stated, politically important and
comprehensible arguments, the details of the agreement, with its
complicated and often highly technical implications, seem to have been
largely irrelevant.

Amery and the SST lobby were even able to win a last battle with the
Treasury; the Treaty contained no provision for a 'break clause',
enabling either party at some mutually accepted point to withdraw from
the programme. Amery and the MoA claimed that this was designed to
ensure that the French could not renege on the agreement. In the event,
and no doubt in the minds of SST supporters, it effectively guaranteed
that as long as the French wanted the project to continue, the Concorde
would be immune to unilateral cancellation by a British Government.[74]

The 1962 Agreement: technical and administrative issues

The treaty was a very brief document to shape the development of
Europe's equivalent to the US Apollo programme and one which linked
for the first time Europe's major aeronautical powers.[75] It comprised a
series of general statements of principle with many details left to be
resolved once the programme was underway. Collaboration was to be
based upon a 'strict' equality between the two states. Because of Britain's
clear superiority in engine technology, the French were allocated 60 per
cent of the airframe and 40 per cent of the engine; but on balance, the
principle of equal sharing of cost and return was intended to be strictly
enforced.[76] Considering the relative weakness of the French aero-engine
industry, conceivably a more calculated approach by the British
negotiators might have been able to exploit this, perhaps forcing a
concentration on the long-range version.

In getting agreement on two versions, a long- and medium-range, the
French, gained a clear victory. They had consistently fought for the
medium-range aircraft which they believed could be produced faster than
the long-range design preferred by the British. Each type would, in fact,
be a hybrid, using as many common components and complete systems as
possible. Development was scheduled to take seven years up to the
delivery of the first production aircraft. In retrospect, British members of
the Concorde design team believe that this was a fundamental mistake,
and a point which should never have been conceded to the French. The
effort involved in concerting two substantially different designs, and the
delay in settling on a definitive long-range version, incurred both
financial and commercial penalties. Had the two companies pressed
ahead from the start with an agreed design, some of the later
environmental and commercial doubts about Concorde might have been
avoided.[77]

The Treaty also only provided the outline of a structure for project management and political direction. It stated that the manufacturers would retain the managerial initiative and day-to-day industrial responsibilities. A trans-national organisation was to be created to be headed by a Committee of Directors, one each for the airframe and aero-engine programmes, both supported by technical sub-committees. The Committee of Directors was supposed to act like the Board of any nationally based private company under contract to Government. It was inevitable, however, that the two Governments would be more than usually concerned with the technical and industrial details of such an important project and, with so many vital interests at stake, in time the distinction between industrial and Governmental responsibilities would become blurred.

The manufacturers were responsible to the two Governments jointly through a Standing Committee of Officials. The Standing Committee was required to monitor and to supervise progress and, where and when necessary, propose measures to ensure the carrying out of the programme. The Standing Committee also delegated specialised matters to a Technical Committee. Interestingly, the British Treasury was not officially represented on the Standing Committee until 1965. It was thought sufficient for the Ministry of Aviation to report back to the Treasury on matters relating to costs and expenditure, a situation clearly unacceptable once the true magnitude of the programme was realised.[78]

Overall, the administrative machinery for the programme at both industrial and official levels fell well short of a fully integrated and centralised system of management. Because the Committee of Directors comprised the senior staff of BAC, BSE, Sud and SNECMA, the responsible Ministries were obliged to send their most senior representatives. The whole composition and arrangement of the management and administrative structure proved to be cumbersome and top-heavy, providing all too many opportunities for Anglo-French rivalry to break out into open conflict. The continuing inter-company rivalry exacerbated these problems and while in time matters would improve, in the early days decision-making was far from easy.[79]

The Treaty contained important omissions; perhaps the most tiresome of these was the failure to allow for intramural costs in assessing the distribution of effort and expenditure between the two countries. Intramural costs related to work done for the Concorde in national research establishments or financed by one Government, but which was not directly attributable to the joint programme. Throughout the development phase, the French refused to detail their intramural expenditure or to allow an assessment of these costs to form part of overall estimates affecting the distribution of work and subcontracts. In spite of periodic imbalances, by the 1970s British officials believed that intramural costs had been roughly equally distributed between the two countries. However, the issue has still to be finally settled and the same officials admit that it would have made for greater trust between the two countries and better accountability if this problem had been anticipated in the original agreement.[80]

The question of adjusting inequalities in costs incurred during development was also left out of the 1962 Treaty. In the event, and to avoid complicated payments across the exchanges, it was decided to even out expenditure through the allocation of sub-contracts. This was not always industrially efficient and sometimes led to major disputes between British and French firms and their respective official patrons. The Public Accounts Committee often expressed its concern at the vagueness and *ad hoc* nature of these procedures. As one report concluded, 'we hope that in all future collaborative projects equitable and economic methods of dealing with cost balances and intramural expenditure will be decided at the outset'.[81]

In general terms, the agreement was far too brief for what was even then an extensive programme. The fact that this was one of the first collaborative projects and patently a vital project to both countries contributed to these weaknesses. Similarly, the urgency of the negotiation may also have prevented a closer and more detailed examination of potential problems. It may even have suited both sides to have kept matters simple. It certainly served as a lesson in future programmes as a system to avoid. It was not surprising, therefore, that in time, as the political and practical problems of directing and monitoring such a complicated project grew, a more streamlined organisation emerged. In particular, the Governments themselves began to impose tighter industrial control over development and to take more detailed interest in the day-to-day management of development.

Reconciling the principle of equality with industrial efficiency was difficult, and a problem which was never entirely resolved. It was an issue which dogged most joint ventures, but it was especially pronounced in this instance. This was, perhaps, inevitable because Concorde was technically such a complex project. As one British analyst has written, it was 'entirely fortuitous that anything like a sensible distribution of labour was achieved on the project', a view echoed by a French observer; 'the principle of equality was prejudicial to a rational distribution of work'.[82] The inefficiency and duplicated effort entailed by these arrangements added between 20 and 30 per cent to the eventual cost of development. But given the project's industrial and political significance any other principle would have been unacceptable to either Government.

At the time Amery had little doubt that the decision to develop Concorde was correct and that the agreement formed a sound basis for this and future objects. At the press conference following the Treaty's signature on 29 November, he averred that the SST was the 'next logical step in civil aviation'. It was also an important step towards a more general commitment between two European states to collaborate in aerospace and other advanced technologies. As Amery put it,

> Even more significant may be the lessons which France and Britain will learn⁻
> from working together on every aspect of a joint project of this size. Our two
> countries were pioneers in the early days of aircraft production. Then, they
> were also rivals. But now the time has come to join forces, if we are to hold a
> leading position in the air routes of the world.[83]

Sadly, de Gaulle's veto of Britain's EEC application in January 1963
robbed the Concorde of its immediate diplomatic value; but British
Ministers took some comfort from his remarks that projects like Concorde
would represent evidence of British determination unreservedly to
embrace Europe. Certainly, the underlying political and financial value
of collaboration would be increasingly significant, if not for this
Government, for its successor. In the last few months of the Conservative
administration, Amery took part in preliminary talks with the French
aimed at launching a wide range of other joint ventures which were
picked up by Labour after their General Election victory in October.[84]

Despite the disappointment at the French veto, the Concorde was itself
regarded as a substantial gain for the United Kingdom. It would not be a
cheap project, but sharing costs with the French would be, it was hoped, a
distinct relief to the British taxpayer. Commercially, with the Americans
also looking to supersonic flight, there could be little doubt that a market
was there for the aircraft. Officials associated with the project at this time
have no regrets about starting development, or about their efforts in
protecting it from what they felt was a short-sighted outlook on the part
of the Treasury. Even then, however, there were no guarantees; the
Americans, aiming at Mach 3.0 and with a larger carrying capacity for
their SST designs, were recognised as being formidable competitors.
Similarly, now that the project began to take on substance and the true
magnitude of the task became evident (or at least came to be viewed more
realistically) estimates of costs were already being revised upwards.
Concorde might have been conceived as a 'supersonic 707' but there were
some who already sensed that it was more likely to be a 'supersonic
Comet'.[85]

By 1964, many of the elements of Government policy towards civil
aerospace, which lasted well into the next decade, had been established.
The principle and procedures of launch aid, as well as a financial
responsibility for the 'buy British' doctrine, were the central features of
the state acting as lender of last resort to private enterprise. There was
nothing over-intrusive about the Government's monitoring of assistance;
the self-policing nature of launch aid effected a nice balance, or so it
seemed, between control and autonomy. By the same token,
compensating the nationalised airlines for procuring 'uncommercial'
equipment (though hardly a compliment to the British aircraft industry)
formalised a public responsibility which, in its earlier ambiguity, had

helped neither the airlines nor the aircraft companies. In the event, although both BEA and BOAC would be subject in the future to more Government directives, changes in the pattern of domestic manufacturing would eventually give them a greater measure of real freedom to procure equipment of their choice. In any case, as R&D costs rose, support through the market was increasingly less significant as a proportion of the total cost of launching a medium to large civil aircraft or engine and purely British launch orders of less importance in decisions to start domestic or collaborative projects.

Finally, the Concorde represented not only a project which would sprawl across the next decade and a half of aerospace policy, but marked a qualitative as well as a quantitative change in Government's relationship with the civil aircraft industry. This was big technology; and civil development would henceforward be important in its own right and not merely a minor offshoot of military activity. It would soon be joined by at least one other airframe project which was equally political if not as financially significant and, more importantly still, by a large engine programme which was both. Together, these three civil projects, Concorde, the Airbus medium-range airliner and Rolls-Royce's family of big fan engines, would help to turn the Government into more than just a lender of last resort, but the lender of only resort for civil aerospace production. By the mid-1970s, the Government would be responsible not merely for a part of civil development financing but for its entirety.

Concorde also indicated that the future development of civil projects, indeed most aerospace activity, would have an international dimension. In many ways, the sheer size and importance of the Concorde made it an awkward exercise in collaboration. The stakes involved were perhaps too high to permit the emergence of a rational industrial or managerial organisation; leadership and technical responsibilities had to be shared equally and it was too early in the learning curve of cooperative ventures easily to establish a more sophisticated approach. On the other hand, its very scale and political importance was a vital catalyst in overcoming domestic resistance to the idea of collaboration, especially in the United Kingdom. For better of worse, directly or indirectly, British civil aerospace development would now have a European dimension and the domestic and international politics of technology would be inextricably interwoven.

3

SUBSONIC POLITICS, 1964–70

The increasing scale of launch costs and the continuing acceptance of international cooperation inevitably brought Government more often and even more decisively into the selection and development of civil aircraft and engines. From Concorde onwards, the launch of civil aerospace programmes was associated with vital technological and industrial assets and important political values. Government had to face a succession of control problems and to cope with the long-term effects and implications of decisions. Civil aerospace after 1964 rapidly became a permanently difficult and problematic aspect of British technology policy. There was a continual need for Ministers to reconcile conflicting domestic interests, and these with differing international requirements. Britain faced recurring problems in deciding how its share of a project should be allocated between the airframe and the engine sectors of UK industry. This was seen most clearly in the case of the European Airbus where the problem was complicated by the preference of Rolls-Royce, Britain's leading engine producer, to establish a permanent place in the US aircraft industry, rather than to participate only in collaborative European projects.

The Labour Party and aerospace

The Labour Government elected in 1964 came to power determined on an expansion and redistribution of national resources allocated to technology. In opposition, the Labour Party had seized on technology as an electoral issue, criticising both the emphases and implementation of Conservative policy. According to Labour, science and technology well used could regenerate British industry and revitalise the economy. The Conservatives had wasted the opportunity by concentrating on defence and 'prestige' projects. The Labour Government, on the other hand, was determined to 'back winners', commercially viable projects and areas of technological innovation which could benefit a wider range of industrial applications. Consequently, it embarked on an ambitious and unrepentantly interventionist strategy to provide British industry with the conditions to advance and to exploit technology. At home, Governmental reorganisation (the creation of a Ministry of Technology), the encouragement of mergers (to increase the capital and productive base for R&D investment) and the identification of 'national champions' (for example, BLMC in cars, ICL in computers and, as we shall see, Rolls-Royce in aero-engines) around which to base public investment. Internationally, the Labour Government responded to the 'technology gap' syndrome by asserting even more strongly than its predecessor the need for European collaboration. This still had a practical purpose, to share costs and widen markets; but like its predecessors, Labour accepted that technology was also politically useful in demonstrating the United Kingdom's value to the European Economic Community. In short, technology was again a strong bargaining card in negotiations to join the Common Market, or as a link if Britain were refused entry.[1]

In general, however, Labour regarded the apparently free-spending aerospace industry with some hostility. Expenditure in the aircraft industry symbolised the waste and mismanagement characteristic of the previous administration. Roy Jenkins, the Minister of Aviation[2] said that the industry had been 'feather-bedded' for too long and it was in for a 'few shocks'. In December 1964 he announced the establishment of a Committee of Inquiry under Lord Plowden to 'consider the future place and organisation of the aircraft industry'. He instructed the Committee particularly to bear in mind the 'possibilities of international cooperation'. Ominously, Jenkins added that decisions on the future of individual projects would not be postponed, but would stand as 'fixed points for their deliberations'.[3] True to his word, by April 1965 a series of military aircraft projects had been axed: however, as we shall see in Chapter 5, Concorde was saved. Against a background of strident Conservative and bitter industrial criticism, Jenkins justified the Government's actions. There had been, he said, simply too many domestic projects based on the 'inadequate' British market. The future lay in joint ventures with other countries which would cut costs and provide larger initial markets. In the interim, however, the Government had to 'clear the ground' before it could start to build.[4] American aircraft were ordered to cover the gaps left by cancellation and Jenkins picked up the negotiations begun by Julian Amery directed at a wide range of civil and military programmes to be built in collaboration with the French.[5] In short, the new Government was determined to reduce the overall burden of aerospace to the Exchequer and to ensure that future investment would be based on a stricter adherence to commercial criteria or promise wider economic and industrial benefits.

The dissolution of the MoA

These principles were to be reflected in the administration of aerospace policy. The continued existence of the MoA was a particularly inviting target for reorganisation. It had long been regarded by the Labour Party as the institutional manifestation of the previous Government's lax

control over its spending in aerospace and symbolised the privileged place
the industry had achieved in the national economy. Tony Benn, as
Minister of Technology, graphically summarised what many in the new
Government felt about the MoA and its representatives. At an SBAC
dinner, no less, he recounted how Ministers of Aviation had been

> ... the most hated and feared Ministers in Government. While their
> colleagues were grateful for anything they could wring from the Chancellor of
> the Exchequer, Ministers of Aviation ran off with sums of money that made
> the great train robbers look like schoolboys pinching money from a blind
> man's tin.[6]

The presumption was that the MoA, a powerful, free-spending but
sectionally orientated department, had been partly responsible for the
inadequacies of the previous Government's industrial and technological
policies. The MoA, it was argued, had been insensitive to the commercial
and economic consequences of overspending on aerospace, particularly
on military and prestige projects. A broader, more comprehensive
approach to the public support of technology and the technology-based
industries was required. As one Labour Minister said of the MoA, 'in
pursuing its sponsorship function of the aviation industry it has failed to
give top priority to commercial objectives and to its wider responsibilities
to the economy as a whole'.[7]

The dissolution of the MoA, and its possible incorporation in a broader
ministry of technology had been considered during Labour's pre-election
policy debate, and reform of the administration of both aerospace and
technology policy generally was high on the Government's agenda.[8] The
new Government had the support of the Treasury in any attempt to limit
the power of the MoA, which was viewed as a formidable lobby forever
advocating expensive and controversial programmes. However, as the
Plowden Report noted, while there was a good case for some change in the
way aerospace policy was administered, allocating departmental
responsibilities for aerospace and aviation, with so many overlapping and
potentially conflicting interests, would not be easy or free from
substantial problems.[9]

Senior officials at the MoA fought any precipitate change, pointing out
how another shift in the location of the people responsible for civil
aviation would have a serious affect on morale and efficiency. In the
event, the MoA survived until November 1966 and the greater part of its
industrial sponsorship and procurement staff remained as a 'solid
phalanx' within their new ministry, a greatly enlarged Ministry of
Technology (Mintech). Responsibility for civil aviation, including
oversight of the nationalised airlines, passed to the Board of Trade (BoT).

The expansion of the Ministry of Technology, the first step on a road
which eventually led to its emergence as a *de facto* 'ministry for industry',
with a vast range of industrial, technological and related administrative

functions, was greeted by Benn as 'significant moment for British technology and the British economy, as well as for the aircraft industry'.[10] The fusion of aerospace sponsorship and procurement with technology policy as a whole was seen as an ideal way of curbing the excess of the former MoA yet bringing its expertise and skills into wider use. For the first time, Benn wrote, 'it is possible to compare projects across the whole field of engineering and to begin the difficult task of evolving criteria which allow intelligent choices to be made between developments in different fields'.[11] However, in view of the sheer size of the old MoA establishment now incorporated in Mintech, some critics did, rather unkindly, but presciently, wonder exactly who was absorbing whom.

The subsequent history of Mintech and Labour's industrial strategy is outside the scope of this book. However, a number of general observations must be made. In the first place, there is considerable doubt whether Mintech did, in fact, significantly improve either the direction of, or emphasis in, British technological development. While there was a distinct shift from military to civil R&D, much of the increased expenditure in the latter was taken up by civil aerospace, and by large, expensive programmes at that. Admittedly, Concorde accounted for much of this, but as even Labour critics pointed out, despite the initial intention to ensure that fewer non-commercial projects received public support, short-term return on public capital was no better in 1970 than in 1964. Similarly, the Government's general success in controlling expenditure in such programmes or in improving accountability generally in large-scale technological enterprises was, to say the least, mixed.[12]

In general terms, then, the Government was determined to reduce the costs of civil aerospace and to improve both the specific and the general return on public money allocated to the industry. At the same time, however, it was vital that the Government gave urgent attention to the launch of new civil projects. As we have seen, two generations of British civil aircraft had failed to achieve a permanent and substantial breakthrough in world markets and it was now evident that both the VC10 and Trident would be unsuccessful commercially. If the civil sector was not to wither away, decisions had to be taken to start on a further cycle of development and production. Costs were rising, even if the market for airliners was continuing to expand at a steady rate. The limited success of past civil projects and the weakness of the defence sector had meant that firms had been unable to accumulate reserves necessary for financing civil development. Similarly, private investment in civil aerospace was deterred by the absence of a good record of profitability. Even following rationalisation, the two large airframe companies admitted to the Plowden Committee that they would not be able to raise even the 50 per cent of launch capital required by the 1960 policy for any totally new programme.[13]

The Plowden Report

The Plowden Report provided the Government with both a diagnosis of past failures and suggestions for possible remedies. Published in December 1965, the report set out in stark terms the problems of maintaining an extensive and sophisticated industry on a small and limited domestic market. In a single, telling sentence it stated that there was 'no predestined place for an aircraft industry in Britain'. Moreover, although there were general economic benefits to the nation from having one, these should not be allowed to obscure the growing burden of costs the industry expected the state to accept. There was general criticism of the Government organisation for formulating and administering aerospace policy, the inadequacy of control over project development and the parochial attitudes of industry and Government to the demands of an international market. There was no case for maintaining an aircraft industry at a size which bore little relation to commercial or economic returns. Plowden went on to recommend the encouragement of further rationalisation, especially in the airframe sector where the existence of competition was neither useful nor real. More controversially, (with Aubrey Jones dissenting), Plowden noted that as the Government already participated to a large extent in the industry's decision-making and provided most of the cash for development, it made sense for the state to acquire some share of the business.[14]

An important theme of Plowden's general recommendations was the need to expand and extend international collaboration. The report advocated a policy of clearly directed and comprehensive cooperation with the industries of Europe. It suggested that this should include 'most of the projects on which the industry will be working'.[15] An alternative option, collaborating with the United States, was considered to be a poor choice, as it was unlikely that the Americans would be interested in joint research, development and production agreements of a size and scale satisfactory to British interests. It was, however, important and desirable that complete units, such as engines and equipment, should be developed and offered for sale in America and incorporated in American aircraft.[16] The lure of the large and profitable American market could not be entirely denied and Plowden clearly saw no danger that this might create tension between a European strategy for airframes and a transatlantic approach for other sectors of the industry.

As far as civil aircraft were concerned, in spite of the poor record in the past, the Committee felt that 'it would be a mistake for British manufacturers to opt out of this field of activity'. Some projects had been successful; many others, however, had been handicapped by having a small home market or as a result of limitations in their original specifications (here Plowden made specific and damning reference to the tailoring of designs for the nationalised airlines). Industry itself could clearly improve its market research and customer liason. In the last analysis, however, the adoption of international collaboration was of special relevance to the civil sector.

Turning to Government policy towards civil aerospace, Plowden saw no reason for any radical change in the system of launch aid, and felt that in most cases the limit of 50 per cent on Government's contribution should be retained. Nevertheless, it ought not to be treated as a fixed and immutable principle, and larger grants should be given in exceptional circumstances. Interestingly, as events transpired, the Committee felt that there should be no need for the limit to be exceeded on aid for engine development. However, both Government and industry had to adopt more stringent tests of commercial viability before investing in new ventures. As a result, the Government would have to undertake a more extensive examination of the prospective market for aircraft and engine projects and adopt a more detailed and positive role in the formulation of requirements. As it was likely that the Government would have to bear a larger share of launching costs and become involved in cooperative schemes with other states, it would also have to participate more actively in the 'country's civil aircraft programme than in the past'.[17]

Plowden's recommendations were accepted in principle by the Government. It accepted that the overall level of public support for the aircraft industry would have to fall, but it endorsed the general case for retaining an aircraft industry with a comprehensive design and production capability. Fred Mulley, the Minister of Aviation, said that the Government would certainly seek to implement Plowden's suggestions to rationalise further the airframe and aero-engine companies as well as negotiating some form of public holding in the former. But above all,

> We must turn to collaboration . . . as the principal means of improving the relationship between the size of the market and initial production costs and as the key to remaining a major force in aviation . . . Britain is unlikely to be justified again in embarking alone on an expensive new project.[18]

Moreover, any project, indigenously or internationally produced, had to show 'good economic prospects', and civil aircraft in particular had to demonstrate clearly defined markets as a precondition for receiving financial support from the Government.[19]

The Plowden report was not well received by the aircraft industry. The overt commitment to collaboration in advance of any firm agreement on specific programmes was seen as a dangerous constraint on Britain's negotiating position, a point emphasised by the SBAC in its response to the report[20] and also by Sir George Edwards:

> I do not recall hearing a French Minister say that it would not be possible for France to undertake projects on her own any longer and that they could only

start if she had a colleague country on which to lean. It is no good going to the table with one's own Government openly professing inability or unwillingness to go it alone.[21]

The Conservatives, naturally enough, were particularly exercised by the prospect of a nationalised or partially nationalised industry. This, they felt, was unnecessary and would entail additional bureaucratic interference in the industry. They too felt that while collaboration was desirable, Britain had to have a strong, independent design capability and be prepared to go it alone if necessary.[22]

The *Economist*, however, argued that the report did not go far enough. The newspaper not only urged outright nationalisation but argued that there was a strong case for Britain concentrating on aero-engines while the French, for example, might specialise in airframe production.[23] This kind of functional specialisation has frequently been put forward as the most rational and efficient form of European collaboration. Aside from the industrial implications of such a radical step, in practice Governments have not been keen to accept this level of interdependence in a key technology. That being said, the possibility of biasing policy towards the aero-engine sector clearly had some logic. The aero-engine sector, especially Rolls-Royce, had distinguished itself in both profitability and technical success. Indeed, many of Plowden's strictures concerning the civil aircraft industry were qualified with glowing references to successful engine developments. Without explicitly stating that this would be the case, the Government accepted that even if the aircraft industry should be maintained, it would increasingly focus policy on defending and promoting the interests of the aero-engine sector – a policy which in the event came to imply giving priority to Rolls-Royce.

In the short term, the immediate effect of Plowden on civil aerospace policy was to provide additional impetus to the talks already under way between French and British officials about the possibility of launching an Airbus type of airliner.[24] The Plowden philosophy also influenced the decision to refuse BAC launch aid for the Superb, a 250-seat design based on the VC10. BAC had made an initial approach to BOAC about the Superb in August 1965. BOAC's chairman, Sir Giles Guthrie, had showed little enthusiasm for the aircraft, suggesting that it would be 15 to 20 per cent more expensive to operate than the Boeing 747, then emerging as the archetype long-range, high-capacity Jumbo jet airliner. Development costs for the airframe alone were estimated to be over £40 million. BAC made it clear that it could not find the 50 per cent contribution required by the launch aid policy; in fact such was the company's financial position that it wanted the Government to pay for the entire cost of launch.[25]

The Government was aware of the implications of failing to support the Superb. BOAC clearly needed a high-capacity airliner which would otherwise entail buying the 747 with an inevitable effect on the balance of payments. Following the cancellation in March 1966 of BOAC's 'suspended' Super VC10 order, unless the Superb was launched Britain would cease to be a producer of long-range subsonic airliners.[26] However, Plowden had distinctly recommended that under no circumstances should the United Kingdom undertake alone a new long-range aircraft; indeed, in the case of large, long-range airliners, even if in collaboration with others, only exceptional market prospects would justify their development in Europe. The Superb was neither collaborative nor did it have a solid potential market. In May 1966, BAC was told that the Government would not provide launch aid for the Superb.[27] Given its cost and poor commercial prospects, this was undoubtedly a sound and realistic decision. Even Boeing would find the launch of its 747 very tough going indeed, and no other American manufacturer felt it desirable to compete with Boeing in this particular market. It meant, however, that Britain had abdicated to the Americans a large part of the market for subsonic aircraft. By accident or design, the British Government had effected a significant change in the character and shape of British civil aircraft development. Henceforward manufacturers would have to concentrate on short- and medium-range airliners where not only had there been more evidence of past commercial success but also, and more importantly perhaps, European partners were readily to be found.

If the Government applied strict commercial criteria to the launch of the Superb, it was still willing to relax them in order to support the development of other civil projects. The context was a familiar one, BEA wanted to buy a number of American aircraft and in June 1966 it announced plans to buy eighteen Boeing 727-200s and twenty-three of the smaller 737-200. Mulley directed BEA to 'buy British', the motive being to ensure that BEA at least continued to support the British aircraft industry and to save further pressure on the balance of payments. Immediately, BEA's Chairman, Sir Henry Millward, claimed that to buy British would affect BEA's profitability. In line with the BOAC precedent, Mulley agreed to compensate the airline, and steps would be taken to enable BEA to operate as a 'fully commercial undertaking with the fleet they acquired'.[28]

To replace the 737s, BEA ordered BAC 1-11-500s, a version of the basic 1-11 specially modified for BEA's requirements. BAC, as mentioned above, were in a poor way financially and moreover had no wish to build an aircraft for which there seemed little demand outside BEA's initial requirement. The Government agreed to support development on the basis of a fully funded programme, at a cost of £9 million. This order did not immediately lead to BEA receiving the promised 'compensation'. The Government claimed that part of its re-equipment programme was still outstanding and in answer to this BEA selected an entirely new British aircraft, the BAC 2-11.[29]

The significance of this decision is that it shows that the Government could be distinctly woolly about exactly what constituted commercial criteria. The Superb notwithstanding, in practice and under certain conditions the Government was willing to continue in the tradition of supporting civil aircraft which while not having an immediate prospect of wider sales, might offer indirect economic benefits and which undoubtedly were important to the overall health of the civil aircraft industry. The BAC 1-11 was showing some signs of achieving a modest degree of commercial success, and would prove that a British firm could design an aircraft to suit a wider market.[30] Continued investment in this aircraft and its derivatives might conceivably have commercial and technical advantages. However, both these decisions showed that where necessary, and when the government perceived that important non-commercial factors were at stake, the notion of commerciality in civil aerospace policy-making would be subjectively interpreted.

The origins of the European Airbus and the Rolls-Royce turbo-fan engine

Plowden's endorsement of collaboration provided the basis for subsequent decisions relating to airframe development. Perforce, British interest was now largely confined to the medium- and short-haul markets. However, while the aero-engine sector (from the autumn of 1966, effectively just one company, Rolls-Royce) was interested in any civil project started in Europe, its adoption of a collaborative strategy was neither essential nor necessarily the most desirable option. Between 1965 and 1967, there were major decisions on large and important aircraft and engine projects. The Government was closely concerned in both, financially and politically. In the event, the relationship between these projects became a major test of Labour's civil aerospace policy where perceptions of commercial and political value were inseparable from the technological choices involved.

The Airbus

Various studies of airline demand made in the early 1960s showed a widespread need for a high-capacity/low-cost airliner for short- and medium-haul routes. In Britain, the Lighthall Committee of the RAE investigating future civil aircraft requirements in 1961, produced an outline of an Airbus type of aircraft. This was followed in 1963 by BEA's specification for an 'Ultra short-haul, low-cost airliner' based on comparable principles.[31] HSA was particularly interested in these concepts having inherited the De Haviland expertise in short- and medium-haul jet airliner design and was itself conducting research along these lines. However, HSA was unable to interest BEA in its early designs as they tended to be bigger than BEA's immediate requirement. BAC was also interested in aircraft to follow the BAC 1-11 and VC10. In France, Sud Aviation, Breguet, North Aviation and Dassault had started similar design studies. As it was clear that the British Government wanted new aircraft launched in collaboration with Europe, both BAC and HSA established contacts with the French. In 1965 Nord, Breguet and HSA announced the HBN-100 design, and BAC and Sud unveiled their 250-seat 'Gallion'.[32]

Official talks paralleled these industrial negotiations: Roy Jenkins, an ardent European, was especially keen to promote a collaborative venture, and in April 1965, on his initiative, a series of Anglo-French meetings discussed the possibilities. On 17 May Jenkins announced that a joint working party would examine 'all aspects of producing a subsonic Airbus'.[33] A number of European airlines also considered the prospects for formulating a common requirement for a high-capacity, medium-range aircraft. However, a symposium held in October revealed considerable differences of opinion. BEA, for example, wanted a much smaller aircraft than many of its colleagues, having earlier rejected an HSA proposal for an 188-seat Airbus type of aircraft. Undaunted, the French and British Governments outlined a draft specification for a 200–225 seat, twin-engined Airbus. Further discussions exposed substantial areas of conflict, especially over the choice of engine. Nevertheless, it was agreed to invite West German participation, and triparite talks were arranged.

By March, 1966, officials were still only able to talk vaguely of 'target objectives' which 'might' lead to a firm agreement. In July, the three Governments agreed on an outline specification for the airframe alone, and selected the prime contractors for its development. As expected, the French chose Sud Aviation (later Aerospatiale), their 'chosen instrument' for civil aircraft. The German Government put forward a consortium, Arbeitsgemeinshaft Airbus, which had been specially formed for the purpose. HSA was selected as the British contractor.

For HSA, the Airbus was a particularly vital project: it had taken over De Haviland's design capability in medium-range civil aircraft. Indeed, De Haviland was originally acquired by Hawker Siddeley in 1960 to balance its predominantly military orientation. Obviously, HSA had an interest in retaining this capability. Moreover, as the Trident was not selling well, HSA was desperate to win the Airbus contract. An internal report pointed a stark future without it;

> We believe that the Airbus is the only new opening for a large civil aeroplane which will be available to HSA for some time. If HSA intend to stay in the mainline aircraft business the Airbus contract must be secured, since there is no other possibility of a direct follow-up to the Trident . . . It represents not only a channel for recovering development money vested in the Trident but, more importantly, a means of establishing HSA in the European aviation future.

HSA was aware that BAC was also vigorously promoting its claims. BAC had existing links with Sud through the Concorde project, and was believed to be in a strong position to win the Airbus. HSA's response was to launch a campaign 'at the highest level' to sell its case, politically, commercially and technically, to the Government. BAC believed that Sud preferred it to HSA, but Hawkers reckoned on the support of the Ministry of Aviation. After all, BAC already had one major civil collaborative project and, with the 1-11, a promising domestic product. In the event, HSA was chosen. According to BAC, this was simply a case of 'Buggin's turn'; it was 'Government *diktat* that Anglo-French cooperation on the Airbus should be with HSA on the UK side'. HSA, naturally enough, believed it was an indication of its greater expertise and commitment to the Airbus concept. HSA certainly had a long and unbroken experience in this range of airliner, but BAC also had a strong record in civil aerospace generally. HSA, perhaps, had the better specific case for having the Airbus, but in the event, the balance of orders between the two major airframe groups was probably the decisive factor in the Government's decision.

The three contractors rapidly established a cordial and effective partnership. Once the industrial alignments were confirmed, they were able to reconcile their different design concepts and quickly produced a common proposal. In October 1966, they announced details of a 225–250-seat, twin-engined aircraft, designated the A300 Airbus. On the basis of this, they formally requested Government sanction and financial support for development.

Unfortunately, the Governments were stalled on a number of issues. In the first instance, they were still debating whether the contractors should make a contribution towards launch costs, and if so, what proportion this should be. Secondly, they were divided on the necessity of establishing a 'base market' for the Airbus, effectively firm commitments from the three national 'flag carriers', Air France, Lufthansa and BEA, to buy it. On both counts, the British took a much stricter commercial stand than either the French or the Germans, who were more willing to pay for the acquisition of a civil aerospace capability. But the most important problem was that the British and the French (broadly supported by the Germans) were at loggerheads over the choice of a suitable engine. The former insisted a European engine, whereas the latter wanted an American engine. More specifically, the French had suggested a collaborative arrangement based on British Siddeley (BSE) and SNECMA jointly building the Pratt and Whitney JT9D under licence. The British Government, however, were determined on having an all-European project centred on Rolls-Royce.[34] The French, although strong advocates of European cooperation, looked on such agreements as primarily a means of enhancing their domestic, independent capabilities. Paradoxically, the French believed that temporary dependence on

American civil aero-engines was better than what threatened to be a permanent reliance within Europe on the technically superior British aero-engine industry. The former would allow the French greater freedom to develop that independent capability, whereas the logic of European technological cooperation would tend to confirm the status quo.[35]

The turbo-fan engine

Without doubt, Rolls-Royce was one of Britain's most prestigious firms. In an aircraft industry often characterised by market failures, Rolls had a substantial record of commercial success. Technically, of course, the company was the equal of any American manufacturer and clearly dominated its European rivals, including BSE, in the field of large civil engines. Rolls was disappointed when BSE won the Concorde contract, but felt that the choice of the Olympus was technically mistaken and that BSE's long-established contacts with the French was a crucial factor in the decision. During the 1950s, Rolls had won a large share of the market for civil jet engines, despite the limited appeal of British airframes and had not suffered from 'tailoring' to anything like the same extent. It had certainly adhered to the Government's private venture policy and had developed the Spey at some cost to itself.[36] With the reintroduction of launch aid in 1960, Rolls hoped for more assistance from Government, but was again disappointed. At one point in the early 1960s, Rolls' Chief Executive, Denning Pearson, wrote to the Ministry of Aviation expressing his concern about Rolls' future and said that the company might be prevented from 'achieving the fullest exploitation of the position which has been won in the world aero-engine business without further Government support'.[37]

Rolls' relationship with Government improved with the change of administration in 1964. Rolls rapidly assumed a privileged position in respect of aerospace policy. The Government not only encouraged Rolls to compete for all of the proposed collaborative projects, but also 'facilitated Rolls' competitive position by being prepared to sacrifice British design leadership to her collaborative partners in return for Rolls' development and production leadership of the power plant'.[38] Only in the AFVG military project had the pattern been reversed, with a British design lead on the airframe and a French lead on engine development. This practice was roundly condemned by many in the airframe and equipment sectors, believing that the sacrifice of design leadership eroded their ability to obtain a 'reasonable share of a joint project'.[39] Nevertheless, as Edmonds notes, Rolls' interests became the paramount feature of Government strategy towards European and domestic aerospace.[40] The merger with BSE in September 1966 reinforced Rolls' importance. This event, in fact, was also closely related to Rolls' attitude towards the European Airbus and its wider corporate strategy for civil engine development.

Throughout the early 1960s, Rolls was developing a large civil engine to replace the Conway. In 1961, the company received £850,000 from the Ministry of Aviation for preliminary work on the RB178. By the end of 1965, Rolls had decided to build a 'demonstrator' engine with half of the cost again provided by the Government. Rolls chose to focus development on a revolutionary 'three-shaft' turbo-fan concept. Rolls believed that such an engine would offer higher thrust, better fuel consumption and less weight.

Market surveys looked promising, and Rolls was especially determined to win a large American contract. The predicted development costs of a large turbo-fan cast doubt on the viability of any programme launched on a British or even a European airframe. Rolls was invited to bid for American wide-bodied, long-range airliners, but was unsuccessful. From this time the company became 'progressively more and more concerned to secure a major order for its big engine in order to maintain its position as a major world aero-engine manufacturer'.[41] As Adrian Lombard, Rolls' chief civil engine designer put it, 'in effect, we have an advanced technical design in search of an aircraft programme'.[42] In a sense, Rolls' plight was similar to that of HSA, but unlike the airframe company, Rolls was looking beyond the European option. However, without any compensating American order, the absence of the Airbus contract would leave Rolls in a decidedly tricky position. A BSE/SNECMA combination based on the JT9D would be even worse.

In December 1965, Denning Pearson, now Rolls' Managing Director, moved at the highest level to head off this threat. Writing to the Permanent Secretary at the Ministry of Aviation, Pearson urged Government action in support of Rolls' bid for the Airbus. He pointed out the existing investment the Ministry had in the RB178 and noted that BSE had not received such assistance or had the same degree of expertise and knowledge as Rolls had. Pearson mentioned reports that BSE was trying to overcome these deficiencies through contacts with Pratt and Whitney. 'We cannot believe', he wrote 'that it would be the policy of the British Government at one and the same time to finance preliminary work on a Rolls-Royce engine and countenance an association between Bristol Siddeley and the main competitor of that engine'. No engine produced by BSE and SNECMA would be a truly European project, they simply lacked the experience to make much contribution to its development. The result would be to give the Americans a foothold inside the British and European market. The obvious answer, according to Pearson, was a decisive step by the British Government to nominate Rolls as the British contractor in any Airbus programme. It would be open to BSE to join in development, but the engine would be a Rolls concept and design leadership would be retained by Rolls-Royce. 'Such a statement', Pearson concluded, 'would also have the advantage of smoking out the

French position as well as eliminating the threat from Pratt and Whitney'.[43]

The Government acted on this advice, at least implicitly, by insisting on a Rolls engine for the Airbus. In any case, Rolls acted unilaterally to remove the danger of a BSE/SNECMA engine. During the summer of 1966, BSE agreed to take up its option on a licence for the JT9D. Whereupon Rolls made a formal offer for BSE. In its prospectus, Rolls pointed out the financial and technical advantages of a merger, but essentially Rolls was more concerned to head off an American Trojan Horse. The merger, finalised in September, was described by *Fortune* as 'ranking among the boldest business operations in recent British history'.[44] The Government welcomed the formation of the new company, and although it had not been consulted on this 'completely commercial arrangement', Ministers had been informed of Rolls' intentions. It had no objection in principle to the merger, which was consistent with the Plowden recommendations on increasing efficiency within the aircraft industry, and would not be reported to the Monopolies Commission.[45]

The merger created, in terms of employees, the world's largest aero-engine company. Rolls now dwarfed any European manufacturer and, with the breakdown of HSA–BAC merger negotiations in 1967, dominated British aerospace. Paradoxically, the Government had actively sought this particular merger which was recommended by Plowden, as well as the possibility of acquiring some public stake in a single airframe company. In February 1966, the Government announced that it intended to negotiate suitable arrangements with BAC and HSA whereby their airframe and guided weapons interests would be amalgamated, with the Government participating in the equity of the new company. Discussions between the parties began in November, with all three appointing advisers from the City to examine matters relating to valuation and compensation. However, it proved impossible to reach agreement on the question of compensation, and without a deep commitment to nationalisation (the Government probably believed the gains would not outweigh the political odium of a contested battle to acquire either company), the Government did not press the case. In December, Benn announced that negotiations had been ended 'for the time being'.[46] Benn in any case, on becoming Minister of Technology in February 1967, did not like the form of nationalisation which had been proposed by the old MoA. In effect, it entailed Government buying BAC from its parent companies, Vickers, Rolls-Royce and GEC, merging it with HSA and assuming a minority shareholding along the lines of BP. Benn regarded this as unsatisfactory, with insufficient Government control over the new company. For whatever reason, however, the failure to create a comparably large airframe company to act as a counterweight to Rolls had a profound effect on subsequent events. It reinforced the singular importance of Rolls-Royce in the Government's aerospace policy and magnified the significance of the firm's turbo-fan engine project: for increasingly the success of the latter depended on the overall health of the former.

Unquestionably, any fears the French had of being permanently subordinate to the British in civil aero-engines, perhaps across the board in all engine development, were reinforced by the Rolls–BSE merger. Indeed, many French industrialists regard it as ending any serious prospect of creating an Anglo-European engine industry, and generally obstructed the evolution of collaboration.[47] Rolls-Royce, unlike BSE, who had welcomed cooperative ventures and had a less overweening view of Europe, was confident of its independent capabilities to the point of arrogance. One ex-BSE executive, for example, was 'greatly shocked' by Derby's attitude to collaboration, '.. with anyone, ... and certainly with Europeans'.[48] Indeed, while the Government may have welcomed the merger, there were some officials at the Ministry of Technology who felt it had closed an important avenue of Anglo-French cooperation. This was confirmed by Rolls' subsequent decision allowing the licence option on the JT9D to lapse.

A Rolls engine was now a prerequisite for British participation in the Airbus. Rolls had proposed the 47,500lb-thrust RB207 (rather more powerful than the 44,000lb JT9D), and the British Government presented this as the only European option. John Stonehouse, the Minister responsible for aerospace, claimed that 'it would be absolute nonsense to build a European Airbus and then fit it with an American engine'.[49] On 9 May 1967, the responsible Ministers from the three nations agreed on the inevitable and predictable compromise. In return for a Rolls-led engine programme, Sud was awarded design leadership on the airframe. The three companies were told to 'proceed rapidly with a joint project definition study of the best possible aircraft capable of being built around two such engines'. The results of this study were presented in July and formed the basis of an intergovernmental agreement initialed on the 25th. After some delay, this was followed by a formal Memorandum of Understanding in September, governing the development of a 300-seat, twin-engined Airbus.[50]

The 1967 Memorandum of Understanding

The Memorandum of Understanding signed on 26 September 1967, between the French, German and British Governments, specified that the cost of developing the airframe, estimated at £130 million, would be shared in roughly equal proportions, with Britain accepting $37\frac{1}{2}$ per cent of the total. Work and responsibility would be similarly allocated. However, the engine would remain a predominantly British project, with the British Government providing 75 per cent of its development costs, put at £60 million. The aircraft was expected to be in service by 1973. It was further agreed that a final decision to produce the Airbus would depend on orders of twenty-five aircraft from each of the three national airlines. These orders had to be confirmed by the end of June 1968 on the completion of the project study phase when firm price and performance data would be available. The three Governments also accepted that they would not support any indigenous project which competed with the A300.[51]

As a Memorandum of Understanding, the agreement was not a binding commitment to produce the Airbus. It was open for any party to withdraw unilaterally from the programme 'should the project run into a major technical or financial problems or should the circumstances of a partner radically alter'. On the other hand, it was necessary for the stability of development that some deterrent be present. Consequently a period of notice was required (at least six months) during which consultations would continue and the country involved would continue to pay its share of R&D costs. It was accepted, therefore, that while Memoranda of Understanding did not have the status of international agreements, 'the provisions relating to the duration of a programme nevertheless represent solemn undertakings which it would be a very serious breach of faith for any country to break'.[52]

The British Government, for example, stressed the significance of obtaining launch orders from BEA, Lufthansa and Air France. These were designed to 'financially establish the viability of the project'. They were said to form 'the market base and ensure the product is not a cost to the economy but a bonus to the three economies involved'. Full profitability, however, would depend on wider sales, and would not rely 'solely on the loyalty of the national corporations'. In fact, the Ministry of Technology calculated that between 200 and 300 aircraft would have to be sold to break even. No specific performance targets were published, but BEA was told that the A300 aimed to achieve a 30 per cent improvement in seat-mile costs over the best current types.[55] In short, the British Government was determined that the Airbus would not be a 'political venture' but would stand as 'an economic enterprise'.[54]

In practice, it was impossible to divorce political considerations from commercial decisions on the Airbus. The Labour Government was at great pains to associate technological cooperation with Britain's application to join the EEC. Throughout 1967, Harold Wilson himself pointed to these burgeoning links as a symbol of Britain's willingness to embrace Europe. Indeed, official reaction to French withdrawal from the AFVG military aircraft programme in July was quite muted given the supposed importance of aircraft to Britain's defence plans. Similarly, the Airbus agreement nicely coincided with the culmination of the Government's Common Market application. In November, Wilson made his famous Guildhall speech unveiling his proposals for a European 'technological community'. But, to no avail, as on the 27th de Gaulle announced his second veto of British Common Market membership.

The cancellation of the BAC 2-11

Quite apart from these diplomatic considerations, the British Government had been quite prepared to play 'techno-politics' over the Airbus, if only to ensure that a Rolls design was chosen as the basis for the engine programme. Similarly, critics of the Memorandum of Understanding had no doubt that ' . . . vital factors have been sacrificed on the altar of short-term political considerations'.[55] It seemed a poor bargain to give airframe design leadership to France in return for 12½ per cent of the cost of producing the RB207. The agreement was, according to *Flight*, 'too high a price for giving Europe a share of British advanced engine technology'.[56] On the other hand John Stonehouse, admittedly one of the more ardent Europeans in the Cabinet, saw the Airbus as part of a wider politico-industrial context. Other projects would follow, and it was, he said, 'a substantial step toward a viable European aircraft industry capable of building all sorts of sophisticated aircraft in direct competition with the Goliaths of the air world, the United States and Russia'.[57]

The Memorandum also required the British Government to insist on a purchase by BEA of an aircraft which was not particularly attractive to the airline and which, indirectly at least, led to the cancellation of another British airliner. BEA executives had been lukewarm about the Airbus from the outset of development but, as one Mintech official put it, 'It was scarcely conceivable' that BEA would not buy the Airbus if it met its design specifications, or if the Government required it to do so. BEA was still waiting for the Government to fulfil the 'Mulley pledge', a capital reconstruction in return for 'buying British'. This had been postponed until BEA had completed its re-equipment plan. The first part of BEA's order was provided by the BAC 1-11-500. Now, BEA applied for permission to buy BAC's new proposal, the 180–200-seat 2-11 which would be powered by a Rolls' advanced technology turbo-fan, the RB211, a smaller version of the RB207 proposed for the A300.[58]

The BAC 2-11, based on 1-11 technology, was deliberately aimed at BEA's oft-repeated need for a 180–200-seat airliner, available for service in the early 1970s. Indeed, BEA attached far more priority to this requirement than that represented by the larger Airbus. As such the BAC 2-11 did not appear to be a direct competitor to the A300, and BAC, BEA and the British Board of Trade all denied any accusation that it was.[59] Nevertheless, the French viewed the BAC 2-11 as a potential diversion of British energies, even if the aircraft did not 'stretch' during development and become a challenge to the A300 at the lower end of the market. Consequently, during the negotiations leading up to the Memorandum of Understanding, the French put pressure on the British Government to stop the 2-11. No acquiescence to such pressure was admitted by the

British, but the BAC aircraft was refused launch aid and, in November, BEA were instructed to order the Trident 3B as an interim aircraft until the A300 became available.[60]

On balance, the BAC 2-11 would have been an expensive aircraft to develop. Although it was derived from 1-11 technology, at least £60 million would have been needed to launch the airframe and £40 million for the RB211 engine which BAC proposed to use, the future of which was still uncertain. There was also some internal criticism of Millward's advocacy of the 2-11. The genesis of BAC's proposal seems to have been a result of direct negotiations between Millward and Sir George Edwards, BAC's Chairman, and the design did not meet with the universal approval of BEA's technical staff. For its part, the Government claimed that cost was the decisive factor in its decision to refuse BAC launch aid. The BAC 2-11 was undoubtedly dearer than the Trident 3B, but it was also a politically expedient decision.[61] Millward viewed its end as a grave blow to both the airline and the British aircraft industry.[62] The Government on the other hand saw it as confirmation of its commitment to the Plowden philosophy and a genuine reflection of technical and commercial prudence.[63]

The Memorandum of Understanding represented the high-water mark of Labour's commitment to European civil aerospace collaboration. Given the cost of launching a large civil aircraft, this was a logical policy to adopt. Whatever the cause of its demise, the BAC 2-11 would have been a retrogressive step. Certainly, HSA accepted that cooperation was the most rational approach to the development of large civil aircraft and its Board had already decided that it was not proper for a private company to accept the financial risk involved of an independent, even launch-aided development of an Airbus type of aircraft. Design leadership was also seen as a *non sequitur*; if collaboration was inevitable, some degree of compromise was unavoidable to reach agreement with foreign firms. HSA resented the fact that Rolls' interests were so dominant in the British Government's deliberations, but it was far more important to HSA that it had some share of the Airbus rather than none at all. In the event, HSA was more concerned that Rolls might be unable to fulfil its obligations towards the European programme and that as a result British participation in the Airbus might be called into doubt.

Rolls' campaign in the US

While the British Government had been defending Rolls' interests in the European Airbus programme, the company had redoubled its efforts to penetrate the American market. This time its target was one of the long-range Airbus type aircraft being proposed by McDonnell-Douglas (the DC10) and Lockheed (L1011). From Rolls' perspective, this was a bid for long-term security. Over 85 per cent of the world's civil aircraft were built in the United States, and American airlines, with a propensity to buy domestic products, represented 65 to 70 per cent of all aircraft sales. The American market was seen as the chief means by which Rolls would remain in the top league of civil engine manufacturers, a point emphasised by senior Rolls management: 'It appeared to us that if we were to stay in the civil engine business which we had built up since the war, we needed to get into a United States-built airframe as first engine choice'.[64]

Initially, Rolls hoped that the RB207 would be suitable for both European and American applications. In January 1967, the company told the Ministry of Technology about a request from Lockheed for a quotation on the RB207. The Government had already indicated that it would provide financial help to produce Rolls' turbo-fan engine. Indeed, as Rolls said it would only be able to find 30 per cent of the launch costs, the Government, Plowden notwithstanding, agreed to advance more than the 50 per cent limit on grants of launch aid to an engine project. As yet, no agreement was reached, but if Rolls obtained a firm order from an American firm, the Government would be 'sympathetic' towards any application for assistance. Rolls was, however, authorised to show the Ministry's letter outlining the position to Lockheed, or any other potential customer, 'if the company judged that it could help in the negotiations'.[65]

By the late spring of 1967, it was evident that Rolls would have to develop a smaller engine for the Americans. Rolls decided that the RB211, a 33,000lb-thrust engine being considered for the BAC 2-11, would be more suitable. The Ministry was informed of this new requirement, and expressed concern that it should not undermine Rolls commitment to the Airbus:

> We would not wish you at present to frame any offer to America of the RB211 in such a way that an acceptance from the aircraft manufacturer concerned could bind you in a contractual commitment. So long as the RB207 remains on offer for the European Airbus, we should not wish its prospects or timetable to be prejudiced by the action of a third party in which we have no say.[66]

So long as Rolls was aware of this caveat, the Ministry was still prepared to give launch aid for the RB211 and a 70–30 per cent split was 'broadly acceptable'.[67] However, the Government's contribution was fixed at a maximum of £40 million, conditional on Rolls getting a firm American order and subject to a close examination by the Ministry of Rolls' estimates. In view of the unusually high preparation required from the state and large sum involved, the Government also expected to relate the R&D levy to the profitability of Rolls-Royce as a whole.

In June, with Lockheed's decision to adopt a three-engine layout, Rolls knew that the RB211 was the only obvious choice for its American offensive. In addition to the unique 'three-shaft' design, Rolls intended to make extensive use of carbon-fibre composite materials (Hyfil) developed by the Royal Aircraft Establishment to save weight. However, empirical data on a three-shaft turbo-fan was limited, and Rolls was offering an engine considerably more powerful than they had ever built before. As the RB211 would have to be available by 1971, executives readily conceded that the programme was ambitious, but they were confident of its feasibility. More importantly, Rolls' top management believed that without the RB211 and an American order, 'Rolls would have very rapidly run down hill to the point where the company would hardly have been viable'.[68] The future of Derby and perhaps 30,000 jobs were at stake: as Denning Pearson later argued, 'Building a new engine would not guarantee we stayed in business. Not building one would certainly guarantee that we went out of business.'[69]

Others have questioned Roll's pessimistic view of a future without the RB211. John Davis, the Conservative Minister for Industry at the time of Rolls' bankruptcy, believed that there had been 'no reason to be sure that the failure to fund the RB211 engine would necessarily have brought about the demise of the aero-engine industry in Britain'.[70] Ian Morrow, eventually brought in by the Industrial Reorganisation Corporation to join the Rolls Board, also felt that it was never impossible to abandon the RB211. He accepted that this might have led to the closure of plant, but this would not have been so 'catastrophic' if, as a result, bankruptcy could have been avoided.[71]

At the time, however, the Government accepted Rolls' view of the world. Tony Benn, then Minister of Technology, recalled how he and his colleagues 'accepted . . . the basic argument that without the RB211 there [would be] no future for the British aero-engine industry whether or not in public ownership'.[72] It was prepared to back Rolls' judgement and saw no reason why launch aid should not be given for both the RB211 and RB207 engines. In July, the Ministry confirmed its offer of £40 million towards the launch of the RB211 and £49 million (subject to European contributions) for the RB207. The Rolls Board decided that a 'dual programme' was feasible and agreed to make formal bids in respect of both American and European aircraft. The Ministry was told of Rolls' decision and gave its approval to the dual programme. In September, the RB207 was, of course, confirmed as the chosen engine for the A300; at the same time, Rolls attacked the American market more strongly than ever.

Rolls' sales campaign was later described as a model for other British firms seeking to win large order from foreign customers. It was a 'total' effort personally led by David Hudie, Rolls' Chief Executive, from New York. But in practice, Rolls was taking dangerous risks to land the Lockheed contract. Even though devaluation helped its competitiveness, Rolls continually shaved its prices and conceded tighter technical and delivery conditions to suit Lockheed. Even Lockheed, and certainly the American aero-engine manufacturers, Pratt and Whitney and General

Electric, felt Rolls' final price of $550,000 for each engine to be unrealistically low. As Edmonds notes, the Americans clearly believed that the British Government was prepared to underwrite Rolls' commitments and 'allowed Lockheed to force the price down'.[73] Rolls also agreed to an offset agreement whereby they would indemnify the London registered company, Air Holdings, in its purchase of thirty L1011s. Although the Government guaranteed a half of the cost to Rolls, up to a maximum of £5 million, and also increased its offer of support on the RB211 to £45.75 million, Rolls was accepting increasingly heavy financial obligations in order to land Lockheed.[74]

There were a few anxious voices back in Derby urging caution. One senior executive was moved to write to Hudie, warning him of the possible dangers of taking on too much. 'I sense', he wrote 'that you and others in New York, under obvious extreme sales pressure, are impatient of what you believe is a conservative commercial outlook back here.' In his opinion the latest predictions of engineering development indicated serious increases in costs and the impossibility of meeting schedules. Rather than being over-cautious, he believed the truth would ultimately be shown to be very much the opposite:

> The latest engineering early-growth estimates were ... not very well considered – they were generated quickly under strong sales pressure, as almost a last desperate throw, and ... were not really subject to a sufficiently critical review ... If this letter has a practical message, it is 'don't give any more away'. There is already a risk you may win a Pyrrhic victory.[75]

Hudie's reply was fatalistic, unless they made concessions, they would lose the contract. 'There would be time enough', he said 'for the critical appraisal after the event if we win, and no need for it if we lose.'[76] Hudie's attitude at this juncture is revealing; the promise of launch aid from the British Government, ostensibly limited as it was, gave Rolls' management the apparent freedom to conduct a ruthlessly risky sales campaign. Indeed, the point is perhaps still more fundamental: did Rolls believe that their relationship with the Government implied a much more extensive commitment to the company and its projects? Later events would indicate that this was the case.[77]

In March 1968, Rolls finally sealed the Lockhead deal amidst much heralding and praise. *Fortune* described it as a 'bold foreign invasion' of a US industry. Announcing the event in the House of Commons, Tony Benn stressed its wider importance to British industry,

> It constitutes a foothold in the American civil market far bigger than anything which we have achieved before. It is of special value to the British economy, and above all, an outstanding encouragement for the skills and technology of British industry.[78]

Sir Denning Pearson (both he and David Hudie were knighted as a consequence of the Lockheed achievement) admitted that this was the fulfilment of Rolls' 'constant and unwavering ambition' to win such a large American order. He also paid special tribute to the help, financial and otherwise, provided by the British Government.[79] Sir David Hudie, perhaps realising the scale of the task now facing Rolls said that success at this level was a most 'exhilarating' experience. This, he said, would be allowed to last twenty-four hours, 'after that one realises one has taken on another immense responsibility'.[80]

Rolls' success was generally well received in Britain. However, the French were less pleased, feeling that the RB211 and the onerous terms of the contract with Lockheed would inevitably divert Rolls' energies and resources from the RB207, and with that, the British Government's interest as well.[81] Sir Denning moved to counter these doubts, stating that Rolls could develop both engines, and, as if to confirm this, committed the company's own capital tó the RB207. Benn also tried to reassure the Europeans of Rolls' ability to develop the RB207 and, for that matter, the Government's determination to stay with the Airbus. 'The securing of the RB211 order by Rolls-Royce does not lessen in any way our support for the European Airbus.' After all, Benn averred, the RB211 was merely a scaled-down version of the RB207. Although it would mean a supreme effort by Rolls, there was 'nothing new about that and we are confident that Rolls Royce can make it'.[82]

Unfortunately, the Airbus encountered problems, and Rolls' reassertion of its interest in the RB207 did refer to this being in spite of the 'political uncertainty' surrounding the A300.[83] Essentially, the manufacturers were concerned with the high cost of the engine, 'which had to be amortised over a comparatively small number of aircraft sales and in their search for low seat-mile costs during the project definition stage, the A300 grew steadily'. The tendency was for them to seek more thrust from the RB207, which, only existing as a design concept, could be 'scaled to meet the demand'. This enabled further airframe growth and a vicious circle set in, with the airlines standing on the side lines saying 'the aircraft is too big'.[84] By the summer of 1968, and the end of the project definition stage, launch costs had risen to £215 million and £70 million for the engine. Firm data on price and operating costs could not be given, and by the July deadline nothing had been resolved. There were also grave doubts about the likelihood of the seventy-five base orders being confirmed. Lufthansa were particularly insistent that they would not buy so many, and that eight was the maximum they would ever need. Sir Anthony Millward said there was not the 'slightest chance' of BEA ordering it by the July deadline. He said he would resist any pressure to do so and would only defer to an explicit Government directive.[85] There were also no orders, and little interest, from uncommitted airlines. The A300 was in deep trouble.

Announcing the increased A300 launch-cost estimates, even John

Stonehouse seemed less enthusiastic about its future. The British Government had continually stressed the 'commercial' criteria which the aeroplane had to meet.[86] Stonehouse was still hopeful that it would be built, but 'we have made it clear that this is not a political project; it is a commercial one. We want to build an aircraft which will be commercially viable and which will be attractive to the airlines to buy it.'[87] On 30 July, the three Governments postponed a decision to produce the A300, giving the manufacturers five months to produce a revised design with substantial improvements in operating economics and more acceptable development costs. With Rolls' future apparently secure, however, the British Government now had less incentive to carry on with the European Airbus. Diminishing interest in Europe generally also tended to remove any remaining inhibitions about cancellation. If the aircraft did not appear to be worth the investment, there were few other reasons to stay with it. However, an abrupt termination of British participation was diplomatically undesirable, apart from any effect it would have on Hawker Siddeley. Consequently, the Government's ultimate withdrawal was somewhat protracted.

Britain leaves the Airbus

Throughout the late summer and into the autumn of 1968, the future of the European Airbus hung in the balance. Of the three Governments, the British were the most sceptical about the aircraft's prospects. According to Richard Crossman, the Cabinet had agreed to an extension of the project definition stage only by a small majority.[88] Hawker Siddeley was also aware of growing opposition to the Airbus in Whitehall. Officials began to express doubts about HSA's ability to produce the advanced, fuel-efficient wing required by the specification. They also questioned the credibility of the French-led consortium as a source of a successful airliner. In short, HSA felt that the Government as a whole was exploiting technical problems, invariably present in the early stages of developing civil aircraft, to justify its diminishing interest in a European programme.

HSA was also conscious of an all-British alternative, the BAC 3-11, which had been unveiled in July. Hawkers believed BAC's timing had been no coincidence, but a calculated move to capitalise on the Airbus's difficulties. Indeed, HSA believed BAC had been tacitly encouraged by official hints that a domestically produced aircraft would not be unwelcome. BAC denied such accusations, and argued that its 250-seat aircraft, which would use RB211 engines, was a fully commercial proposition. The choice of the RB211 over an initial preference for an American engine, however, was a deliberate attempt to ensure greater Governmental interest. BAC claimed that with its contacts in the United States built up as a result of selling the 1-11 to American airlines, it had a better chance of penetrating the American market. BAC also said that the project would be started as a normal launch-aided programme, and asked the Government for half of the estimated cost of development. Additionally, BAC set themselves a minimum order of fifty aircraft before it would formally request aid.[89]

The Government certainly had substantive grounds for believing the Airbus to be a dubious commercial proposition. There were no additional orders besides those expected from the three national airlines, and even these were still not guaranteed. Lufthansa was successfully resisting pressure from Bonn to confirm its order, and BEA made it clear from the design's advent, that it preferred the BAC 3-11. Indeed, Millward described it as a 'sensible' proposal and began actively to lobby the British Government for permission to buy the aircraft. One suspects, however, that matters would have been less uncertain had the future of Rolls' civil engine business still depended on the A300.[90]

The Lockheed order had removed Rolls' worries about remaining an important manufacturer of large civil engines. The existence of a second project, the RB207, in fact, was a growing embarrassment. As the French had predicted, the Lockheed contract, with its stringent conditions, was diverting an increasing proportion of Rolls' energies and capacity. The larger RB207 was also becoming technically superfluous; the RB211 was bound to increase in power as Rolls responded to Lockheed's requirement for an engine for the longer-range L1011 while the Airbus designers were looking for ways of breaking out of the vicious circle of an ever larger airframe. The Europeans' problem, therefore, could be solved by using the same engine. Growing suspicion that Rolls was 'playing both ends off against the middle' and was keen to jettison the dual programme had already surfaced at HSA. Eventually, through top-level contacts, HSA tackled Rolls directly. As a result, HSA knew that the Airbus design team would have to begin serious consideration of alternative engines.

Apart from the conscious and contractual priority Rolls attached to the RB211, the company's financial position was not satisfactory. A second, large commitment would represent a considerable strain on Rolls' capacity. In the summer of 1968, Rolls had to make a £20 million rights issue and had to find a further £10 million through debenture placing. Technical difficulties with the RB211, particularly with the Hyfil turbine blades, were causing severe problems. Detailed costings of full RB211 development, including the effects of Lockheed's additional requirements, showed an increase of £19.2 million over their initial estimate. By November, Rolls also knew that Lockheed wanted the up-rated RB211 two years earlier than expected. Despite appeals to Government for help in covering the £40 million over seven years which it would cost, Rolls had to shoulder the extra burden alone in order to protect their original investment.[91] While this meant that a suitable RB211 would now be available for the A300, these financial and production problems were rendering Roll's commitment to the Airbus increasingly untenable.

In November, Henri Ziegler, President of Sud Aviation, predicted that major changes would be made in the A300 programme. A smaller design would shortly be presented, and he hinted that it might be offered with a choice of engines. The British response to Ziegler's remarks were predictable. John Stonehouse said that any change in the status of Rolls-Royce required the unanimous consent of all three Governments. Other official spokesmen referred to the explicit specification of the RB207 as the Airbus engine in the Memorandum of Understanding.[92] Details of the new design, designated as the A300B, revealed that its capacity would be fixed at 252 seats, and although the RB211 was selected as the launch engine, alternative engines would be available on later versions. The A300B was a clear return to original design concepts, and airline reactions were more favourable. Dropping the RB207 was reckoned to save £70 million alone, and the smaller design brought airframe costs down to £170 million.[93]

Describing the changes to the House of Commons, Benn argued that the A300B had created a 'new situation' which would have to be studied at length. He could not commit the Government to the A300B without a careful and stringent economic analysis. He warned that the proposal would have to be considered against the need to contain public expenditure.[94] Rather than accepting the changes as the result of the delayed project-definition stage, the Government used the A300B to reopen the whole question of British participation in the European programme. For instance, when the BAC 3-11 was first revealed, the Government had said that it was a 'separate consideration' from the A300. Now, Benn asked the French and Germans to include it in any discussion of the A300B. Benn also wanted to renegotiate Britain's financial and work-sharing arrangements and, especially, to limit the Government's total obligation to the programme.[95]

Britain's partners, however, regarded the A300B as an extension of the A300; renegotiation or even further talks about launching the aircraft, was unnecessary. Delay would simply weaken the aircraft's commercial position. The French refused to consider the BAC 3-11 as an alternative basis for a collaborative venture and gave the British until the end of February to decide whether or not they wanted to stay in the Airbus programme. The German Chancellor, Dr Kiesinger raised the question of British participation when Harold Wilson visited Bonn in February, but Wilson's response was unenthusiastic. Indeed, at a concluding press conference, Wilson said that his administration would not spend money heedlessly on aerospace. Collaboration especially, he said, was ' . . . a desert track littered with the whitening bones of abortive joint projects mostly undertaken at high cost'.[96]

French and German patience finally ran out in March. Jean Chamont,

the French Minister of Transport, said pointedly that they were not going
to go on 'begging the British anymore'. At a final tripartite meeting Benn
made no concessions. Reporting to the House of Commons, he again
stated that the British Government had to 'reserve the right to choose an
aircraft which might make a profit . . . in my judgement the greatest
policy disaster would be if we were to abandon economic criteria in the
investment of public money in advanced technology'.[97] Shortly after this
abortive meeting, the French and Germans agreed to go ahead with the
A300B, reapportioning Britain's share of development costs and
production work.

Reasons for withdrawal

The Labour Government felt that the Airbus lacked sufficient political
or technological value to outweigh what was regarded as an unpromising
commercial future. Nevertheless, the manner of its withdrawal was
somewhat disingenuous. The Government evidently hoped to avoid, or at
least mitigate, the obloquy of an open breach with their European
partners. The Airbus, technically at least, had failed to meet the
conditions of the Memorandum of Understanding, but if Rolls' future as
a worl .-class manufacturer of civil aero-engines had still been at stake,
doubtless commercial criteria would have been more liberally interpreted.
John Stonehouse for one believed that the Cabinet had never really been
more than tentative in its support for the Airbus;

> The prejudice against the aircraft and European collaboration amongst
> British ministers was really quite extraordinary. It was only by a very narrow
> majority in the Cabinet Committee that it was agreed that I should go to the
> meetings to begin negotiations . . . when I left to become P.M.G. the Cabinet
> Committee concerned decided to withdraw from the Airbus . . . They said at
> the time that they could not see sufficient sales, but the real reason for
> cancelling the British participation was that they were against it from the
> beginning.[98]

Stonehouse's view is probably overstating any initial opposition to the
Airbus but, unquestionably, later attitudes were increasingly conditioned
by diminishing support for, and interest in, European cooperation
generally. The Airbus had certainly been launched at a time when the
Labour Government had been most keen on Europe. It represented an
embodiment of Harold Wilson's European Technological Community
and epitomised the Plowden philosophy on civil airframe development.
Moreover, an Airbus had a prosaic image which was more in keeping with
Labour's view of a socially useful, commercially desirable technology.
However, events since Plowden had made it clear that the 'collaborate
or perish' philosophy was no longer operative. The Elstub Report,
published in 1969, suggested that the 'attractions of collaboration' had
tended to 'obscure its disadvantages'. The report argued that the delay

and inefficiency associated with joint ventures were not always sufficiently balanced by the gains from cost-sharing and wider initial markets.[99] For the Government, Benn said that even if collaboration was still their general policy, it would be so only 'where appropriate'. There were sound reasons for encouraging cooperative activity, but there was no 'automatic bar or rigid policy laid down by us that rules out all-British projects'.[100] Similarly, as the Airbus began to run into severe difficulties during the summer of 1968, Ministers like Dick Crossman were seeing signs of a second Concorde, or at least a possible repetition of the civil aircraft failures of the 1950s. On the face of it, all previous performance indicators suggested that Rolls was far more likely to get a project right and produce a commercially viable product than the airframe sector, even without the addition burden of collaboration. Moreover, much of the steam had gone out of Labour's general commitment to Europe. Although the effects on Britain's erstwhile partners in the Airbus and on prospects for future collaboration ruled out a precipitate decision to launch the BAC 3-11, the cooperative dimension no longer had the strength it once had to influence policy.

HSA was extremely disappointed and very bitter about the outcome. The company was, as one executive recalled, 'left holding the baby'. The HSA Board decided that they would stay with the Airbus, believing that the A300B would be successfully produced and that a profitable, privately financed sub-contract could be negotiated. HSA duly obtained a fixed-price contract for the A300B wing and wing box. It was also later invited by the Franco-German consortium (formally constituted in December 1970 under French law as Airbus Industrie) to act as a design consultant and to join the marketing team. HSA's contract, although it protected the firm's investment in subsonic airliner development, gave it no say in policy decisions; nor did it guarantee its participation in later versions of the aircraft. This was a clear case of Government gainsaying the commercial judgement of a manufacturer. HSA was confident, even if some Ministry officials were not, of producing its advanced, fuel-efficient wing and that the aircraft as a whole was a sound proposition. More importantly, by negotiating a private arrangement with Airbus Industrie, HSA was prepared to back its opinion with its own money. British withdrawal also cost the domestic equipment and avionics industries some £100 million worth of orders.[101] Airbus Industrie selected the General Electric CF6 to replace Rolls, with SNECMA eventually signing a joint production and development agreement with the Americans.

The engine question was the crux of the matter. The thrust of British negotiating tactics had been to secure Rolls as the sole source of engines for the A300. Even without the Lockheed contract, the decision to offer the RB211 on the A300B as the launch engine but not necessarily as the sole choice, would have reawakened suspicion of French motives. The market for civil aircraft was increasingly demanding multiple engine choice and clearly Rolls' monopoly on the Airbus would eventually have been challenged. However, the Airbus was no longer of overriding importance to Rolls' future and was already seen as an extra burden for a stretched development programme. There was point, perhaps, to being the launch engine for a large American project with what were seen as solid commercial prospects but not to fighting a corner on what seemed to be a less than promising European enterprise.

In retrospect, the Government's support for Rolls-Royce and its campaign to win a major American contract was always potentially in conflict with the European orientation expected of the airframe sector. However, at the time the Government was assured by Rolls that it could manage to develop engines for both European and American aircraft. Conflict between the two elements of policy only became fully apparent when this confidence was later shown to be misplaced. Admittedly, the Government was always likely to give priority to Rolls-Royce and the difficulties experienced by the Airbus made the choice that much easier; nevertheless, it is clear that the Government traded off the interests of the airframe industry against those of Rolls-Royce. In the longer term, the final decision to withdraw from the Airbus marked a divide in civil aerospace policy. Although in competition this time, BAC and HSA would increasingly concert their design activities and actively seek further links with Europe. Rolls, on the other hand, would continue with its American strategy. In future, however, the Government would not find it so easy to prefer one sector over the other. In the short term, it had to resolve the growing crisis at Derby caused, paradoxically, by the RB211 and the contract with Lockheed.

The BAC 3-11 was not an immediate beneficiary of British withdrawal. BAC pressed ahead with a major sales campaign, but by the end of 1969 it was still short of its self-imposed minimum launch order. Nevertheless, in December BAC believed that the aircraft was showing sufficient promise to warrant launch aid. A request for £70 million was submitted to the Ministry of Technology. Government spokesman gave it a cautious welcome, saying that the application would be 'studied very carefully'. Subsequent discussions were described as a 'very good example' of industry–Government cooperation. As would be expected, BAC's supporters continually stressed the proposal's commercial viability and how, in a domestic project, public expenditure would be more easily controlled and monitored. BAC also said that they would seek risk-sharing partners from abroad. For its part, BEA continued to stress the importance of a positive decision on the 3-11 both to itself and to the British aircraft industry. BAC's commercial assessment had some support from Ministry experts who, although fearing the effects of intra-European competition, felt that the BAC 3-11 was a sounder proposition than the A300B. But the Government, wholly aware of the need for a speedy decision, would not rush into a large financial commitment 'without strict economic analysis'.[102]

As we have already noted, the Government was not entirely unaffected by the likely response of the French and Germans to an immediate decision to support the 3-11. In spite of Britain's rebuff by de Gaulle over membership of the Common Market, technological cooperation still had a wider political value. The British Government had no wish needlessly to antagonise the French or Germans who were still actual or prospective partners in other projects. Later the Government also had to consider the effect of HSA, whose arrangement with Airbus Industrie was not supported by launch aid. In any case, in the light of Rolls-Royce the Government had to evaluate the BAC 3-11 with great care: as we shall see in a later chapter, the Ministry had steadily improved their techniques for assessing launch aid proposals, and submissions were scrutinised much more rigorously than had been the case earlier in the 1960s.

The BAC 3-11 was going to face tough competition from the A300B. Despite BAC's claims that it had the superior market contacts with American customers, HSA's continuing links with the Airbus, and to be fair, Aerospatiale's own commercial experience with the Caravelle, gave the consortium a solid basis from which to seek commercial credibility. BAC, although receiving some encouragement from the Government, was not going to have an easy ride. By March 1970 estimates of BAC 3-11 airframe costs had risen to £100 million, to which had to be added a minimum of £30 million for developing a suitable version of the RB211 engine. Orders for the BAC 3-11 stubbornly stuck below fifty and, as one observer put it, the launch of the 3-11 was turning into a 'dour struggle'. By June BAC was confident that launch aid would eventually be forthcoming. (This view is confirmed by Charles Gardner in his history of BAC, who argues that Benn in particular was prepared to fight for the aircraft in Cabinet [C. Gardner, *British Aircraft Corporation*, London 1981, p. 180].) The General Election then intervened, returning a Conservative Government. A decision on the BAC 3-11 was deferred pending evaluation by the new administration. In December 1970 the Government rejected BAC's request for assistance, as well as an invitation to rejoin the Airbus programme. By then, of course, Rolls' financial problems were such as to deter any new expenditure on civil aerospace.[103]

Labour's decision in 1969, reinforced in 1970 by their Conservative successors, left the British airframe industry in some disarray. Moreover, the effect on European civil aerospace development was equally profound. These events, according to an EEC report, represented a 'severe conflict of political and commercial interests (which) divided the European industry'.[104] They left the British civil aerospace industry with diverging interests and orientations, a state of affairs which determined the context of Government policy throughout the next decade. Of course, one can debate any number of hypothetical cases where Government policy might have differed. If either HSA or BAC had been able financially to launch an Airbus type of aircraft without involving either an excessively high public contribution or the complications of collaborative politics, the Government's attitude towards Rolls may have been less influential on whether such a project was started. Alternatively, if BAC and HSA had been involved in a collaborative programme as a single, rationalised company, a negative decision would have threatened a much larger technological and industrial asset. Ultimately, however, the determining factor was the relative importance of Rolls and either one of two smaller firms not as dependent on a single civil project for their future survival. Paradoxically, the British public sector airlines appear to have derived the most benefit from this split. Henceforward, it would be increasingly difficult, though not entirely impossible, for the Government to apply a simple 'buy British' policy to airline procurement. British Airways, as BOAC and BEA were to become in 1972, found itself with a much wider scope for manoeuvre and choice amongst competing Anglo-European and Anglo-American projects.

In general, the events surrounding the launch of the RB211 and the Airbus showed the increased politicisation of civil aerospace during the 1960s. This was an inevitable consequence of the greater financial burden of civil projects and the international implications of development. This was precisely what Plowden had predicted. What was absent, however, was any clear sense of policy coherence. This was in fact noted by the Select Committee on Nationalised Industries in relation to the Government's policy towards BEA. After examining the conflict between BEA and the Government over the airline's re-equipment programme, the Committee recommended an end to the 'fiction of BEA formulating an independent procurement policy while the Government is formulating a conflicting policy which they are in a position to compel BEA to adopt'. Instead, the Government ought to formulate a coherent strategy for civil aerospace in which all concerned should participate.[105] The large-scale administrative changes of 1964–6 appear to have made little difference to the policy process for civil aerospace. Indeed, the one agency supposedly designed to provide a general forum for policy debate and discussion, the Transport Aircraft Requirements Committee, gradually lost what little significance it had had, to disappear quietly in the early 1970s. Civil aerospace policy remained a basically incremental process, but given the long-term consequences of these decisions, in retrospect, they were perhaps the most crucial of the entire post-war period, setting as they did the parameters for later debate and policy choice.

4

GOVERNMENT, ROLLS-ROYCE AND THE RB211, 1962–71

Tony Benn, Minister of Technology from 1967 to 1970, described the collapse of Rolls-Royce as a 'management failure, commercial failure and financial and technical failure'.[1] Its immediate cause was indeed the financial and technical strain of developing the RB211 engine for Lockheed and there were undoubted weaknesses in the Rolls management structure. Yet, while Benn was correct in his judgement, he should have admitted that the affair was also a major Governmental failure. The partnership between Rolls and the Government was central to the company's success in winning the Lockheed order and launch aid was essential for developing the RB211. Even if, in the event, Rolls presumed too much of the relationship, Government was responsible for the impression that their financial commitment to the RB211 programme was deeper and more comprehensive than it actually was. The project similarly exposed the limitations of launch aid policy when applied to large-scale projects and the overall weakness of 'self-monitoring' approaches to the sponsorship of civil aerospace. Although subsequent examination of the Concorde will show that direct and detailed supervision did not guarantee adequate control either, this experience still demonstrated the need for closer Government involvement in all phases of project selection, company tendering and programme development in any large civil project which required its aid; lessons which were, in fact, later incorporated in launch aid procedures.

The Lockheed contract

Rolls-Royce fought a sustained and hard campaign to achieve a long-standing corporate objective, a major order by an American airframe manufacturer. Assistance in various forms from the British Government was essential in securing the Lockheed contract. Rolls' ruthless, perhaps even reckless tactics in the face of competition, its willingness to shave its prices, to accept ever more ambitious technical requirements and production schedules, has already been noted. When Rolls had to fulfil the terms of that contract, increasingly the company found that its targets were, in fact, impossibly difficult to meet.

The contract with Lockheed, and the terms of the launch aid

agreement with the Government, defined the context in which Rolls had to develop the RB211. Rolls' management knew that producing the engine would be difficult. The contract with Lockheed was a fixed-price agreement with only a limited provision for inflation. It also contained strict and onerous penalties in the event of any failure to comply with its terms. The whole programme gave Rolls little leeway, financially or technically, if it encountered major problems. The company could rely on the Government for 70 per cent of the £60.25 million which Rolls estimated the engine would cost. Indeed, giving such a high proportion of launch costs for a new project was unusual. However, in this case, the Government took into consideration the ' . . . very great importance of their project in the future engine strategy of Rolls-Royce'. It was also influenced by the significance, especially to the balance of payments, of such a substantial breakthrough in the American market.[2] But, in theory, Rolls had to accept the risk of any cost-overrun and, of course, the effects of any penalties incurred under the contract.

The Government was not involved in the detailed negotiations between Rolls and Lockheed. The contract was a matter for two private companies; the Government, therefore, claimed that it had 'no responsibility of any kind' for the contract or its provisions. The Ministry of Technology was aware of some of its general features, for example that it was a fixed-price contract. In fact, the Ministry did not see a copy of the full text until six months after Rolls had signed it, although a close examination made no difference to the Ministry's opinion of the project's viability.[3] Officials had also known about Rolls' stream of concessions, but these were regarded as a 'necessary prelude to getting the contract'. As one official recalled, Rolls were up against 'some pretty tough opposition' and their actions were viewed as being comparable to similar offers being made by P&W and GE.[4] The American engine manufacturers felt that Rolls' final offer on price and delivery was, in fact, quite unrealistic. Certainly, Lockheed was very satisfied with the terms; according to one executive, it was the 'best price deal we have ever made'.[5] The Ministry, however, had complete confidence in Rolls' judgement of its commercial interests.

It was more than probable, then, that both Rolls and Lockheed believed that the British Government, even if they did not know its details, condoned the terms of the contract.[6] More importantly, both parties perceived a deeper commitment from the Government to the RB211 than was usually evident in launch-aid projects. Put bluntly, both Rolls and Lockheed negotiated in the belief that the British Government would guarantee any cost-overrun on initial estimates. As Edmonds points out, there were good grounds for such an assumption; the Government had clearly associated themselves with Rolls, the RB211 and the company's long-term survival.[7] The company was the cornerstone of many Government policies, in defence, aerospace, technology and industrial development. Lockheed officials were invariably invited to discuss the RB211 with senior civil servants and Ministers. Sir Denning Pearson certainly believed that Dan Houghton, President of Lockheed, formed the impression that the Government's commitment to Rolls went beyond the formal provisions of a launch aid agreement.[8]

Undoubtedly, experienced industrialists should have been aware of the dangers in taking political rhetoric at face value. For example, only two months before Rolls' collapse, Benn was attacking the Conservatives for not supporting Rolls more strongly in the face of growing financial difficulties. Once launch aid had been granted, he said, 'we became partners with Rolls and Lockheed in selling the aircraft'.[9] Yet Benn also had no doubt that both Lockheed and Rolls knew 'what the terms were. They clearly understood what was at stake in launching the aircraft under those conditions because we had discussed them beforehand.'[10] The Government recognised that Rolls would be fully stretched, but for reasons we will discuss shortly, they believe that Rolls would be able to develop the RB211 without further assistance. Benn was quite sure that the Government had been careful to limit the extent to which Rolls would be 'entitled to draw on the public purse'.[11] Perhaps he should also have limited the Government's association with a famous industrial coup.

The RB211 and launch aid
The conditions referred to by Benn were commonly attached to all launch-aided projects, and had been formulated when launch aid was reintroduced in 1960. The nature and operation of launch aid was described in chapter 2, but at this point a brief recapitulation would be useful. The Government gave launch aid on the basis of a fixed percentage of an initial cost estimate. Ministry officials evaluated a proposal submitted by the manufacturer, mainly to insure that the company were not inflating their figures to cushion them from the effects of a cost-overrun. Once a sum was agreed, no more money would be available; any cost-escalation would have to be borne by the company. This was the supposed 'discipline' of launch aid, to protect public money, to encourage managerial efficiency, and to obviate the need for elaborate monitoring procedures. Essentially the Government always assumed that a private firm would know its own best interests and would not, in a rash, ill-considered venture, put at risk its own survival.

In the case of the RB211, therefore, the Government had to assume that Rolls was prepared 'in absolute good faith' to accept the terms of launch aid agreements 'which imposed all the risk on the company'.[12] This may well seem naive, but the Ministry did not see its function as a shadow management team, nor did officials have the commercial experience of the Rolls Board. The company was regarded as the body 'best placed to take those commercial judgements of marrying the risk between the contractual terms and the difficulties of the programme and its ability to meet it'.[13] In theory, the launch aid system was seen as a good (perhaps even the best) compromise between the need for managerial autonomy in technical and commercial decision-making, and the requirements for accountability in public expenditure. But clearly much depended on both the quality of managerial judgement and the determination of Government in adhering to a limited commitment.

Even without any evidence of special Government favour, Rolls might have been excused some expectation of additional aid in the event of difficulties. Launch aid was only an administrative device, and in the brief history of the 1960 policy, there had already been a number of useful, if indirect precedents. Where it had been expedient to do so, Governments had mitigated some of the 'disciplines' of launch aid.[14] There was no real barrier, other than political will, to giving more money over and above the original agreement to a company in trouble.

Moreover, for Rolls, the psychological climate in which it operated gave good reason to suppose that the Government would never 'pull the rug out' in the event of a major crisis.[15] No matter what Government spokesmen may have claimed later, the company had a 'faith in Government support which exceeded anything that the Government was prepared to do in the end'.[16] Significantly, John Stonehouse, the Minister responsible for aerospace at the time, suggested that even if the Government had not given an open-ended commitment there had been 'an implicit undertaking that if Rolls-Royce was unable, from its own limited funds, to see the RB211 contract through . . . the Government would look extremely sympathetically at providing assistance to see it through'.[17]

Rolls was aware that the contract with Lockheed was risky; figures then available suggested that if the RB211 overran by a factor of two, two-thirds of Rolls' net worth would be tied up in the one project.[18] Rolls probably envisaged that if the worst did happen, and its financial position deteriorated, this would be such that a modest level of additional aid from the Government would be enough to see them through. At heart the company had overwhelming confidence – perhaps to the point of arrogance – in its ability to complete the RB211 programme. The Dual Programme for the RB211 and the RB207 was some evidence of this; but Rolls was also prepared to take on another large order for the RB211, from Douglas for the DC10. It was, perhaps, fortunate that Rolls in this instance was unsuccessful.[19]

A lot hinged upon the accuracy of Rolls' estimates of costs and the time they would take in developing the RB211. This was, and still is for that matter, an aspect of aerospace development prone to miscalculation. The problems of cost/time escalation were well known throughout the aircraft industry and to Ministry officials responsible for Government-funded projects. In defence programmes, usually organised on a 'cost-plus' contractual basis, remedies for time slippage could be 'bought' at the expense of higher development costs. Large cost-overruns were certainly not rare. Evidence presented by the Downey Committee in 1966 showed that the British norm for cost-escalation was about 280 per cent. American experience indicated that anything between 350 and 650 per cent could be expected in large, complicated projects.[20] Rolls had never had to work under a fixed-price contract for such an important order, and the company was also embarking upon the most advanced civil engine in its history, incorporating a number of hitherto untested design concepts. As Ian Morrow later pointed out, the risk may well have been justifiable, but 'its magnitude should have made them pause'.[21]

However, by British standards, Rolls' experience of cost escalation had been fairly benign. The firm's record in this area showed that, on average, Rolls engines had been produced with less than 100 per cent cost-escalation and usually on schedule. Rolls had encountered some problems with earlier civil engines; for example, the Tyne and Spey had given cause for alarm in the early stages of development. The Spey especially had at one time threatened the company's financial stability. On the other hand, the Dart and Conway engines had been very successful. Indeed, paradoxically the Spey gave Rolls additional assurance when it contemplated the task posed by the RB211. Despite those initial setbacks, the Spey had been built within both time- and cost-estimates, and went on to become one of Rolls' most profitable products.[22]

The RB211 was, as already mentioned, Rolls' most ambitious civil design and had no direct antecedents. Estimates of performance, development times and cost were based on parametric studies of the Spey and earlier, smaller turbo-fan designs. At an early stage, however, Rolls cancelled a three-shaft demonstrator engine, a decision which Sir David Hudie described as 'one of our greatest mistakes'.[23] The company's ability to surmount development problems was also severely handicapped by the death of Adrian Lombard, Rolls' chief civil engine designer, with a brilliant reputation for trouble-shooting problematic engines.[24]

Rolls, therefore, undertook the Lockheed contract with little direct empirical data on the RB211, or its essential design features. The information derived from the Spey proved totally misleading. Sir Denning Pearson later admitted that, even allowing for the increase in size of the RB211 over the Spey and contingencies added by Rolls to their parametric studies, the relationship between the two engines gave a false impression of future problems, and of Rolls' ability to overcome them.[25] Rolls was subsequently accused of being a firm run entirely by engineers with engineers' enthusiasm for accepting, and even seeking out, difficult technological challenges. This implied the possession of great technical skill but an unfortunate tendency to disregard economics. Sir Denning Pearson, for example, said that if Rolls had been run by accountants, they would never have built the Spey.[26] Then, Rolls had escaped the financial consequences of a major programme in difficulty, but this time it would not be so fortunate.

As far as the Ministry was concerned, Rolls' estimates were optimistic but not 'unreasonable'. The RB211 was clearly a substantial leap forward in the 'state-of-the-art', and the Ministry had access to research which showed the limitations of carbon-fibre composites. Officials were also well aware of the problems of cost escalation in large-scale projects.[27] Indeed, there were a few sceptics within the Ministry, but these were 'lone voices' amidst a general consensus supporting Rolls' judgement. The Ministry too had been impressed by the way Rolls had solved its problems with the Spey and believed that the RB211 set objectives, which, even if taxing, were not beyond Rolls' abilities.

In any case, as launch aid procedures then stood, the Ministry was not required to conduct an intensive technical or commercial investigation of Rolls' submission. Officials were more concerned to confirm that Rolls really did need such a large proportion of the engine's launch costs in aid. As a result of consultations with Rolls' bankers, they had found that the firm's financial position precluded a more conventional 'half and half' agreement. On the other hand, they had not seen it necessary to evaluate the effects of a major programme failure on Rolls' long-term viability. That again was not their responsibility, although the ability to survive such a catastrophe would be essential if Rolls was not, at some future date, to confront Government with an appeal for help. The Ministry certainly lacked the manpower and expertise to 'second guess' Rolls' estimates.[28] In any case, Rolls-Royce was its own guarantee of sound and accurate technical and commercial decision-making; the firm's reputation, prestige and history gainsaid any residual doubt. As Benn himself conceded, Rolls' status in the aircraft and engineering industries was a crucial factor in the decision to back the RB211. 'I was', he said 'dealing with not only the most famous British engineering company, but a company that had a blue-chip reputation. I am afraid those factors influenced me. I would not have done this with any tin-pot company.'[29]

The IRC loan

Even by June 1969, there were signs that Rolls' original estimates were inaccurate. Although termination of RB207 development towards the end of the year eased some of Rolls' development problems, the earlier-than-expected need to invest in the uprated RB211 virtually offset these gains. Revised calculations of the total programme costs suggested that the engine would cost just under £100 million. There were also some signs that Rolls would be hard-pushed to achieve a profit on the first RB211 production run. Rolls' Financial Director warned that the company stood to lose at least £16.5 million on the Lockheed contract of contractual penalties. However, the Rolls Board seemed to be fairly optimistic that these setbacks would be surmountable. The task was 'difficult but achievable'. In September, however, Sir David Hudie reported that the completion of the RB211 now represented a 'formidable task and we are putting the programme on an emergency basis'.[30]

Rolls was refused aid by the Government for the more powerful version of the RB211 required by Lockheed for the long-range L1011, and money for other applications was also refused. In an effort to cut costs and to improve its overall financial position, Rolls embarked upon an intensive corporate economy drive. Dividends for 1969 were reduced by 1 per cent and Rolls' total workforce was reduced through redundancies. These were only short-term palliatives, and Rolls warned the Government that it would need a substantial injection of fresh capital to overcome cash-flow problems. The Government was clearly faced with the dilemma of allowing Rolls' position to deteriorate to the point of crisis, threatening a wide range of policies, and of course even more redundancies, or acceding to the company's request for more money for the RB211. The Government side-stepped the inevitable breach of launch aid procedures by asking the Industrial Reorganisation Corporation (IRC) to investigate the company and to recommend what action should be taken in order to help Rolls.

The IRC had been established in 1966 to 'promote industrial efficiency and profitability' through the selective application of public funds in industry. The IRC was designed to help in the reorganisation of British companies and to encourage more effective exploitation of new technologies and production techniques. Increasingly, the IRC played an important role in arranging and financing mergers, supporting new ventures and rescuing ailing but industrially significant firms. In short, by 1969, the IRC was a vital instrument of an active, interventionist Government; in effect its merchant bank. As such, the IRC insisted on a complete investigation of an applicant's financial status and its management. Companies in the private sector were naturally wary of the IRC, viewing its role as an extension of the sponsoring Ministry. However, by strictly protecting the confidentiality of any information provided by a company under investigation, and by giving the Government only a summary of its final report, the IRC was able largely to overcome the suspicions of private industry.[31] In the Rolls case, the IRC was able to act as an intermediary between the company and the Government, considering Rolls' financial position as a whole and not just specifically the problems engendered by the RB211. However, although any aid provided by the IRC would depend on a thorough examination of Rolls, the Ministry would still be without a detailed picture of how the RB211 programme was faring and of the effects of major problems on the company's future status.

The IRC completed its review of Rolls-Royce in December 1969, and the Minister of Technology duly received a summary of its report. There was no specific mention of the RB211 and its problems, but reference was made to the heavy reliance placed by Rolls on its successful completion. Rolls' difficulties, according to the IRC, went beyond a short term liquidity crisis; 'it is clear that the size of the problem is such that only strong measures with substantial backing will produce results'. In view of Rolls' importance as a national technological asset and the company's contribution to the balance of payments, the IRC felt justified in recommending a loan of £10 million to Rolls. On the other hand, the IRC were concerned that Rolls' management did not appear to be fully aware of the seriousness of their position. Consequently, the loan was conditional on changes being made in the firm's managerial and financial procedures. In particular, the IRC insisted on having its own nominees on the Rolls Board.[32]

The IRC's Chairman, Sir Joseph Lockwood, later admitted that he had not believed Rolls' forecasts, and had been very concerned about the quality of Rolls' internal financial reporting.[33] Although Benn also said that he too had noted 'manifest financial accounting weakness', the Ministry of Technology accepted the IRC's summary.[34] From the Ministry's perspective, the report revealed a 'tight but not catastrophic' situation, which could be ameliorated if the IRC loan and its associated conditions were implemented.[35] The withholding of the full IRC report has been criticised as an example of inadequate public accountability. Certainly, the Rolls case did illustrate the limitations of monitoring launch-aid projects, but it is unlikely that the situation would have been materially altered at this stage by a fully detailed submission by the IRC to the Government. At best, 'it could have provided fair warning of the way things would end'.[36] Conceivably, the Government would have been required earlier to recognise the inevitability of even greater demands on the public purse from Rolls to finance the RB211 programme. Lockwood, for example, believed that Rolls was rapidly reaching the point at which the company would no longer be a 'viable entity'. He felt then that the Government would eventually have to finance Rolls on a regular basis, or see the company sold to an American buyer or merged into a European consortium.[37] Perhaps if such sombre realism had been made more explicit, the events of January 1971, could have been anticipated and the outright collapse of Rolls averted. This would have entailed negotiating with Lockheed for easier contractual terms, but given an open declaration of Government support for the RB211, this surely was not an impossible task.

With the benefit of hindsight, it is easy to pinpoint this as a moment when such an orderly response to Rolls' deepening crisis could have been mounted. However, at the time Rolls still did not fully appreciate the danger it was in. The Board hesitated for some weeks before accepting the IRC loan. Sir Denning Pearson objected to the imposition of an IRC nominee on the Board, a move which he interpreted as a step towards more direct Government involvement in the affairs of the company. He urged instead, that Rolls seek alternative sources of capital.[38] But Rolls' position was such that the IRC's offer had to be accepted. Under pressure from Benn, Rolls acceded to the terms of the IRC loan and appointed Lord Beeching to the Board and Ian Morrow as Joint Deputy Chairman. Morrow's task was to take 'special responsibility for strengthening financial control and forward planning'.[39]

Rolls' financial management was undoubtedly under some strain. The company still argued that it could make a profit on the RB211; but in order to do so, it had to forecast returns across the entire lifetime of the engine, perhaps over twenty years. Rolls also had to represent an increasing proportion of the R&D costs as corporate assets. Indeed, by the summer of 1970, almost the whole sum had been 'capitalised' in this fashion. Launch costs were now in excess of £150 million. The IRC was unhappy about so much of these costs being capitalised and suggested that part of Rolls' expenditure on the RB211 should now be written off.[40]

Publicly, Rolls radiated guarded optimism. In the spring of 1970, shareholders were told of the difficulties associated with any large project like the RB211, but that the company had adequate working capital to meet current demands. Sir Denning Pearson admitted that RB211 costs had risen, but he was confident of eventual success so long as the Government continued to invest in civil aerospace. He reiterated the mutual benefit of repayable launch aid and averred that the partnership between Rolls and the British Government had 'proved successful in the past and should so continue'.[41] Despite these confident remarks, the Board was awakening to the growing crisis. Owing to technical failure, the 'Hyfil'-based engine had already been abandoned, and although (on Lockheed's insistence) a titanium back-up programme was available, the change-over caused further delay and additional expenditure. Programme costs now stood at over £169 million and the RB211 was six to nine months behind schedule. For the first time, serious consideration was given to the implications of abandoning the project.[42]

The Conservative rescue package

While in Opposition, the Conservatives had gradually adopted a philosophy of 'disengagement' designed to end, or at least severely to limit Government involvement in private industry. However, senior Party spokesmen viewed aerospace, along with other examples of high technology, as a special case, warranting aid from the state. In the same way that American taxpayers supported their advanced technologies through defence and space contracting. ' . . . we are more or less forced to do the same thing – and with a smaller choice of firms. We recognise that as client or through the NRDC, Governments should back carefully selected new developments beyond the timescale of private enterprise.'[43] Following their election victory in 1970, the Conservatives accepted that aid for civil aerospace should continue, but they also wanted to ensure that money would not be wasted on uncommercial activities. They certainly had no intention of taking on open-ended commitments. Concorde, of course, absorbed a substantial proportion of the money the new Government were prepared to allocate to civil aerospace. The still-growing costs of this aircraft would necessarily influence actions in respect of other projects. For example, BAC's outstanding request for launch aid for the BAC 3-11 was seen in this context. However, the Government soon found that Rolls' continuing problems required urgent considerations and potentially represented another large claim on public expenditure.

Immediately after the election, Sir Denning Pearson wrote to the new Minister of Technology[44] to seek an assurance that the Government would continue to support Rolls' R&D programmes. The IRC, shortly to be abolished, also submitted its final appraisal of Rolls' financial status. Sir Joseph Lockwood drew attention to the deterioration since the IRC's initial report. He described how 'subsequent developments have confirmed our misgivings and cost-escalation has been such that the company has recently not been recovering even prime costs on the basic RB211 contract'. In August, Morrow confirmed this sombre assessment. Reporting to the Ministry, he stated that the situation was 'much worse than previously supposed'. Every engine constructed for Lockheed was now expected to show a substantial loss. The Ministry immediately instituted a full technical and financial investigation of the RB211 programme.[45]

Up to this point, officials had relied on Rolls to provide the necessary data for periodic checks on the course of development. This again was not unusual; launch-aid projects, remember, did not require elaborate and detailed monitoring procedures. The Ministry had also accepted the IRC's judgement of Rolls' future position as being difficult but not disastrous. The intensive review conducted by Ministry officials with the full cooperation of Rolls, brought results which 'surprised and shocked' the Government.[46] In September, there was more bad news, with the publication of updated cost-estimates. These showed that Rolls would need at least £170.3 million in order to complete the programme. Even if the Government agreed to support the RB211.61 for use in the BAC 3-11, Rolls faced a critical short-term liquidity problem. The Rolls Board also concluded that if any further delays occurred in the programme, they would have to approach Lockheed for some relaxation of contractual obligations.[47]

The Government agreed that additional aid would have to be provided. Negotiations began between Rolls, its bankers, the Government and the Bank of England. Sir Denning Pearson was told that more changes in Rolls' senior management would be required as a condition of any further help from the Exchequer. Consequently, Lord Cole became Chairman and Morrow took over as Chief Executive.

On 30 September, Lord Cole saw the Prime Minister, Edward Heath, who assured him that Rolls would now receive additional support from the Government. This was confirmed in a letter to Lord Cole from Heath's Permanent Secretary:

> The Prime Minister said that, in view of the damage to the national interest which would result from Rolls-Royce defaulting on the contract with Lockheed for the development and production of the RB211-22 engine, he would regard it as reasonable for Rolls-Royce to ask the Government to meet part of the overrun on development costs for the engine.'[48]

Lord Cole was further informed that the Government would not be prepared to meet the whole of the overrun, nor could it accept 'an open-ended commitment'. Help for Rolls would, similarly, depend on steps being taken to put 'the management of the company on a proper footing'. It would also be conditional on the results of an investigation conducted by a firm of independent accountants. In return, the Government undertook to give, in launch aid, 70 per cent of the £60 million still to be found of the overrun on R&D costs attributable to the RB211. The Government would also adopt a 'reasonable approach' towards contributing to any further escalation. Detailed arrangements made by the Ministry of Aviation Supply – which replaced the Ministry of Technology in 1970 (see Chapter 7) – would provide for the repayment and the phasing of aid. It was also agreed that the Rolls-Royce dividend would be limited in the coming year and, 'no doubt, for some years to come – to the minimum needed to maintain trustee status'.[49]

Rolls obtained a further £10 million from the Midland and Lloyds banks, and the Bank of England weighed in with another £8 million. The Industry Minister, John Davis, tried to separate the Bank's contribution from the Government's; 'It is difficult for me to say exactly in what guise the Bank saw itself acting but it was acting as a banker. It was, therefore, not drawing on its public institutional character in this particular operation.'[50] A nice distinction, perhaps, but rather unconvincing. In any event, the Government were directly or indirectly responsible for putting together a major rescue package for a private company and, even more so than its predecessor, wanted closer scrutiny and control over its investment.

The Minister of Aviation Supply, Frederick Corfield, announcing these arrangements, claimed that it would be a 'grave mistake if we were to allow these difficulties entirely to overshadow the record of the past'. Rolls-Royce was no 'lame duck'; the Government had every reason to believe that the firm would overcome its present difficulties. The alternative was to put at risk the Government's entire investment in the RB211, the future of vital defence interests and the possible destruction of the company. Corfield, however, reiterated that implementation of the package would depend on the review of Rolls by Sir Henry Benson, the Senior Partner of Cooper Brothers and Company, Chartered Accountants.[51]

This caveat was an important one, for Lockheed, then experiencing its own financial problems, was worried about the future of the RB211. Rolls assured Dan Houghton that, with the additional capital which would shortly be available, the engine was safe. Evidently, Houghton again failed to appreciate the significance of the qualifications attached to Government's additional support for Rolls. He was left, therefore, with the impression that the Government was unconditionally committed to the RB211 and willing to support the programme to a successful conclusion.[52] In the aftermath of the Rolls bankruptcy, a Government spokesman said that they had not given, nor could they have given, such an unlimited guarantee. Corfield himself stated that although he had indeed seen Houghton at the time, 'I am certain as I can be that he was fully aware of the situation . . . We made it clear that we were worried about the Rolls-Royce situation and that we could not offer an open-ended commitment. There must have been a misunderstanding or some misreporting.'[53] Whatever the truth of the matter, Lockheed still did not realise that Rolls-Royce was not 'synonomous with HMG and that if further financial difficulties arose, the company would not be "bailed out" by HMG'.[54]

The cancellation of the BAC 3-11

With the Government assuming a larger and more expensive share of the RB211, Ministers were not inclined to support more claims on public expenditure from the civil aircraft industry. This had a serious effect on the airframe sector as it meant that no aid would be given for large civil projects. The most obvious casualty was the BAC 3-11, but hopes of an early return to the European Airbus were also thwarted.

Paradoxically, the return of a Conservative Government had been seen by some as a sure sign of increased support for the domestic aircraft industry. The Conservatives had traditionally been firm advocates of aerospace development; as one observer put it, 'If the Church of England was the Tory Party at prayer, then the aircraft industry was the Party at work.' There was indeed strong support for the BAC 3-11 from the Conservative backbenches, as well as a standing request from BEA for permission to order the aircraft. BAC, for their part, claimed to have forty-five definite orders for the 3-11, and had showed willingness to back the project with their own money to the tune of £3 million already spent on preliminary technical and commercial development. It had also reached tentative agreements with Jugoslavian and Romanian companies to cooperate in its production in risk-sharing contracts.[55]

There were other, less encouraging factors. The new Government was

determined to limit public expenditure, and even if the aerospace industry
was regarded as a special case, the Government would be in no hurry to
add to its commitments in this area. Secondly, the Prime Minister was
personally dedicated to achieving UK membership of the EEC. He, and
his Cabinet, would not lightly contemplate any action which could
needlessly damage relations with the French and the Germans. The BAC
3-11 was a direct competitor to the Airbus, and the French particularly
would resent the sponsorship of a project which might damage the latter's
commercial prospects. Finally, the Airbus consortium invited the British
Government to rejoin the programme, thus presenting the Cabinet with a
direct and awkward choice between the all-British BAC 3-11 and a
European aircraft in which, it will be recalled, HSA was already
participating as an important British subcontractor.

The invitation from Airbus Industrie, backed by a promise of financial
assistance from the German Government to build a suitable version of the
RB211 engine for use on the A300B, was a direct challenge to the BAC 3-
11. According to supporters of the British project, the 3-11 was an asset
too priceless to be 'traded away for Common Market entry'.[56] Sacrificing
the British aircraft industry, it was rather dramatically suggested, would
be a poor opening to negotiations with the Europeans, a step which could
'so easily become a precedent for still more damaging concessions'.[57] The
influential American journal, *Aviation Week and Space Technology*,
joined in the debate with an editorial stating that without the 3-11, the
British aircraft industry faced the future 'as only a bidder for bits and
pieces of joint European programmes', and, consequently, it could not
'avoid degrading its present technical capabilities.'[58]

HSA, with its long-standing commitment to the Airbus, also lobbied
hard. Members of Parliament received a briefing which argued that BAC
had underestimated the cost of the 3-11 and stressed the absurdity of
British support for a second European airliner. Firm advocates of
European industrial and technological collaboration, such as
Christopher Layton, put the case for the Airbus in a wider context.
Independent development was no longer feasible, and the long-term
future of the aircraft industry lay in the evolution of permanent trans-
national companies. Full membership of the Airbus consortium would be
an important contribution in this process.[59] The debate became quite
intense, with each side arguing that theirs was the more commercial and
economic project. It was, as one HSA executive put it, 'a competition for
the esteem of the British Government'.

BAC had stressed that it would provide half of the necessary launch
capital, but the company was also under pressure from its shareholders to
obtain the best possible arrangement from the Government. BAC, a
holding company for the aircraft interests of Vickers, English Electric
(GEC) and Bristol Aeroplanes (since 1966, held by Rolls-Royce), was in
the event only prepared to put up 40 per cent of the money required to

develop the 3-11. If, as the manufacturer suggested, the aircraft was such a sure-fire winner, the Government rightly wondered why it was not prepared to find half. The Ministry, in the light of what was happening at Rolls, also wanted proof of BAC's ability to carry the costs of an overrun or major programme failure. The Ministry of Aviation Supply finally agreed to negotiate on the basis of a 60 per cent grant of launch aid provided that BAC's shareholders increased their equity in the company by £50 million. Grudgingly, they accepted this request, but GEC, in the person of the Chairman, Sir Arnold Weinstock, made it quite clear that it opposed any substantial increase in BAC's civil business.[60]

The Government considered the two projects throughout the autumn of 1970. There was strong pressure from the Foreign Office and the British Embassy in Paris to stop the BAC 3-11, but although there were some indications that the Government favoured the A300B, negotiations with the French and Germans scheduled for November, were postponed. The decisive factor, however, was Rolls-Royce. In December, Corfield announced that neither aircraft project would receive Government support. The A300B had indeed been the aircraft most likely to have received support, but there had been too many unknowns about its eventual cost, especially if it had been fitted with an RB211 engine. The total cost of the BAC 3-11 and its RB211 engine was estimated to be over £140 million. This, Corfield said, was simply too expensive. In short, the Government had to take into account 'the large sums of money already being devoted to the support of civil aircraft and engines and to bear in mind other calls on public funds'.[61]

The decision pleased few in the British aircraft industry. HSA's position in the Airbus consortium would have been strengthened and would have guaranteed its participation in further development of the aircraft. BAC had no subsonic project for the 1970s and with one shareholder eager to end civil development entirely its future was bleak. French officials, of course, were pleased to see the threat of competition from the 3-11 removed.[62] Although the 3-11 was not the last proposal from BAC, or the last British airliner conceived outside a collaborative framework, its cancellation marked the end of an era of independent British civil aircraft designed for major airline customers.

The collapse of Rolls-Royce

Events following the November rescue operation moved rapidly to a final dénouement. Even while Sir Henry Benson was conducting his investigation of Rolls' financial position, matters took a sharp turn for the worse. Sir Henry had already formed the opinion that the additional aid promised in November would not be sufficient. In January, revised estimates produced by Rolls showed that it would need nearer £110 million rather than the £60 million provided for by the November agreement. (Table 2 summarises programme estimates between 1968 and January 1971.) Moreover, Rolls reported that 'there must be considerable risk that we will not satisfy the programme as written'.[63] Unless Lockheed and its customers were prepared to accept a six- to twelve-month delay in delivery, Rolls faced heavy penalties under the terms of the 1968 contract. Lord Cole said that there were only two courses of action: abandon the engine or negotiate with Lockheed for contractual waivers. The first option would cost £300 million in compensation; failure to achieve the second, would entail £50 million in charges.

Table 2 RB 211-22 Launch cost estimates, 1968–January 1971 (1973 prices)

	Engine [a] (£m)	Launch cost to two years in service — Thrust reverser and pods (£m)	Total (£m)	Continuing development costs (£m)	Total launch costs (£m)
1968					
September [b]	74·9	7·3	82·2	7·1	89·3
1969					
June	84·1	6·1	90·2	9·4	99·6
1970					
January	91·5	6·9	98·4	9·4	107·8
March	119·1	6·2	125·3	9·4	134·7
April	119·1	6·2	125·3	26·5	151·8
July	136·7	6·3	143·0	26·2	169·2
September [c]	137·5	6·6	144·1	26·2	170·3
1971					
January 18	160·3	8·3	168·6	34·1	202·7
January 25 [d]	154·2	6·9	161·1	34·1	195·2

Notes
[a] In the case of the RB 211-22, only costs classified in the table as engine launch costs were eligible for launching aid from HMG.
[b] The original -22 launch cost estimate submitted to HMG.
[c] Submitted to HMG in connection with grant of £42 million additional launching aid.
[d] Assumes a six-month delay in the programme.
Source Flight, 9 Aug. 1973.

Ministry officials were greatly shocked by this sudden, appalling crisis. Their technical staff had given an optimistic prognosis for the engine, and they had no 'prior knowledge or indication' of this near-fatal financial position. Indeed, until January the Ministry still held hope for recovering the launch aid over the lifetime of the RB211. Since 1968, the Mintech had had two senior officials from its Engine and Aircraft Directorates working full time on the programme. Their primary concern, however, had been the examination of Rolls' short-term borrowing requirements and not the company's overall and longer-term financial position. What overwhelmed the Ministry was the speed and totality of Rolls' problems. Although many of these had been fermenting for months, they were apparently manageable. Then, 'most things with the RB211 moved in the wrong direction' and Rolls began to 'get up' against these contractual time-limits.[64] The banks moved to limit Rolls' overdraft facilities, and the Ministry realised that bankruptcy was a strong possibility. Both they and Rolls were increasingly conscious of the fact that Rolls might be in contravention of section 332 of the 1948 Companies Act, making it illegal to carry on business and incur debts when, to the knowledge of the directors, there is no reasonable prospect of the company being able to pay them.[65]

The alternative was for Government to assume full responsibility for the RB211 and any claims Lockheed might make against its contract. The Cabinet was obviously concerned not only about the financial implications of such a step, but also the effect of bankruptcy on vital defence interests. When the Rolls Board met for the last time on 26 January, Sir Henry Benson had already suggested that the appointment of a Receiver might now be inevitable. The Board accepted that a selective take-over by the Government could not be ruled out. They decided that a Receiver would have to be called in, but set a date for early in February, giving the Government and Lockheed time to discuss a way of saving the RB211.

Morrow had already tried to persuade Lockheed to renegotiate the contract. Clearly, had Rolls been able to increase the price paid for each engine and to avoid incurring contractual penalties, there would have been a good chance of averting the eventual collapse. Houghton's response was that Lockheed had a contract and 'they expected it to be carried out'. Morrow told him of the threat of bankruptcy, but Houghton, even at this late stage, still believed that the British Government would never allow Rolls to go bankrupt. He knew that Rolls was having some problems, but he had no idea that the 'difficulties were so great that Rolls could not perform under contract'. Houghton thought that Morrow was bluffing, and that the only consequence likely to follow holding Rolls to the original contract was that Lockheed would obtain its engines at a bargain price. He refused point blank to consider renegotiation.[66]

Bankruptcy

On the 29th, the Cabinet decided against intervening to save Rolls-Royce from bankruptcy. This was later described as a necessary step to avoid an unknown largely open-ended obligation on behalf of a private company. It would not have been, according to the White Paper on the Rolls collapse, 'a responsible use of public funds to assume a very large unquantified commitment either by supporting the company with funds which it had no prospect of repaying or by the Government taking the company over and thereby making itself responsible for all the company's debts and obligations'.[67]

Bankruptcy allowed the Government to negotiate with the Receiver for the selective purchase of Rolls' assets, especially those related to defence or public international obligations. The Government accepted that it must try to reach a satisfactory agreement on the RB211 with Lockheed, but would assume no prior responsibility for the engine or Rolls' obligations to Lockheed. Because of the diplomatic implications, Heath immediately contacted Washinton. In the absence of President Nixon, Heath told Henry Kissinger, the President's National Security Adviser, of the threat to the RB211. No special effort was made to inform Lockheed, Dan Houghton being due to see officials on 2 February for a routine meeting.[68]

On the 2nd, Houghton was told that Lockheed would have to relinquish all claims under the existing contract and to accept a delay of up to twelve months on the delivery of production engines. Houghton, 'dazed and shocked' by the news, had already spent a harrowing period trying to bolster Lockheed's own shaky financial position. He could not reach an agreement without further consultations with his Board, Lockheed's bankers and their customers. Consequently, the Government said it had no alternative but to allow Rolls to go ahead with bankruptcy proceedings.[69] As Lord Beeching later observed, Rolls' drift towards bankruptcy had the elements of a Greek tragedy. Nobody involved wanted to have the law applied to this case: 'It would have been much more satisfactory for everybody if we could have turned a "Nelsonian blind eye" and gone on negotiating our way out of the position.' But once the full depth of Rolls' financial plight was known and with the Government set against bailing out the company, it was the Board's duty to make it known that Rolls could not meet its liabilities.[70]

The official announcement that Rolls' affairs were to be placed in the hands of the Receiver, Rupert Nicholson, knocked nine points off the Financial Times share index. Dan Houghton was particularly and personally hurt by the decision. He had already battled to keep Lockheed afloat in the face of mounting financial problems and now he again had to meet expensive claims from Lockheed's airline customers.

Up to the last, Houghton had believed that the British Government had stood as guarantor, implicitly if not explicitly, for the RB211 programme. His official response to the bankruptcy concluded with this telling observation:

> We were completely surprised and appalled at the precipitant decisions made by the Rolls-Royce Board and the sudden withdrawal of the British

Government's financial support for this key industrial firm. The Government's stand today represents a distinct change from its announcement last November . . . We deeply regret that this great British company with its long and proud reputation should be brought suddenly into such a desperate position.[71]

Other American reactions were less restrained: 'this is the sort of thing you would expect from an underdeveloped country'.[72] And the President of TWA said that Britain's reputation as a trading nation had been irreparably damaged. In Britain, *Flight* felt shamed by the event: 'in the most ruthless industrial decision even taken by a British Government, Rolls-Royce was allowed to fail and a contract with a customer repudiated . . . This was not Britain's proudest moment.' Rolls-Royce, for its part, deeply regretted 'the loss and embarrassment which will result from the failure of the company to meet its obligations'.[73] Sadly, on the day the Receiver was appointed, tests at Derby confirmed that the RB211 would be a technical success.

Houghton and Nicholson discussed the chances of saving the RB211 contract. Nicholson recognised that the Government needed a 'clean sheet' before it would be willing to pick up the threads of the RB211 programme. Houghton appealed to the Receiver not to cancel the contract, but he could only offer terms which Nicholson felt to be unacceptably restrictive and inimical to British technological interests. Sadly, Nicholson had no alternative but to renounce the 1968 contract.[74]

On 4 February, Frederick Corfield outlined the measures the Government proposed to take in regard to Rolls-Royce. They were, as the Cabinet had already considered, to be based on a selective nationalisation of the company. In order to ensure 'the continuity of those activities of Rolls-Royce which were important to our national defence, to our collaborative programmes with other countries . . . the Government have decided to acquire such assets . . . of the company as may be essential for these purposes'. He repeated that the Government had no liability in respect of the contract with Lockheed. However, urgent discussions would be held with both Lockheed and the American Government to obtain a mutually satsifactory solution.[75] Later, in a nod of apology for the rather shabby way Houghton had been treated, Corfield expressed his deep regret that Lockheed were 'not given more notice of this calamity'.[76]

The Government did not regard the acquisition of Rolls as a usual form of nationalisation. Corfield described it as being 'somewhat different to the normal form of public ownership'. This was not a case of taking over a going concern and paying compensation to the shareholders. The Government was simply buying the assets of a liquidated company from the Official Receiver, the value of which would be subject to negotiation. Rolls-Royce (1971) Ltd would remain a limited-liability company, but with the state as the sole shareholder. The Government hoped that this would not remain the case indefinitely, but that private capital would eventually invest again in Rolls-Royce. The Government also believed that the new arrangements would strike a balance 'between the need for control over public expenditure, and the need to develop a proper commercial approach to the company's trading activities'.[77] As we shall suggest in a subsequent chapter, nationalisation, however formulated, was in itself no easy answer either to the short-term problems of controlling projects at Rolls-Royce, or for the aerospace industry in general where civil projects were concerned. Nevertheless it did reflect, even in a Conservative administration, a growing realisation that there were limits to Government disengagement where civil aerospace was concerned.

Corfield also hoped that with the bankruptcy, Rolls would be more amenable to European collaboration. Indeed, he referred to the RB211 as an obstacle to joint ventures, 'sapping both its resources and its energies'.[78] Benn, of course, attacked this view, arguing that the engine was itself a 'priceless European Asset'. It indicated Rolls' technical supremacy and represented a foothold in the American market. The RB211, he said, was the British equivalent to the Airbus: 'The Europeans are quite content to use their Governments' money to subsidise the airframe to hang an American engine on, but they do not want us to put our money, through Rolls, into the L1011.' Benn urged the Government quickly to confirm its support for the RB211 and reach an agreement with Lockheed.

The Opposition was clearly suspicious that the new Government's avowed intention of joining the EEC would mean sacrificing what it regarded as a major commercial breakthrough and, whatever its tragic consequences, one of the high points of the previous Government's industrial policy. It was difficult, however, for Labour spokesmen to condemn or criticise the actual act of nationalisation. The whole episode was deeply embarrassing to both major political parties, exposing the Government to the inevitable irony of nationalising one of the pearls of private enterprise and the Opposition to revelations of mismanagement which it had failed to recognise and to remedy effectively. It was, in fact, left to the Liberal leader, Jeremy Thorpe to pass an unbiased judgement on the bankruptcy and nationalisation of Rolls-Royce. 'Bound up in these events', he declaimed 'is the good faith and commercial credibility of this country . . . Bankruptcy is the only form of suicide permitted by the law to put a firm out of its agony; but it is also the only way in which a firm, and sometimes indirectly a country, may renege on its responsibilities and its liabilities.'[80]

The decision may not have been, as Benn later suggested, an exemplary measure designed to serve as a warning to other firms of the dangers of relying too much on the state, the so-called 'lame duck' approach to companies in difficulties. Nor was it a deliberate attempt to 'make possible the merger of a truncated Rolls-Royce with a European aero-engine company'.[81] It was, however, certainly the ruthless act noted by *Flight*. By allowing Rolls to go into bankruptcy, it was able to get its 'clean sheet'. The dangers of taking on the RB211 as it stood were obvious; Lockheed was in a vulnerable position and was itself near to collapse with the Tristar's future doubtful. There was some risk, therefore, that the Government might have found itself left with obligations to Lockheed's creditors and with no aircraft for the RB211. Finally, the direct costs, even without penalty charges, of developing the engine had yet to be accurately assessed and represented a large but uncertain claim on the Exchequer.

Sir David Hudie felt that the Government was not right to let Rolls go: 'a Government with more experience would certainly have hesitated longer before allowing that to happen. And I believe that if they had thought about it a bit more they would not have done it'. Harold Wilson, then Leader of the Opposition, was not so sure: 'we would have had the same advice and . . . we would have taken it'. As far as Morrow was concerned, the Government 'had no option, given that we could not have renegotiated this contract'. Corfield concurred: the crux of the matter was the extent to which a private company could become entirely dependent on public money. The Conservatives never expected to have to nationalise a 'lame duck', but 'once you have decided you cannot run a private organisation entirely on Government money, it is almost the logical inevitability'. There was some concern expressed by the Foreign Office at the likely affect on Lockheed and relations with the United States. But Corfield argued there really was no alternative to bankruptcy and nationalisation: 'The only alternative would have been an enormous Government subvention, . . . [and] the criticism that you were putting taxpayers' money into private shareholders' pockets would have been almost unanswerable.'[82]

The question remains, however, whether this was the only realistic course open to the Government. We have already mentioned the uncertainties surrounding the RB211, the L1011 and the costs which might have been incurred by hanging on too long. But what were the alternatives? For example, when the Government finally reached an agreement with the Receiver over the value of Rolls' assets, he was able to pay between 10p and 30p for every £1 share. It was regarded as such a generous settlement that speculation was rife that the company need not have gone into liquidation. In the event, there were special reasons why the Government allowed such a settlement and the Receiver himself said that on 4 February, 1971 the firm was 'hopelessly insolvent'.[83] Certainly, in view of the huge contractual penalties hanging over Rolls, even if the legal position had allowed any leeway, bankruptcy was the most obvious outcome.

Was there an alternative to nationalisation? Selling the company to the highest bidder was one possibility, as part of a European consortium perhaps; it was, it should be recalled, one of the options suggested by Lockwood and the IRC. But who would have been prepared to assume the responsibility for such an extensive and basically unsound enterprise? The Americans clearly thought that there were already too many aero-engine manufacturers serving the world market for civil engines; and it surely was not politically acceptable for a major British defence contractor to fall into the hands of foreign, even allied ownership. Similarly, while the Government might have hoped that following bankruptcy Rolls could extend its links with European companies, prior to bankruptcy few Europeans, Governments or private companies, would have looked on Rolls as a good risk, politically or financially, or would have been able to meet a reasonable asking price for Rolls' assets. Surely, in the light of Britain's rather shabby departure from the Airbus programme in 1969, the French would have hardly been prepared to pull British chestnuts out of the fire. So, if the Conservative Government was not going to let Rolls-Royce stand as one of the 'lame ducks', ripe for destruction, it had had little alternative. To allow the total collapse of Rolls was ruled out. The company was a special case, a technologically advanced company with a future, as well as being demonstrably vital to the nation's defences. In this respect, the Government's stance on Rolls was not a reversal of policy in the way that action over Upper Clyde Shipbuilders would be.[84] Cynical or not, the Government's action had the effect of putting Rolls on a stronger footing with regard to Lockheed, even if it was a case of creating a partnership in misery. More importantly, perhaps, nationalisation did at least help to clarify the Government's exact status with respect to both companies. Many of the causal factors in the affair had been due to the ambiguity of their earlier relationship; henceforward, the Government would play a full and open part in the negotiations and, consequently, would be clearly associated with any agreement to relaunch the RB211 for the Tristar. In the last analysis, the Government was unwilling to bite the bullet of inflicting major surgery on the aerospace industry, at least to the point of ending large civil aero-engine production. Indeed, the Government quickly sought to secure the RB211 programme. Having assured themselves that the RB211 was technically sound and that the delay in development would be within the six months already estimated, the Cabinet felt sufficiently confident to approach Lockheed for talks on a new contract. Calculation also appeared to show that of the £120 million estimated for development, £100 million had already been spent and that losses on the first series production would be £80 million. Some of the unknowns began to disappear.

Early in March, talks were opened between Lockheed and DTI officials. The British suggested setting up a joint company to manage and finance the RB211. They also wanted to increase the contracted price for each unit, mutual guarantees of programme security (both the RB211 and the L1011) and that Lockheed waive any claims for penalties on the old contract. Lockheed found these terms unacceptable and said that in any case it could not raise the capital necessary for a joint company. The British Government was faced with a choice between ending the RB211 or assuming its full cost themselves, always assuming that the L1011 itself was safe, as Lockheed's problems were patently worsening. Consultations between the Defence Secretary, Lord Carrington, and the Attorney General in Washington with senior Federal Government officials and Lockheed executives failed to clarify matters, and although work continued on the RB211 under Government indemnity to the Receiver, the Cabinet was not yet prepared to commit any more money until they had a 'guarantee from the other side' that the L1011 would go ahead.[85]

After further hard bargaining between Department officials and the Lockheed management, on 11 May a new contract was agreed, with revised prices and delivery times. Lord Carrington had already obtained assurances from the American Government that it would authorise a loan guarantee worth $250 million for Lockheed. On the strength of the new contract and the American assurance, the British Government took over Rolls' aero-engine assets, including the RB211 and from 23 May was officially responsible for the engine and its development. This was, perhaps, a little premature, as the Lockheed loan guarantee still had to be approved by Congress. The legislation was greeted with much opposition and its passage was always in doubt. However, by a single vote, the Senate agreed to the guarantee and on 14 September, the new contract between Rolls-Royce (1971) Ltd and Lockheed came into force. The deal was estimated to cost the Government £170 million, to be offset by profits on spares and additional sales of the RB211. In the event, even the first batch of RB211s earned a profit.[86]

The Government summarised its reasons for nationalising Rolls Royce and renegotiating the Lockheed contract in the following terms:

The failure of the old Rolls-Royce company had confronted the Government with a situation of immense gravity, affecting not only our own armed forces and national airlines, but many overseas governments and airlines as well. Our reputation as a trading nation and leaders in technology would have been damaged if the Government had not stepped in quickly and effectively to preserve the physical resources of the company and to provide finance and leadership on a new basis.[87]

While Benn probably exaggerated the effects of the Government's actions when he said that it 'destroyed' its credit with the United States Government and 'Rolls' credit world-wide', it was by any standard, a pretty sharp piece of business practice. The Government did get by *force majeure* a better contract with Lockheed and saved a major national technological asset. It was not, however, one of Britain's finest hours.

As far as Rolls was concerned, Morrow felt that the bankruptcy was a salutary lesson to the company. It administered 'a very necessary shock to Rolls-Royce'. Hitherto, it had been a complacent, often arrogant organisation; 'this shook them out of it'. The result was a better, more efficiently managed operation.[88] The Government would also learn some important lessons from the affair. In particular, the Government had to recognise that the RB211 had exposed severe limitations and weaknesses in the self-monitoring procedures of launch aid. Although there had been signs throughout the late 1960s that all was not well with the system, the Rolls collapse demonstrated the need for a major reappraisal of the 1960 procedures.

Launch aid and the lessons of the RB211

The RB211 programme revealed above all the need for a more comprehensive initial examination of a company applying for launch aid, especially if the project looked like absorbing a large proportion of the firms' capital. The devastating lesson of the RB211 was that Government could not rely on managerial realism avoiding unacceptably high risks, which could place unacceptable demands on company viability in the event of a dramatic increase in costs or following some other instance of programme failure. With the benefit of hindsight, it was all too clear to officials at the DTI that when they were required to deal with really large demands from industry, greater emphasis had to be put on assessing the applicant's overall financial status. In the Rolls' case, 'we did not deploy the right resources and depth of investigation which might have prevented us from getting it wrong'.[89] It is clear from the above that the Government and the officials at Mintech were influenced by the record and reputation of Rolls for 'delivering the goods'; any residual doubts about the magnitude of the task before the company and its ability to complete it successfully melted in the face of Rolls' confident assurances that it was within the bounds of the possible. The prevailing belief, stated by Sir Robert Marshall, Permanent Secretary at the DTI, was that the company had much more to lose than the Government, even though its contribution to the costs of developing the RB211 was initially only 30 per cent, and that it was better placed than the Ministry to make the necessary technical and commercial judgements. This trust, Sir Robert agreed, turned out to be misplaced and was plainly wrong.[90] In short, any guarantee that the public liability at stake in the programme was limited and would be protected by the self-discipline of private enterprise broke down.

The solution seemed to be fairly simple, to improve the methods by which launch aid contracts were allocated and to tighten monitoring procedures once the project was underway. Indeed, as we shall examine in a later chapter, this was precisely what the Conservative Government insisted upon.[91] Even before the full extent of the Rolls failure was known, some measure of reform had already been instituted to increase the depth of departmental examination of requests for launch aid. Throughout the 1960s there was a steady increase in the number of staff responsible for commercial and technical evaluation. Their methods and techniques also grew more sophisticated; as one official put it, 'In the early 1960s we did not adopt anything like the depth of market survey or the depth of technical investigation or financial investigation of firms that have been adopted in recent years.'[92] It was also suggested, though without supporting evidence, that within Mintech, the aviation department not only considered the effect of a proposal on the civil aerospace programme, but also its potential impact on industry as a whole.[93]

The absence of launch-aided projects after 1967 was cited as evidence that they had tightened up evaluation procedures. For example, officials claimed that the BAC 2-11 had been rejected because its case had not been strong enough commercially and that this had also applied to the BAC 3-11. In both instances there had been some commercial doubt about BAC's proposals, but it was somewhat disingenuous to ignore the plain fact that political factors had helped to determine the outcome on both occasions. As far as other proposals were concerned, including a version of the BAC 1-11 which, unlike the 1-11-500, the company felt would be commercially viable, the Ministry had said that the company could and had to do it alone. In a number of smaller projects officials had also felt that the manufacturer concerned could raise the capital from private sources.[94]

There was no hiding the fact, however, that the RB211 had shown the limitations of financing large-scale programmes through launch aid to private industry. There was, perhaps, an upper limit on the size and cost of a civil aircraft or engine for which the 1960 procedures were suitable. One industrialist feels that Rolls' disaster undermined what had been an ideal balance of aid and accountability for the more modest airframe projects of the 1960s. Again, in retrospect, officials recognised that the RB211 might have been better controlled with a more direct and detailed system of monitoring. However, and in the circumstances a vital observation, to have adopted measures such as those used on the Concorde from the outset of the RB211 programme, the whole character of the relationship between the Government and the company would have changed.[95] By availing himself of the accuracy of *post facto* judgement, Benn also admitted that this was precisely what should have happened. The company should have been nationalised in 1968 and the Government should have assumed responsibility for the entire programme. On the evidence available, no such recommendation appears to have been made or considered. Put bluntly, in 1968, even in 1969, the Government, the Ministry of Technology and Rolls were confident that the system was working and there was no need for such a radical change in either policy or monitoring procedures. It took the failure of Rolls to confirm again Plowden's judgement that Government would have to accept a more active and overt role in project selection and programme management.

In their report on the Rolls bankruptcy, MacCrindle and Godfrey noted that the affair called into question the 'suitability of companies in the private sector to undertake contracts committing a substantial proportion of their resources to the achievement of major advances in sophisticated technology'.[96] Clearly, it made little sense to them that the Government, by encouraging firms in such fields and at the same time by limiting support to a fixed sum, could hope to avoid disaster. Launch aid, for example, had the commendable objective of limiting public expenditure and was ostensibly a facility for instilling 'commercial discipline' in publicly-financed civil projects. However, it did require adherence to the firm, and perhaps questionable, notion that in the event of a major failure, the company had to bear the entire risk of failure. Any ambivalence or equivocation on this question would inevitably tend to undermine that discipline and encourage, perhaps, the assumption of greater Governmental support than was intended. Writing from the perspective of an ex-Cabinet Minister and Chairman of the Public Accounts Committee, Edmund Dell nicely summarised this problem:

> The success of such an approach depends on whether, in the last resort, the Government can in practice limit its commitment and wash its hands of failure. If it cannot, and if in addition the past commitment is very large, it will be well advised to face the reality of the situation, accept the fact of unlimited commitments, and draw the appropriate conclusions for the exercise of responsibility.[97]

Whether public ownership by itself could have ensured a different outcome is a more problematic question. We will see in Chapter 7 that nationalisation does not guarantee the absence of corporate or administrative error in these fields. Similarly, it remains open to considerable doubt whether closer monitoring generally might have effected a different result. The Concorde experience surely stands as powerful evidence to the contrary, and it is to that programme and its control which we now turn.

5

CONTROLLING CONCORDE, 1962–81

The development of the Concorde sprawls across the greater part of the period covered by this book. In Chapter 2 we examined the origins of the British SST and the establishment of a joint programme with the French. This chapter, however, focuses on the management and control of the programme between 1963 and 1980. Although some reference is made to the trans-national aspects of development, as well as to Concorde's wider commercial and political context, the emphasis is primarily on the relationship between the British Government and its domestic contractors. We start, however, with a brief survey of the main events between 1963 and 1981. The reader seeking a more detailed history of the Concorde since 1962 is again advised to consult the existing literature.[1]

Cost-escalation and commercial failure

Concorde is one of the most technically advanced aircraft ever built. In one analysis it is ranked first in terms of the level of innovation required by its development.[2] It remains one of the very few genuinely supersonic aircraft, that is to say, capable of sustained supersonic speeds over long distances.[3] In order to achieve this, the Anglo-French design team had to overcome a number of extraordinarily difficult engineering tasks. The whole exercise represented a continual struggle to reconcile two entirely different design requirements, sustained supersonic flight and subsonic airport approach and landing patterns. It was the largest supersonic aircraft ever built and had to meet the stringent safety standards of civil operations. It has needed highly sophisticated systems and components. Above all, the engine manufacturers had to convert an essentially military engine, where supersonic thrust could be 'bought' for short periods at the expense of high fuel consumption and frequent maintenance, into a civil engine capable of sustained supersonic power, with acceptable direct and indirect operating costs.

Sir Richard Melville, Permanent Secretary at the Ministry of Technology, rated Concorde second only to the US space programme in technological complexity. In his view, many of the subsequent 'difficulties of cost estimation and cost control . . . should be considered in this light'.[4] There is a direct relationship between the degree of technological complexity of a project and the likelihood of cost-escalation, and estimating the future costs of large scale technology can never be easy. Accuracy is not helped either by the natural optimism which sometimes surrounds development and the less ingenuous tendency of technological lobbyists to underplay the drawbacks, financial or otherwise, of launching a new project. Both factors combined in the case of Concorde to make the initial cost estimates virtually worthless. The suspect nature of the estimates available at the time the Conservative Government entered into its binding agreement with the French was conceded by Sir Richard Way, the Permanent Secretary of the MoA from 1963 to 1966. It was, he said, 'very provisional indeed . . . it was . . . more than a little more, but it was not a great deal more than an inspired guess'.[5] As the 'technical sketch' filled out, a clearer picture of costs would emerge. In the case of contemporary domestic projects, this principle was linked to a series of milestones, where progress and costs could be reviewed and, if necessary, could provide an opportunity to terminate development. However, the British Government became fully committed to Concorde before any of these more detailed evaluation stages had been reached.[6]

The cancellation crisis of 1964

In March, 1964, when Amery announced that the French had agreed to concentrate on the long-range version, he also revealed that this would now cost £250 million, compared with the £85 million figure given in November 1962. This was much closer to the more pessimistic assessments made in the late 1950s, but it was still far short of what the project would actually cost.[7]

Nevertheless, the new estimate was already high enough to enrage critics of the project. In the run-up to the 1964 General Election, Labour spokesmen made considerable capital out of the Conservative Government's commitments to wasteful 'prestige projects' like Concorde. Soon after its victory in the October election, the Labour Government announced a wide-ranging review of all aerospace programmes. Concorde was already vulnerable to this review, but a rapid deterioration in the balance of payments with commensurate pressure to cut public expenditure, increased the new Government's resolve to cancel Concorde.[8]

The MoA was divided on the issue; the department's technical people were still heavily in favour of the aircraft, but many senior officials with fewer career and personal ties with the programme were more worried about the aircraft's ultimate cost. The Minister, Roy Jenkins, was an ardent European and generally in favour of collaborative projects. However, he was determined to stop Concorde, even though he was aware of the effect of such a move on Anglo-French relations. For the first time, then, Concorde was faced by a combination of a sceptical Minister and opposition from influential officials within the MoA.

In the event, the attempt to withdraw from the programme was managed in an extremely inept fashion. In October, the French Government was informed of a request from the British to 're-examine urgently the Concorde project' only twenty-four hours before details were published in a White Paper on public expenditure cuts. Only then did Jenkins go to Paris to put the British case for cancellation. His argument was based on the rather optimistic belief that the French would recognise that the long-term interests of Anglo-French cooperation would benefit from a review of a project about which, he claimed, they both had 'legitimate doubts'.[9]

The French response was short and to the point. In their view, the 1962 Treaty had committed both parties to design and to produce a supersonic airliner. If the British attempted to renege on this agreement, then they would be taken to the International Court of Justice where damages would be sought equivalent to the estimated cost of completing the programme. At home, the British Government faced pressure from BAC, BSE and the trades unions to save the project. The Foreign Office and the Foreign Secretary, Michael Stewart, also warned of the damage unilateral cancellation would cause to any hopes of joining the EEC. Ultimately, the Cabinet accepted the Attorney-General's legal opinion that the French would have a strong case to put before the ICJ, and that withdrawal would not save much money. Announcing the Cabinet's capitulation, Jenkins tried to make the best of things. He told the House of Commons that 'we had, and we still retain, some doubts about the project. We have, however, been much impressed by the confidence of our French partners.' The Government would stand by its treaty obligations.[10]

Of course, even if the French had taken the British to court, and that might have been a bluff, the cost would have been small in comparison to the final cost of developing the Concorde. Certainly, as one senior British civil servant believed, the Cabinet was 'over-impressed' by the lawyers. Equally, through its inept diplomacy, the British Government may well have lost an opportunity to make common cause with those in the French Administration who were also sceptical about the project.[11]

Clearly, the Government was aware of the political costs of pressing its case, either in respect of any EEC negotiations or in relation to starting other collaborative ventures. To some extent, these factors would have influenced the decision irrespective of a formally binding treaty. However, its existence undermined the case for calling the French bluff. Paradoxically, it did help the Government to retreat with some grace from its abortive talks with the French.

This was a turning point in the history of the Concorde; there would be no greater opportunity to stop the project. When, in 1967, the continued deterioration in Britain's economic fortunes required further expenditure cuts, Concorde's future was again in doubt. Significantly, there was every indication that the French too were concerned at the growing cost of development. By then, however, an extensive industrial infrastructure had grown up around the programme in both countries, and even if British interest in European collaboration was then waning, the industrial and technological momentum behind Concorde was difficult to resist. Indeed, in spite of well-publicised leaks that both Governments seriously considered cancellation, Concorde again survived. Indeed, in 1968, the two Governments agreed to arrange finance for the first stages of production.[12]

Concorde's defenders have argued that the binding nature of the agreement brought a vital degree of political stability to what was a very complex technical and industrial task. This was undoubtedly true, but it does raise important questions of accountability and control. Naturally, the engineers and industrialists involved in such projects would prefer safeguards against politically inspired cancellation. On the other hand, where very large sums of public money are involved, the taxpayer must also have protection against the possibility of runaway costs. The more so in this case, because the original launch decision was based upon very limited data.[13] Significantly, all subsequent collaborative agreements contained some provision for periodic reviews of progress, and opportunities for withdrawal from the programme concerned. Political and industrial pressure would still constrain a Government's real freedom to take such extreme measures. However, without any power to cut its losses, or to take account of changed circumstances, Government has a much reduced ability to control events and to sanction the dubious programme. Without such power, it faces the prospect of seeing any supervisory or monitoring system, however sophisticated it may be, reduced to merely recording the rising costs of development and, retrospectively, explaining why the increases have occurred.

Cost-escalation

The broad outline of Concorde's cost-escalation is widely known. Between November 1962 and May 1972, cost estimates rose from £150 million to £970 million. A large increase occurred between 1965 and 1968 (see Table 3), of which a substantial part can be attributed to inflation and currency fluctuations (see Table 4). However, during this period there were also costly changes in the design of airframe, engine and major systems. In fact, during this period development became sufficiently detailed to enable more realistic assessments of costs to be made. At this point a domestic programme, or a collaborative project with some provision for withdrawal, would probably have faced cancellation. But as we have seen, the aircraft again survived rumours of the axe.

The first major technical problem appeared in 1964. In order to meet the American FAA's demand for a bigger fuel reserve, the manufacturers were forced to make the first of a number of increases in fuel capacity.

Table 3 Concorde cost estimates, 1962–72 (1973 prices)

Date of estimate	Total (£m)	UK share (£m)
Nov. 1962	150–70	75–85
July 1964	275	140
June 1966	450	250
May 1969	730	340
May 1972	970	480

Source   HC 335/353 (1972–3). p. xi.

This naturally incurred penalties in terms of increasing the design's all-up weight with a commensurate effect on costs. Worse still, in 1967 it was discovered that the aircraft as conceived would have difficulty in meeting its payload and range targets. Substantial modifications had to be made to the pre-production prototypes. This included a redesign of the wing and an extension of the rear fuselage section. Other problems appeared in main systems which 'rippled throughout the programme', bringing more changes and increasing costs still further.[14]

'Civilianising' the Olympus proved to be equally problematic. Measures designed to reduce noise and smoke emission, an increasingly important sales requirement, were more difficult to achieve in practice than had been originally expected. The cancellation of the military Olympus in 1964 also transferred all of the cost of proving the basic supersonic engine on to the civil programme. Above all, as the airframe grew larger and heavier, the engine had to keep pace. BSE (Rolls-Royce) and SNECMA were under continuous pressure to increase the Olympus' thrust, necessitating large changes in the engine's design. The cost of developing a civil version of the Olympus was originally put at £12 million, but, according to Knight, 'what had been initially regarded as a comparatively simple and inexpensive task ultimately accounted for nearly half the total Concorde programme'.[15]

Although by 1968 hopelessly behind the schedule laid down in the 1962 agreement, subsequent development went reasonably well and there was no repetition of the 1966–7 design crisis. The first French-built prototype 001 made its maiden flight in March 1969, followed in April by 002, the British-built aircraft. In 1970, the Concorde flew supersonically, and by mid-March 1975, the Concorde test fleet had achieved a total of 3,762 hours. Technically, it was now apparent that the Concorde would be an unequivocal success. However, by 1970 it was equally clear that the return on development, either directly or indirectly, would at best be very limited.

In 1971, the Conservative Government attempted to assess the full cost and the wider benefits of Concorde. The Prime Minister, Edward Heath,

Table 4 Causes of Concorde cost-escalation (1973 prices)

Changes in estimates	Changes in economic conditions [a] (£m)	Programme slippage (£m)	Cause of escalation		Other adjustments (£m)
			Revision of estimates (£m)	Additional development tasks (£m)	
Nov. 62 to July 64 £m 170–275	18	–	47	40	–
July 64 to June 66 £m 275–450	34	–	38	103	–
June 66 to May 69 £m 450–730	107	–	57	115	–
May 69 to May 72 £m 730–970	83	26	22	70	39
	242	26	165	328	39

Note
[a] Changes in the levels of wages and prices of materials and in exchange rates.
Source HC 335/353 (1972–3) p. xii.

asked the newly formed Central Policy Review Staff (CPRS) headed by Lord Rothschild to undertake a review of the project, including 'technical, economic, financial, industrial and employment factors'. The CPRS would also have to consider Britain's 'contractual and general political relations with the French'.[16] In the event, the CPRS concluded that there was still a good case for pressing on with the aeroplane. Quite apart from any contractual obligation to the French, the CPRS felt that the programme formed the basis of an important European technological effort, and, though difficult to quantify, contributed extensively to the country's technological and industrial standing.[17] The Government duly authorised further production expenditure under the Concorde Aircraft Development Act of 1973. This allowed the Secretary of State for Industry to give loans and guarantees up to £250 million, extendable to £350 million.

Commercial failure

The purely commercial case for Concorde had long since collapsed and the Government could hardly expect to recoup much of its costs through the levy nominally attached to the selling price of each aircraft (fixed in December 1971 at $22 million). Indeed, back in 1967, the PAC was told that the Government hoped to obtain a return of one-third of its investment from sales, but by 1969, it was conceded that it would obtain a 'good deal less'. According to the Treasury, it was more likely that there would be a 'thumping loss' on the project.[18]

In 1964, the manufacturers had been confident that Concorde's sales would excede 150 copies, even against competition from the proposed American SST. An elaborate option system gave every appearance of solid market support. In fact, most of these orders were 'protective' and meant little more than places in a hypothetical production queue. Only the two national airlines, BOAC and Air France, could be considered guaranteed customers. BOAC was sceptical of the whole concept, but an early clash with Amery silenced any public criticism of the aircraft. However, BOAC was assured by officials that if it had to have the Concorde against its commercial judgement, 'the Government will have to reimburse them'.[19]

Between 1964 and 1970, Concorde's commercial status grew ever more ambivalent. The advent of the wide-bodied aircraft, and changes in the pattern of air travel towards mass transport indicated that the classic 'curve of speed' was of less significance to the airlines. Worse still, environmental criticism threatened to ban overland supersonic flight, thereby reducing the value of SST operation. Concorde's prospective customers, already under financial pressure as a result of buying both long- and medium-range wide-bodied aircraft, began to cast anxious glances at both the initial and operating costs of an SST fleet.

In 1973, the option system collapsed. The American environmental lobby had already forced the cancellation of the American SST, and there was a strong movement to stop all SST operations into key US 'gate ways'. This was especially strong in New York, the most important East Coast airport. At the same time PanAm, as ever the market leader, was in financial difficulties. With Concorde presenting increasing economic and political problems, PanAm decided to cancel its options. A flood of cancellations followed, and by 1974 only Iranair and the Chinese People's Republic, outside the home airlines, were still formally committed to the aeroplane.

The fuel crisis engendered by the Yom Kippur war and the rocketing price of aviation spirit was a further blow, and it was questionable whether the Concorde could be flown at a profit at all. Legal action by the New York Port Authority also continued to threaten Concorde's operation on the most profitable of the North Atlantic Services. Although the Federal Government, under pressure from the French and British Governments to abide by international agreements on access, conceded a probationary period of flights into Washington, it could not override local jurisdiction in New York without the matter being tested in open court.[20] Certainly, British Airways (formed in 1972 on the merger of BOAC and BEA) was increasingly doubtful about the commercial viability of supersonic operations. The increased cost of fuel, combined with the uncertainties over major routes suggested that British Airways (BA) would be more than likely to lose heavily on its Concorde flights. In 1973 BA had obtained some financial protection against losses, but the airline was publicly unhappy at having to accept what it felt to be a loss-making aeroplane.[21]

The Heath Government made every effort to support and protect the Concorde's commercial position. Michael Heseltine flamboyantly 'sold' Concorde, wooing airlines and trying to negotiate overland supersonic corridors. However, in 1974, Labour was returned to office and Tony Benn, in the 1960s an enthusiastic supporter of Concorde, became Secretary of State for Industry. In a dramatic exercise of open Government, Benn for the first time publicly revealed the total programme costs of Concorde.

The 1974 statement and review

Benn's statement, and a more detailed report published soon after, showed that the total development costs for the existing version of the aircraft was an unrecoverable £1,070 million: in addition, 'British Airways estimate that the operation of Concorde could substantially worsen their financial results, possibly by many millions of pounds a year.' The manufacturers had also proposed a series of modifications to reduce noise levels and increase the aircraft's range which would involve a further £167 million, which prudently could be expected to rise towards £220 million by the time development was complete. On the basis of

various assumptions about the aircraft's selling price (ranging between
$40.25 million and $47.50 million) Benn claimed that Concorde could
only be produced at a loss. At 1974 prices, the potential loss on production
would be, for sixteen sold, £200 to £225 million; for thirty-five, £260 to
£300 million; and for one hundred Concordes sold, £120 to £250
million.[22] The manufacturers' estimates of sales were also believed to be
unduly optimistic and failed to take sufficient account of the effects of
noise and pollution restrictions, the consequences of improved versions
of existing jets coming into service and the impact of increased fuel costs
on all facets of airline operation and procurement. It was difficult to
assess 'how far any of the manufacturers' estimates of passenger demand
will be translated into existing sales of the improved version, but the
effects of the above factors could be to reduce sales substantially'.[23]
Inevitably, the Government again seriously considered cancellation.

BAC responded in forthright terms: the commercial outlook, although
not promising, was not yet disastrous and the Government itself could
take a more active part in easing Concorde's access problems. It
challenged BA's pessimistic estimates on operation, suggesting that
Concorde's flights could break even on 50 per cent load factors.
Furthermore, any threat to Concorde's production would have an
adverse effect on employment; some 21,000 jobs at BAC alone were
directly related to Concorde. It was also noted that the Government had
allowed only £80 million in cancellation charges, and past experience
showed such figures invariably grew when finally settled. Similarly, no
account had been taken of additional charges which might be payable to
the French.[24]

Concorde was again saved partly by the French Government's
determination to see the programme through to the bitter end and partly
because the British Government ultimately fought shy of the social costs
of cancellation. In July 1974, Harold Wilson met President Giscard and it
was agreed to complete the first phase of Concorde production. However,
no more were to be built unless *both* countries accepted that this would be
worthwhile. In 1976, the PAC was told that if the last five of the sixteen
production aircraft were sold at an 'escalated price', production losses on
the agreed programme would excede £200 million. There was little
chance even with a substantial new order that further production could
be undertaken without incurring heavy losses.[25] Finally, in March 1979,
the Government agreed to write off the £160 million cost to BA of buying
Concorde and its spares, in return for 80 per cent of any surplus earnings.
In the event, between 1978 and 1981, BA recorded losses of £14.5 million
through operating Concorde. For the financial year, 1980–1, the support
and operational costs of Concorde were estimated at £34.86 million.
Although BA put a brave face on its Concorde operation, the aircraft
continued to be a drain on public expenditure.[26]

The 1962 Treaty also continued to cast a long shadow. In April 1981, the Industry Committee of the House of Commons reported that intramural expenditure was still severely unbalanced between France and Great Britain. It was estimated that for the years 1981–3 the United Kingdom would spend £94 million in support of the entire Concorde programme, while the French would spend £48.8 million. By 1983, Britain would be paying over 58 per cent of Concorde's support costs. The disparity was to some extent a result of the original distribution of work. Britain had proportionately more of the engine than the French, and this would be where most of the support costs would lie. The French have never agreed to a system of adjusting imbalances in expenditure of this sort, and in spite of continual effort, British officials have yet to resolve the issue.[27]

The Industry Committee was even more surprised to discover that the 1962 Treaty still appeared to commit the British Government to support the aircraft in service 'until such time as either Government takes the decision to cease the project or . . . until an airline decides that it wishes to cease operating. 'It was admitted that this could mean supporting the aircraft for thirty years. The original agreement appeared to bind the British to the French, who had showed little desire to stop flying Concorde. Again, a unilateral action by the British could lead to action by the French to obtain compensation. Nevertheless, the Committee recommended that Concorde operations should cease. It recognised that there were difficult contractual problems involved, but it was also of the opinion that the Department of Industry had been less than honest in calculating the cost of maintaining or stopping the programme. At a time when public expenditure was under rigorous examination, 'we find it remarkable that the Concorde project appears to have been immune from such appraisal'.[28] To the end, it would seem that Concorde retained both a charmed life and officials prepared to defend it.

An account of the Concorde programme, even one as brief as this, almost always seems to convey an impression of inevitability, a runaway technological juggernaut against which Governments were either helpless or unwilling to stand firm. Looking back one can rail against the insanity of the 1962 Treaty, or the culpability of those who launched a project on the basis of such limited data with no provision for second thoughts. Of course, once the agreement with the French had been signed, a unilateral decision to stop the project was never going to be easy. The problem grew steadily more intractable as the programme acquired an industrial, technological and social momentum. Whether significant savings would have been made by cancelling the project once the prototype had flown is conjectural and subject to different and often highly subjective assessment. Even now, if the House of Commons Industry Committee's report is to be accepted, some savings can be expected by cancellation.[29] In 1964, cancellation would have saved money; and even without the benefit of hindsight, the danger of a large escalation in costs was realised by many in Whitehall and Westminster. In the event, it was again the perception of political and technological costs, and especially the former, which turned the tide in favour of continuing with the aeroplane. Cancellation would have brought a difficult period in Britain's relations with the French, and certainly it would have damaged Labour's chances of gaining entry to the EEC. Probably, however, the worst that it could have done would have provided the French Government with an easier way of rejecting Britain's application. It would have been a difficult decision, but equally it was one which should have been made. In the last analysis, the Government funked the best opportunity to stop Concorde.

Programme monitoring and management

If the broad outline of Concorde's technical and commercial problems is fairly well known, the relationship between the British Government and the two main contractors, BAC and Rolls-Royce, is less so. The experience with Concorde provides an important and useful comparison with other, more conventional projects started in the 1960s which were financed and monitored by risk-sharing launch aid agreements. From the outset, the Government accepted that it would have to provide most of the money for an SST. Consequently, development would inevitably require a monitoring system as extensive and as elaborate as one which would be employed on a large-scale defence programme.[30] The two Governments involved in the project agreed that as both sides had the same incentives to minimise cost escalation and to achieve maximum industrial efficiency, it would not be worth the effort and extra complications to set up a common monitoring system. Instead, both would rely on usual domestic practice, leaving the Official Committee to oversee the performance of British and French contractors and to discuss generally national cost estimates.

The monitoring system

A special Concorde Division was established within the MoA (later Mintech) to supervise the British side of the programme. The Concorde Division also provided British representatives for the technical sub-committees of the Official Committee. Originally, the British Project Director (from 1966 to 1971, James, later Sir James Hamilton) was responsible only for technical questions. Later, as design gave way to the more expensive development phases, he also acquired the responsibility for all administrative and financial matters relating to Concorde. In total, the Concorde Division comprised some fifty officials; in addition to his own team, Hamilton could call upon expert advice from the Research Establishments and from the rest of Mintech's aerospace staff. This was particularly useful where the engine programme was concerned.

The Concorde Division remained together throughout the lifetime of the aircraft. Even in 1971, when departmental responsibility for the administration of civil aerospace contracts passed to the Ministry of Defence, the Concorde Division stayed with the DTI. Concorde was made an exception because in this instance it was felt unwise to separate the policy and executive aspects of development where the two were so closely related. Later, in 1976, the Concorde Division was transferred to the MoD(PE). By then, only a few major policy issues were left to be resolved.[31] As a result of this administrative stability over the years, the Concorde Division built up an expertise which enabled it to deal on roughly equal terms with those directly involved in the development of Concorde.

The official system of monitoring and control was, however, slow to evolve. As late as 1965, the Comptroller and Auditor General (CAG) noted that there was no fully costed technical plan. The Ministry argued that such a plan was not appropriate to a collaborative programme, but that there was a separate British management document where quarterly returns from the manufacturers were checked against estimates. In addition, regular meetings were held between the Ministry team and the contractors. The CAG felt that this was not entirely satisfactory and urged the adoption of a more detailed and specific system of comparing progress against costs.[32] As a check on the adequacy of cost control in general, in 1965, a high-level Anglo-French team of officials visited the four prime subcontractors, and nine of the larger ones. They concluded, however, that in most firms the methods adopted for Concorde appear to have been an advance on previous methods. Even the Treasury officials said they were 'reasonably satisfied' with the monitoring system.[33]

In spite of this fairly promising start, as costs began to rise and a number of design problems implied the likelihood of still larger increases in the future, Mintech officials grew apprehensive about the speed and accuracy of cost reporting from the two British prime contractors. In 1967, the Ministry made 'strong and successful' representations on the matter to the manufacturers. For its part, BAC said that before 1967 it had simply been unable to define suitable areas for detailed cost reporting. These, in fact, were only identified as a result of actually working on the aircraft over a period of time. The company also told Mintech that there had been some difficulty in recruiting sufficiently qualified and experienced staff to undertake these functions. In February 1967, however, BAC were able to appoint a Director specifically responsible for Concorde cost control. As a result the Ministry began to receive more detailed information.[34]

Eventually, the British system of technical-cost control was based on an elaborate scheme of individual 'design areas' or 'chapters'. There were fourteen chapters, containing up to fifteen main 'task areas' under a task sponsor, further subdivided into over 200 more detailed categories. Eventually, the Ministry required quarterly costs against actual expenditure up to the completion of each task. Each task sponsor at BAC worked to a series of milestones determined as a result of consultations with the Ministry. Regular meetings were held to review progress against these milestones. BAC also used a full range of advanced management techniques, PERT, (Programme Evaluation and Review Technique) Critical Path Analysis and so forth; but the milestone system provided the real 'guts of control'. It enabled the Ministry to ascertain 'precisely when each milestone had been reached, and when necessary to discuss the position with the task sponsor in the particular area'. There were 700 of these milestones and they were sufficiently detailed and specific to 'drive BAC nearly mad'.[35]

The Ministry, however, was far happier once such detailed information was available. On occasion, the Concorde monitoring team was extremely concerned that BAC had become seriously late in reporting its expenditure, and, at the same time, had been gravely underestimating the manufacturing costs of major design modifications. It was discovered, for example, that BAC had done work worth £4 million which had not been authorised. Even though the work was not unnecessary, the Ministry was disturbed that this could occur, and felt that it would not have happened if the company had reported on time. BAC was reprimanded and told that it would be in breach of contract if it did not obtain prior approval for all development work.[36] Of course, it was precisely the need for formal authorisation during a complex R&D programme which really did 'drive BAC nearly mad', and highlighted the tension inevitably present in trying to reconcile official control and managerial autonomy.

There were certainly legitimate grounds for debate between the BAC and the Ministry of Technology over the degree of depth and detail required to monitor the programme adequately and effectively. BAC preferred to employ people in areas other than cost reporting, especially when there were so many more urgent technical problems needing attention. The Ministry disagreed; the firm employed too few staff to operate its cost management system. Officials felt, for example, that BAC's PERT system was not capable of reacting quickly enough to problems, and was insufficiently comprehensive. BAC responded by claiming that generally its line management was already well able to report costs and that the Ministry's criticisms had coincided with a number of acute technical crises which had diverted staff from administrative duties.[37]

Although the Ministry did concede that BAC was preoccupied with urgent technical problems, between 1966 and 1967, the reporting procedures had simply failed to work. The essence of the problem, according to one official, was 'how much information the Department could reasonably ask for in the circumstances where a highly complex project was being carried out'. However, at the time there had been a 'fairly harsh and really rather unpleasant series of talks between the Director General (Concorde) and the Managing Director (BAC). It was something very near to a major clash of wills as to what was to be done and whether what ought to be done would be done.'[38]

In passing, it is worth noting that during the 1960s the use of advanced management systems such as PERT had attracted a certain amount of perhaps unwarranted praise. This reflected a current fashion in some quarters of British Government and public administration to employ more 'rational' methods in the control of large-scale programmes. This was a consequence of an awareness that traditional methods had not been particularly successful in many new contexts. It was also a result of earlier experience and experimentation with these techniques in the United States, where PERT, Critical Path Analysis and their derivatives had acquired a high reputation following their use in American defence programme management and procurement.[39]

In Britain, Concorde was one of the first projects in which these techniques were used. Paradoxically, although Mintech initially insisted on building into Concorde an 'enormous PERT system', officials grew increasingly sceptical about its ultimate value. According to one, it was perhaps regarded with too much reverence. Such techniques had some use, but the figures changed so rapidly and development became so complicated that the contractors sometimes appeared to 'hide behind PERT', covering up delays in reporting significant events beneath a welter of data. Eventually, the Concorde Division insisted on a much simpler system, which it found to be a better way of supervising progress, effectively dispensing with PERT. In retrospect, the application of sophisticated management techniques was most relevant to projects which, even if large in scale, contained relatively fewer major innovations than Concorde. Concorde tended to defeat such systems because it contained just so many technological unknowns.

BAC and Mintech eventually compromised on how much detail was required of the firm's cost control system. The company tightened up its cost reporting procedures, but the Ministry allowed BAC line managers to perform this function without requiring the deployment of additional supervisory staff. They all reported to a central cost control organisation responsible to senior management who, in turn, passed on the information to the Ministry. Officials were gratified by the improvement in the quality, reliability and accuracy of the data they received. The firm was also less reluctant in its response to requests for information. Although by 1969 it was officially stated that the system was not far off as 'good as we could make it', the Ministry was never entirely satisfied with the standard of cost reporting.[40] Part of the problem was that officials had to 'learn' how best to control such an advanced and complex project. Equally, the contractor also discovered that methods used on Concorde could not simply be extrapolated from past experience on other civil or even military programmes.

It should also be recorded that relations between Sud and BAC improved in the course of development. Some of the old animosities between them slowly diminished to be replaced by a mutual respect for each other's engineering and technical abilities. The actual demands of working together, as well as presenting a common front to outside threats to Concorde, helped to forge a better relationship. Accelerating costs, a broader appreciation of the magnitude of the task and political sensitivity to criticism induced much needed reforms in the systems of trans-national management and control. The Committee of Directors was gradually superseded, and in 1966, a Concorde Executive Committee was formed, bringing a more direct and integrated approach to technical decision making. This was still unsatisfactory, and by 1969 the two airframe contractors had appointed full-time Concorde directors with enhanced responsibility for coordination of work, with authority to take immediate decisions on matters of joint policy.[41] Although the Concorde would never be regarded as a good example of managing a collaborative programme, by the early 1970s something more like a rational and efficient trans-national management structure had evolved.

On the official side, in 1966, the Standing Committee of officials was reformed as the Concorde Directing Committee (CDC) and increasingly it delegated more authority to its technical sub-committee. This was formalised as the Concorde Management Board (CMB) with a British and a French Director. As the project slipped behind schedule and costs rose, the CMB took a much firmer line with the prime contractors, forcing programme decisions and insisting on further internal changes to improve management efficiency.[42]

For example, towards the end of the 1960s, the British side of the CMB urged BAC to bring the Concorde team at Filton under closer supervision. The Ministry particularly wanted to see the amalgamation of the Filton and Weybridge financial units into a single accounting body. The result was the appointment of a Project Director responsible to BAC's Managing Director. A procurement controller was also introduced to improve control over subcontractor costs. The BAC Board had already been considering such a reorganisation, but the problem of forging BAC out of a number of proudly independent units had obstructed rationalisation. The Filton team had also been led by the indomitable Archibald Russell, and with his retirement in the mid-1960s, Weybridge found it easier to bring his fiefdom under stronger central direction from Weybridge.[43]

The procedures used to monitor the engine programme were somewhat different. This was primarily due to the way in which aero-engines in general are developed. The basic approach is continually to test components to the point of failure, until full performance and reliability targets are reached. Under these circumstances, the Government accepted that the day-to-day monitoring used on the airframe was not suitable for the Olympus. There were, therefore, fewer meetings between Ministry officials and Rolls-Royce. The Ministry was not entirely satisfied with this and in the late 1960s, a firm of management consultants were called in to examine the management systems used by Rolls. Its report recommended the use of procedures similar to those employed at BAC. Rolls spent some twelve months trying to implement these suggestions, but after considerable effort they were found to be impracticable. In the event, Rolls and Mintech agreed to use a simpler system derived from the one used on the Pegasus engine. Mintech officials felt that this reform had been successful, and that they received more accurate information as a result.[44] The Olympus was still most closely supervised civil engine programme BSE/Rolls had ever built. Even when Rolls accepted an incentive contract, tight official monitoring continued, a state of affairs which Mintech admitted was 'unusual'.[45]

The long struggle with BAC over cost reporting, the abortive attempt to employ airframe monitoring techniques at Rolls and the general pressure on the contractors to change or improve their internal practices, illustrated the dilemma of control and autonomy in a major civil programme sponsored by the state. Certainly, as far as Rolls was concerned, officials felt they had gone as far as they could to ensure adequate control 'without usurping the functions and responsibilities that must fall on the company's own management'.[46] Some senior industrialists believed that generally in the case of Concorde the Ministry had gone too far. Knight was particularly forthright about what he felt to be over-elaborate Government monitoring. He cited one example of how BAC could not spend more than £10,000 without explicit prior approval, and how obtaining this often led to long delays. Knight's opposite number at SUD (Aerospatiale), he said, had to face fewer officials and the responsible French Ministry was far more willing to take the contractor's word on technical and managerial issues. Knight conceded, however, that the British Government did at least pay for work done with greater alacrity.[47]

But Concorde was not a run-of-the-mill, launch-aided civil aircraft, and a tighter monitoring system was inevitable. Quite apart from the magnitude of the public investment involved and the size of the industrial effort concerned in its construction, the degree of cost-escalation encountered worried even hardened Mintech officials into close attention to detail. Moreover, and more positively, the Concorde was quite unlike most civil projects aimed at an open commercial market in that Government was involved in development from its inception.

Officials were, it will be recalled, largely responsible for selling the idea to Government as well as protecting the SST from Whitehall enemies. Concorde was not only a great industrial and technological enterprise, it was also an administrative legacy handed down through generations of civil servants and Government scientists. In addition to the genuine expertise accumulated within the MoA and Mintech, this continuity of involvement enabled officials with some justice to claim that developing Concorde was a partnership between themselves and industry.

The partnership necessarily continued into the industrial phases of development if only because of the value to industry of the services provided by the Ministry of Technology. The facilities and information available through the RAE and other Research Establishments, produced data and gave advice to industry and Government alike. British officials were far better placed than their French colleagues, who lacked direct access to public research facilities of this quality, to examine and comment upon technical issues. When developmental problems were referred to the Research Establishments the Ministry would receive the results of research at least as early as, if not before, the contractor. Not unnaturally, officials backed by their own experts and experience would form their own conclusions about possible changes or improvements in the aircraft's design.

Cost-plus or incentive contracting

The Concorde could not be regarded in any sense as a 'normal' civil programme. The size of the Government's investment automatically put it into a special category. Moreover, the reluctance on the part of the prime contractors to accept anything but the most limited form of incentive contracting was not conducive to a more relaxed approach to monitoring on the part of the Government. In Concorde's initial stages, industrial contracts had been awarded on a 'cost-plus fixed-fee' basis, but the Conservative Government did intend that firms should eventually make some contribution to launching costs.

Not unnaturally, the manufacturers were reluctant to change from cost-plus contracting to a less comprehensive method of financial support. Even though BAC had every confidence that the programme would be profitable its position was clear; the company had no objection to providing up to half of the costs of launching conventional aircraft, but the SST was such a leap in the dark that it would be 'improper' for BAC to risk large sums of its shareholders' money on the project. As Knight later observed, Concorde was not 'a fit project for shareholders' investment, no more than I think the US space activity is'.[48]

Both Labour and Conservative Governments hoped to avoid an agency relationship with private industry. It was recognised that this would necessarily lead to an undesirable blurring of public and private responsibilities, putting 'commercial judgements in the Government's hands'.[49] Some, perhaps even a large, degree of Governmental involvement was unavoidable, but incentive contracting might have helped to reduce the adverse effects of a fully funded programme as well as increasing managerial efficiency. The problem was to establish a realistic level of incentive. The size and magnitude of the project clearly precluded a really substantial private contribution. On the other hand, the incentives had to be sufficiently biting to 'really put the firms at risk'.[50]

Discussions on this question between the two Governments and the prime contractors were 'prolonged and difficult'. Between 1964 and 1966 progress was officially described as 'disappointing'. The plain fact was that the manufacturers 'required a considerable amount of confidence themselves before they were willing to go over to incentive contracts'. In short, they 'showed a singular unwillingness to accept risk-bearing contracts', until the technical uncertainty surrounding the Concorde had been much reduced by actual development.[51] Eventually, all four prime contractors were 'summoned together and strongly addressed' by the Concorde Directing Committee who firmly told them that some form of incentive contract would have to be introduced.[52]

Actually negotiating an acceptable incentive contract nevertheless proved to be a protracted exercise. Under the circumstances there were few sanctions available to the Governments short of halting the programme until the manufacturers capitulated. After a detailed investigation of alternative formulae by British and French officials, in the winter of 1968 the two Project Directors 'cooked up' a simple system of incentives. It was based on a reimbursement of manufacturing costs, with the incentive provided by setting a diminishing rate of profit as costs escalated beyond a percentage of an agreed target. If this cost target was exceeded or performance slipped by 15 per cent or more, the contractor would only receive a fixed fee. Target costs could only be altered if approved design changes were likely to increase manufacturing expenditure. The individual company was free, of course, to spend its own money to achieve better performance figures, thereby earning a larger profit on the contract. It was hardly a stringent form of incentive contracting, but Ministry officials believed that 'it got the worst of the old cost-plus out of it'.[53]

In practice, the companies appeared to lose very little if they slipped behind on the contract. Although in theory, profitability could come down to nothing if a firm's costs continually exceeded 15 per cent, the Ministry conceded that if this was the case, the project would have reached such an exceptional level of cost escalation that the project would have faced outright cancellation. The Public Accounts Committee was somewhat sceptical of these 'incentives'. Under close questioning from the Committee, officials conceded that the system contained only mild penalties but, nevertheless, an incentive was still present because the full-risk rate of profit was sufficiently attractive to encourage the attainment of technical cost targets.[54] In the case of the Olympus, the Ministry was unable to obtain even such a limited form of incentive arrangement. A similar variable profit scheme was proposed, but the engine programme encountered so many difficulties that the effectiveness of any incentive system was nullified. As most of the problems were the result of design changes and matters outside the control of Rolls-Royce and SNECMA the firms were entitled to a continuous revision of target costs.[55]

In the later stages of development, attempts were made to improve on this system. In 1971, the DTI tried to obtain a fixed-price contract for 60 per cent of the work needed to complete airframe development. But even then, with technical uncertainty much reduced, the Department was not optimistic about negotiating an unqualified fixed-price agreement. At this point, further discussions were suspended in view of the attention being given to the possibility of a more advanced Concorde. In July 1974, when final production authority was given, most of the outstanding R&D was either well-advanced or near completion. Consequently, it was agreed that it made little sense to change from the existing formula at that late stage.[56]

An even more determined effort was made to tighten up contractual arrangements in the production phase. The 1968 Industry Expansion Act authorised the provision of £100 million to BAC and Rolls-Royce in interest-bearing loans, the exact amount taken up to be determined by the number of aircraft sold and the terms of payment agreed with the airlines. Both the British and the French Governments agreed that any losses on production should not be subsidised.[57] Similarly, while BAC and Rolls-Royce were to lease £30 million worth of special tools, they were expected also to raise an additional £25 million from private sources to finance production (although, in fact, this was guaranteed by the Government). Later, the 1973 Concorde Aircraft Act increased the loan provision to a maximum of £350 million.[58]

Production agreements were signed on the assumption that the manufacturers would accept a share of the risk of production once the first twenty aircraft had been sold. This assumed, of course, that there would be a long and profitable production run. The collapse of Concorde's market in 1973, forced a review of production schedules. While it was agreed to keep both production lines open, arrangements for financing the construction of aircraft based on sales of a hundred or more copies were 'no longer appropriate'. Under these circumstances, the Government had to accept that BAC and Rolls would have to be paid a fixed management fee for production.[59] There was some consolation in the fact that the Department of Industry had been able to negotiate an incentive contract for the last three British-built aircraft in addition to an earlier incentive agreement negotiated with Rolls governing production of the Olympus. The Department of Industry regretted the failure to achieve a more extensive use of incentive contracting for production, but the collapse of the Concorde's market and the decision to curtail production made this inevitable.[60]

Looking back on Mintech's and the DTI's efforts to achieve incentive contracting, one official felt that it was difficult to see what alternative there had been to the limited form of incentive they had been able to achieve 'which would not have been more expensive to the Government. I think that in the circumstances probably the best efforts were made to secure a reasonable incentive, and some desire to save some expenditure'.[61]

The Public Accounts Committee was generally dismissive of the Ministry's incentive arrangements. It pointed out that any contract based on a fixed fee, no matter how much the rate of profit could be varied by performance, could hardly amount, strictly speaking, to a true incentive contract. Where, as in the case of the Concorde, 'there is a guaranteed minimum profit the incentive to reduce costs diminishes as the costs approach the level at which the minimum profit operates and disappears completely when that level is reached'.[62] At best, it could only have had a marginal effect on the contractors and certainly made little difference to the relationship between industry and Government as far as control and monitoring of the programme was concerned.

One cannot doubt the good faith of all involved, and clearly the contractors had responsibilities to shareholders not to act imprudently under pressure from the Government and assume a greater risk than they perceived to be safe. Officials were certain that the manufacturers had tried their hardest to make the Concorde a success, and they had been 'extremely concerned about the rising costs'. There was, for instance 'no question of the firm(s) doing their work as slowly or as expensively as they like'. Although they clearly gained technologically from the enterprise and many specialised facilities were paid for as a consequence of developing the Concorde, the companies had substantial material assets tied up in the programme; 'they have tremendous vested interests in making the thing a success and a tremendous risk should it fail'.[63] This kind of commitment was not easy to quantify, especially when by BAC's own admission such advanced projects were really quite essential if they were to remain in the forefront of aerospace technology.[64] If the taxpayer was going to subsidise the acquisition by private enterprise of the skill and expertise necessary for commercial survival, logically private companies should be expected to pay for the privilege, or accept tighter control over their affairs, which a genuinely risk-sharing agreement might have avoided.

From an industrialist's point of view, Knight presents a case for maintaining the right of a management to manage, irrespective of the source of risk capital. However, where this involved a lot of public money, there was no easy way to reconcile this principle with the demands of public accountability. In projects like Concorde, Governments had to keep an eye on their investment.

But in this case, I think it is a very difficult problem because although it is perfectly correct to say that the Government is putting up all of the money and

BAC is simply spending it and, therefore, the Government should be taking the major decisions and if it is going to take the major decisions it must put itself in the position where it had the knowledge to do so, the fact of the matter is that the company is likely to know much more about the job in all its aspects than officials however, intelligent they might be . . . I think it is a very difficult one to work and I do not think we have probably yet got the right solution for it.[65]

One senior British official, reviewing the long struggle to obtain an incentive contract, was always conscious of BAC's limited financial base and that this conditioned the degree of risk the Ministry could realistically expect BAC to accept.[66] Although the Government may have hoped to avoid an agency relationship, and to limit its involvement in commercial and technical decisions, in the end it had little alternative but to accept both as necessary, if unpalatable, facts of life.

Costs and control, an evaluation
In retrospect, officials working on the Concorde programme had grave doubts about the possibility that they could ever have brought the project under control in any real sense of the term. With estimates so unreliable, any pretence of achieving an effective check on costs, certainly for main programme development, was rather absurd. As one put it, 'If you feed in underestimates, your control system is obviously ineffective.' Moreover, insistence on ever tauter administrative measures to monitor costs, paradoxically may have exacerbated the problem. If the base figures needed for cost control tended to become virtually meaningless, monitoring was largely a case of keeping a reasonably accurate score of rising costs. The best one could do was to ensure that 'work has been done and deciding whether that work is necessary, whether it was done as expeditiously and efficiently as could be expected, and whether it has been costed properly'.[67]

The sheer scale and complexity of the programme affected the ability of officials and industrialists alike to come to terms with the difficulties of control. It certainly made cost-estimation very difficult indeed. It may also have been fruitless to expect a normal relationship between Government and contractor. This type of project, with so many risks and uncertainties was, perhaps, 'outside any form of contractual control'.[68] One clearly senses, in fact, a kind of fatalist desperation amongst the officials who had to explain the how and why of Concorde's mounting costs and diminishing sales prospects. Knight does admit to some over-optimism in BAC's approach to costs, but this was no ordinary technological punt launched by extravagant manufacturers. The fact of collaboration also served to exacerbate any purely domestic difficulties. As we have already noted, the specific circumstances surrounding the Concorde agreement removed any real Governmental sanction until the agreed programme had run its course. However, in the end, and as critics of advanced technological projects often note, they seem to acquire a momentum and life of their own, operating outside any conventional notion of managerial or political control.

There is no disguising the fact that Concorde, for all the early hopes of obtaining a direct or indirect return on a massive investment, has been a gross commercial failure, a monument to techno-diplomacy and the determination of expert after enthusiast to fight for the survival of a 'technically sweet' project. Using a discount factor based on various interest rates between 1962 and 1976, Henderson calculates that the true cost to the British Government alone may have exceeded £2000 million. He goes on to suggest that under the most favourable assumptions, the value of externalities to the United Kingdom could have been no more than 1 or 2 per cent of the total, and more likely to have been a net loss.[69]

Henderson also reminds us that the original objective of building Concorde was as a civil, commercially orientated investment project. Indeed, the aircraft was designed to 'sell speed' and, it was hoped, to do this sufficiently well for it to be profitable. Instead, as Henderson succinctly observes, 'in so far as we regard Concorde as an investment project, then on the evidence presented here I think it must be judged to have failed; and it has failed in a rather conspicuous way and at appallingly heavy cost'. Such a gross failure, he concludes, can only be regarded as a net loss to the nation's prestige and a blow to any image of technical and commercial competence the country would have hoped to project. The pure technical achievement was superb and impressive, but Henderson ends by citing Sir Alan Cottrell; the Concorde was simply a 'tragic waste of national resources'.[70]

The general impact of Concorde on the civil aircraft industry is equally difficult to assess; its supporters argue that the Concorde was a necessary technological vanguard, which the aircraft industry needed to improve its overall competence. On the other hand, others within the industry believe that the Concorde deprived other, potentially more valuable, projects of finance and technical support.[71] Certainly, if one accepts Henderson's assessment, the expenditure incurred must have had a gravely distorting effect not only on the civil aircraft industry but on Britain's overall technological effort during the 1960s and early 1970s. As far as collaboration was concerned, Concorde served as a classic example of how not to organise a trans-national programme. Similarly, while the industrialists learned mutual respect, the Concorde probably helped to cloud political perceptions of the value of collaboration and undoubtedly clouded the British Government's view of projects like the Airbus.

Concorde and public accountability

In his book on European technological collaboration, Williams argues that the Concorde highlights the often grave difficulty which the British

Parliament has in securing accountability for large-scale, publicly funded technology. Apart from one important gap in the 1960s, the project was subjected to a close and frequent examination by the Public Accounts and Estimates Committees. Despite this scrutiny, the House of Commons often had difficulty in supervising adequately this expensive and controversial use of public money. The work of the Committees was certainly hampered by the lack of a full and frank disclosure of information. William cites the 1969 PAC report which criticised the Government for not providing revised estimates of costs for three years, although in the interim there had been a massive increase in development costs. In Williams's opinion, the Government itself could be blamed for too readily accepting official advice that confidentiality was necessary to protect its position in regard to negotiating incentive contracts with the manufacturers. Surely, Williams argues, the companies would have been able to calculate the contingency being allowed for cost increases by the Government. In effect, only Parliament and the public were left ignorant of these matters. Similarly, given the Government's contemporary attempts to cancel the aircraft, there was no reason to have kept these things secret just to please the French. The House of Commons, as well as the Comptroller and Auditor General, might have been more alert during this period, but clearly, the main source of the accountability problem lay in Whitehall and not Westminster.[72]

Without doubt, the various Parliamentary Committees investigating Concorde encountered genuine and severe problems in getting the data needed for the exercise of accountability. In 1972, as part of its general survey of public money in the private sector, the newly formed Expenditure Committee considered, along with other civil aircraft and engines, the Concorde programme. In spite of some tough questioning, the Committee was unable to discover from officials the costs of engine development separated from those of total programme costs; nor were they able to discover details of the pricing policy then being adopted for the sale of production aircraft. In both cases, the officials giving evidence again argued that such disclosure would weaken the Government's position in relation to both the manufacturers and prospective customers. According to DTI witnesses, if the Government revealed its pricing policy, it would have to make known the percentage in the price which was given over to the R&D levy. If this became widely known, the airlines would naturally seek to have it removed from the price they would actually pay for the aircraft. The Committee was also anxious to discover the related information about estimated production losses if sales fell short of expected numbers. Both issues, production financing and pricing policy, involved substantial risks, and particularly at risk were large sums of public money. According to Sir Samuel Goldman from the Treasury, assessing such risks was the 'essence of entrepreneurship' and required confidentiality. The Committee, however, observed that while they were prepared to accept the 'entrepreneurial role of the Government in the case of Concorde' they also believed that the public should nevertheless 'be fully informed of the risks being taken with their money'.[73]

The Committee conceded that there were difficulties of confidentiality involved in any matter which concerned Britain's partnership with the French, but again they could not absolve the Government from its duty to the British House of Commons. The Committee was equally unimpressed with official pleas that disclosure would endanger the Government's negotiating position with the manufacturers and customers, or that it would have made cost control even more difficult. Concorde was virtually a monopoly product and prospective buyers were not able to 'shop around for an alternative'. Secondly, as there was no question of recovering more than a small proportion of R&D costs through a sales levy, 'there can be no element of true profit about which there would be room to argue'. A wider and more general appreciation of the true costs of developing the Concorde, the Committee felt might also have led to a greater degree of public pressure on the manufacturers to cut costs and manage the project more efficiently.[74]

The Committee was also exercised by the fact that Sir Robert Marshall, giving evidence for the DTI, was unable to cite another parallel case in any other field where national security was not at stake and where Parliament had been denied such information. Even when reading the dry transcript of the Committee's proceedings, one can easily sense the growing frustration and anger of its members in the face of official reluctance to give details of cost-escalation and commercial arrangements. On one occasion, its Chairman, William Rogers, was moved to comment on an official's reluctance to speak openly,

> I realise the policy is not yours, or certainly not yours alone, but I must say for myself that I think it is the most outrageous example of Parliament being denied information about public expenditure since John Hampden refused to pay ship money.[75]

The Committee did not want to be accused of 'knocking' Concorde, nor did its members feel that information had been held back simply to prevent Parliament from being frightened into abandoning the project. However, where so much expenditure was involved Parliament had a basic obligation to seek, and to comment upon, accurate and contemporary information. More fundamentally, 'continuous and informed Parliamentary and public comment is essential to the proper control of future large-scale projects of this kind'.[76]

When in 1974 Tony Benn made what was then the fullest statement of Concorde's costs and commercial problems, he referred specifically to the need to improve future decisions on the project by adopting a more candid approach to information disclosure. Although some were intensely critical of Benn's figures and assumptions, the actual act of opening up the programme to public scrutiny was broadly welcomed. *Flight International,* long an advocate of open Government on aerospace matters, believed that concealment worked to the long-term disadvantage of the aircraft industry. Sooner or later, its editor wrote, 'the lid blows off and everyone gets hurt, not least the aircraft industry'. Public confidence and support for aerospace had been eroded by a series of such events. Hiding the true facts induced 'sloppy management and eventually flaming rows ... Openness, by demanding more skilled and professional management, may not ensure success but it will give it a better chance.'[77] Earlier, the journal had also suggested that a Minister facing a complicated technical question needed the widest range of advice possible. Although the technical civil service was competent and experienced, alternatives should be canvassed from other, equally qualified sources. Obviously, the danger of institutionalised advice was that it might be based on departmental policy or the unrestrained enthusiasm of a number of committed officials and scientists. Increased public awareness of the issues might at least mitigate this danger to some degree.[78]

This latter point is at the heart of Henderson's perceptive comparative analysis of the Concorde and the Advanced Gas-cooled Reactor programmes. Both were large-scale, costly and, ultimately, commercially as well as economically dubious enterprises. 'Key decisions in both cases were taken in secret by a close circle of scientists and officials with vested interests in getting positive decisions.' Ministers came and went, hardly ever staying long enough to gain more than a limited understanding of the technical and commercial factors involved. Politically, however, they usually had a deep interest in the appearance of success and progress or, at the very least, accepted the classic Whitehall dictum of arguing one's departmental corner. Over time, the progression of Ministers and, eventually, even officials diluted responsibility, the net result being that the organisations concerned could 'cover their tracks far too easily'. Above all, obsessive secrecy made learning from experience difficult and tended to narrow the options available to decision makers.[79]

My own view is that these judgements are undoubtedly accurate and proposals from various quarters to improve the provision of information on key issues of public policy – open government – are necessary to insure adequate public accountability and, it should be emphasised, to encourage better decision-making. It should not be seen on the other hand as a panacea, an easy solution to many complex issues. If there had been a wider awareness of the technological and commercial risks entailed by the launch of an SST and, consequently, an appreciation of the likely costs involved, there might have a closer, more critical scrutiny of the decision and its assumptions. By the same token, if there had been an open discussion prior to the signing of the Anglo-French treaty, the dangers of accepting a binding agreement at that stage in the development of the aircraft might have been more readily apparent, and the Government encouraged to negotiate a more flexible arrangement. On the other hand, the political perceptions and diplomatic arguments which influenced the decision might still have been sufficiently strong to have produced the same outcome. However, genuine accountability requires at least some degree of prior consultation and information, and neither was present in this decision.

Later in the programme's history, matters are less easy to evaluate; for dominating any question of control and accountability was the fact of the binding international agreement with the French Government. It is difficult to see how greater disclosure would have had a direct impact on controlling either cost-escalation or improving the technical decisions affecting development. Indirectly, had disclosure led to increased public pressure against the aircraft, this might have strengthened the Government's resolve to test the French on the question of cancellation. Of course, by 1968, the perhaps intangible political benefit attached to stopping the Concorde also had to be balanced against the real costs, industrial and social, of dismantling a large and growing industrial infrastructure – questions which would have given any Government pause for thought before wielding the financial axe.

The Expenditure Committee's view that more information about the industrial side of the programme would have encouraged greater cost-consciousness and industrial efficiency on the part of the British contractors has some validity. As a sector, the aircraft industry ultimately depended on public expenditure for its survival; it might have encouraged its critics both on the political right and left, if private industry had been shown to be so unwilling to accept some of the risks when presumably, there was still some prospect of commercial return, and by their own analysis, substantial technical and industrial benefits to be gained. Yet again, one should not overestimate the power of public opinion in these matters; the financial dangers of becoming too committed to the success of the Concorde had dominated BAC's and Rolls' approach to the project and these might very well have outweighed any fear of attracting public opprobrium.

There is a fundamental principle here, however, which transcends an hypothetical assessment of the effectiveness or otherwise of more openness in the Concorde programme. The scale of the investment and the magnitude of the cost-escalation as much as the apparent uselessness of the control system applied by the Government, all suggest that the ethical desirability of knowing what was happening to public money supersedes any question of either maintaining the diplomatic niceties or defending what was, in any case, an increasingly invalid argument about maintaining commercial confidentiality. If nothing else, fuller, earlier disclosure would have shown, perhaps only as a warning, the apparent impossibility of bringing such a complex and uncertain project under control. This, in turn, might have induced a more sceptical view of Rolls' ambitious technical and commercial objectives for its big fan engines. Access to information, and then what to do in the light of the data received, was also at the heart of the RB211 affair. Here the issue was complicated by the fallacious belief that Rolls, because of its own substantial financial commitment and its reputation for managerial competence, knew what it was doing. There was, of course, the additional point that both company and Government misperceived the exact nature of the financial relationship linking them to the project. The upshot was that the Government did not actively seek more information about the true state of affairs at Derby until it was really too late, by which time its whole civil aerospace strategy hinged upon the success of Rolls and the RB211. As Edmonds points out in his study of the RB211, the affair raised many questions about public accountability in a Government-orientated company. These ranged from its internal management, through the differing perceptions about the strength of the British Government's commitment to support it indefinitely, to the company's place in a much wider techno-diplomatic context.[80] More than Concorde, which was from the start a Government-funded, Ministry-directed exercise, the RB211 touched upon the difficult and problematic relationship between the state and a privately run industry where public money was used to finance large-scale civil and commercially orientated projects. However, the Concorde in spite of its military-style monitoring system was still ostensibly a civil programme aimed at fulfilling commercial or economic goals. Together with the RB211, as well as the abortive European Airbus, the Concorde set new problems for Government if it was to remain a lender of the last resort to a privately owned civil aircraft business.

To many in the Labour Party, the Rolls bankruptcy, Concorde and the Government-financing of civil aircraft generally, was increasingly seen as a clear case for public ownership. The scale of public investment in private firms and the Government's reliance on private decisions about publicly financed programmes was so grotesquely out of balance that nationalisation was a necessary and painless regularisation of private industry's dependence on the state. Public ownership, it was agreed, would also enable the Government to strike a better balance between control and autonomy; the Government could retain its existing ability to determine strategic questions and pass judgement on individual projects requiring aid, but if public money was being spent in public sector enterprises, tight, and perhaps counter-productive monitoring would be less necessary. Events would show that such hopes were over-sanguine; in the case of complex, high-risk technologies what mattered was not ownership but the scale of the commitment involved. Ultimately, the problems encountered during the 1960s stemmed from intrinsically difficult technical and management tasks compounded by the diplomatic and political context of development. These facts would not be significantly altered, either by Rolls' nationalisation or by the creation in 1977 of a publicly owned British Aerospace Corporation.

6
GOVERNMENT AND CIVIL AEROSPACE IN THE 1970s

British civil aerospace policy in the 1970s was to some extent a natural progression from the previous decade. Past technical and commercial choices inevitably cast a shadow across subsequent decisions. The financial commitments to the RB211 and to Concorde continued to have a significant effect on the resources which were available for civil aerospace generally. More subtly, the experience of Concorde's cost-escalation and the trauma of Rolls' bankruptcy, influenced political and industrial attitudes, engendering a noticeably more cautious and conservative approach to civil aerospace. The broad division of interest between the airframe and engine sectors also continued to shape the basic context within which decisions for British civil aerospace were made. However, matters were made much more complicated by the existence of a wider range of collaborative options, both European and American. The technological and commercial environment was also radically affected by the energy crisis of 1973 and its aftermath.

The Conservatives and civil aerospace, 1971–4

Ministers and officials alike were 'shaken stiff' by Rolls' collapse and the enforced nationalisation of one of Britain's most prestigious private companies. The successful outcome of negotiations with Lockheed gave the government a breathing space, but with 30 per cent of Rolls' turnover tied up in the RB211, the firm's future viability was mortgaged to the continued development and eventual profitability of the one programme. Rolls would need more money to improve the basic engine and to match new airliner designs, and there could be no guarantee that any of these would be commercially successful. It was certainly believed that the first 555 RB211s for Lockheed would be produced at a loss, but there was every chance that in time (over some ten to fifteen years) the engine and its derivatives would earn substantial sums for both Rolls and the state. The problem was, of course, riding out the immediate short-term difficulties. Measures could be taken to improve the quality of Rolls' management and to tighten Departmental control (from 1970, the Ministry of Aviation Supply and then, from 1971, the Department of Trade and Industry; in 1974 Trade and Industry separated to form two

Departments of State), but if the Government was going to maintain a strong, civil aero-engine capability, and that seems to have been unquestioned, it knew it would have to judge Rolls and its products by less than strict commercial criteria.[1] At the very least, the RB211 was going to be a major fixed commitment for the Government.

Another heavy demand on public money was obviously going to come from Concorde. If the RB211 had some promise of showing a return, the prognosis for Concorde was much less hopeful. In Chapter 5 we noted how in 1971–2 the total costs of development had crossed or would shortly cross the £1000 million mark. On top of this, the Government knew that production costs would exceed £200 million for Britain alone. At least until 1973, Ministers might still be hopeful that the aeroplane would sell in some quantity, but whatever its ultimate sales were, the project was a second huge and continuing claim from the civil aerospace industry on the Exchequer. In spite of their determination to 'disengage' from private industry, and even before the Rolls bankruptcy, the Conservatives were aware of the special problems faced by high-technology companies. Projects like the Concorde and the RB211 did need a special approach, and 'even within a general policy of non-intervention' the Government accepted that 'aerospace may have to be treated differently from other industries'.[2] However, the Government drew a line at more open-ended commitments, and if its freedom was constrained by existing projects, a price would have to be exacted in respect of new ones.

Indeed, the effects of these 'pressing and immediate' demands were felt particularly by HSA and BAC. The likelihood of limited assistance for new projects was a fact of life in the early 1970s, a point sadly conceded by Sir Arnold Halls, Managing Director of HSA:

> The realities today, I suppose, are that the Concorde and the RB211 together will fully absorb what is available (from the state) and therefore . . . in British practice today . . . unquestionably other projects are going to be and are being starved . . . I do not think they are being starved because someone made a policy to do so . . . I think that is so because it has come to that.[3]

HSA was at least still in touch with the A300B Airbus programme. The company had negotiated what became a very lucrative subcontract with Airbus Industrie financed with its own money. In due course, it also became a design and marketing consultant to the consortium. BAC, on the other hand, had nothing certain with which to follow the 1-11 series. This, naturally enough, was very worrying to BAC executives; but even HSA would still need to look to Government for future projects. According to Geoffrey Knight of BAC, unless the United Kingdom matched European levels of support for civil aerospace, British industry would soon drop from the first rank of civil producers.[4] Given the existing expenditure on civil projects, however, the Government was in no hurry to extend aid for new developments. It was, as one senior official put it, a 'dire time for the aircraft industry generally'.

Civil aerospace under scrutiny

The shock of Rolls' collapse, the appalling escalation in the cost of producing Concorde as well as the poor record of return on state aid to the industry throughout the 1960s also led to a wider and often critical examination of civil aerospace, and of Government support for it. For example, in the early 1970s the House of Commons Expenditure and Public Accounts Committees investigated state-assisted civil aerospace development. DTI officials naturally tried to present a strong case for public investment in civil aerospace. In evidence to the Expenditure Committee, Sir James Hamilton, a Deputy Secretary at the DTI, stressed the value of civil production to the balance of payments. Technological spin-off and the maintenance of employment were advanced as other reasons for supporting civil aerospace. Ultimately, however, the chances of winning a large share of an expanding market was still the principle argument in favour of aiding development. This, he suggested, was why 'it would not be wise in the national interest to opt out of the civil aviation business at this time'.[5]

On the same day Sir James was giving his evidence, his superior at the DTI, Sir Ronald Melville was appearing before the Public Accounts Committee. He too emphasised the importance of exports and import saving as a justification for giving launch aid, even to apparently unsuccessful projects: 'the general theme or philosophy underlying launch aid has been more than anything else the earning of foreign currency or the saving of imports of aircraft from abroad'. Sir Ronald also described how civil work aided military projects, citing the RB211's contribution to the RB199 and research work on the Trident wing, having been of great value in the MRCA programme.[6]

The MPs did not find the official case entirely convincing. One senior Labour member of the Expenditure Committee, Joel Barnett, made a particularly telling observation:

> if we ever got to the happy situation of not having balance of payments difficulties, then what you are virtually saying is that there are only minor reasons why any government . . . should maintain an aircraft industry.[7]

The Public Accounts Committee also concluded that launch aid seemed to have been little more than an implied subsidy for unprofitable and uncommercial projects.[8] Both criticisms were hotly disputed by Hamilton and Melville. Sir James hastened to assure the Expenditure Committee that 'the profitability of the design' was an 'extremely important factor in the whole assessment' made by his Department of a launch aid proposal. For his part, Sir Ronald claimed that launch aid had always been a risk-sharing partnership between state and industry and never, in any formal sense, a permanent subsidy.[9] The continuing contribution to exports, despite Barnett's aside, was not to be gainsaid, and the future market for civil aircraft would be a powerful incentive to stay in the business. However, no one could be sure that the mistakes of the past or errors of technical and commercial judgement would not be repeated. More jaundiced observers were more likely to share one Treasury official's view of the optimistic predictions from the DTI: 'One can always hope that the next [project] coming along is going to repeat the success of the one or two that have been successful. One fears very much, however, that it is more likely to repeat the failures.'[10]

For its part, the Government was also worried about the level of expenditure on aerospace and the return on state aid for civil projects in particular. This concern was first reflected in a review of the organisation of defence procurement and civil aviation policy conducted by Derek (later Sir Derek) Rayner.[11] But more importantly in this context, in 1972 the Cabinet asked Sir Robert Marshall, the Permanent Secretary (Industry) at the DTI, to lead a full scale interdepartmental inquiry into the state of the British aircraft industry and to make recommendations on future policy. Although Marshall's findings were not published, the Committee evidently discussed the fundamental question of whether or not to continue to support a large-scale, comprehensive industrial capability. In spite of some doubts, it was accepted that there was insufficient cause to run the industry down, and that civil aerospace was at least equally as defensible as the military side.

Bridge-building with Europe

The perennial question of reducing the cost of development directed Marshall to re-examine international collaboration. The problems of the 1960s notwithstanding, there was still a strong case for extending the principle of international collaborative projects. However, officials were divided between broadening existing links with Europe and the possibilities of opening up new avenues across the Atlantic. In the event, and certainly in the short term, with the Government's general commitment to Europe well established, the European option was politically the more favoured of the two. Yet, as will become evident, this would not be an unconditional acceptance of European collaboration, nor would it deny either transatlantic or indigenous civil programmes.

The Government's existing commitment to the principle of European collaboration was clear enough. In December 1970, when the decision not to rejoin the Airbus was announced, Government spokesmen quickly reaffirmed their belief in European cooperation.[12] Indeed, there was a strong current in favour of promoting more permanent forms of industrial association. David Price, an Under Secretary of State for Trade and Industry, suggested that 'we must think seriously of the possibilities of international companies with, ideally, integrated managements, financial and physical resources operating with optimum efficiency in our mutual interests'.[13] Industrial integration was enthusiastically promoted by Michael Heseltine, the Minister responsible for aerospace. He resurrected the spectre of the 'American challenge' and urged the formation of a single aero-engine company and two airframe groups in Europe.[14]

Despite these fine words, the Government did little actively to encourage cross-national rationalisation. In some respects its actions seemed to contradict them. For a start, in the light of the Marshall report, the Government's primary objective was to maintain a comprehensive, balanced and independent industry. There was no specific plan to push British firms into integrated groups.[15] Indeed, from contemporary moves to unite HSA and BAC, it seemed as if the Government was more concerned to press for domestic consolidation than to forge permanent international links. Moreover, decisions on individual projects were firmly disconnected from the Government's negotiations for membership of the EEC and British participation in any joint venture would depend on its satisfying strict commercial criteria.[16]

Both BAC and HSA were involved in discussions about new cooperative ventures. Early in 1970, HSA and Dornier formed the CAST design study group and later the same year BAC joined MBB of Germany, CASA of Spain and the Swedish firm of SAAB in a similar consortium designated 'Europlane'. By September 1971, the Europlane group had completed a preliminary design and market study for a 200-seat airliner powered by Rolls RB211-24 engines.[17] BAC put considerable effort into Europlane, but largely because it lacked French participation, the British Government made it clear that approval for launch aid would be hard to obtain. As far as the French were concerned, their interests centred on the A300B and they did not regard Europlane with much favour. The Director of Airbus Industrie, Henri Zeigler, argued that Europlane was a divisive element in European aerospace. Although BAC contended that it would not be a direct competitor to the A300, Airbus Industrie felt that two similar European civil aircraft projects was 'a nonsense'.[18] In the event, Europlane was stalled by the 1973 fuel crisis, but in any case it, and CAST, were very much on the fringe of European civil development and were hardly comparable to the maturing Airbus programme.

Any hopes of re-establishing Rolls' civil links with Europe were even more rapidly and comprehensively dispelled. In the months following its bankruptcy, Government and independent observers alike believed that Rolls might now be able to find its rightful place within a European context.[19] Early in 1972, officials from Derby had a number of conversations with SNECMA and other European companies about rationalising European engine-production. They tentatively agreed that any new European airframe project should be complemented by a joint engine proposal. Only if this was subsequently rejected by the airframe companies concerned would they be free to offer an alternative, either individually or with an American partner. If a pooling of interests was not feasible in the short term, the companies agreed to consider a looser, Panavia type of organisation.[20]

In the event, French actions prevented these preliminary ideas from being realised. Given SNECMA's existing ties with GE, they were probably doomed from the outset. With the active support of the French Government, SNECMA negotiated an extension of its existing agreement with GE (to build the CF6 for the A300B) to include the design and development of a new 'ten tonne' (22,000lb thrust) engine, designated the CFM56. GE welcomed the arrangement as it reinforced its foothold inside the European aircraft industry. The French, on the other hand, saw it as an important part of their challenge to Rolls' European monopoly as a major centre of civil aero-engines.[21]

Rolls was not unduly bothered by the breakdown in these discussions. The firm recognised that while there were few alternatives to European competition in military projects (the Americans were simply not interested in joint ventures and the British Government was firmly committed to European collaboration for all major defence projects), civil engines were a different matter. There were distinct technological and commercial advantages in collaborating with an American company and, as GE demonstrated, American firms were keen to obtain access to European money. Rolls saw Anglo-American cooperation as being 'between equals'. In certain areas, according to Rolls' Chairman, Sir Kenneth Keith, 'they are better than us, and in certain areas, we are better than them'. The problem with European collaboration, he said, was that it was usually in a 'one-way direction, with Rolls-Royce on the giving end'. Even if the airframe industry had to collaborate on large-scale civil projects, Rolls could credibly compete on 'all fours' with the 'big two' American companies, GE and Pratt and Whitney (P&W).[22] Consequently, in the spring of 1973, Rolls opened negotiations with P&W with a view to building an engine similar in size to the GE–SNECMA CFM56.

The HS146

Paradoxically, for all its expressed commitment to Europe, the Government's only positive decisions on new aerospace projects related to essentially domestic products, HSA's HS1186 (Hawk) strike-trainer and the HS146 feederliner. As Williams observes, the HS1186 was a milestone in British aerospace policy, being the first independent project started in the UK since the early 1960s. Although the choice of the Rolls/Turbomecca Adour engine 'allowed some flavour of collaboration to persist', it was in direct competition with a Franco-German project.[23]

Hawker Siddeley's civil venture caused even more concern amongst

European manufacturers. There had been a number of independent military aircraft produced in Europe during the 1960s, usually by the French, but it had been generally assumed that civil projects would invariably be collaborative. Moreover, the HS146 would again compete with a European project, the VFW-Fokker 614, being built by a consortium of German, Dutch and Belgian companies. European objections were even more pronounced because the 614 would use the M45M engine, partly developed by Rolls. Short Bros of Northern Ireland was also a subcontractor on the airframe. The HS146 also had the domestic 'political disadvantage' of proposing to use an American Lycoming engine instead of a Rolls or European alternative.[24]

HSA's request for launch aid put the British Government in an awkward position. It was officially in favour of extending collaboration and Government spokesmen had frequently criticised the duplication to be found in European aerospace. HSA did offer a share of the 146 to other European firms, but there was little response. Reaction from Dutch and German companies building the VFW-Fokker 614, a direct competitor to the 146, was, understandly perhaps, less than welcoming. Support for the 146 contradicted the Government's declared position on collaboration. On the other hand, HSA was owed a few favours. It had used its own money to stay in touch with the most important civil cooperative project currently under development. Over the years, it had received less than BAC in terms of launch aid. The company also had a rigorous, 'hard-nosed' approach to civil aerospace which was very attractive to Whitehall. Finally, to those in the industry at large who had been critical of the sacrifices apparently made by British firms in order to further collaboration for political reasons, the 146 represented an important gesture of independence. This was, in the words of one industrialist, an opportunity to end Britain's sad history of being a 'tail-end Charlie' to Europe.[25]

In September 1973, the Government agreed to provide launch aid for the HS146. Announcing the decision, Heseltine said that he was convinced that the aeroplane had 'excellent prospects for success both technically and commercially, and that it will bring great benefit to the British aircraft industry as a whole'.[26] Government spokesmen also sought to justify the HS146 in European terms. Neither that, nor the earlier case of the Hawk, denied the importance or the general desirability of collaboration. However, there were different levels of cost and complexity in aerospace production, and some were more suited to collaboration than others. Projects like the Airbus and Concorde unquestionably had to be joint programmes; still more advanced projects would probably require transatlantic cooperation. At the other end of the technological spectrum, however, there were opportunities for purely domestic programmes which might but not necessarily, have some degree of commercially based, cross-national subcontracting. The Government also wanted to ensure that any future civil project was commercially sound. Collaboration was economically desirable for the larger classes of aircraft. It did not greatly increase the base market for the smaller type of airliner, and the cost of collaboration would be disproportionate to any advantages accruing from joint production. In short, the Government argued that a viable national project was far better for the United Kingdom and Europe than an unsuccessful cooperative venture.[27]

The energy crisis and civil aerospace

The three years following the Rolls bankruptcy had been something of a transition period for British civil aerospace. With important projects launched during the 1960s only just entering advanced stages of development, it would necessarily have been a time for preliminary research work on the next generation. The doubts and uncertainties engendered by the Concorde and the RB211 exacerbated the industry's credibility problems with a new Government and politicians generally. However, by 1973, the Government was groping towards a policy for civil development, based on a mixture of domestic and international projects. Although British companies were still on the periphery of major European civil activity, both HSA and BAC were involved in discussions, and the former still had a important role in Airbus Industrie. The launch of the HS146 and the steady improvement in Rolls' position were also promising signs of a revival from the low point of 1971. The events of late 1973 and early 1974, however, returned matters to a state of flux.

The energy and economic crises following the Yom Kippur war in October 1973, threw the aviation business into confusion and dramatically changed the context of civil aircraft development. In the first instance, the airline industry was hit by a massive increase in the cost of fuel and later suffered from a slump in air travel induced by the wider economic recession. This blow came just as airlines were beginning to recover from cash-flow and over-capacity problems of the late 1960s. In 1973, traffic grew at an annual rate of 11.3 per cent, still three points short of the 1960s average, but in the next two years, the rate was 5.0 and 2.0 per cent respectively.[28] Airlines immediately sought to cut back on their orders for new equipment and airliner sales inevitably dried up. In the longer term, escalating kerosene prices increased the premium on fuel-efficient aircraft. Manufacturers were already having to meet new environmental demands, especially from the anti-noise lobby, but these new conditions forced major changes in many of the assumptions governing future development.

In Britain, the HS146 was a direct casualty of the energy crisis and its aftermath. Under the double impact of inflation-induced uncertainty about costs and the slump in airliner orders, HSA felt that the 146 was too risky. In 1974, the company decided to cancel the project. This did not meet with the approval of the new Labour Government, which, for a variety of non-commercial reasons, wanted the programme to continue. In the event, full development was 'suspended' pending a decision by a future nationalised British Aerospace Corporation (BAe).[29]

In short, the end of the Conservative Government marked a very anxious time for the British aircraft industry. In the words of a senior British civil servant, it was 'very difficult to see any light, politically, financially, technically'. For Government and industry alike, the uncertainty usually associated with the launch and development of civil aircraft and engines had increased with dramatic suddenness. In retrospect, the discontinuity in the airline replacement cycle caused by the 1973–4 crisis, probably worked to the advantage of the British airframe industry, allowing it to recover much of the ground lost in 1970. At the time, however, no such silver lining was readily observable. Energy price inflation, economic disruption at home and turbulence in the market place, were factors hardly conducive to business confidence and the launch of expensive new civil projects.

The emerging options 1974–7

The problems facing the British civil aerospace industry in 1974 were therefore to a large extent a product of the technical and commercial uncertainties affecting all concerned with civil aerospace and civil aviation. The aircraft and aero-engine manufacturers found it difficult to discern a clear pattern in the market. All companies were agreed that once the airlines began to buy they would do so in large numbers in order to replace ageing and obsolete equipment with a new generation of quiet and fuel-efficient jets. Conversely, was it better to extend the life of existing designs through modification or with the production of derivatives, or to launch an entirely new project? The former was the cheaper option, but if an entirely new aircraft was produced substantially superior to it, the market could be lost for a generation. Starting from scratch, on the other hand, carried the grave risk of committing large sums of money to a project which might not enter the market at the right time with the right mix of design features. Invariably most firms tried to delay decisions on new ventures until the market position became clearer. In the interim, European and American firms began a protracted period of 'feeling out' new designs and possible collaborative agreements.

The American 'Big three', McDonnell-Douglas, Boeing and Lockheed, began to promote design studies in a bewildering proliferation of configurations and designations. Boeing was especially active, touring airlines, and manufacturers in Europe and Japan with a whole series of design studies. The 7X7 was a generic name for a family of 'rubber aircraft', designs varying in capacity from 175 to 200 seats, with twin- or tri-jet layout. The 7X7 eventually led to the 767. Boeing was also interested in a derivative of the 737, a stretched 737-300. This in turn became the 7N7, a 125–180-seat narrow-bodied proposal. This concept was later launched as the 180-seat 757.[30]

All three of the American giants were interested in forming some form of design or production consortium with European firms, either singly or in a group. While the main efforts of the French and German aircraft industries were concentrated on the A300 programme, the British were still only on the fringes of European civil development. Britain's options, therefore, could be presented as a straight choice between expanding its ties with Europe or, as Rolls-Royce would urge, to follow its lead and to join an American based project.

The Group of Seven

The commercial and technical uncertainties engendered by the energy crisis had a salutary affect on the European aircraft industry. In spite of the continuing technical success of the Airbus and the fact that it stood a good chance of selling well when the market recovered, its makers were aware that American competition would be fierce. Similarly, BAC and HSA were very conscious of their vulnerability without a major civil programme to carry them into the 1980s. In September 1974, European and British firms took the initiative and formed EURAC, a design consortium commonly known as the Group of Six. Early in 1975, the Group of Six became the Group of Seven with the inclusion of Dassault. Besides Dassault, the Group of Seven comprised BAC, HSA, Aerospatiale, VFW-Fokker, MBB and Dornier. This was the first design consortium to include all the major European civil manufacturers and was in advance of any specific airline or Governmental request for proposals. With recent history in mind, Alan Greenwood of BAC summed up the attitude of the British participants: 'it would be fatal to form competitive partnerships, cut our own throats and hand the market to the USA on a plate'.[31]

In spite of initial progress towards the formulation of joint strategy and tactics, the Group of Seven faced a number of difficult problems. First, there were wide and genuine differences of opinion about future demand and the technical requirements of new airliners. Second, there was the question of relating any new project to existing programmes. As a majority of EURAC were members of, or associated with, Airbus Industrie, a consensus favoured basing discussions on the A300 and its derivatives. This immediately raised the issue of Britain becoming a full member of the AI consortium, opening up a whole range of problems.

The newly elected Labour Government was not prepared to enter precipitately into new and far-reaching collaborative agreements. Its priority was to steer BAC and HSA into a single, publicly owned company. The Government was quite happy for BAC and HSA to discuss the matter with their European colleagues, but Ministers made it clear that no firm decisions could be taken until after nationalisation. Lord

Beswick, Minister of State at the DoI, and from December 1975, Chairman-designate of British Aerospace, recognised that planning the future of the civil sector would be the most difficult and contentious issue facing BAe, but while airlines were not yet ready to order the new airliners, there was little urgency to reach definite conclusions. He was sure, therefore, that there would be no 'planning gap' between then and BAe's vesting day, scheduled for early in 1977.[32]

By the end of 1975, however, BAC and HSA were less sanguine about the effects of postponing decisions. There was an increasing danger that delay in settling European proposals would trigger off unilateral approaches to the Americans. The big American companies were themselves actively seeking partnership agreements. Their interest and motives had been evident from the early 1970s. Like P&W and GE, the airframe companies were aware that the ever rising costs of launching civil projects and the risk of failure had become dangerously high even for them. International cooperation would not only provide access to the public funding which European firms received from their Governments, but it would also serve to head off, and perhaps to nullify, growing European competition. American manufacturers were also concerned that unless they formed links with European companies, protectionist sentiment amongst some European industrialists and Governments might lead to measures aimed at penalising American imports.[33]

From a European perspective, there were attractions in forging transatlantic links. If the Americans hoped to by-pass through cooperation potential protectionism, then some Europeans saw an ideal opportunity to penetrate the tough and already virtually closed American market. Similarly, the overall technical and commercial strength of the American aircraft industry offered European companies, especially the smaller and technically less advanced firms in Italy and the Benelux countries, a short cut to commercially viable civil aircraft production.[34] If to these advantages was added that of avoiding the protracted political wrangles which seemed to be the inevitable adjunct of European collaboration, transatlantic agreements could easily be seen as a more fruitful way of resolving any domestic economic and industrial problems associated with civil aerospace.

On the other hand, European collaboration, for all its attendant difficulties, was a known factor and, as the Airbus was demonstrating, a European project could obtain commercial and technical credibility. Conversely, cooperating with American firms had its drawbacks. European firms would be expected to meet far stricter and more stringent production and cost targets than they were used to, and if this suited domestic critics of waste and inefficiency in civil development, Governments would still have to guarantee tight contracts and underwrite the risks of failing to meet their terms. Employment and technological development would also depend on American attitudes and decisions. Once an independent design and production capability was lost, recovery after any break with the American partner would be difficult, if not impossible; it would certainly be very costly.

The Spinelli Report

The dangers of bilateral cooperation between European and American firms were pinpointed in the EEC Commission's *Action Programme for European Aerospace*, published in October 1975.[35] This report, commonly referred to as the Spinelli Report (after the Commissioner responsible for Industry and Technology) contained a clear warning of the risks being run by a disunited European aircraft industry. It was the culmination of some eight years of active interest in aerospace on the part of the EEC Commission and both presented a diagnosis of the problems of European aerospace, and outlined a comprehensive set of proposals designed to overcome them. As the Commission was unable politically to lay claim to any military or procurement functions, the Spinelli proposals were primarily directed at civil aerospace. The Action Programme however, tended to reflect existing projects and proposals, with little attempt to rank them. It also advanced a very extensive role for the Commission in directing community finance for civil development; a sensitive area over which member states proved unanimously unwilling to relinquish sovereign control.

Nevertheless, Spinelli made the point that as far as their civil aerospace policies were concerned, the EEC Governments were at a crossroads; 'If they refuse to seize the new opportunities offered and continue to pursue divergent national policies, this could lead to the disappearance of an autonomous European aircraft industry, thus damaging the economic, political and social fabric of the Community.'[36] The position had been bad enough in the past, when the separate national industries of Europe had competed against each other, and when *ad hoc* collaboration had sometimes left a residue of bitterness and conflict. There were some signs that lessons had been learned, but the present uncertainties over future European civil projects created new dangers. As one of Spinelli's staff put it, there was 'a strong possibility that this hard-won experience might be thrown away by a precipitate rush to embrace the American option'.

British airframe constructors, either individually as HSA, BAC or collectively in BAe were inclined to view American collaboration with caution and even with extreme suspicion. One of the clearest expositions of the airframe sector's dilemma was given by Handel Davies of BAC in evidence to a House of Lords Select Committee. It is worth quoting at some length.

> The advantage of a European policy, if it could be made to work, would be that we would be collaborating or trying to collaborate with companies which are roughly the same size . . . We are able to develop organisations in which there is a good standard of sharing of design responsibilities, for example, so

that if we wish to maintain an industry in the United Kingdom which continues to carry out research development, as well as manufacture and support, then a European policy would stand a good chance of doing so . . . If we collaborated with the United States it would inevitably be collaboration with a more powerful partner . . . we would undoubtedly be junior partners. We would perhaps on the design side be able to and be allowed to carry out detailed design of parts of the aircraft and so on, but we would certainly have no vital controlling part of the overall concept . . . So for that reason my own company has had a preference for attempting to build up the European industry rather than to make collaborative arrangements with the United States.[37]

Davies's opinion was shared by Sir Peter Fletcher of HSA. He, like many in British industry, did not fully accept the need for centralised European direction as envisaged by Spinelli. Nevertheless he felt that the Americans were simply trying to secure a foothold in Europe by offering industrial and commercial inducements which, though attractive in the short term, could over a longer period be of less and less benefit, and would turn out to be a net loss to European industry.[38]

Official and quasi-official attitudes to Spinelli tended to reflect Sir Peter's scepticism about the role of the Commission in sponsoring civil development. For example, the British Government was uneasy about an undercurrent of anti-Americanism which it perceived in the Spinelli Report. For the Conservative Opposition, Lord Carr also attacked the insularity of the approach advocated by Brussels. It typified, he said, 'the very worst kind of inward-looking approaches which so many of the opponents of the Community feared'.[39] A senior British official suggested that references to Euro-American collaboration were only added at a late stage to accommodate existing Italian contracts with American firms. The same official, however, saw great advantages in European manufacturers adopting a multilateral approach to cooperation with the United States; if only because 'they might get better deals if they negotiated collectively . . . rather than individually'. This 'negotiate from strength' case was put particularly well by Allan Greenwood of BAC. He suggested that outright competition with the United States was likely to prove counterproductive for Europe, but it was in the interest of all European firms to create a 'powerful and united European industry with a broad design capability . . . to enable us to have a more meaningful dialogue with the American industry if or when the opportunity arises'.[40] Sadly, in the view of many in the United Kingdom not only had Spinelli overplayed his hand (by demanding an unrealistic accretion of Commission authority) but his report had also been too eager to establish at all costs a European policy, and had tended to ignore the real advantages to both American and European companies of a broader-based transatlantic cooperation.[41]

Notwithstanding its faults and over-ambitious goals, Spinelli's proposals focused attention on the real problem facing European civil aerospace; namely that while Europe was facing increasing pressure from the United States and although decisions were urgently required on individual projects, there was still insufficient movement towards a concerted civil aerospace effort. There was an ever present danger that one country, as a result of domestic interests and slow progress at the European level would break ranks and join an American partner. As Sir Peter Fletcher of HSA put it, 'there is over-capacity throughout Europe. This generates problems ... where companies are hungry for work; pressures get greater and greater and this tends to push them out into fragmented or isolated positions which they feel they must accept, rather than sticking to the coherent ones.'[42]

The French break ranks

There were already signs that a common European approach was under attack. Towards the end of 1975, the French had made it increasingly clear that they were unhappy with the state of European negotiations. Aerospatiale and Dassault were suffering from a slump in orders and over-capacity in the French aircraft industry was approaching crisis proportions. Jacques Chirac, the French Prime Minister, said that while he hoped France would remain firmly committed to Europe, the French Government would support its own industry and would 'turn to other partners in other places' if this was the only way to secure French interests. In particular, the French Government showed some interest in collaborating with Boeing, while Dassault was conducting its own bilateral negotiations with McDonnell-Douglas, hoping to revitalise the ailing Mercure programme.[43]

In February 1976 it appeared that the break had been made. Aerospatiale announced that it had signed a letter of intent with Boeing. Boeing were to be offered a share in the design and the production of a smaller version of the A300, the B10 (later designated A310) then being considered by AI. In return, Aerospatiale would take part in the 7N7 programme. A closer inspection of the letter of intent revealed that it was far short of a firm commitment by either party. There was considerable doubt about France's ability to make promises on behalf of Airbus Industrie.[44] As far as Boeing was concerned, it had yet to explore all its options in Europe, and talks were already planned with the British for the spring. Although the French Government was unquestionably serious about its threat to press ahead with the next generation of aircraft with an American partner if necessary, Aerospatiale's announcement was probably designed more of a warning that there was a limit to French patience. Six months later, however, the French would again announce an agreement with an American company, but this time with rather more definite intent.

Of course, the British Government could have resolved the issue by taking the initiative on a European-based programme. However, it was still not ready to commit itself. As the manoeuvring between British, French and American firms quickened in pace, the British Government was naturally concerned to maximise its return, commercially, industrially and politically, from any new investment in civil aerospace. Government spokesmen said repeatedly that the British civil aircraft industry must retain its independence. Cooperation was necessary, but British industry ought to be able to collaborate on equal terms with any prospective partner 'either across the Channel or across the Atlantic or elsewhere, if appropriate'.[45]

In the short term, the British Government used the signs of French impatience to urge the speedy passage of the Aircraft and Shipbuilding Industries Bill which was meeting fierce opposition both inside and outside Westminster. If this domestic matter was not resolved, the British aircraft industry could find itself 'excluded from major new developments which could bring jobs and ensure the continuation of an important technological capability. The very future of civil aircraft manufacturing in this country is at stake'.[46] The Government conceded that it was prepared to give very serious consideration to rejoining the Airbus programme as a full partner and it encouraged BAC and HSA to produce a joint policy document in advance of nationalisation. This expression of good will was unlikely to impress the French, who wanted actions not words.

The crux of the matter — Airbus Industrie or Boeing
In May 1976, Lord Beswick met General Mitterand, President of Aerospatiale, to discuss prospects for European collaboration. Beswick told Mitterand that BAe had every intention of focusing its efforts on a European programme. These assurances failed to satisfy the French Government. It wanted a clear declaration from the United Kingdom Government that it would support the Airbus unconditionally, and that this ought to be confirmed by BA ordering either the A300 or the B10.

Events were rapidly assuming the familiar shape of European techno-politics, with its mixture of industrial, technological and political self-interest, European idealism and hard cash. There was a clear difference of opinion between the British and the French over what was meant by rejoining the Airbus programme. The British Government was only interested in the B10 (A310), and wanted to negotiate British participation in this separately from Airbus Industrie and the A300, in which HSA already had a lucrative stake. The French argued that it would be absurd to establish a new consortium to build the A310; Airbus Industrie had gained credibility as an efficient and effective manufacturing and commercial entity, a reputation which would be dissipated by the existence of two similar but separate organisations. Equally, if BAe was to join Airbus Industrie, neither it nor the British

Government could expect special treatment or have a privileged position within the organisation. The French Government felt that this should entail the payment of an 'entry free' (a contribution of between £100 million and £200 million towards sunk costs of the A300B programme) as well as Britain's share of launching the A310, put at between £60 and £100 million. It also wanted to renegotiate HSA's original subcontract with Airbus Industrie, worth at least £130 million. The British Government was naturally eager for BAe to retain the rights to this contract, but the French argued that as a full member of Airbus Industrie, BAe could hardly expect to remain a subcontractor to the same consortium.[47]

Officially, the British Government remained non-committal. The Department of Industry recognised Airbus Industrie's success in managing the A300B; it would certainly be 'a good example for the future', and it was 'quite possible for that sort of structure to do more than one project'. However, the first step in a new project was to negotiate directly with the manufacturers and Governments concerned. The form of industrial organisation should be settled later. It might then be found that Airbus Industrie was the best administrative umbrella for further development. As far as financial matters were concerned, while the Government accepted that it might be reasonable for Britain to contribute something towards Airbus sunk costs, exactly how big this should be was a 'very large question indeed'. The total programme costs incurred by the Europeans in developing the A300 had been high and the British Government was unwilling to finance French and German 'learning costs' in building up their civil aircraft industry. British Airways also made it quite obvious that it did not have a requirement for the A300 or, for that matter, the A310.[48]

The nationalisation Bill had also run into trouble. As a result of effective opposition to the shipbuilding half of the legislation, vesting day for BAe slipped by twelve months to early 1977. On the one hand, the delay in settling the ownership and organisation of the industry made decision-making difficult. On the other hand, it may not have been an entirely unwelcome diversion. During this 'feeling out' period, there were a number of crucial questions to be resolved before the British Government could be sure that the Airbus was the most attractive alternative available. For instance, at the same time as Beswick was assuring Mitterand of BAe's likely interest in a European programme, he, the Organising Committee for British Aerospace and officials from the DoI were having exploratory talks with Boeing. The British too wanted to keep their options open. The protracted struggle to nationalise BAC and HSA could, therefore, be presented as a legitimate excuse for procrastination.

If this was the case, French actions again made the running. In August 1976, Dassault announced that it would be collaborating with

McDonnell-Douglas on a development of the Mercure, designated the Mercure 200. Dassault stated that Aerospatiale would have up to 40 per cent of the production work, and that a substantial proportion would be 'available' for other European firms. The agreement apparently had the full blessing of the French Government. Dassault's Group of Seven colleagues were very angry that the French company could break ranks without prior consultation. The British in particular felt that they had gone out of their way to incorporate Dassault, even though it had very limited experience of building civil aircraft. Aerospatiale was not entirely happy with Dassault's initiative and it certainly seemed to end any chance of the latter cooperating with Boeing.[49]

The effect in Britain was to intensify interest in what Boeing had to offer. In preliminary talks Boeing had outlined the basis for a design and production partnership on the 7N7. Boeing would lead the programme – that was not negotiable – but BAe was offered design leadership on the wing section and a substantial part in general assembly work. If sales warranted it, Boeing would be prepared to locate a second production line in the United Kingdom. Boeing presented the offer as a wholly commercial venture and claimed that it would be a major share in one of their main civil programmes for the 1980s and 1990s.[50]

The Boeing option had obvious attractions; the company's record as a manufacturer of successful civil aircraft and its current position as market leader was bound to impress a Government more used to commercial failure in civil aerospace. Boeing's offer was also roundly supported by Sir Henry Marking, Chairman of British Airways. In his view, which he made clear to BAe in no uncertain fashion, the 180-seat 7N7 was the only project which was likely to be suitable for BA's future requirement in this class. More important still, perhaps, Boeing said that the 7N7 could use the Rolls-Royce RB211 engine.[51]

Rolls' American strategy
We left Rolls in 1973, poised to begin negotiations with P&W about a joint programme to develop a new 'ten tonne' engine. P&W was eager to match GE's success in establishing a foothold in Europe, and also wanted to gain access to new sources of finance for the development of an advanced series of new civil engines. Rolls too wanted to extend its range of products, especially with an engine smaller than the basic RB211. Talks centred on P&W's JT10D design, an engine which would be comparable with, but somewhat smaller than the CFM56. It was hoped that the two companies would be able to establish a collaborative programme whereby functional responsibilities would be divided equally, but with P&W retaining overall managerial responsibility for the project. From Rolls' perspective, the long-term advantage in this arrangement would be that they would be able to offer the right mix of engine options to Boeing for their next generation of airliners. Both firms were also

interested in drawing in other European firms, such as MTU and Fiat, thereby creating an alternative European–American axis to the GE–SNECMA link.[52]

The Labour Government welcomed Rolls' efforts in the United States. Even though the Treasury was somewhat sceptical of the JT10 proposal, the Government gave Rolls every encouragement in its efforts to reach an agreement with P&W. There was still some reluctance to finance Rolls more than twelve months at a time, a limitation which could have caused some difficulties in formulating a long-term development programme with P&W. Eventually, the British Government agreed to provide Rolls with its share (roughly 34 per cent) of JT10D launch costs, which were estimated at around $250 million. Rolls' Chairman, Sir Kenneth Keith, was very happy with the outcome, and suggested that henceforward, 'all major commercial engines will be undertaken as trans-Atlantic collaborations'.[53]

Notwithstanding the JT10D, Rolls was also interested in further developments of the RB211. The uprated RB211-524 was already being built for use on the long-range Lockheed L1011, and as a possible alternative engine for the Boeing 747. Equally important, Rolls wanted to produce a 'cropped fan' de-rated version of the RB211, the 535. Like the JT10D, this was aimed at one of Boeing's new designs. Although it would overlap the 28,000lb thrust JT10D, Rolls felt that the 535 was too large to be considered as a direct competitor to the joint venture.

In 1976, Rolls secured two important victories for the RB211. BA specified the RB211-524 engine for its second batch of 747s. This gave Rolls access into one of the most important current airliner programmes; it also reinforced its position in respect of Boeings' future projects. However, Government finance for the 535 was conditional on a second airline selecting Rolls-engined 747s. Keith accused the Government of showing insufficient resolution and failing to recognise a major commercial opportunity. The condition had been insisted upon by the Treasury, believing that Rolls had overstated its likely share of the market. The Government, however, later relaxed the two-order condition and Rolls got its money on the strength of BA's order alone.[54]

In June, PanAm selected RB211s for its order of long-range L1011s. Again, the British Government helped Rolls to secure the contract against stiff competition from GE. In this instance, the ECGD was authorised to give PanAm an unprecedented £250 million guarantee for the loans it needed to buy Rolls-powered L1011s. GE claimed that the British had unfairly exploited a subsidy to sway PanAm, whose financial position was far from healthy. Rolls was unrepentant; this type of financial tactic was not unknown in the United States and, as the only non-American engine manufacturer, it had to offer something to overcome entrenched competition.[55]

When Boeing suggested that Rolls might provide an engine for the

7N7, the British Government had already shown itself willing to back Rolls hard in the American market, either as a collaborative partner or as a direct competitor with GE and P&W. In one package, the Government would be able to satisfy all three elements in British civil aviation. Rolls certainly regarded any European programme as, at best, a secondary outlet for its products, and by itself an inadequate base for its technical and commercial future. British Airways was more than keen to confirm its American orientation and to keep its distance from the Airbus family. The key question was to what extent the fledgling BAe could and should be brought into transatlantic collaboration in support of Rolls' and BA's commercial interests. Gerald Kaufman, Minister of State for Industry, tried to strike a neutral tone. The Government, he said, was aware of the need for an independent civil airframe industry and of the dangers of becoming too dependent on the United States. Nevertheless, there was a limit to the price which could be paid for independence. Where new civil projects were concerned, 'we are not going into prestige but to make a profit and secure employment'.[56]

The advantages of a link with Boeing seemed less obvious to BAe. Boeing was determined to lead the programme. BAe might be given an important place in the design process, but overall responsibility for the vital integrating functions would remain with Boeing. In effect, BAe would be a subcontractor to a dominant and perhaps unreliable partner, a status which might threaten the long-term health of BAe's civil capability. BAe feared that its ability to design, produce and market a complete civil aircraft would be progressively eroded by the contract with Boeing.

The harmful effects of subcontracting to Boeing could be mitigated by resurrecting the 146 programme. Although this was not comparable in size or technical importance to the big wide-bodied projects being considered by Boeing or Airbus Industrie, it did offer BAe a means of keeping its broad-based civil interests intact. There is no evidence to suggest that the 146 was used by the Government to sweeten the Boeing option; in all probability they were separate issues. However, in July a further £2½ million was authorised to cover the cost of additional 146 development. This did not mark the aeroplane's relaunch. It was officially regarded as a way of maintaining the 'momentum of the holding contract with HSA until BAe could make a recommendation about its future'.[57] At the same time, BAC designers were proposing a 150-seat aircraft, the X-11, based on 1-11 technology. Again rather larger than the 146, and certainly at a less advanced stage of development, this too represented another possibility for the Government if it wanted to balance any subcontract arrangement with an American company.[58]

Although by the end of 1976 the exact direction to be taken by British civil aerospace in the 1980s was still not decided, a number of alternatives had emerged and the period of 'feeling out' various options was drawing to a close. The Government was increasingly aware that the time for decision was imminent. Thankfully, the protracted legislative battle to nationalise HSA and BAC was coming to an end (vesting day for BAe was now set for early 1977) and both the Government and BAe would shortly be in a position to undertake firm commitments. This was emphasised by Eric Varley, the Secretary of State for Industry. 'Six months ago,' he said in December 1976 during a closing debate on the Aircraft and Shipbuilding Industries Bill,

> there was relatively little firm activity on future projects, but the outlook for aircraft manufacturing companies, Governments and airlines is now quite different. They are beginning to enter into serious negotiations, which will lead to the formation of new groupings to produce the new generation of civil aircraft.
>
> Through the Organising Committee, the British aircraft industry has been involved in useful and promising discussions with a number of potential partners. These are now moving beyond the exploratory stage, but they will make their alliances with others if the future organisation of our industry remains in doubt.

The next few months, Varley concluded, would bring new opportunities for the development of British technology and employment in the aircraft industry which the United Kingdom could ill afford to miss.[59]

The existence of American options for many European airframe and engine companies made this round of civil aerospace decisions significantly more complicated than that of the mid-1960s. Then, the British Government had been able to make relatively straightforward choices between one European and a domestic project, with Rolls' needs as a criterion. This time there was a much wider range of possible manufacturing alignments. More important in terms of British policy, the nationalised and rationalised British airframe industry was politically and industrially far better placed to defend its interests as it saw them than BAC and HSA had been in the previous decade. Rolls would not be so easily able to influence the direction of civil development, nor Government able to override determined opposition from BAe.

The decisions, April 1977 – December 1979

In April 1977, British Aerospace formally came into existence. The future of its civil operation was still highly uncertain, however, and both BAe and the British Government faced far from simple decisions. Boeing's opening offer was already on the table; Lockheed and Douglas would shortly present similar proposals for Anglo-American cooperation. The Government also had to accommodate Rolls' interests and to finance British Airways' short- and medium-haul re-equipment programme, both strongly biased towards American options. On the other hand, there were the various European alternatives which had been under consideration for much of 1975 and 1976, rejoining the Airbus programme proper, contributing to a derivative Airbus, or embarking upon any one of a number of entirely new proposals.

The European front had been thrown into some confusion by the French *démarche* of August 1976. However, in May 1977, following the breakdown of negotiations between Dassault and McDonnell-Douglas, the situation became even more fluid. The French Government instructed both Dassault and Aerospatiale to seek European partners and, to this effect, the latter proposed another new design, a 135–170-seat airliner designated the A200. The A200 was aimed at complementing the A300 series and was to be built within the existing Airbus Industrie consortium. The French regarded British participation as important but not indispensable, and their position that Britain must become a full member of Airbus Industrie remained unchanged. A condition which, in their turn, the British were not yet prepared to accept.

BAe would not be drawn therefore on the invitation to participate in developing the A200. Although more inclined towards European rather than American collaboration, BAe executives wanted to consider very carefully the terms on which they might enter a European programme. They were certainly not going to be swayed by 'international politics' or by any 'European dream'. Indeed, BAe was rather sceptical of the A200's commercial viability, and both the Boeing 7N7 and its own X-11 concepts were more promising.[60] A threat to make VFW-Fokker instead of BAe the European centre of wing design and production on the A300 programme was not taken seriously, at least in the short term. While there was no doubting the skill of the German–Dutch company, the old HSA design team was way ahead of any comparable unit in Europe, and their expertise would make a considerable difference to the time and cost of developing a new wing for any European project. On the other hand, the BAe Board did not think that Boeing's offer, then the only substantive alternative, was very attractive either. Boeing was certainly not going to concede to the British anything like an equal status in design and development, and BAe felt that nothing less than full partnership would ensure that it would not become an expendable subcontracting appendage to the larger and more powerful American firm.[61]

The JET design consortium
The main area of uncertainty was which, if any, of the European alternatives offered the best prospect for BAe. To help clarify this, in June 1977 BAe joined another design study consortium, the Joint European Transport (JET) group. JET's remit was to consider all the main ideas for a 130–170-seat aircraft, to be built either by the Europeans alone, or as a bloc with the Americans. Discussions would not prejudice any decision on the larger A310 or, for that matter, British partnership with Boeing on

the 7N7.[62]

At an industrial level, JET made substantial progress, and by December 1977 the companies were ready to discuss more detailed aspects of development aiming at project definition by the spring of 1978. Politically, matters were not so easily resolved. Although the JET had the blessing of HMG and, as evidence of British goodwill, Kaufman announced that there was no question of launching the X-11, the Government was still unwilling to accept Airbus Industrie as the main centre for European civil development. He was definite in one thing, namely that BAe must have a major role in the design and development process. 'I have no doubt', he told Parliament, 'that BAe, as the largest aircraft manufacturer in Europe, will feel that it is entitled to a substantial part of the work on any aircraft which may eventually be launched.' Indeed, if negotiations proved fruitless, even the X-11 could 'return to the front of the stage.'[63]

It was debatable whether the Government seriously contemplated launching something as large as the X11 independently from Europe or the United States. Quite aside from the cost of developing it, BAe was itself likely to be divided over the project.[64] However, the Government was not going to submit to French pressure which could entail large financial commitments to the sunk costs of the Airbus programme, or to confirm Aerospatiale as the focal point for all future European civil aircraft production. This was not just a matter of prestige; the British Government wanted to protect a wide range of technological and industrial interests and any hint of junior status in Airbus Industrie could affect Britain's share of equipment contracts and the place of Rolls-Royce in future European ventures. Similarly, there were some voices within the British Government, primarily from the Treasury, who were not happy with the quality of financial and commercial control within Airbus Industrie.

Joining Airbus Industrie was a negotiable issue, if Britain could obtain compensation elsewhere. The JET programme offered just such a potential for a trade-off. In return for design leadership and final assembly, the Government offered to carry 40 per cent of programme costs; and, if this was accepted the British might be prepared to consider joining Airbus Industrie in order to build the A310. The French Government, however, would not budge on the question of Britain's 'entry fee' to the Airbus programme, even if, as Aerospatiale suggested, the British might pay a larger proportion of A310 costs instead. Nor, for that matter, were the French happy to allow British design lead on JET or final assembly to be located anywhere but at Toulouse.[65]

In an attempt to break the deadlock, the issue was discussed at the Giscard–Callaghan summit in Paris during December 1977. There was no specific report of progress, but the two heads of government said that they were going to ask their respective industries to work hard in order to 'reach a conclusion as quickly as possible' on the question of collaboration. Callaghan added that he hoped that an agreement would be reached by late spring, but he stressed that it must be on a 'commercial basis'.[66]

The organisational problem and its implications, however, were not to be solved simply by exhortation. There were good commercial reasons why any new airliner should be seen to be part of an existing and now credible consortium. The British accepted as much when BAe said that any new project would be best marketed as part of a family of European airliners, just as Boeing's strength often lay in its range of aircraft from the small 737 to the Jumbo 747 airliner. But, as BAe argued, it was still possible to establish a family of projects without necessarily using an existing consortium structure. Indeed, it might be a grave mistake to 'centralise operations' on Airbus Industrie, which was there primarily to sell the A300. It would perhaps, be advantageous that the Europeans should seize this opportunity to create a wider organisation consisting of each participating company and country. Airbus Industrie would then be 'under this central umbrella organisation along with any other management'.[67] This compromise proposal failed to impress the French, and even if it had been accepted, there was still the question of Britain's contribution to Airbus' past costs. There was a growing danger that both Governments were hardening their positions to the detriment of the progress being made at the technical and industrial levels.

Boeing makes its offer

In February 1978, Boeing made a formal offer for the British to participate in their 180-seat narrow-bodied aircraft, now designated the 757. Boeing would still be responsible for project management and lead the design team. Final assembly would also be in the United States. Tooling and engineering standards would be set according to Boeing's requirements and practices. Any contract between it and BAe would be a firm, fixed-price agreement, in dollars. The price agreed between the two parties would not be allowed to exceed Boeing's estimated in-house costs apart from a reasonable sum allowed for profit and inflation. Finally, Boeing stated that the Rolls RB211-535 would be selected as the 757's lead engine.[68]

The 757 order was now even more important for Rolls than when it had been suggested earlier that the RB211-535 might be used on the 7N7. During 1976, Rolls and P&W had begun to drift apart. As Boeing's design studies had all tended to increase in size, P&W had naturally wanted the JT10D to grow as well. Rolls, on the other hand, had reached the conclusion that the RB211-535 was likely to be the most suitable engine for any of Boeing's medium-range aircraft. Rolls suggested that the joint programme should, therefore, be centred on the British engine. P&W did not see itself as a junior partner in a British engine. P&W also felt that it needed a 'new-new' engine to retain its place in the civil market. Conversely, the Rolls management was increasingly uneasy about risking money on another large and unproven design. Rolls also believed that P&W was setting an over-ambitious and highly optimistic development and production schedule. As Rolls thought it had detected airline resistance to the prospect of another new turbo-fan with its attendant teething problems, the Rolls Board decided that it would be wiser to opt for a cheaper and more cautious approach and to develop RB211 technology. The formal break came in the spring of 1977. It was described by both sides as 'amicable' and future links were not ruled out.[69]

With the breakdown of the P&W agreement, Rolls needed the 757 order to maintain the momentum of its civil programme and especially to launch the 535. Rolls was able to convince the National Enterprise Board (NEB), its formal owners since 1974, of the case for the 535, and preliminary research work had already been financed. Once Boeing's proposal was formalised, Rolls immediately approached the DoI with a request for the £250 million needed for full development. Rolls was going to face intensive competition from GE and especially from P&W with its uprated JT10D. The struggle was again seen in terms of corporate survival. As Sir Arthur Knight, then a non-Executive Director of Rolls (later Chairman of the NEB) recalled, Sir Kenneth Keith's view of the 757 order was unequivocal: 'if we do not get these orders there will be no Rolls-Royce at all in three years' time'.[70]

This may well have been overstating the importance of the 535, but Rolls certainly lobbied hard to win Government approval for the money needed to build the new engine. Members of Parliament were circulated with details of the 757 contract suggesting that Britain stood to gain some £5 billion in earnings from the deal over twenty years. Sir Kenneth Keith stressed its importance to Rolls' long term future and how the 535's selection as lead engine in a Boeing aircraft would guarantee the commercial success of the whole RB211 family. An unofficial memorandum, though issued with the blessing of the Rolls Board, was circulated to MPs with Rolls-Royce factories in their constituencies. The authors pointed out Boeing's dominant position in the civil airliner market and emphasised American claims that sales of a 757-type aircraft could exceed 1000. If BAe were to join in the 757 programme, Britain would be responsible for 55 per cent of the project and that would generate between 14,000 jobs for Rolls, and 9000 for BAe.[71]

Rolls' case was endorsed by the new Chairman of the NEB, Sir Leslie Murphy. In his first annual report, he gave strong support for the company's American strategy. In announcing the NEB's approval of Rolls' corporate plan, which gave a prominent place to the 757 order, Sir Lesie said that he believed the American programme would not only be commercially advantageous to Rolls, but would certainly provide more employment in the British aircraft industry as a whole than any European alternative. In evidence to the PAC, Sir Leslie said that the vital objective was to get into the American market, 'this is where the business really is'. As far as the 535 was concerned, 'the potential prize is very large indeed, and it could transform the whole profitability of Rolls-Royce if we could make an impact on the American market'. The opportunity to collaborate in an American airliner was an 'unprecedented' chance for BAe and should, in his judgement, 'be taken with both hands'.[72]

BAe's response was equally emphatic. In Lord Beswick's opinion, it was impossible to predict future employment with the kind of accuracy which Rolls and Sir Leslie Murphy appeared to be suggesting. He was especially upset by Sir Leslie's intervention: 'It is wrong to claim such figures with this degree of precision. Have the NEB the facts on which to make such claims? I say, flatly, no.' BAe, he believed, should not become dependent on Boeing, especially as the Americans had admitted that the 757 might not be as important as either of its two other new designs, the 767 and the 777.[73]

More important, BAe's management was hardening against the Boeing offer on principle. They had found Boeing's proposals 'increasingly less attractive' during their negotiations in 1977. In essence, Boeing's best offer involved BAe in little more than manufacturing the main wing section. Besides having full responsibility for the management of the programme, Boeing was also insisting on retaining complete control over sales and marketing. BAe argued that it must have some share in the marketing of the aircraft in order to maintain its own commercial expertise and contacts with airline customers.[74]

Some officials, and not a few members of the Cabinet, felt that BAe simply feared the commercial and industrial discipline of working with Boeing. If BAe joined the 757 programme, it was suggested that it would be unable to meet the terms of a fixed-price contract or Boeing's delivery schedules. The claim that BAe would lose design capability was nothing more than a cover for the firm's lack of confidence and an irrational fear of Boeing. Yet a closer examination of the terms offered by the Americans did indicate that BAe was being asked to meet targets which Boeing itself would find hard to meet. For instance, BAe would have to design and produce the newest element in the 757 design, the wing section (most of the remaining aircraft was derived from existing technology) at prices based on estimates derived from Boeing's calculations of *total* programme costs thereby hiding the true cost of developing the wing. According to BAe's calculations, Boeing and BAe differed by 30 per cent on estimates of the cost of producing the wing section. BAe's analysis of comparative costings showed that American firms, even with their generally higher productivity, would be unable to produce a new wing at the prices demanded by Boeing. BAe also pointed out that it would need a large investment programme to cover the cost of new plant and the company would have to adopt new and costly techniques and procedures (some of which BAe claimed were less advanced than its own) in order to meet Boeing's requirements. In short, if BAe accepted the American offer, the company had every expectation of incurring a heavy loss on the deal. Moreover, BAe had no guarantee that it would be selected for any subsequent programme. In short, there was no question of BAe being 'scared of Boeing'; it was simply a bad business proposition.

Boeing sweetened its offer by suggesting that BAe could be responsible for flight testing and for some 757 final assembly. BAe was also offered a share of the existing and very successful 727 and 737 programmes. Boeing argued that the 757 was likely to outsell any comparable European project (from the JET range) and for a share of development costs put at between £150 and £200 million, BAe could earn up to £1,000 million over the lifetime of the programme. Boeing moved to counteract BAe's fears that subcontracting would lessen design capability, by claiming that American firms had subcontracted on Boeing projects without losing expertise. Boeing also contended that the 1978 offer did give more design and management responsibility than earlier proposals. At the same time, Boeing attempted to increase the pressure on BAe and the British Government to make a final decision by announcing that unless it received a positive reply by May 1978, it would start to look for suitable American subcontractors and BAe would lose its 'exclusive' position.[75]

BAe was not impressed by Boeing's 'improved' offer. In its view, there was no change in the area of overall design and management responsibilities and, unlike many of Boeing's traditional subcontractors within the American industry, BAe had expertise in the design and development of complete civil airframes which it was determined to protect. The threat of looking elsewhere for partners was also regarded as a bluff (an opinion shared incidently by the DoI). The opportunity for Boeing to secure a firm foothold in Europe, as well as having access to British money for part of what was a very expensive range of designs, was believed to be too great for the Americans to forgo easily. Officially, BAe said that it would continue to examine Boeing's offer, but the company said that it had to bear in mind commitments made in principle to its JET partners. Indeed, not only were BAe's European prospects brighter than they had been in 1977 (possibly because of the Boeing offer, the French Government had said that BAe might be allowed design leadership of a JET project) but McDonnell-Douglas had also asked BAe to consider joining it as a full partner in a longer-term airliner project. This also had the advantage of complementing any European programme. As a BAe spokesman put it;

> We are by no means foreclosing our option to collaborate with Boeing, McDonnell, Lockheed or anyone else. But we have an agreement taken in

good faith, that we will first explore with our European partners the possibility of building in collaboration with them a European aircraft in the range of 150–160 seats and we are going to honour this agreement.[76]

Now that it had closely examined Boeing's offer, BAe clearly recognised that its interests lay within a European framework. Executives believed that they could negotiate an agreement with the Europeans that would not only protect BAe's design and development capability, but which would also be profitable. Faced by two differing views on transatlantic cooperation, Rolls' and BAe's, the British Government would either have to choose between them, which in effect meant imposing American cooperation on BAe, or seeking some compromise which would satisfy both. Matters were further complicated by British Airways' re-equipment requirements which were all directed to the purchase of American aeroplanes.

BA had already clashed with British Aerospace over its order for new short-haul airliners. In November 1977, BA had served notice that it intended to seek approval from the Government to order Boeing 737s, a deal worth £120 million. BAe replied that the airline could buy BAC 1-11-500s instead. Although the 1-11 was cheaper than the 737, BA claimed it was less competitive and was much the noisier aircraft (an increasingly important criterion in the selection of new airliners). It had been more than ten years since the last occasion on which a nationalised airline had been forced by Government directive to 'buy British' and BA was determined to keep its hard-won commercial autonomy. The airline had a pretty firm idea of what it wanted for its future fleet of aircraft, and, in many respects, differed quite markedly from other European airlines in terms of seating capacity and delivery times for new types. Obviously, the Government had the power to insist on a 'buy British' policy, but could expect a hard and politically bruising battle with BA. At the very least, the precedents of the 1960s would force the Government to compensate BA for its supposed loss of commercial advantage. Similarly, although the case of the 737 was clear enough, for its larger aircraft where was the 'buy British' principle to lie, with Rolls or with BAe? Ross Stainton, BA's Chief Executive, accepted that a decision to buy Boeings might hurt BAe, but 'our job is to say what is best for British Airways'. If BA was to remain an efficient and profitable airline, it had to be free to select the most suitable aircraft for its routes. This might have unfortunate consequences for BAe, but the airline could not afford to get 'very emotional about it'.[77]

In the event, the Government postponed its decision on the 737, for it was evident that the Cabinet wanted to avoid a fight with BA. There was a consensus against a 1960s style directive and in favour of allowing BA commercial autonomy in fact as well as in theory. The delay in giving BA permission to buy the 737 proved to be more a question of timing than of any real opposition to the order.

BA's request for the 757 was regarded in much the same light, but it was politically rather more sensitive given French interest in BA's order for one of the European projects. In April 1978, BA formally asked for the 757 as well as pressing for a decision on the 737. BA firmly rejected the A300 as a possible alternative and stated that the A310 was not only dearer than the 757 but that the CFM56 engine would add greatly to BA's running costs. There was some chance that BA might have a requirement for one of the JET series, but its choice was the least preferred of those under discussion by the manufacturers. According to Stainton, the British civil aerospace industry would be best advised therefore to foster transatlantic cooperation.[78]

For its part, the Government was well aware that it might not be able to satisfy the three public corporations. All would be involved and consulted in the process of decision making but, as Edmund Dell, the Trade Secretary, noted, 'the interests of these bodies do not always coincide'. Equally, in such an important and complex area of policy, the Government did not want to arrive at its decisions 'in a hurry'.[79] The Government was acutely conscious of the fact that it was about to authorise some very long-term and highly expensive purchases and investments and that similar decisions in the past had led to very mixed outcomes. Leslie Huckfield, Under Secretary of State at the DoI expressed this feeling very well when he told the House of Commons that these decisions:

> will be the last major ones of the present century. Therefore, while I accept that it is important that conclusions should be reached as a matter of urgency, I suggest that it is just as essential that we get the ultimate answer right.[80]

There was, however, a limit to the patience of Britain's potential partners. At the end of May, Boeing announced that it was starting preliminary talks with American subcontractors, and in June, the French and German Governments told the British that in order to match the Boeing 767, they intended to launch the A310 with or without BAe. To expedite matters, in the event of BAe not joining the programme, Airbus Industrie was also preparing to shift wing design and manufacturing from BAe to VFW-Fokker. BAe immediately warned the British Government of the financial implications of not moving quickly to join the Europeans, while Rolls and its supporters urged it to choose the Boeing route and thereby re-establish a degree of coherence in British civil aerospace policy.[81]

A month later, the French and Germans attempted to force the British into a decision. On 7 July they announced that the A310 would be launched. The question of British participation was left open, but BAe had to join Airbus Industrie as a full partner. There was no question, for instance, of continuing to build wings for the consortium as a subcontractor.[82] This decision virtually ended the prospect of an early launch for a JET design; indeed, all work on JET development had already been suspended while the British decided whether to join the Boeing 757 programme. The Franco-German initiative showed that their primary interests and resources would be directed at the larger A310 and the consolidation of Airbus Industrie. It also meant that the British Government, if it was to accept BAe's judgement, would have to tackle directly the question of joining Airbus Industrie and face French demands for a back payment to Airbus programme costs.

The decisions

The matter now became the subject of a high-level debate throughout the summer of 1978. Discussions centred on a Cabinet sub-committee chaired by the Prime Minister, James Callaghan, which consisted of the Chancellor of the Exchequer, Denis Healey, Edmund Dell, Eric Varley and Harold Lever. This was backed by an *ad hoc* Cabinet Office group with representatives from the Treasury, the Foreign Office, the Departments of Trade and Industry, the Ministry of Defence and the Central Policy Review Staff (CPRS). Initial feelings were strongly in favour of accepting the offer from Boeing, or at least one of the American options. The strongest advocates of the transatlantic strategy were from the Treasury team, who were most attracted by the commercial discipline promised by the Americans and dismayed at the prospect of negotiating a back-payment with the French. The Treasury also led the attack against BAe's claims that it would suffer long-term damage by cooperating with Boeing. BAe was hardly ever likely to launch another large civil aircraft outside a partnership agreement, and inevitably BAe would suffer some loss of expertise. The Foreign Office played a straight European bat, pointing out the political advantages of getting back into AI. The DoI, with a foot in both camps, tried to be neutral, but many officials were inclined towards the commercially more attractive prospect of cooperating with Boeing. Dell and the Department of Trade were determined that BA should be allowed the equipment that it wanted. However, on the industrial question Dell's preference was that BAe should join up with a stronger rather than a weaker partner. Callaghan himself was also attracted by a transatlantic arrangement, even if the chosen partner was not necessarily Boeing. McDonnell-Douglas's offer, which by now included a package of other collaborative proposals, was particularly tempting.

BAe would, however, resist the imposition of a decision against its better judgement. Its Chairman was particularly incensed by the prospect that his Board's first major decision might be overruled by the Government. He had been a member of that Government and his original appointment had been criticised as an attempt at indirect Governmental intervention in the affairs of the aircraft industry. Consequently, he was bound to be highly sensitive to any threat to BAe's commercial autonomy.

The insistence on defending BAe's design capability might have reflected a degree of irrational pride in independence, but his opposition to the Boeing contract was primarily on commercial grounds. He genuinely feared that unless BAe could join as an equal partner in any collaborative exercise, the United Kingdom would lose vital industrial and technological expertise which, if not in the short-term certainly over the years, would entail a net loss to the nation.

Beswick's stance, as well as the unanimous support of the BAe Board, impressed Sir Frank Berrill, Director of the CPRS, whom Callaghan asked to evaluate the various options. Berrill also began his investigation with a predisposition towards the Boeing contract, but he was influenced by BAe's firm and unanimous advocacy of the European option. It would certainly be regarded as a matter of confidence. The BAe management had carefully considered from all possible angles the respective merits of the Boeing and the European projects. The Boeing contract presented substantial risks for the Corporation, either because it could entail a loss of technical and commercial expertise, or because its terms might put BAe in a similar position to Rolls-Royce in the late 1960s. For the Government to overrule this consensus would probably have been a resignation issue, certainly for Beswick, and perhaps for the BAe Board as a whole.

Berrill's close examination of the available data also raised doubts about the validity of the claims used to support the American option. Indeed, it was increasingly clear that the conflicting predictions about employment and commercial return from either the 757 or the A310 were based on highly speculative assumptions. In the last analysis, many of the arguments hinged upon the respective reputations of Boeing and the European consortium. There was no doubting Boeing's past success in selling civil aircraft, and the future success of the 757 tended to be seen as a natural progression from the 707, 727 and 747. However, this was not an inevitability, and Boeing also had the larger 767 to consider, a project it regarded as being more important than the 757. On the other hand, Airbus Industrie's credibility as a centre for civil aircraft production was steadily increasing. There were a number of unpalatable aspects attached to Britain's membership of the consortium, but these were negotiable points, especially as the British could count on the active support of the German Government against French intransigence. On balance, therefore, Berrill reported rather more favourably abour the A310 than had been expected.

In the event, most witnesses agree that Berrill's conversion to the A310 was important, but the really crucial element in the final decision was the personal intervention by Helmut Schmidt, the German Chancellor and a personal friend of James Callaghan. Schmidt told Callaghan quite bluntly that in the present climate of Britain's relations with the EEC, a 'European gesture' would be more than welcome and would bring wider political advantages to the British. He also appealed to Callaghan to join in the A310 programme as a means of limiting French influence over European civil aerospace policy. With at least half of the Cabinet away, a decision to rejoin the Airbus programme was made during August. Schmidt's appeal, Berrill's conversion and the resistance of the BAe Board had finally defeated a strong coalition in favour of transatlantic cooperation.

In the event, the Government structured its decision so that everybody got something. A package of decisions emerged during the summer and early autumn. Even before its final decision on the A310, the Government announced in July that BA could have its 737s; simultaneously the Commons were told that BAe would be allowed to relaunch the HS146, which it had requested in March. This would cost BAe £250 million, the expenditure for which was to form part of BAe's approved capital investment programme but which would, in the first instance, be financed from BAe's own resources. Additional finance, if required, would be available from the National Loan Fund.[83] The 146 relaunch was made in advance of firm orders. It was a risky decision, and it met with some opposition from the Treasury and the MoD(PE). Nevertheless, BAe believed that the 146 would attract customers once it had been built. BAe's assessment was backed by the American company, Lycoming, which provided the engine and which took a risk-sharing subcontract on the project. The Government accepted BAe's judgement on the matter. After all, this was precisely the kind of independent commercial decision that the publicly owned company was expected to take, and rejection by the Government could have been interpreted as a lack of confidence in the corporation's judgement.[84]

In September, the Government revealed its decision on the A310 and the RB211-535. The Government said it would invest at least £750 million in civil aerospace over the next decade. The bulk of the money was allocated to British Airways for the purchase of Boeing 757s and to Rolls-Royce for the development of the RB211-535 engine which would be the 757's lead engine. This would be dependent on the Rolls-engined 757 obtaining a second order from a major airline, but this was generally seen as a foregone conclusion. BAe would be allocated £100 million to pay its share of A310 costs. The decision was warmly welcomed by both Rolls and BA. Sir Frank McFadzean, Chairman of BA, later of Rolls-Royce, was particularly pleased, as it enabled BA 'to continue on a very long and close association with Rolls-Royce'.[85] Less charitable observers perhaps felt that the Government had taken an easy way out. As Arthur Reed of The Times wrote, 'After many years of argument over whether Britain should look to the United States or Europe for partners in a new generation of aerospace products, this country has emerged . . . facing both ways'.[86]

Finalising BAe's membership of Airbus Industrie

A number of issues had to be resolved before BAe could officially rejoin the Airbus programme. The outstanding problem was the question of Britain's contribution to Airbus programme costs. As a concession to the French position, the British Government announced that in addition to the £100 million for future development, it would also offer £25 million towards 'work in progress'.[87] But would this sum, a token effort by contrast with the historical costs of A300 development, satisfy the French? The French Government was certainly unhappy that the British were not only supporting a possible competitor to the A310 but that BA was to buy it. As one French spokesman put it, 'I can hardly see how an agreement can be reached if it were confirmed that British Airways is buying the new Boeing 757, which is a rival to the new 200-seat Airbus B10.'[88] More talks would have to be held before Britain could join the A310 programme, and in the interim Airbus Industrie was directed to continue with its preparations to transfer wing development to the VFW-Fokker plant at Bremen.[89] Just how much of this was Fench-inspired bluffing was hard to tell. BAe's expertise was as valuable as ever if the A310 was to be launched in time to match Boeing. The British Government's £100 million was equally attractive, especially to the Germans, whose expensive policy of building up a civil aircraft industry would receive a welcome injection of new money. Nevertheless, Lord Beswick was worried about the delay. BAe's financial and technical resources could still be placed behind alternatives but, he admitted, 'There are in reality, few, if any left.'[90]

The French were motivated by more than a few suspicions about British intentions; lessons of the recent past no doubt coloured French attitudes to the negotiations. Certainly, by deciding to re-enter the Airbus programme, the British Government had implicitly conceded an important point to the French; namely that Airbus Industrie would remain the focus of European civil development. However, the real sticking-point appears to have been French perceptions of Britain's willingness to stay with the Airbus and not, at some time in the future, to be again diverted by the interests of Rolls-Royce. What the French wanted was a way of limiting any threat of British disruption or procrastination on the A310.[91]

Helmut Schmidt was again an important actor in mediating between the British and French Governments. Indeed, at crucial points over the next few weeks, Schmidt's intervention was vital in preventing negotiations from breaking down. The trick was to establish an arrangement by which French suspicions could be assuaged at an acceptable cost to the British. A formula was eventually hammered out whereby BAe joined Airbus Industrie as a full partner in development, but with certain limitations on British rights. The British were assigned 20 per cent of the voting rights on the Airbus Industrie Supervisory

Board, and although all decisions would in theory require more than 80 per cent of the available votes, thus giving the British a veto on development proposals, in practice it was agreed to retain the existing 75 per cent majority. In effect, this prevented the British from obstructing decisions on either the A310 or the A300. These restrictions would remain in force until August 1981 in the case of the A310 and permanently so far as the A300 was concerned. However, all limitations on British rights would lapse on the event of the 150th sale of the A300 or an order for either aircraft from British Airways. All parties agreed not to participate in any project likely to compete with one of the Airbus Industrie aircraft. Membership of the Airbus Industrie consortium would naturally guarantee the option of a share of any future development.[92]

The full cost of British participation in the A310 was put at between £200 and £250 million between 1978 and 1984, the money to be made available under section 45 of the Aircraft and Shipbuilding Act. This should be contrasted with a German estimate of total A300/A310 programme costs of over £2,000 million (equivalent to the cost of Concorde development and production).[93] Further developments of the Airbus family were envisaged, but these would require the approval of the three Governments.

Significantly, the allocation of profits on the A300 and 310 were to reflect past contributions to the entire programme. The levy on sales would be distributed between the partners according to a formula based on present contribution to the programme and each member's share of past losses incurred during development. When the losses had been fully recovered, profit-sharing would then revert to a strict proportion of current contributions.[94] The British Government also announced that it was to make a one-off contribution of £50 million as an entry fee to Airbus Industrie. On 27 October, the British Government announced that terms had been reached and that BAe would become a full member of Airbus Industrie on 1 January 1979.[95]

BAe regarded this agreement as offering 'important new openings for the rest of the British aerospace industry and all who work for it'. Joining Airbus Industrie would stabilise employment levels in the corporation. Throughout its campaign to join Airbus, BAe argued that the A300/A310 series would be a profitable venture; ultimately, BAe and the Government would have their investment repaid. By 31 December 1980, Airbus Industrie had sold 227 A300s, with another 91 on option. Comparable figures for the A310 were 76 sales and 64 options. Equally important, the Airbus had begun to make significant inroads into the American market. However, according to one calculation, it should be added that for the Airbus programme as a whole to break even, some 880 aircraft would have to be sold. Naturally, by the terms of the 'November Agreement', the United Kingdom Government would begin to receive a return on its investment rather earlier than that, but this would not begin before 1985.

In these terms, although the cost of the A300/A310 would be high, Britain would not be carrying anything like the same burden of past development costs as its partners were.[96]

These decisions appeared to fix the pattern of British civil aerospace well into the 1990s. The airframe sector had assumed its perhaps natural place as a major element in the European aircraft industry. For all the British wavering on the matter, Airbus Industrie was a solid basis for development, and it would have been absurd to undermine its commercial and technical credibility by building the A310 under a different umbrella organisation. Airbus Industrie could well become one of the two most important centres for civil aerospace over the next decade, and BAe should be able to hold its own technically and industrially within the consortium. Much will hinge on the continuing availability of money to finance BAe's share of further AI developments. Capital already committed to civil projects will depress corporate profits throughout the early and mid-1980s and the cost of existing programmes will require additional borrowing.[97] Throughout 1980, AI was actively considering the launch of more A300 derivatives and a new 150-seater, the A320. The cost of BAe's participation in these could easily match that of the A310. In reptrospect, the 1978 decision to 'buy' into Airbus Industrie appears to have bound the British Government to consider a non-finite number of subsequent commitments. It may choose not to accept these as they arise. However, without a substantial share of any new project, BAe's stake in AI would diminish and make it more difficult to influence consortium decision-making. This could not only harm BAe itself, but make it more difficult for other British companies to secure important subcontracts. In short, British Government has got to adjust itself to a relatively new aspect of European technology policy-making, a phenomenon which might be called the politics of the permanent consortium.

Rolls-Royce, of course, re-emphasised its American orientation, and showed that it still regarded Europe very much as a secondary market for engines. In January 1981, Rolls received a substantial setback by losing its monopoly of the 757. After a fierce battle between P&W and Rolls, both Delta and American Airlines selected the JT10D (PW2037). Rolls has also found its dominant position on the L1011 under threat from GE.[98] Given the success of the Airbus family and the launch of the 150-seat A320, Rolls may yet come to regret its dismissive attitude to the European airframe industry. Rolls will face strong competition from American manufacturers in its chosen area of concentration, it will also meet increasing competition from the French in Europe. In the ten years since its bankruptcy, Rolls has regained much of its earlier confidence. However, like BAe, its future will largely depend upon the continued support of the British Government. The dilemma for the Government is that while the financial demands of the industry are unlikely to diminish, the momentum of development tends to require unhesitating and unequivocal decisions. In the 1970s, the British Government responded positively to the civil aerospace industry, but as past experience has shown, dependence upon Government inevitably adds one more uncertainty to an already highly problematic commercial and technical environment.

7

FROM PRIVATE TO PUBLIC ENTERPRISE, THE MONITORING AND CONTROL OF CIVIL AEROSPACE, 1970–81

Chapter 6 was devoted to the 'strategic' aspects of civil aerospace policy in the 1970s; this chapter is concerned with 'tactical' issues related to the monitoring and control of project development. It will be recalled that during the 1960s, a number of limitations were revealed in both private and public procedures for monitoring and controlling civil aerospace programmes. This experience encouraged the Government to seek changes in its approach to the supervision of civil aerospace. In spite of some fairly substantial reforms, the difficulties associated with the control of large-scale civil projects continued to give cause for concern. Similarly, although by 1977 both airframe and engine sectors were publicly owned, this did not resolve the dilemma of control versus autonomy in the management of, and responsibility for, project development.

Administrative reform 1970–6

The Rayner Report
Soon after the 1970 General Election, the new Conservative Government announced that Derek (later Sir Derek) Rayner, Managing Director of Marks and Spencer, would be investigating ways and means of improving the Government's machinery for the sponsorship of aerospace and procurement for the Services. His report was published as a White Paper in April 1971.[1] The most fundamental change suggested by Rayner and implemented by the Government, was the separation of executive and policy functions; the Ministry of Aviation Supply, created as a temporary measure in 1970, was dissolved with all defence-related activities, procurement, contract supervision and the R&D establishments, passing into the hands of the MoD. Ministerial and departmental responsibility for aerospace policy was assigned to the Trade and Industry Department (DTI), which had been formed out of the old Ministry of Technology and Board of Trade. Within the MoD, a specialist Procurement Executive (MoD(PE)) was established to oversee all Government contracts with the aircraft industry, civil as well as military.[2]

The DTI would still have a small, specialised commercial and technical evaluation staff to advise the Secretary of State on policy for the industry generally, and to assess 'The likely future needs of the civil air transport industry and of other civil customers of the aerospace industry in order to arrive, in consultation with the procurement organisation, at a programme of support which would provide the best balance between these needs, the technical possibilities open for meeting them, and the finance and resources available for the purpose'. However, this should not duplicate the 'considerable resources and expertise' of the MoD(PE). Concorde was the single exception; in this case, policy and execution were so closely related that Rayner felt that separation of the official team into separate divisions could prove counterproductive.[3]

As far as civil development was concerned, it was up to the DTI to identify particular demands and requirements from industry, to decide whether or not to provide financial assistance and to allocate resources accordingly. It was the MoD(PE)'s job, however, to tender and monitor contracts with individual companies (either publicly or privately owned) and to provide a prior assessment of a project's technical prospects and continuing status. The resolution of any conflict between the DTI, the MoD and the MoD(PE) would, according to Rayner, be best provided by a permanent Joint Ministerial Board. In the event, the JMB was one of the few proposals made by Rayner which was not accepted by the Government. Evidently, most officials felt that existing channels provided by the Cabinet and Cabinet committees would be adequate in solving any problems of coordination or conflicts of interest.[4]

According to Sir Robert Marshall, the Permanent Secretary at the DTI, the main aim of the division was:

> primarily to get clarity in policy-making away from the involvements and pressures which will undoubtedly occur if one is in the business . . . It is more difficult to sit back and try to evaluate dispassionately the things which need to go into policy-making when one is involved day by day with the persons in the industry, undertaking very difficult tasks which engage all their being, to a certain extent their emotions, and one gets caught up in this.[5]

In separating these functions and by creating a department devoted to the procurement process, Rayner hoped in the first instance to limit the traditional preoccupation on the part of both user and industrial sponsorship departments with technological advance at the expense of financial and economic considerations. He was, at the same time concerned that any reforms in the procurement system should not lead to the 'progressive erosion of the Government's civil aerospace interests'.[6]

Rayner said that he had been tempted by the possibility of making the MoD responsible for all aerospace matters. However, on balance he had concluded that this might have led to conflict between the MoD's duty to provide the best and cheapest equipment for the Services and an obligation to promote the interests of the aerospace industry. Rayner also accepted that policy towards the aircraft and aero-engine industries should be integrated into Government policy for manufacturing and technology generally, and it was desirable, therefore, to distinguish clearly between the cost and requirements of the defence effort and civil, commercially orientated activities. In short, even if technically speaking, civil and military aerospace were 'indivisible', there were different policy issues to be accommodated.[7]

Reforming launch aid procedure — the HS146

One immediate effect of these changes was that the MoD(PE) became responsible for monitoring launch-aided programmes. This coincided with a general tightening up of procedures governing both the granting and supervision of launch aid. The RB211 affair had already led to changes in the way launch aid was administered, and this experience continued to affect Government determination to improve the system. The basic principle of launch aid remained untouched and giving a fixed sum at the outset of development was still regarded as the crucial sanction to instil commercial discipline in companies. This was emphasised by Cranley Onslow, an Under Secretary of State at the DTI:

> We are dealing with commercial concerns with contracts made by the Government with such concerns. It would be wrong and foolish to suppose that such contracts secure for a company a cloak of immortality making it immune from the realities of the commercial world.[8]

It was vital, however, that the ambiguities surrounding the Government's support for Rolls-Royce during the 1960s should never be repeated. In future, any launch aid contract would clearly specify from the outset the responsibilities and obligations of both parties regarding the project and towards each other. Onslow was adamant that the relationship between state and industry 'must be made so clear that the prudent industrialist cannot unwittingly blunder into a situation in which he finds he has put himself at risk'.[9]

Some of the changes favoured industry, while others improved the Government's position. For instance, there would be some provision for adjusting the terms of the contract if a firm encountered difficulties in developing a project and came under financial pressure. On the other hand, industry no longer had preference over the Government in terms of getting its money back from a launch-aid programme. The most significant change in the system was that there would be a much more rigorous and comprehensive examination of a company's financial status before launch aid was given. This was a direct result of the Rolls experience, which showed just how important it was for the Government to be fully aware of both the risks the applicant company was planning to carry, and its ability to survive a major programme failure.[10]

There was, in fact, just one new project during the 1970s to receive launch aid, the HS146. In 1973, development costs were estimated at just over £90 million. The Government's contribution was firmly and unambiguously fixed at 50 per cent of estimated costs and HSA guaranteed that it would carry the burden of any cost escalation. HSA was able to assure the DTI and the MoD(PE) that it had sufficient financial cover to assume this risk. Indeed, Sir Arnold Hall made it known that the company could have covered the entire cost of development, but had applied for launch aid to ease cash-flow problems and to spread, but not avoid, the risks involved. Launch aid did provide a degree of protection for HSA, but the Government could be assured that its money was being invested in a 'safe' company. Michael Heseltine, the Minister responsible for aerospace, was impressed by HSA's 'commitment' to the project and he told Parliament that the DTI was satisfied that the firm had the 'necessary financial resources to undertake the project on these terms'.[11]

The contract between HSA and the DTI also defined clearly the rights and obligations of both parties in the technical and commercial decisions relating to the 146. The manufacturers would have full autonomy in technical and commercial matters, but would be obliged to provide both the DTI and the MoD(PE) with adequate data on progress, and to inform them of any change in the status of the programme. The contract specified in great detail the type and quality of the information which HSA had to pass on to the two Departments but both sides agreed that they had to avoid 'over-inspection' of the programme by officials. For instance, in evidence to the Expenditure Committee, a DTI witness had stated quite bluntly that:

> however elaborate the monitoring arrangements set by a government department the primary responsibility for getting the thing right must lie with the firm and it is extremely important not to blur the responsibility between the government department which is providing some of the money and the firm. There is a danger that excessive monitoring could do that and make the firm's management a little less efficient.[12]

With the experience of the RB211 always in mind, Government Departments would naturally want to adopt a stricter regime than in the past. Monitoring by the Procurement Executive of the 146 or any other project was now based on matching technical progress and cost performance against detailed estimates. These would be reviewed at quarterly intervals and if the Procurement Executive spotted any problem which might cause the project to 'slip into non-viability', the manufacturer had to convince them that matters were under control. In the event that the explanation was unsatisfactory, the Procurement Executive, with the approval of the DTI, could halt or delay progress payments until the issue had been resolved. In the view of the officials involved, these procedures required no more attention to progress chasing, or the provision of any more information than an efficient manager would need to do his own job properly.

The HS146 was an ideal programme for the Government to finance; the manufacturer was known to be a cautious judge of market opportunities; the 146 would cost just too much for private enterprise to finance comfortably, but the company clearly had sufficient capital to survive any major upset, and it was sufficiently within the technical state-of-the-art to monitor with confidence. HSA and the Government had also negotiated a contract which, in theory, would be less likely to lead to a conflict of interpretation, and would not encourage the former to assume too much of the state for additional help in the event of programme failure. HSA, on the other hand felt secure in the knowledge that it would be responsible for all 'strategic' decisions, including cancellation if, in its opinion, the 146 was no longer viable. It was over precisely this aspect of the agreement, however, that HSA and the Labour Government, elected in 1974, came into conflict.

HS146, cancellation and 'suspension'

The 1973 oil crisis and the resulting slump in the demand for civil aircraft hit the HS146 just as HSA's sales campaign was getting underway. Sales projections began to look very bleak indeed. Britain's own economic problems also began to have a serious effect on the project's viability. The sharp rise in the rate of domestic inflation affected cost estimates, and the target price of £1.75 million per aircraft could no longer be guaranteed. There was, in short, no sound basis for sales contracts and no reasonable short-term hope for orders. The impact of inflation on a civil programme had been graphically demonstrated by the RB211 and HSA was determined at all costs to avoid a similar experience. In July 1974 HSA warned the DTI that the 1973 contract could no longer justify continuing with the project. The company proposed a mutual termination of the agreement or a renegotiation of its terms. In August, HSA conducted a full-scale review of the programme; various projections showed a dramatic worsening in cash-flow over the 1974–8 period. Development costs could surpass £92 million, possibly rising to over £200 million and the market looked very unsettled. The project was no longer viable, and the review confirmed that cancellation, causing 250 immediate redundancies, with more to come as other projects wound down without a replacement project, was far better than risking the whole HSA group by continuing with the 146.[13] HSA denied that the threat of nationalisation had anything to do with its decision, though obviously any extra capital tied up in aerospace would be subject to problematic negotiations over compensation. The 146 was simply a sick project getting sicker.

The new Secretary of State for Industry, Tony Benn, saw the problem differently. Employment and the existence of HSA's civil design

capability within a nationalised airframe group were factors that had to
be weighed against commercial uncertainty. Benn took the position that
HSA must be held to the 1973 agreement against the company's perhaps
better judgement (many officials were also sceptical of the 146's future).
Benn told HSA that he found its arguments to be 'not wholly convincing'
and he decided to institute a 'careful examination of their case and the
wider issues involved'.[14]

The issue triggered off an exchange of letters between Sir Arthur Hall
and Benn, with both sides accusing the other of contravening the spirit, if
not the letter, of the 1973 agreement.[15] Benn also argued that the future
rate of inflation was conjectural and could 'hardly form the basis of a firm
and hurried recommendation to cancel'. It was dangerous, he said, to
assume that the present level of inflation 'makes it necessary to
automatically destroy projects upon which the long-term health of British
industry depends'. Sir Arnold was equally forthright, the agreement gave
HSA autonomy to determine the project's commercial and technical
ability. HSA had, in effect, fulfilled its obligations and the firm expected
the Government to accept its judgement.[16] HSA certainly had no fear of
legal action in respect of the contract and, it was suggested, might well
have relished its 'day in court'.

Just after the second General Election of 1974, in October, HSA
decided to cancel the 146 unilaterally. On the 14th, the DTI was given
notice that work would cease on the 21st and simultaneously, HSA would
terminate and compensate its subcontractors. Benn, however, was under
considerable pressure from the Unions representing HSA employees
affected by the decision, and Labour MPs with HSA factories in their
constituencies also lobbied the Minister. Some estimates put the long-
term job loss as high as 20,000 with another 10,000 in supporting
industries. There was also a grave risk to the continued existence of
Hatfield as a design and production centre.

The Government conceded that 50:50 funding was no longer an
acceptable basis for development but equally it could not agree to a fully
funded programme. A compromise was reached whereby full-scale
development was 'suspended', but with the Government continuing to
finance further design work and market studies. HSA would pay between
£6 and £10 million in compensation to its subcontractors and the £4
million already given in launch aid would be subject to future
negotiations between HSA and the DTI. The Government's view was
that it had to maintain 'this type of capability in the civil aircraft
industry'. But even more significantly, perhaps, it had to give the Board
of a publicly owned industry every opportunity of reviewing the 146 at a
later date 'in the light of its plans for the industry as a whole'.[17]

The decision to suspend development of the 146, even more so Benn's
pressure on HSA to continue, was clearly motivated by non-commercial
criteria. HSA felt that the 146 was no longer economically viable, and

according to the launch aid policy it had a right, and even an obligation perhaps, to cease work on the project. Politically, however, this was not acceptable to the new Government and it wanted HSA to press on regardless in order to protect employment and an important design capability. On the other hand, the Government was unwilling to provide an open-ended commitment to HSA, presumably because this was at odds with impending nationalisation. It was, to say the least, an odd situation with an undercurrent of personal and ideological animosity between the two parties. The broader significance of these events, however, was that to the last, and despite administrative reforms, launch aid to the private sector was vulnerable to external events and non-commercial interests. No matter how the monitoring procedures were improved, or policy making rendered more 'dispassionate' by separating policy formulation from execution, the relations between state and industry were still highly problematic, a situation which Labour's nationalisation Bill tried to resolve.

Nationalising the airframe sector

From the early 1970s, Labour spokesmen had again begun to argue the case for nationalising BAC and HSA.[18] With Rolls-Royce already in public ownership, the continued existence of a privately owned airframe industry largely dependent on public money seemed increasingly absurd. Nationalisation would, it was claimed, legitimise that dependence and improve the accountability of publicly sponsored programmes. Nationalisation of both the aircraft and the shipbuilding industries was included in the Labour Party manifesto for 1974. Following their second General Election victory in that year, the proposal to nationalise the two industries in one piece of legislation was announced in the Queen's Speech in November 1974.

In January, Benn published draft legislation, accompanied by a consultative paper, outlining the rationale and the likely operation of the two public corporations, British Aerospace (BAe) and British Shipbuilders. More details were given during subsequent debates on the Bill. The underlying argument for nationalising the aircraft industry was that there really would be little effective change from the present relationship between the Government and the industry. As in the past, the Government would continue to play a major role in strategic planning for the industry, and as a main customer and financial sponsor it would inevitably play an important part in major investment decisions. The Government was conscious of the fact that for the first time it would be directly concerned with the industry's civil, commercially orientated business and that historically public ownership had not always been synonymous with effective commercial decision-making. Nevertheless, nationalisation was presented as a means of resolving problems which in the past had damaged relations between the state and companies receiving launch aid. Public ownership, it was argued, would lead to greater rather than less managerial autonomy in civil development. It would certainly not undermine the industry's ability to make its own commercial judgements. Public ownership would also finally complete the rationalisation of the airframe sector which had long been recognised as being financially and technically desirable, but which had not been accomplished by private enterprise.[19]

The intention was to create a flexible and adaptable organisation, capable of responding quickly in a highly competitive environment. The powers given to the Secretary of State would be the minimum required to secure the Government's influence over corporate strategy and to protect public investment. The consultative paper, for example, made it clear that the Government believed nationalisation would bring a greater degree of public accountability to an industry which depended to 'an unusually large extent on Government purchasing and Government financial support of various kinds'. On the other hand, the Government would give the company 'the greatest possible freedom consistent with public accountability and Government policy.[20]

The new Secretary of State for Industry, Eric Varley (who replaced Benn in June 1975), continued this theme in introducing the Bill's first reading. Such an industry, he said, so dependent on the state, could no longer be regarded as 'a genuine example of private enterprise'. He also confirmed that nationalisation should resolve many control and accountability questions. In the past, huge amounts of public money spent in private industry required detailed monitoring. However, once this money was 'channelled into a publicly owned undertaking, the accountability can be at the strategic, corporate level and the substance of accountability can be maintained and improved, but the detailed intervention and monitoring by the Government under public ownership can be dispensed with'. As far as new civil projects were concerned, it was not the Government's intention to monitor them closely at 'factory level, as has been the case of necessity in the past'. A simple merger of HSA and BAC, he added, would have still left confusion in the roles of Government and industry which, especially in project choice, had 'bedevilled the industry'.[21]

Later, Varley also stressed the advantages of taking 'key strategic decisions on a coherent basis'. For example, he noted that until very recently BAC's and HSA's 'international collaborations and discussions have been uncoordinated, if not actually competitive'. This had been changing for the better, and now this improvement would be reinforced and confirmed. Referring to the current state of play regarding future European and American civil projects, it was necessary for the United Kingdom, both at an industrial and at a Governmental level, to speak with a 'single authoritative voice'. The HS146 affair, he asserted had shown the limitations of the private sector in launching civil projects. Indeed, without public ownership, the Government could see 'little prospect of major new civil aircraft projects'.[22]

The Government would exercise strategic control through its power to appoint the Chairman and Board, and through its approval of British Aerospace's annual corporate plan, its capital investment and R&D programme and the Corporation's operational budget. The Secretary of State for Industry would also approve all new civil projects, while the Secretary of State for Defence would have similar authority for military aircraft and engines. The Industry Secretary would also have powers to direct the Corporation 'in the national interest'. Finally, British Aerospace would be answerable directly to the Secretary of State and, unlike Rolls-Royce, would not be supervised by the National Enterprise Board (NEB).[23]

Industrial and Conservative critics of nationalisation were not over-impressed by either the Government's diagnosis or its prescription for the aircraft industry. Decision-making, it was claimed, would inevitably be slow and cumbersome – a problem endemic to all nationalised enterprise. The Government was also accused of slandering the industry's commercial record. Speaking from the Opposition front bench, Michael Heseltine believed that the Government's intention to limit its interference in BAe's internal affairs was a charade. No major decision in a nationalised industry could be taken unless it had been approved by Ministers and officials. The promise to abstain from detailed control was a 'pious thought' which would 'last as long as the first crisis'. That, he said, would 'bring a demand from the Secretary of State for Industry for cash, and the Treasury will respond with the ruthlessness with which it controls the rest of the public sector[24] Heseltine also attacked the appointment in December 1975 of Lord Beswick, then a Minister of State at the DoI, as Chairman-designate of BAe. Although Beswick had a long-standing interest in aviation matters, his selection was seen as evidence that the Government, despite its protestations to the contrary, was going to interfere in the day-to-day affairs of the Corporation.[25]

Monitoring British Aerospace's civil programmes
The various decisions made during 1978 showed that the strategic relationship between Government and industry differed very little from comparable project choices in the 1960s, (or the 1950s for that matter). The fact that BAe was newly nationalised did provide Beswick and his Board with an additional lever in the fight to secure re-entry to the Airbus programme, but the dynamics of the choice were not significantly altered by public ownership. With Government commanding the source of launch finance, this was inevitable. However, the moot question was whether the creation of BAe effected significant changes in the balance between control and autonomy at a 'tactical' level.

In practice, there has hardly been either sufficient time or a variety of examples of civil development to prove the case conclusively one way or the other. Re-entry to the Airbus programme represents a different order of problem, and the HS (BAe) 146 has been the only indigenously directed civil programme launched (or rather, relaunched) since 1977. The formation of BAe led to the abandonment of launch aid for civil airframe development. Launch aid, BAe senior officials believed, was no longer appropriate to a nationalised corporation. As part of the public sector, it was regarded as a 'dishonest' arrangement which did not provide an adequate sense of commercial discipline. From the outset, BAe set itself the task of raising from its own resources development finance for the 146. On the other hand, money for the A300/A310 was arranged through Section 45 of the Aircraft and Shipbuilding Industries Act. This provided a limit of £50 million which could be granted by the Secretary of State on his own authority. Anything over this sum required full Treasury review and approval. As BAe was also required to submit its annual and rolling plans for DoI inspection, there seemed a satisfactory number of check points to secure strategic accountability without the additional controls associated with launch aid.[26] On a tactical level, BAe was allowed more autonomy to evaluate and to control its own development work. In the case of the relaunched 146, as one official put it, 'the reins are a lot looser'. The DoI could still call for a full MoD(PE) assessment, but this was hoped to be the exception rather than the rule, particularly as Beswick was known to be sensitive about official interference in management activities: 'we shall expect the fullest consultation and cooperation with our sponsoring department, but also the clearest devolution of authority and responsibility'.[27]

The position on collaborative projects was rather different. When the British re-entered the Airbus consortium as a full partner, although HSA had been closely associated with the programme since the 1960s, they joined an established collaborative structure. They also found the French well entrenched on the various technical and official sub-committees. BAe was fully integrated into the industrial and technical management processes, and British Government officials joined the inter-Government Supervisory Board. In theory, the United Kingdom acquired comparable rights and status to the French and the Germans. However, the French continued to control the Secretariat of Airbus Industrie, and some British officials believed that this enabled the French to structure the technical and administrative context in their favour. Consequently, the British have sought to internationalise the Secretariat and to bring it into line with the rest of Airbus management.

In terms of programme control, there was some concern that French and German industrial and technological ambitions have tended to allow a much freer attitude to cost control and pricing policies than was acceptable to British practice. However, AI has sought to present itself as a wholly commercial enterprise, capable of matching American standards of efficiency, productivity and cost control. On the other hand, with three Governments so closely involved in the development of Airbus, and with so many vital long-term technological interests at stake, undoubtedly the consortium may be under pressure to relax a strict commercial regime. More significantly, perhaps, proposals to launch variants of the A300 and A320 family, or new projects for that matter, come out of a trans-national system where one Government may find itself facing pressure to make a positive decision from its own industry, the international consortium and other Governments. At both a tactical and a strategic level, membership of AI has made it more difficult for the British Government to retain control over events.

BAe has been in existence for only a short period of time. It is not yet possible to assess fully the claims made at the time of nationalisation that public ownership would improve the quality of both tactical and strategic accountability without undermining corporate autonomy. The 'privatisation' of BAe in February 1981 by a Conservative Government introduced another variable, and with a promise from Labour that they will 'renationalise' the company when they are next in office, the ownership question has not yet been settled. On the basis of the limited evidence available, however, the ownership of the aircraft industry has had some effects on the formal relations between company and sponsoring departments, but has had little effect on the working relationship between the two parties. Strategically, of course, the interaction between the state and industry was effectively the same. At this level, however, the relationship was always determined by financial dependence and not ownership.

Monitoring Rolls-Royce, 1971–80

In the case of Rolls-Royce, we do have more information about the relationship between a nationalised aerospace company and the Government. Following the bankruptcy in February 1971, Rolls was reconstituted as the publicly owned Rolls-Royce (1971) Ltd. The formal relationship between it and the Government was based on a Memorandum of Understanding published in September. This specified the rights and obligations of both parties. It stated that Rolls should continue to operate as if it was a privately owned enterprise, and that the Government did not intend to become involved in the day-to-day management of its affairs. However, as the firm's only shareholder, its banker, principal military customer and source of launch aid for civil projects, the Government expected to be consulted on the company's forward planning, and about any financial commitment entailed by new developments. Rolls was also expected to provide the Government through the DTI with full information about it operations.[28]

Initial problems

By early 1972, a general system of reporting and monitoring had been agreed between Rolls and the DTI, but the DTI was still worried by the weakness of Rolls' internal management. In particular, officials were concerned that while they might be receiving a sufficient quantity of information, its accuracy and relevance was suspect. This concern was shared by Rolls' new Chairman, Sir Kenneth Keith. On his appointment, he immediately examined the quality of progress reports and planning documents he received, and which the DTI also required for its monitoring procedures. He found that he could have little confidence in their accuracy and felt that it would be 'misleading and undesirable that the Government should go on receiving reports which he regarded as unsatisfactory'. As a result, in November 1972 Sir Kenneth stopped the flow of information between Rolls and the DTI until he could effect reforms and improvements inside Rolls.[29]

This was essential for the proper conduct of Rolls's business as much as for effective Government monitoring of its activities. Part of the problem with the privately owned company had been the weaknesses of its own management systems, which had exacerbated any difficulty and ambiguity in the relationship between Rolls and the Ministry of Technology. Sir Kenneth was well aware that both Rolls' commercial and technical survival as well as the Government's ability to monitor complex programmes depended on internal reform. By October 1973, he was able to provide the DTI with both a general ten- and a more detailed five-year forward plan. The DTI was also happier about the state of Rolls' internal procedures, but officials were still not entirely convinced that all was well. The official view was that as the quality of Rolls's own management was perhaps more important than the DTI's monitoring system, it had to be water-tight. The DTI was keeping a close eye on these matters when the election of a Labour Administration led to further changes in the relationship between the company and the Government.[30]

In spite of these 'strategic' problems, the DTI and the MoD(PE) were much happier with the control of the RB211. From May 1971, RB211 development was governed by a new contract administered by the Procurement Executive. Rolls was expected to follow agreed technical cost programmes and to seek prior approval for any changes to them. Officials had complete access to information, and could attend any company meeting about the engine. There were also regular meetings between the company's representatives, the Procurement Executive's RB211 Project Director and his team of officials and technical advisers. In effect, the RB211 was being treated as a military programme, and not as a normal, launch-aided civil project. The DTI and the Procurement Executive reported that they were pleased with the engine's progress, having noted few technical or financial problems between 1971 and the end of 1973.[31] Relations between Rolls's line managers and the

Procurement Executive team initially were somewhat cool, but they eventually established a cordial and productive relationship. Undoubtedly, even though Rolls had been humbled by bankruptcy, its senior managers were still proud of their earlier independence and took some time to appreciate fully that the development of the RB211 had become a true partnership between Government and manufacturer.

The continuing problems with both Rolls' internal procedures and official monitoring during this period were demonstrated by the Anglo-French M45H project. Rolls had inherited the M45H from BSE following the merger in 1966. In 1971, Rolls-Royce (1971) refused to undertake further development of the engine, which had been selected for the German–Dutch VFW-Fokker 614, unless the Government financed production, at an estimated cost of £11.2 million.[32] Because of the collaborative links, as well as the promise of a commercial return, the Government agreed to Rolls' request.

Rolls provided a fully costed technical programme, presumably similar to that produced for the RB211. The DTI and the Procurement Executive were quite happy with the control of launch costs, but the estimate of production costs was substantially wrong. By the beginning of 1974, new estimates showed that the company would have a peak deficit of over £28.8 million on M45H production. It turned out to be £35.9 million.[33] An internal inquiry into the Procurement Executive's monitoring procedures discovered that the two-monthly progress reports had not updated changing estimates of future production costs and that Rolls' own internal system was again at fault in producing misleading and optimistic data. Insufficient account was taken of the impact of the 1973 energy crisis and the onset of a high level of UK domestic inflation. The project's specific managerial problems had also been affected by the general uncertainty inside the company about the effectiveness of its management procedures. As the Public Accounts Committee put it, 'The company admitted that there had been inadequate liason between their financial and engineering staff, and that their reviews had not always been based on realistic assumptions.' There were mitigating circumstances; the collaborative dimension had not helped in the provision of accurate data, as some problems with the airframe had affected the engine programme. Similarly, the Procurement Executive was not caught by surprise as officials were aware from an early stage that some increase in costs could be expected owing to technical difficulties. However, they had to wait to discover by exactly how much the costs would actually rise![34]

Nevertheless, the Public Accounts Committee was somewhat disturbed by this very substantial increase in costs, in spite of what seemed to be a fairly close system of official monitoring. The prime objective of monitoring, after all, was to give sufficient early warning of cost increases, their magnitude and other developmental crises so that the sponsoring department would have adequate time and information to decide whether 'to continue with a project on an agreed basis of financing or to cancel it with a minimum of further expenditure'.[35]

Significantly, the option of cancelling the M45H was ruled out, largely on political grounds. In 1972, the Government did consider terminating the project, but it was decided not to risk certain 'defence considerations connected with the Government's relations with Germany which were thought to be paramount at the time'.[36] In effect the Government abdicated its ultimate sanction and final instrument of control. Time and time again, it is evident that unless Government is prepared to terminate a programme, monitoring becomes a matter of keeping a score, auditing rather than controlling. In a more limited sense, the M45H served notice that close monitoring notwithstanding, things could still go wrong. It was obvious that no one could afford to be sanguine about the continuing difficulty of managing and monitoring civil engine projects.

Rolls and The National Enterprise Board

The Labour Government elected in 1974 was committed to a deliberate strategy of intervention in industry and intended to establish a National Enterprise Board (NEB) to act as an investment bank, development agency and holding company for ailing and convalescent companies. The new Government decided to place Rolls in the hands of the NEB. This was a surprise to Sir Kenneth Keith, who evidently had been assured by the Prime Minister himself that the status quo would obtain for Rolls and it would remain directly under the control of the DTI.[37] The NEB could certainly provide Rolls with adequate funding but its presence as an intermediary in decision-making and monitoring was not welcome. According to Sir Kenneth, 'we have come a long way towards making Rolls-Royce long-term viable' and the relationship between Rolls and the DTI had worked well. He could not see what role the NEB could play: 'Two people cannot run a business. Rolls-Royce is a complex business. We understand it – and we cannot be backseat-driven by people who do not.'[38]

Eventually, after a personal intervention by the Prime Minister, Harold Wilson, Sir Kenneth, Lord Ryder, (the Chairman of the NEB) and the Department of Industry arrived at a second Memorandum of Understanding. This was broadly similar to the original terms of reference established in 1971 between Rolls and the Conservative Government. Rolls was again expected to act as a commercial enterprise and had full autonomy to run its operations. As sole shareholder and the major provider of money for development, the NEB had to approve appointments to the Company's Board, and its long-range and annual plans. Rolls was also obliged to provide the NEB with such information as to enable it to monitor the firm's performance and financial progress. For any project exceeding £5 million, Rolls were expected to inform and seek the approval of the NEB and the Secretary of State for Industry.[39]

On all major issues, Rolls had to deal with the NEB, but any discussions between the NEB and the Industry Department on matters affecting the firm, Rolls had the right to be represented. Similarly, the Chairman of Rolls had direct access to the Secretary of State, provided the NEB Chairman was consulted first and had the opportunity to attend if he wished. In addition, of course, there were day-to-day contacts between Rolls and the Department of Industry as the sponsoring department for the industry, with the Ministry of Defence (Procurement Executive) on matters relating to contracts, the monitoring of military projects and launch-aided civil programmes (pre-eminently, the RB211) and the Foreign and Commonwealth Office for matters relating to overseas sales and international programmes. The NEB's supporting staff were also to have technical and financial discussions with Rolls so that they could properly advise their Chairman. In conclusion, 'both the NEB and RR71 will do their best to make the relationship a harmonious one'. The Department of Industry believed that they had established a balance between giving Rolls the necessary freedom of action in a highly competitive environment and enabling the NEB to exercise its statutory duties.[40]

It was inevitable, however, that Rolls's relationship with the Government, on both day-to-day matters and questions of strategy, could be complicated by the existence of the NEB. The sheer complexity of Rolls' business and the traditional links the company had with many Government departments, could render the NEB's position intolerable. The Procurement Executive reported to the DoI, but not to the NEB. Sales of civil and especially military engines tended to be matters of direct Government concern. The DoI was also better placed to negotiate with the FCO on Rolls' behalf and, if necessary, to press the Export Credits Guarantee Department for help in financing Rolls' export business.

The Department of Industry was at last fairly satisfied with Rolls' internal procedures and controls. On the verge of transferring responsibilities to the NEB, officials said they were 'well content with the monitoring arrangements'. They also felt that Rolls' traditional technical enthusiasm which, in the past, may have affected the company's attitude towards financial discipline was now matched by a better sense of economic realism. It was assumed that the NEB would use a similar monitoring system, but the Department was worried that the presence of the NEB would add another layer of administration in managing the aero-engine sector. This, it was said, could 'easily make everybody's job more difficult'. 'But under these circumstances, it will be the tasks of the civil servants and the members of the NEB to make the system work as smoothly as possible'.[41] For his part, Lord Ryder was impressed by Rolls' management and with the way they had tightened up 'enormously on their control mechanisms on all the financial aspects'. He certainly believed it was necessary for the Chairman to have his own technical staff to advise him on his new responsibilities. Without this the NEB would be a 'sitting duck' for a company wanting to blind them with science. Similarly, in spite of his initial troubles with Rolls, Lord Ryder believed that there was no firmer advocate of the NEB than the Rolls Chairman, Sir Kenneth Keith.[42] The concordat reached between Ryder and Keith was no more than an uneasy truce; in essence, the triangular relationship between the NEB, Rolls and the Government, was unstable and would add little to the latter's ability or otherwise to monitor Rolls' major decisions.

The Boeing Contracts

The most important investment decisions taken by Rolls during this period were, of course, those relating to the RB211-524 and 535 engines and the contracts for both with Boeing. In December 1977, the NEB and the DoI discussed means of financing future development through a combination of launch aid, equity capital and loan finance. The NEB wanted to set overall financial targets for the company, but the DoI felt it was 'inappropriate' to specify detailed financial objectives until all concerned had a 'clearer idea of possible future development expenditure'. During 1978, such a picture began to emerge: commitments to the 524 and 525 engines would entail just over £500 million at 1978 prices.[43] The necessary capital would be based on a total launch aid agreement covering the period 1978–83. This was then regarded as a fixed sum for all civil engine development. The intention was to prevent Rolls accepting over-ambitious targets. Similarly, anything other than the RB211 series would have to be financed by other means.[44]

Rolls believed that it would earn 10.9 per cent and 11 per cent on the capital devoted to the 524 and 535 respectively. The DoI felt that this was somewhat optimistic, even over the lifetime of each engine. Indeed, officials were inclined to treat the possible outcome of both with more caution; 'we thought that it was prudent to allow for a higher cost, because all past experience is that projects of this kind take more than the company assumes'. The DoI estimated that the programmes would not be profitable until the early 1990s compared with the company's view that the turnround would occur in the later part of the 1980s. For the company as a whole, the DoI expected it might be returning 10 per cent on capital by 1981.[45] By December 1979, the DoI had revised its forecasts; not only would profitability on the RB211-524 and 535 engines be delayed until the late 1990s, but also the company would be facing losses on operations well into the 1980s.

Rolls' difficulties stemmed from the terms of the contracts with Boeing to produce the RB211-524 and, especially, the 535 engine. No party to the decision, the company, the NEB, the DoI, nor the Cabinet, doubted the importance of these contracts to the continued health of British civil engine manufacturing. Nor was it the case that Rolls made unrealistic assumptions about development costs or time, the fatal weaknesses in the original agreement with Lockheed. The crux of the matter was the assumption made in relation to the exchange rate and Rolls' decision not to cover its foreign exchange risk on the forward currency market. In outline, Rolls agreed prices with Boeing with sterling worth $1.80, with a possibility of it rising to $1.90. Rolls had hoped that a weak pound would have helped to overcome the disadvantages of a higher rate of inflation relative to the United States, and its poorer level of productivity compared with its major American competitors. In the event, the strength of sterling grew steadily during 1979 and accelerated to over $2.30 in 1980. Although there were hopes that British inflation would begin to fall in the mid-1980s, Rolls would find it difficult to reach American productivity standards in the short term, even though in late 1979, with union support, Rolls implemented a major campaign to increase its efficiency and reduce unit costs. However, as DoI officials noted, if sterling remained at $2.30 for any length of time 'it would have a very serious effect indeed' on Rolls. Similarly, if improvements in productivity were not achieved, 'I think that we should be in serious trouble.'[46]

The factors leading to this rapid turnround in the strength of sterling were clearly outside Rolls' control. The impact of North Sea Oil and the new Conservative Government's high-interest-rate policy both inflated the value of sterling. This exerted a toll on British industry generally, but especially on export-orientated firms like Rolls. The net effect was to prevent an early chance of Rolls returning to profitability. The 1979 annual report showed a pre-tax loss of £58.4 million, largely attributable to the dollar-priced RB211 contracts. In April 1980, the Government did help Rolls to some extent by providing an extra tranche of £180 million in launch aid, and waived its rights in respect of the R&D levy on engines ordered during 1979. The DoI still had every confidence that it would recover the investment in the RB211 over the lifetime of the programme, but this would not be easy while sterling remained overvalued.[47]

Rolls' assumption of a $1.90 pound was based upon extensive consultations it had in late 1977 and the spring of 1978 with the NEB, the DoI and the Treasury. This was in response to a criticism from the NEB that Rolls had not discussed in sufficient detail the economic assumptions on which its long-term planning had to be based. In rejecting the company's 1977–81 plan, the NEB had specifically referred to the exchange rate as a factor in Rolls' calculations.[48] This time, Rolls was aware of the need to consult all concerned on the exchange-rate assumptions it was using to plan its operations. However, and this was a crucial qualification, these discussions were held in respect of Rolls' general forward planning, and were not related to any specific contract or contracts.

Estimates of sterling's future value ranged from the NEB's prediction of $1.82 in 1978, steadily devaluing to $1.67 in 1982, to the Treasury's more conservative $1.90. A consensus formed around an average sterling value of $1.80. Moreover, in Rolls' own review of all available forecasts, not one contradicted the official view of a declining exchange rate. As one Treasury official put it, although the Treasury had felt that Rolls was being a little optimistic about a falling sterling rate, 'nobody contested at all the downward trend'.[49] On the basis of these assumptions, Rolls negotiated its contracts with Boeing, and as a senior DoI official admitted, 'we did not demur from the assumptions that they were making'.[50]

The second, and as it turned out, the most crucial element in Rolls' decision to base its contracts on a $1.80 exchange rate was the choice not to cover forward on the exchange markets. This would effectively have fixed Rolls' exchange risk at $1.80 and protected its contracts from the consequences of a rise in the value of sterling. According to the PAC, normal commercial practice was to protect corporate earnings and net assets by seeking to avoid undue currency risks.[51] Similarly, in his evidence to the Committee, Sir Frank McFadzean, Sir Kenneth Keith's successor at Rolls, drawing upon his experience in the oil business, said that it was his policy to minimise risks which were 'extraneous to the actual business I am doing'.[52] Rolls' decision had been determined by three considerations. First, by operating in the spot market, it hoped to use the fact that the exchange rate was directly affected by the relative inflation levels between the United Kingdom and its major trading partners, to compensate for Britain's very high rate of inflation and the company's lower productivity compared with its American competitors. Second, given the unanimity of forecasts, Rolls did not believe that in the foreseeable future, the value of sterling would appreciate to any significant degree, and that the risk to Rolls was minimal.

The third, and perhaps most compelling reason for Rolls' decision, was past experience. As McFadzean explained, the company had expected to incur a large loss on the original contract with Lockheed. In the event, the first 555 engines supplied for the L1011 had earned a £54 million profit, a positive shift of nearly £100 million. The biggest single ingredient in that swing 'was the fall in the rate of exchange'. If Rolls had covered its risk then, it and the Government would not have had the benefit of a depreciating currency. Rolls did try to take out some insurance against an appreciation in the value of sterling by asking permission from the Bank of England for the right to close its forward position if the pound began to move upwards against the dollar. As this entailed the Bank's agreement to what would have been an 'official' speculative move against sterling, Rolls' request was denied. However, Rolls believed on the basis of the best advice available that the risks of not covering forward were negligible.[53]

The NEB and the DoI were not party either to the negotiations with

Boeing or the decision not to cover forward. According to McFadzean, even the full Rolls Board had probably not discussed the details of the contracts, although he did add that this was not so unusual in large companies.[54] Officials agreed that the adoption of a policy on forward cover was the sort of decision 'for the management of the company to take', but the PAC wanted to know exactly what the Government did know, or was expected to know, about what one of its members called 'this hair-raising decision'.[55]

Sir Peter Carey, the Permanent Secretary at the DoI, argued that if one wanted Rolls to operate commercially in competition with foreign private sector companies, the Government had to have, and to show, confidence in its management. He said, 'You must leave certain major decisions to the Board of that company.' The key to such a relationship was in the establishment of a 'framework of surveillance'. If the DoI or anybody in Government were 'involved in decisions about every contract taken, we would have been involving ourselves in the day to day management of the business. It was not part of the arrangements to do that.' The DoI was bound to be concerned about the company's affairs because of the expenditure involved and because it was ultimately responsible for launch aid policy. However, the DoI felt that it would have been over-extending its remit to have been 'engaged in any detailed discussion on individual contracts'. With hindsight, Sir Peter conceded that it might have been 'sensible' for the DoI to have taken a closer look, but at the time officials had been satisfied that 'that was the proper way in which Rolls-Royce should operate'. They certainly had had no qualms about accepting the judgement of Sir Kenneth Keith and his Board. It was not a 'blunder', as one member of the Public Accounts Committee put it, but clearly, it was a 'pity' that everyone had accepted the assumptions on which the decisions were taken.[56]

Barry Jones, a Labour member of the Committee, still found it difficult to accept that in regard to one of Britain's biggest export-aerospace contracts, the DoI was not 'following almost day-to-day the progress leading up to these decisions. Sir Peter reiterated that they had been aware of the principles on which Rolls was conducting its business, but the 'conclusion of a contract for the sale of engines' had to be left to the company. The DoI knew it could not do a better job of running the firm than an independent, commercially orientated Board. Even the Treasury admitted that there had been nothing wrong in theory with the DoI's monitoring. If anything, it was 'just a case of simple misjudgement by the company'.[57]

From NEB to DoI control
Officials did not seek to dissociate themselves from the general responsibility for all that happened, 'whatever the technical and formal position is about monitoring'.[58] However, a strong undercurrent of

implied criticism of the NEB can be discerned in the DoI's evidence to the PAC, to the effect that its presence had made the exercise of oversight 'at one more remove' rather more difficult than it might have been. Certainly, McFadzean felt that it had been superfluous and had represented an unnecessary layer of management between Rolls and the sponsoring department.[59]

The original decision to place Rolls in the hands of the NEB had not been welcomed by the company, and at the time the DoI hinted at possible problems inherent in the triangular relationship, between itself, the NEB and Rolls. Up to 1978, an uneasy truce reigned, and the NEB was a valuable ally backing Rolls' American strategy. However, after the 1979 decisions, relations between the company and its nominal owners, began to deteriorate. To some extent, this was a clash of personalities between Sir Kenneth Keith and Lord Ryder's successor as Chairman of the NEB, Sir Leslie Murphy. Essentially, Sir Leslie felt that his job and that of the NEB was to keep a tighter check over Rolls' affairs than Sir Kenneth was prepared to concede.[60] Conversely, Sir Kenneth disparagingly referred to the NEB as a 'bureaucratic contraceptive' and sought to limit the NEB's ability to intervene effectively in Rolls' affairs. The existence of direct links between Rolls and the various Government departments helped to make the NEB's position increasingly awkward, while Rolls believed that the NEB was taking its data, its five-year plan and quarterly reports, and presenting these to the DoI with the NEB's own recommendations. The situation, as one official put it, tended to become a 'bloody mess'.

In the summer of 1979, Rolls' deteriorating financial position and the advent of a Conservative Government brought matters to a head. In his annual report for 1979, Sir Leslie said that Rolls ought to adopt 'a more stringent application of financial disciplines'. The NEB rejected Rolls' request for additional money and, at a press conference, Sir Lesie added that it was time for the company to realise 'that it is not any good Rolls-Royce thinking that it can always hold out its hand and get more from the public'. Sir Leslie felt that Rolls had underpriced its contracts, had insufficient control over its finances and had not taken adequate steps to improve productivity.[61] He also had grave doubts about Sir Kenneth Keith's judgement, and it was reported that he had sought his replacement before the General Election in May. Sir Leslie wanted to appoint a Chief Executive and to gain access to details of Rolls' contracts; changes which Sir Kenneth stolidly resisted.[62]

The struggle between Rolls and the NEB was very embarrassing to the new Government. It certainly wanted to reduce the role of the latter, but at the same time it was determined to reduce the role of the state in industry generally. Nevertheless, in this case, its sympathies tended to lie with Rolls, and Ministers favoured bringing the company back under the direct control of the DoI. There was some disquiet about Sir Kenneth Keith's style of management, indeed the Treasury evidently agreed with the NEB's view that Rolls had underpriced its contracts. DoI officials also agreed that there was a need for 'tight financial control and tight production control' as well as further improvements in productivity. In November, Sir Kenneth announced that he was retiring early, apparently in return for a promise from Margaret Thatcher that Rolls would be taken out of the hands of the NEB. His successor was Sir Frank McFadzean, whose approach to the job of running Rolls was rather tighter than his predecessor's.[63]

The Government's decision led to the resignation *en masse* of the NEB Board, and accusations that the DoI would be a 'soft touch' for Rolls. The DoI resented this slur on its critical faculties. There was no question of the DoI substituting an 'inexperienced civil servant's' view of Rolls for the NEB's 'hard-headed businessman's approach'. DoI officials were equipped, and would equip themselves further, 'to carry out a conscientious monitoring function'. The Department's own expertise could be supplemented by that of the MoD(PE), and it would also call upon the Industrial Development Unit, headed by a merchant banker, to help in assessing Rolls' future performance. In terms of staff support and experience of civil aerospace, the DoI felt that it was better able to supervise Rolls than the NEB had been.[64]

With Rolls once again the direct responsibility of the DoI, officials were determined to use the lessons of the Boeing contract to influence the way they monitored the company. However, the DoI still had no intention of paralleling management operations with a detailed examination of Rolls' day-to-day activity. The exact relationship had to be discussed with Rolls, but it was hoped that the DoI would have access to information about individual contracts, and to have the opportunity to comment upon them. Nevertheless, both parties agreed that this would still only relate to contracts which raised 'exceptional issues' and that the DoI would not interfere in negotiations with potential engine buyers. McFadzean was quite blunt on the matter: 'as Chairman of this company I have no intention of going and clearing everything with civil servants; otherwise I would never run the company . . . Goodness gracious me, you would never run a business on that basis.[65] In his view, if the Government was dissatisfied with the way Rolls was being managed, the only legitimate course of action was to change the management.[66]

There is a strong temptation to compare these events with those leading up to Rolls' collapse in 1970. The heart of the matter is again a contract with an American firm, in which erroneous assumptions are made about vital economic data. The sponsoring department is again largely unaware of the details of the contract. The NEB also provides some parallels with the role played by the IRC. Yet the two cases are really not that similar. McFadzean rightly noted that the original Lockheed agreement represented a gross underestimation by Rolls of the technical difficulties entailed by building a large new engine from scratch.[67] In 1978, the RB211 was known and tested technology, and Rolls could be sure that any derivatives would perform as predicted, and development times were largely predictable.

Whatever criticism might be levied at Sir Kenneth Keith, he and his senior managers were confident that these decisions were within the bounds of an acceptable degree of risk. His reforms had made a considerable difference to the quality and structure of Rolls management. There was no question that he and his team were not aware of the risks they were running. In the event, the decisions to assume a $1.80 parity and not to cover forward, were undermined by events outside their control. Moreover, they had taken expert advice and had amended their assumptions accordingly. No one in fact, had been in a position to 'outguess the market'.[68] From this perspective, they had taken a valid commercial risk, which, had it come off, would have led to high praise for their business acumen and financial prescience.

Currency fluctuations can, and do, work both ways. By the late spring of 1981, the pound was drifting downwards, and in June fell quite sharply to $1.90. Improvements in productivity made by Rolls have also helped to achieve a complete turn round in the company's general financial position. Pre-tax losses for 1980 were halved over the 1979 figure to £27 million and McFadzean could announce that the firm was back on course for a return to profitability early in the 1980s. However, in his view, the pound was still too hard against the dollar, and did not help Rolls in its battle with GE and P&W to sell engines.[69]

In spite of this later recovery, the 1978 decisions still left something to be desired. The PAC conceded that the nature of Rolls' business left it vulnerable to long-term economic factors and that it had received unanimous advice about the likely trend in the exchange rate. In these circumstances 'we do not think that the company's commercial judgement should now be criticised with the benefit of hindsight'. However, Rolls' actions were unusual, and since the change in management, the practice has been to protect earnings by seeking to avoid undue currency risks.[70] Civil aerospace contains sufficient risks and uncertainties without compounding the problem by speculating against the rise and fall of currencies.

As far as the DoI's monitoring of these decisions was concerned, the PAC did not think that anybody had blundered. Nor did it deny the undesirability of officials involving themselves in the day-to-day management of a company like Rolls. Nevertheless, there were weaknesses in the DoI's monitoring of Rolls' commercial policies, 'particularly where these are capable of having material effect on overall results and its requirements for external, including Exchequer, finance'. There was also a strong sense that DoI officials sought to ascribe many of the problems to the existence of the NEB. There were anomalies and tension in the triangular relationship between the NEB, Rolls and the

DoI. The NEB in particular found it difficult to break into long established and complicated linkages between the company and the various Government departments with which it had dealings. However, its existence or otherwise was not the sole reason for the failure in supervision. It was clearly a function of the degree of freedom Rolls expected and was given to make its own commercial decisions.

This case demonstrates that there is no easy way of reconciling the dilemma of control versus autonomy in this type of high-risk, high-technology industry, whether publicly or privately owned, a company in receipt of public money must still be able to respond to what it sees as its technical and commercial imperatives. The official view is that Government cannot control companies such as Rolls more tightly without a serious loss of corporate autonomy. While Government itself is not equipped, administratively or politically, to supplant the industrial decision-maker, it has little alternative but to place its trust in the managerial skill and judgement of others.

8

CONCLUSIONS

It has become very clear that the reasons why successive Governments have supported British civil aircraft and engines go well beyond the application of simple commercial criteria. Although the starting point for any decision to aid a particular project was usually its likely profitability, the Government, 'because it is the Government', had to look at 'other aspects of the national interest' as well.[1] Indeed, the rationale for assisting civil programmes has been consistent with the thesis that Governments can and should intervene in the market to promote broader economic and social values inherent in technological innovation which, for structural or behavioural reasons, the market has failed to attain. Consequently, the notion of a direct return on investment has been qualified by reference to an 'acceptable' return.[2] In practice, the acceptibility to the Government of a civil aerospace programme will depend upon a number of factors. These factors, 'externalities' in the jargon of economists, may not have an explicit or quantifiable commercial value, yet they are assigned subjective or qualitative values. The externalities for civil aerospace have been defined in terms of employment, the relationship, technical and productive, between civil and military development, and the generation of technological spin-off into industry generally. Factors of prestige and diplomacy have also been invoked in civil aerospace decisions. Similarly, investment decisions have also been affected by political commitments to the rationalisation and nationalisation of the aircraft industry.

Interestingly enough, with very few exceptions, individual decisions to help the development of British civil aircraft and engines have been based upon estimates of a project's likely profitability. Realisation has rarely matched expectation, as only two post-war civil projects, the Viscount and the Dart engine, have repaid public investment in civil aerospace. Some have got close, others may yet do so, but generally speaking, the direct commercial return has not been satisfactory. (See Table 5) However, officially, the commercial case for launching civil projects includes the direct and indirect effects of civil aerospace on the balance of payments. While some analysts would regard this as one of the 'externalities', figures presented to Parliamentary Committees suggest that the overall earnings from exports and from 'import saving' have been large (See Table 6). Of course, virtually any domestically manufactured

Table 5(a) Government contributions to and receipts from the launching of civil aircraft and aero-engines, 1945–74

Type		Contributions to 31/3/74		Receipts to 31/3/74	
		Current prices (£m)	At 1974 input prices (£m)	Current prices (£m)	At 1974 input prices (£m)
Aircraft					
Shetland					
Sandringham					
Solent	1945	2·25[d]	11·7	n.a.	n.a. [a]
Tudor					
Air Horse					
Apollo	1948	1·25	6·5	nil	nil [a]
Brabazon	1948	6·45	32·8	nil	nil [a]
Hermes	1949	1·3[d]	6·4	n.a.	n.a. [a]
Comet 1-4	1956	10·25	38·0	4·1	12·2
Ambassador	1951	1·85	7·6	·15	·4 [a]
Princess	1961	9·1	47·1	nil	nil [a]
Viscount	1951	1·8	8·4	3·0	9·8
V-1000	1955	2·35	7·8	nil	nil [a]
Twin Pioneer	1955	·05	·1	·05	·1
Britannia	1955	6·4	24·8	5·1	16·0
Rotodyné	1956	3·05	7·8	nil	nil [a]
Argosy	1961	·1	·2	nil	nil
Herald	1962	1·1	3·0	·05	·1
VC 10	1963	10·25	27·1	1·05	2·1 [a]
Trident	1965	26·1	53·5	·75	1·6 [a][b]
BAC 1-11	1965	19·05	45·3	3·3	6·1 [b]
Islander	1968	·05	·1	·05	·1 [b]
Jetstream	1968	1·2	2·4	·1	·2
A300B	1968	1·15	2·2	nil	nil [a]
HS146	1972	1·25	1·6	nil	nil
Concorde	1968	233·8	406·8	3·15	5·8 [a][b]
Total		340·15	741·2	20·85	54·5 [c]
Engines					
Dart	1949	5·3	21·7	8·45	20·8
Proteus	1950	19·45	72·2	3·5	9·2 [a]
Eland	1952	10·9	34·8	·05	·1 [a]
Tyne	1958	4·0	12·6	2·1	4·0 [a]
Orien	1959	4·75	14·9	nil	nil [a]
Avon	1958	8·5	26·7	6·95	17·1
Conway	1960	6·65[d]	15·9	5·85	13·4
Spey	1965	9·9	23·7	6·6	11·2 [b]
RB178	1967	1·3	2·8	·1	·1

Table 5(a) continued

Type		Contributions to 31/3/74		Receipts to 31/3/74	
		Current prices (£m)	At 1974 input prices (£m)	Current prices (£m)	At 1974 input prices (£m)
Trent (RB203)	1968	2·5	5·1	·6	1·0
RB207	1968	2·0	3·8	·05	·1
M45H (for VFW 614)	1973	6·6	8·6	nil	nil [a][b]
RB211	1971	146·7	224·4	6·25	10·4 [a][b]
Olympus 593 (for Concorde)	1968	178·1	297·0	nil	nil [a][b]
Total		406·65	764·2	40·5	87·4 [c]
Overall total		746·8	1,505·4	61·35	141·9

Notes
The date shown in the type column is about the mid-point of the development programme.
[a] denotes a subjective judgement that motives other than the commercial success of the project in question were responsible for the contribution.
[b] denotes projects from which appreciable further receipts may accrue.
[c] The totals shown are incomplete.
[d] Provisional estimates.

Source   N. K. Gardner, 'The Economics of Launching Aid', in A. Whiting, *The Economics of Industrial Subsidies*, London, 1976.

product represents an 'import saver', and there are other export-orientated sectors which have not had the same degree of assistance. However, it has been pointed out that like most high technologies, civil aerospace does have a particularly favourable ratio of imported materials to export price.[3] There is no doubting, however, that in various periods since the war, the balance of payments has possessed a high political salience. Although with the advent of North Sea Oil surpluses this has diminished, concern for the trade figures in manufactured goods is still high. In any event, the balance of payments has been used to justify public expenditure on apparently unprofitable projects, and was seen as the primary reason why the United Kingdom should remain a producer of civil aircraft and engines.[4]

Employment has been another particularly sensitive factor in civil aerospace decisions. Although employment on civil projects cannot easily be separated from that related to military production, there is some indication that the decline in employment levels attendant on reductions

Table 5(b) Department of Industry expenditure on civil aerospace, 1974–7 £ million (1977 survey prices) (net)

		Aircraft and aero-engines R&D (£m)	Concorde (£m)	RB211 (£m)	Other projects and assistance (£m)	Total (£m)
1974–5	Loans	–	–	1·9	6·0	4·1
	Grants	–	–	–	–	
	Other	28·9	119·3	77·0	23·3	248·5
1975–6	Loans	–	–	−3·8	27·7	23·9
	Grants	–	–	–	–	
	Other	22·0	94·8	1·0	65·6	183·4
1976–7	Loans	–	–	−2·3	−6·0	−8·3
–		–	–	–		
	Other	19·9	48·9	12·1	5·7	86·6
1977–8	Loans	–	–	−0·9	–	−0·9
	Grants	–	–	–	–	
	Other	15·7	41·2	−1·4	3·4	58·9
Total outgoings		86·5	304·2	90·1	131·7	62·5
Total receipts				10·3	6·0	16·3

Note Negative figures indicate receipts.

Source HCD 944, 20 February 1978 (written answers), cols 475–6.

in the demand for military equipment has been cushioned by civil activity.[5] (Table 7 provides total figures for employment in the aircraft industry.) Certainly, specific events such as the review of Concorde in 1967, the RB211 rescue packages, and the launch, suspension and relaunch of the HS146, have been heavily influenced by the regional impact of cancellation on jobs. Similarly, the debate over the A320 and the Boeing 757 contained deliberate attempts by the protagonists to use hypothetical calculations of employment in their 'bid pitching' directed at the Government. Again there is no reason to suggest that civil aerospace is any more important a source of employment than any other manufacturing sector, but there has been a broad political concern for job creation in 'expanding' technological sectors in the context of a shrinking national industrial base. Individual centres of civil development, such as Hatfield, have also been located in areas of marginal constituencies.

The other externalities can be briefly summarised. The importance of the links between civil and military development should not be overstated. There is a technical and industrial advantage to be derived from having both capabilities, but this is more likely to benefit the civil side than the military. The requirements of civil and military are different, and have tended to become more specialised over the last two

Table 6 Civil aircraft, engine parts – exports, imports and import saving, 1946–70, 1971 prices

(£m)	1946–52 (£m)	1953–5 (£m)	1956–60 (£m)	1961–5 (£m)	1966–70 (£m)	Total
Exports	117	79	345	381	776	1,700
Of which, exports of 'aided products'	62	62	268	283	564	1.240
Civil imports	44	39	116	139	282	620
Import saving (i.e. sales to home market)	93	57	234	324	269	977

Source   HC 347 (1971–2), p. 377.

Table 7 Employment in the aerospace industry, 1948–78.

Year	Number (thousands)	Year	Number (thousands)
1948	172	1964	267
1949	183	1965	259
1950	179	1966	249
1951	193	1967	254
1952	236	1968	250
1953	262	1969	246
1954	279	1970	235
1955	295	1971	219
1956	308	1972	208
1957	312	1973	202
1958	301	1974	210
1959	292	1975	211
1960	291	1976	206
1961	304	1977	199
1962	292	1978	198
1963	270		

Sources   1946–65, Cmnd 2853 (The Plowden Report);
1966–78, The Sorris Report, EEC 1971; SEC(76), EEC 1976; CSO Annual Abstract of Statistics, 1980.

decades. In some respects, to have a military capability does not require an elaborate and expensive civil sector, but an ambitious civil programme would be difficult without some military activity. The position is somewhat more complicated in the case of aero-engines than in airframes, but generally speaking, British civil aerospace has been regarded as a useful outgrowth of a defence industry retained for 'strategic' reasons. It has also been asserted that the technical and organisational demands of civil aerospace, like many advanced technologies have encouraged technical and commercial progress in other industries. The exact value of spin-off however, has been the subject of much controversy and the relationship between the innovatory capacity of one area and that of another has not been fully explained.[6] Clearly, those companies most likely to benefit are those already established as subcontractors to civil aerospace programmes. There is also, as we shall consider below, an opportunity cost involved in tying up a large proportion of Britain's skilled personnel and technically qualified manpower in any of the aerospace sectors. Within a collaborative context, the maintenance of a strong technical capability has also been seen as desirable if Britain was to remain an attractive partner in cooperative ventures, and a significant participant in collective decision-making. This may be so, but it does beg the question why Britain should have a civil capability in the first place. Although officially prestige as such has almost invariably been dismissed as having little significance in decision-making, certainly individual Ministers have often been quick to associate themselves with the launch of key projects, and to take pride in, as well as to derive political capital from technological achievements. The diplomatic potential of some projects has not been denied, and civil collaborative programmes have had a general or specific relevance to Britain's evolving European policies. Neither prestige nor diplomatic values, of course, can be quantified and in general much of the case for maintaining a civil aerospace sector has depended upon a subjective and disputable viewpoint that it represents a national technological asset with an intrinsic value to be weighed against individual commercial failures.

The question remains, therefore, whether all or most of these externalities could have been achieved equally well or more effectively had similar amounts of public money been spent elsewhere. More fundamentally, has civil aerospace fully justified the taxpayer's money allocated to it, and is it likely to do so in the future? In these respects, Government support for civil aerospace, along with other advanced technology, including military aviation, has not gone unchallenged. In 1965, the Plowden committee concluded that there was:

> no predestined place for an aircraft industry in Britain. The economic justification for the industry receiving more Government support than other industries must rest upon whether it provides particular benefits to the country. There are such benefits ... But the present degree of support is already higher than these benefits justify, and in future the value of these benefits seems likely to decrease.[7]

Hartley, for example, is highly sceptical of the value and utility of a state-supported aircraft industry, civil or military. In particular, the argument that Government should assist the development of civil programmes because private capital is deterred by the level of risk involved is to 'misunderstand the allocative role of the private capital market. If a project or enterprise is commercially sound, or the expectation of profits high enough, private capital will invest in high-risk activities.' Launch aid, however, contributes to a situation where the 'incentives and "checks" that the British system places on the efficiency with which resources are used are thus destroyed or weakened'. Even more bluntly, Hartley believes that launch aid involved the state in an area which would appear to be the obvious preserve of the private sector. The result, he argues, has been the 'creation of an environment which restricts consumer preferences and emphasises technological advance financed by the taxpayer'.[8]

As Hartley sees it, since past policy had failed to achieve satisfactory results, either commercial success in the case of civil projects, or the provision of cost-effective equipment for the Services, it would be better to cut the ties between state and industry, and to allow the latter to find its own salvation. His recommendation is that the Government should let the free market decide on the future of civil projects, while adopting an open competitive approach to military procurement. Industry would inevitably face a much reduced status and would have to seek commercially based partnerships with European or American companies. The change would force the industry to attend more closely to commercial realities, increase business efficiency, and relieve the taxpayer of an unnecessary and expensive burden.[9]

Gardner is another very critical of aid given since 1945 to civil aerospace. Although writing in a strictly private capacity, as a DoI economist, his views deserve to be given due weight. After reviewing the case for, and the practice of, providing launch aid between 1945 and 1972, Gardner concludes that the commercial return on public money has not been good enough to justify the expenditure. Moreover, in his judgement, 'the net effect of aerospace launch aid has been a loss of national welfare'.[10]

Gardner and Hartley have grave doubts about both the principle of the policy and its implementation. Both feel that the availability of public money simply reduced the risks of development to the point that companies were able safely to launch commercially marginal projects. The system, in Gardner's opinion, tended to persuade firms to 'undertake projects which would otherwise have been commercially unattractive even if they had offered no threat of insolvency'. In the early 1970s, the RB211 experience induced a more cautious attitude in both industry and Government. There were also changes to launch aid which increased the incentive for firms to behave more commercially. Nevertheless, Gardner implies that the continued provision of aid has insulated the civil sector from the market to an unhealthy extent. Even more damning, if the promotion of externalities was the primary objective of policy, launch aid has not been the best way of achieving it; 'launch aid is unlikely to have been the most effective way of pursuing goals which were not specific to the supported projects – simpler and more direct instruments were available to promote foreign exchange earnings, preserve employment or support an infant industry'.[11]

This, of course, is the heart of the matter. Unless a high value is assigned to externalities, the case for supporting civil aerospace may be difficult to sustain. Eades, for instance, is extremely dubious about claims that technological choices can, indeed ought, to be made on the basis of externalities. Although his main target was the American SST, his arguments are of interest here. Federal aid for the SST, he feels, would have been a dangerous precedent for the United States. The market was not convinced that civil supersonics were commercially viable, and that the search for wide economic benefits in such an enterprise was a doubtful exercise. In this case, the externalities were suspiciously imprecise in value, and largely immune to objective analysis. They were, however, always available to balance commercial scepticism and, as Eades puts it, in this and other cases, 'if care is not taken, externalities will be discovered primarily where it is politically advantageous to discover them'. The market for civil aircraft was usually able to identify viable projects. On the other hand, there were many cases in the civil aerospace market where projects had been produced as a result of Government aid given on the grounds of market imperfections, and in which the 'pessimistic judgement of the market' had been fully vindicated. 'Indeed', he concludes, 'the entire post-war British experience can be viewed in this light.'[12]

On a broader front, a number of studies of the macroeconomic effects of the extensive commitments to aerospace and similar technologies have tended to be highly critical of such investment. Since the war, this has amounted to a large proportion of all R&D expenditure, and the claim is that the country has not received an adequate return on its investment in terms of economic growth. It is also suggested that other, potentially more productive industries have been starved of resources and aid.[13] Pavitt is particularly scathing. In his view, there is no reason to believe that 'a reduced Government commitment in these high technologies will harm Britain's long-term economic performance, or the strength of its industrial technology'. The opportunity cost of Britain's past investment in high technology has been considerable and 'more attention and resources should have been devoted to improving industry's performance in other innovation-intensive sectors of the economy, which have been the basis of most of our competitors' growing industrial strength over the past twenty years'.[14] These arguments have, in turn, been questioned by apologists for the aircraft industry. In their view, the critics have underestimated the value of aerospace to the balance of payments, and the spin-off effects of investment in this type of advanced technology.[15]

Nevertheless, a significant body of opinion believes that the United Kingdom has not received value for money from Government investment in aerospace and nuclear engineering, by a long way the two most important areas of publicly financed technology.

As a jaundiced guardian of public expenditure, the British Treasury has rarely been impressed by the non-commercial factors used to justify expenditure on civil aerospace. Officials have consistently queried projects and policies which have not shown, or in their opinion, were unlikely to show a profit. Put bluntly, the Treasury feels that there are no good reasons for having a civil aircraft industry which does not make money. Institutionally inclined towards a conservative approach to public expenditure, it has been less enthusiastic than spending departments about even the balance-of-payments benefits of civil aerospace. Officials certainly disliked the 'buy British' policy, and have long championed commercial autonomy for the air corporations.

It is also evident that many in the Treasury have accepted the macroeconomic criticism that money spent in this area has had a counter-productive effect on the economy as a whole. In February 1979, a Treasury memorandum from the Permanent Secretary, Sir Douglas Wass, to his opposite number at the DoI was 'leaked' to the *Guardian* newspaper. In it, Wass criticised a number of Government-financed industrial programmes, and especially the decisions to launch the RB211-535 and the BAe 146, and to join Airbus Industrie. They were, he said, likely to prove heavy loss-makers and designed simply to protect jobs. Wass concluded, either we must accept the unsatisfactory macroeconomic performance that goes with the acceptance of the projects quoted; or we must try to find the means of influencing the decision-making process so as to ensure a higher rejection rate in the future'.[16]

The 'Wass Report' was roundly criticised by industry and, later, by members of the Government. Indeed, in retrospect, one ex-Minister called it 'industrially illiterate'. The thrust of the counter-argument was that the Treasury had always taken a short-term view of a very long-term industry, where commercial returns are spread over decades. In 1979, one can look forward to the end of the century, and see the possibility of substantial profits on all of the projects criticised by Wass. The Treasury can, of course, point to similar opportunities in the past which in the event failed to materialise. This is the crux of the matter, for clearly, any criticism of expenditure in civil aerospace would be confounded by a commercial breakthrough over the next decade or so. However, to stand any chance of achieving one, the British Government must continue to invest in civil development. Because so few projects have reached a plateau of revenue-earning from spares and replacement orders, the United Kingdom must face these heavy initial costs without the benefit of a foundation of commercial success. This is the legacy of failure which the current generation of projects has still to overcome, and, in many senses, has to live down.

In spite of this record, there has been a fairly widespread political consensus about the desirability of supporting civil programmes. Some projects, especially in the early years of a new administration, have been stopped, or have faced cancellation. However, irrespective of their ideology, politicians have usually discovered and often actively embraced civil aerospace. They seem to find it hard to resist the continuing demands for more public assistance. One interesting exception is Edmund Dell, who as Secretary of State for Trade, and as a Chairman of the PAC, has seen this issue from both sides of the accountability fence. Dell believes that Government has pursued a chimera in sinking money into a limited number of high-technology industries. The whole pattern of post-war industrial policy, he suggests, has been distorted by the unparalleled and largely mistaken commitments made to aerospace and nuclear engineering.[17]

There have been even more cynical descriptions of politicians' motives for supporting technology. Lord Beeching, for instance, said that Government had wasted an 'enormous amount of money on things justified by the pursuit of advanced technology – an almost childlike desire to play with toys'.[18] Or, as Jewkes remarks, British Governments have readily 'fallen victim to what might be called the hocus pocus of discussion on technology'. The upshot, he continues, is that we find 'major decisions being made by statesmen because they feel in their bones, or if you will pardon the vulgarity, they have a 'gut feeling' that this or that course is correct'.[19] The only surprising thing, perhaps, is that politicians still cling to the need to present their actions as being commercially sensible. For this, Beeching has one possible answer: 'there are many things which the Government may consider to be desirable, for a variety of reasons, which are not commercially viable, so as to make the decision to proceed easy'.[20]

Inevitably, the problem for the decision-maker and analyst alike is to evaluate often questionable data. Henderson's cost-benefit analysis of the Concorde suggests that we should be careful of attributing high values to non-commercial factors in civil aerospace decisions. Admittedly, Concorde has lacked few of the balance-of-payments advantages associated with conventional projects. Nevertheless, Henderson's calculations show that many other externalities do not stand up to strict examination.[21] However, cost-benefit analysis, even when as cautiously presented as Henderson's, is more of an art than a science. The qualitative aspects of technology, the subtle effects of innovation and its consequences for the economy as a whole, are impossible to assess accurately. Henderson argues that the final test of a commercial project is its sales record. But invariably there are powerful voices urging the significance of other values, and short of a radically new and better approach to cost-benefit analysis, it will remain a highly subjective technique.

In the last analysis, the justification for supporting civil aerospace, depends upon Government accepting and believing in the valuation put on the benefits to the economy of any advanced technology, and the short-term social costs of allowing roughly a third of the aircraft industry to collapse. There is, in fact, a strong perception that aerospace, civil and military, is the kind of industry that the United Kingdom must have in order to survive as a manufacturing nation. For whatever reasons, traditional industries and low-technology sectors are in decline, and threatened by low-cost producers in the near- and newly industrialised states. In these circumstances, high technology appears to be the only route for economic growth in the future.

The Commission of the EEC evidently accepts this argument on behalf of western Europe as a whole: 'It [the aerospace industry] is one of the chief representatives of a type of employment – highly skilled, commanding sophisticated technologies and a high level of investment – toward which the Community must necessarily move in the future as the industrialisation of the Third World proceeds and a wider division of labour unfolds.'[22] As other industrialised states, economically more successful than Britain, Japan for example, appear to be set on acquiring such a capability, it would seem to be an act of egregious folly to abandon hard-won expertise and experience in a high-entry-cost technology like civil aerospace. It may well be that the newcomers, and here we should include West Germany, will only discover the heartbreak of civil aerospace. Nevertheless, it would take a very courageous decision on the part of a Government to opt out of civil aerospace. Conventional wisdom, supported by other constraints, suggests that for the moment the weight of circumstantial evidence will justify further expenditure in civil aerospace.

In any event, the persistent application of externalities in the rationalisation of public money spent on the advanced technologies may be easier to decry than to prevent. Sir Alan Cottrell, who as an ex-Scientific Adviser to Government has some experience of such matters, believes that it is only natural for politicians to give the greatest weight to 'political and social factors with which they are most familiar'.[23] Henderson too, it will be recalled, said as much about the Conservative Government's approach to the SST in the early 1960s. Cottrell, however, is more sweeping in his final observation: 'Robert Oppenheimer once said that if a project is "technologically sweet" it is irresistible; but in practice the converse is often true – if a project is politically or socially sweet, then it is strongly favoured to go forward even if it may be unsound technology.'[24]

There is no unequivocal, quantifiable case for maintaining a comprehensive civil aerospace capability in Britain. Governments, however, have rarely been compelled or have chosen to consider the matter synoptically. Still rarer has been any attempt to place civil aerospace in the context of a national strategy for technology. The pattern of policy has been incremental and sectoral. According to one senior official, this is the only way it can be done. 'It is only by looking at specific projects that one can see whether one can make a balanced judgement in terms of resources.' There is some awareness of opportunity costs, as well as the demand on resources implied by a project decision over a decade or so; but such concerns are generally confined to the aircraft industry independently of industry as a whole.[25] For better or for worse, British civil aerospace policy is the cumulative effect of successive project choices. As launch costs have grown, the development of one aircraft or engine was more likely to be affected, technically, commercially or politically than another. This has created dilemmas for Governments, conscious if only in a general sense, of a limit to public money available for civil aerospace. Individual projects have been rejected or discarded, but no Government appears to have seriously considered abandoning the principle of supporting civil aerospace.

A continuous sequence of British Governments since 1945 have accepted, sometimes reluctantly, the arguments for having a civil aerospace industry and for providing some form of aid. The rationale for assisting civil development, either directly or indirectly, has remained virtually unchanged since the post-war recovery programme. The only substantially new element has been the collaborative dimension, and this has usually reinforced rather than undermined the strength of political commitment to civil projects. Under the circumstances, one might legitimately wonder just how much freedom of choice has actually been available, or has been perceived to be available. In his analysis of British nuclear power decisions, Williams notes how Ministers found it 'difficult' to free themselves of the 'constraints in the situation they inherited'. Once a number of crucial decisions had been made, a 'clockwork' was wound up which 'thereafter remorselessly unwound'.[26] There is a danger of over-simplifying complex issues by ascribing the whole problem of controlling advanced technology, to the power of 'technological determinism'. However, in many technologies the complex of institutional, technical and personal commitments to a particular line of technological development in time amounted to a virtually irresistible force. In civil aerospace, Ministers coming to the area freshly elected or appointed did find a number of options either foreclosed or limited by past events and existing commitments.

The Concorde is a fine example of how Governments can become 'locked in' to a long-term programme, and lose most of their freedom to manoeuvre and their ability to command events. Over the years, successive Governments found it increasingly difficult to break the apparent stranglehold of political, industrial and technological factors which always seemed to defend the Concorde against cancellation. One might suggest the same of the RB211, although here we are also dealing with a particularly important company as much as a single project. Nevertheless, try as Government might to place, as one civil servant put it, 'a ring fence' around expenditure devoted to the engine and its derivatives, consequential funding always seemed to be required. It is apparently hard to challenge the argument that such expenditure is necessary to capitalise upon prior development. This may border on a case of throwing good money after bad, but once the really big money has been allocated, many of the subsequent claims may be only relatively small additions to the total cost of development. Once Governments become heavily involved in such serial development, it is again very difficult to abandon prematurely what is presented as a promising and potentially lucrative line of research. It is even harder to abandon entirely what is perceived to be a vital asset, in which important employment and technological interests are felt to be at stake.

The international dimension exacerbates this problem. Although formal collaborative commitments are particularly significant, involving as they do inter-Governmental negotiations and agreement, publicly supported commercial contracts also exert implicit constraints on Governmental choice. The most notorious example of the former case is Concorde. One of the crucial elements in the 'locking in' process was the 1962 Treaty. Without a formal break clause, once the Labour Government failed to call the French bluff, it always seemed as though there was no real alternative but to see the project to a conclusion. As long as the French wanted to continue, the British seemed compelled to follow. When both might have been tempted to curtail development, other considerations stayed execution. The international ramifications of the Rolls bankruptcy also influenced Government actions regarding the RB211. Although the initial contract with Lockheed was repudiated, the interdependence of engine and aircraft development invoked similarly interdependent obligations for the British and American Governments. Again other factors were involved, but the British Government was very aware of the damage to Anglo-American relations outright cancellation would cause.

In general, the move towards international collaboration in aerospace during the 1960s and 1970s, brought a set of constraints on policy-making which affected civil development. These were again hardly deterministic, but under certain circumstances, they could condition Ministerial attitudes to projects. The hesitations over the BAC 3-11 were caused partly by the harmful affects its launch would have on Britain's European partners in existing programmes and in future collaborative proposals. International agreements can, and since Concorde invariably do, contain break or review points. However, the existence or not, of a formal break point does not necessarily make it easy for the Government to abandon its partners. Broader diplomatic considerations, implications for one's future reputation in other projects, as well as the need to protect past investment, can conspire to reduce a Government's freedom of choice.

Now that Britain is a full member of the Airbus consortium, the Government will face a series of pressures from both its own airframe industry and its European partners, to invest in further developments of the Airbus family. For example, the industrial launch of the 150-seat A320 has already pre-empted to some extent political decisions. Although the Thatcher administration would like to see BAe raise the necessary capital privately, a failure to join, or decisions limiting BAe's participation, may incur diplomatic costs, or more likely trigger unilateral actions which would seriously reduce BAe's position and status in the consortium.

Decision-making in an area like civil aerospace is also undertaken in an environment characterised by a high-level of technical and market uncertainty. The rate of change of both factors creates conditions and pressures which are simply outside the unilateral control of either Government or industry. This is especially so of middle-range states such as the United Kingdom, where the pace and direction of change is to a large extent set by others, particularly by American manufacturers and airlines. Occasionally, British firms have been able to secure a technological or market lead, but unfortunately, they have rarely been able to capitalise on and to reinforce their advantage. In the 1950s, the eclipse of the turbo-prop and the tragedy of the Comet were both examples of this problem. The failure of the medium- and long-range turbo-prop was partly due to unforeseen technical difficulties, but it was also due to the unexpected popularity of jets, even on routes for which they were not economically suited. More recently, the 1973 energy crisis threw both the airline market and the civil airliner and engine manufacturers into a period of frantic turmoil, and delayed the introduction of a new generation of aircraft. Paradoxically, this delay was probably beneficial for British civil aerospace as it to some extent mitigated a period of domestic political and industrial upheaval. Such dramatic changes in the context of development are however, rarely so benign or so convenient.

This problem is not confined to Britain or to civil aerospace. In his study of the French Government's attempts to promote an independent electronics industry, Zysman shows how the state, 'accustomed to imposing its will on the market place, has been unable to alter the structure of international industry or to isolate French firms from its pressure'.[27] The British aircraft industry has been all too aware of the effects of uncertainty. All aerospace projects are affected by it. However, it tends to be felt more acutely in the civil sector, where time and performance cannot easily be traded off against cost – a fact which Rolls discovered in the late 1960s. When problems do occur, British firms, and by implication, British Governments, have less room to manoeuvre. There are other constraints closer to home. Particular attention has been directed at the existence and influence of distinct and identifiable 'technological lobbies'. The presence of highly motivated individuals and well-placed groups within the bureaucracy committed to important programmes and design concepts has been noted in studies of British nuclear power decisions.[28] Others have argued that this is a characteristic of most of the well-established areas of publicly supported technology.[29] Undoubtedly, such a constellation of Government experts and officials, as well as industrialists with a stake in development, was associated with the Concorde. Other examples in the civil aerospace sector are harder to prove. There have also been conflicting and contradictory elements amongst those who might be called the civil aerospace lobby. There have been differences of opinion over particular projects, and between those officials responsible for 'sponsorship' and those employed to monitor civil programmes. Above all, the bifurcation of engine and airframe interests (not to mention the plaintive cries of neglect from the avionic and equipment sectors), the conflicts between Whitehall, individual companies and the nationalised airlines, and the existence of competing firms, has ensured that the lobby has contained a degree of pluralism. What is perhaps easier to demonstrate is the presence of an institutional bias towards civil aerospace in general, which, by having long-standing organisational and personal links between Government and industry, presents a strong case to Ministers.

The presence of a solid group of officials and Research Establishment scientists devoted to the promotion and administration of aerospace policy ensures that the civil sector has a sympathetic hearing inside Government. In fulfilling their 'promotional' obligations, officials are bound to be sensitive to the need to protect industry's 'seed corn', a comprehensive design, production and marketing facility – for once dispersed, its resurrection may be impossible and, unquestionably, very expensive. This was particularly so in the lean years between 1960 and the mid-1970s. The failure of the Comet, VC10 and Trident types had left the industry without profitable designs to carry them through into the next, and still more expensive generation of aircraft and engines. Admittedly, Rolls-Royce was in a sounder position, coming through the 1950s with a series of profitable engine programmes. However, Rolls and the two new airframe groups, BAC and HSA, were all motivated in the 1960s to protect and to advance their civil design capabilities and then fought hard to get Government backing for civil projects. Although in specific cases, companies would be more or less successful in convincing officials of the strength of their cause, the general principle of maintaining a capability was accepted as a legitimate criterion in decision-making. In this respect, civil aerospace has been more fortunate than some other technologies which have lacked comparable official patronage.[30]

The existence of these technological, international, environmental and institutional constraints does not entirely remove the possibility of choice. It certainly does not preclude tension and conflict between the Governmental or political interest, and the industrial or technical. For the manufacturer, whether publicly or privately owned, the actions of Ministers and Governments are major elements of 'external uncertainty' in technological development, where the market and rate of technological change already provide considerable risks and uncertainties.[31] Sir Arnold Hall conceded that this might be inevitable but it still made poor engineering sense.[32]

Projects are subject to the vicissitudes of changing political priorities. In civil aerospace as in other areas of British technology, there is a line of cancelled projects and discontinuities in development to gainsay an obvious technological or institutional determinism. The need for consistent political support in civil aerospace was reconised in the Elstub Report. As Government and industry were in partnership in 'one of the most competitive markets, there is a fundamental need for an overall policy if their combined efforts are to achieve the best results'.[33] Elstub was looking back over the 1950s and early 1960s, certainly a period of great uncertainty in Government policy towards all aspects of aerospace. However, the *ad hoc* priorities of later years showed that Elstub's strictures had a continuing relevance.

On balance, the instability which Elstub criticised, and the political uncertainties perceived by industrialists in the 1960s, seem to have diminished, while the constraints imposed on Government by domestic and international commitments have grown. Hard-nosed attitudes to public spending may help to instil some credibility in threats to hold the line on the increasing cost of civil aerospace. Such a policy may make the companies concerned 'think twice before doing too much', but as officials readily concede, if things were to go wrong, Government would still find it difficult to deny help and further assistance. The partnership between state and industry in the promotion of civil aerospace, not without its ups and downs, has the weight and momentum of past commitments, traditions and expectations. Governments, irrespective of ideological shading, have accepted, or have come to accept, the reality of this partnership.

The experience of British civil aerospace also points to a broader phenomenon. Where the state and an industry have been so closely associated for so long, almost inevitably their interests and obligations will begin to converge. While both the British aircraft industry and its Governmental sponsors have sought commercial return from their efforts in civil aerospace, both are also united in perceiving an intrinsic value in its promotion. This does not mean that there are no disagreements, but that there is a general movement towards complementary and symbiotic behaviour. This interfusion of political and corporate activity has occurred in many high technologies and, with variations from country to country, it has happened in most western industrialised states. This has been described by Abraham as a situation where 'essentially corporate objectives are pursued through machinery mainly designed for the political system, and where political aims are exercised through business organisations'.[34] According to Bruce Smith, the interpenetration of public and private sectors has become so great that the distinction, ideologically often so important, is no longer an 'operational way of understanding reality'.[35] This has been variously defined in terms of the 'New Political Economy', the 'New Public Sector', or the 'Contract State'.[36] The basic thesis is the same; modern societies have evolved close, functionally indistinct partnerships between the state and powerful economic units, where ownership is irrelevant to their working relationships and the distribution of decision-making power. In this context, the crucial problem relates to the provision of public accountability and the degree to which Government can and should be responsible for the outcome of publicly financed programmes undertaken by industrial actors.

The most crucial aspect of this relationship has been the extent to which Government should become involved in the technical and commercial decision-making associated with specific projects. This has been summarised in terms of a dilemma between the need for official participation and monitoring, and the desirability of allowing the executive agent autonomy to fulfil his specialised functions efficiently and effectively. In the case of British civil aerospace for most of the post-war period, certainly once the recovery programme with its much criticised centralised monitoring and control procedures had ended, officials have been reluctant to 'second guess' the technical and commercial judgements of industry once a programme has been authorised. Even in the prior appraisal of proposals put to Government for launch aid, at least until the Rolls case, officials tended to defer to the expertise of manufacturers. Their task was primarily to counter any obvious over-optimism on the part of the contractor, and to spot any general weakness in the technical and commercial case for a particular project. Towards the end of the 1960s, and certainly after the Rolls affair, there was a much more detailed and a wider examination of projects. Similarly, for the very large programme, or where the responsible department suspected the quality of industrial management, there was a tighter and more comprehensive monitoring of development. Yet even then, officials were conscious of the limitations of their own expertise, and of the dangers of removing responsibility from the executive agent. The problem, of course, has been in finding the correct, or most effective and efficient, balance between control and autonomy.

In the 1950s, the private venture policy inevitably reduced the role played by officials in monitoring development. However, the absence of some form of official responsibility during this period might have contributed to the misjudgements associated with the specifications of crucial projects. For example, the MoS had reservations about the Trident, but under the terms of reference then governing civil development, there was little it could do to affect the course of events. A consultative body such as TARC was hardly better placed, especially when it lacked credibility with either the airlines or the industry, and any growth in its functions was regarded with some suspicion and hostility by officials.

Similarly, the actions of Ministers throughout this period in applying indirect pressure on the airlines also raised delicate questions of accountability; especially as the airlines were consistently told both that they should act in a fully commercial fashion and that they would have the freedom so to do. In practice, this was all too often more honoured in the breach than in the observance. The experience of supporting British civil aerospace through intervention in the public sector market reflects that of other publicly financed technologies. There have been comparable problems in the nuclear, telecommunications and computer industries, as well as in some 'lower' technological sectors. Successive Governments have vacillated over the degree to which the nationalised industries should support British technology, at what costs, and over who should bear the responsibility for the decision and any unfortunate consequences. A strong lobby, usually led *sotto voce* by the Treasury, has pressed for commercially orientated procurement policies. The experience of civil aerospace illustrates the dangers of trying to have it both ways. Few involved in the wrangles over directed or influenced purchases, compensation and the aftermath of unfortunate decisions, would regard the experience as anything less than unedifying, and at worst damaging to all parties.

The procedures established in 1960 were undoubtedly an attempt to get the best of all possible worlds. The responsible Ministry was an effective participant in the decision-making process, but the primary source of monitoring and control would be provided by the 'natural' self-discipline of commercially realistic private enterprise. The problem with this approach was that it did not guarantee that companies would be 'realistic', nor did it make allowance for Government's own willingness to by-pass its provisions. In the worst case, that of Rolls and the RB211, the relationship was fatally ambiguous. The company overestimated, or were encouraged to overestimate, the strength of Government's commitment. The Government lacked sufficient knowledge of Rolls' true state to anticipate major problems, or to take avoiding action before the crash came. By the 1970s, launch aid as conceived in 1960, was recognised as being suitable only for modestly sized programmes. It certainly lost its value as a self-monitoring device, as the relationship between

Government and contractor became much closer.

The experience of Concorde, treated from the outset as a military project with full monitoring procedures, was no better. The sheer size of the programme, the number of technical unknowns it contained, and the convolutions of its trans-national management system, put it beyond any conventional problem of control and monitoring. It was certainly unsuitable for the application of normal launch aid procedures. It was hoped that the companies involved would accept some degree of risk-sharing, but as we have seen, this proved impossible to achieve. Incentive contracting was resisted and the system eventually employed hardly put the main contractors at risk. Over the years, BAC and Rolls did commit personnel and plant to the project; in that sense corporate assets did become tied to Concorde. It was, however, the programme which created the commitment and not the other way round, and technically, most contractors gained much from contributing to the project.

Public ownership was seen by some as a possible answer to the dilemma. According to this thesis, the stumbling block had previously been the fact of public money being allocated to private sector contractors. Once public money was entirely devoted to a public sector industry, there would be less need for close monitoring. In the case of British Aerospace, the validity of this argument has yet to be proven one way or the other. Indeed, the 'privatisation' of BAe has only served to cloud the issue still further. While wholly owned by the state, the impression was that BAe was conscious of a looser relationship with Government. However, there has been little actual experience of civil projects developed under this regime. Moreover, there has yet to be any major crisis which might put a 'hands off' relationship under stress.

The history of Rolls-Royce in the 1960s and 1970s, under both private and public ownership, suggests that the problem of control and autonomy is an issue which transcends ownership. An effective balance between Government and company over the exchange of information, and the rights and obligations of each in key managerial decisions, has yet to be worked out to the complete satisfaction of either party. Scale and complexity are the crucial variables, not the fact of ownership. Large sums of public money and the technical and commercial uncertainties associated with high technology make it difficult for Government and industry to avoid getting in each other's way, or to view decisions from different perspectives.

For instance, according to Sir Arthur Knight, one-time Chairman of the NEB and, up to 1978, a non-Executive Director of Rolls-Royce, monitoring decisions before they are taken is 'unlikely to improve the decision-making process'. On the other hand, the monitoring of individual decisions after they have been taken is of 'limited value'. In Sir Arthur's opinion, managers of the required ability to handle programmes of great complexity are 'frustrated by the diversion of effort which monitoring involves and will be increasingly deterred from accepting responsibility where monitoring becomes excessive in their view'.[37] But clearly, Governments are vulnerable to the misjudgement of autonomous managers. At the very least, Ministers expect notice of any sudden and disastrous programme failure. More important, the natural enthusiasm and commitment of the engineer and industrialist, all too often as much a source of weakness as a positive quality in technological development, needs some external restraint and monitoring when the ultimate cost of a bad decision is borne not by the company or private risk capital but by the taxpayer.

Officials associated with civil aerospace have unquestionably acquired greater competence and technical expertise in evaluating the technical and commercial prospects of new projects, as well as in understanding the complexities of developmental management. This improvement has been due to better technique and the sheer professionalism of civil servants who have spent their careers associated with aerospace and related technologies. It is also the result of often painful lessons delivered by a number of expensive failures. There is still a limit, however, to just how much we can and should expect of Government in carrying any responsibility for technical and commercial decisions once a project has received its official sanction. In practice, one senses a degree of fatalism in some official and political circles about a system which, no matter how much one tinkers with it in detail, cannot respond adequately to the problems of controlling large-scale and very expensive technology. Back in 1967, the then Conservative spokesman on aviation matters, Edward Carr, argued that no post-war Government had been able to get to grips with these problems. The issues were 'rooted in the inappropriateness of the Whitehall system itself, a system which was developed in the far-off days for entirely different purposes and conditions when the problems of Government participation in the selection and control of advanced technological projects were not so much as dreamed of'.[38] Even if this may be a rather extreme view, it is not very comforting to feel that Government is still more aware of its dilemma than nearer a solution.

Under these conditions, the provision of an adequate level of public accountability becomes quite crucial, yet it has tended to be one of the first casualties of technology policy. This is, of course, part of a wider problem afflicting modern Government. In his classic study of public accountability, Normanton argues that the steady accretion of institutional power, the extension of Government into wider areas of social and economic activity, and the expansion of public expenditure generally, have gone 'wholly beyond the traditional limits of accountability'. 'Big Government' requires a more balanced and comprehensive approach to accountability and control, one which must look beyond matters of simple financial regularity to the 'consequences of planning decisions'. He too feels that nationalisation alone does not necessarily improve things. Although public ownership is often justified because (as in the case of aerospace) it would seem to bring 'powerful economic forces within the scope of public accountability . . . the mere act of nationalisation does not make an enterprise accountable'.[39] However, these problems are exacerbated by the scale and complexity of advanced technology.

There are certainly limits to the scope and role of Parliament in fulfilling its public-accountability functions. As in many other areas of technological decision-making Parliament has not been a particularly effective monitor and guardian of public expenditure. Its Select and Public Accounts Committees have periodically, but spasmodically, investigated civil projects. The PAC has been especially concerned with the cost-escalation and programme-control of Concorde. Since the bankruptcy and nationalisation of Rolls-Royce, it too attracted considerable attention from the PAC. We have already discussed the specific inadequacies of Parliamentary scrutiny in regard to Concorde, where there was a real problem in gaining access to official information. Similarly, although a more complete picture of Rolls' operations and problems emerged from the PAC's reports in the 1970s, the time for Parliament to have asked pointed questions was before 1971. However, Whitehall is institutionally disinclined to proffer timely and relevant information. It is still more difficult for Parliament to get to grips with the assumptions on which policy is based, and to trace the interplay of official and quasi-official advice to Ministers. While attitudes are slowly changing, there is still a deep suspicion of full and regular disclosure on a routine and unprompted basis. Without proper access, Parliament inevitably faces a major structural impediment to its examination of civil aerospace programmes or policy.

Of course, Whitehall's defences, formidable though they may be, are not the only reasons for the weakness of Parliamentary accountability. The tendency for Parliamentary Committees to focus on individual projects is itself a limitation. Since the war there have been only a small number of general investigations of civil aerospace policy. The Estimates Committee looked at transport aircraft policy in the early 1960s, the PAC investigated launch aid in the early 1970s, and in 1972 as part of its wide-ranging survey of public money in the private sector, the Expenditure Committee considered various aspects of civil aerospace. Finally, the Select Committee on the Nationalised Industries, in its various reports on the air corporations, has made reference to civil aircraft manufacturing. The latter certainly revealed much of interest about the relationship between the airlines, manufacturers and Government, but of course its primary interest has always been the efficiency or otherwise of airline operations. However, it is worth comparing the more complete and forthright account of the policy issues which appears in the Select Committee's report on BOAC, presented in the aftermath of the airline's

1962 financial crisis, with the more guarded review of the same events in the slightly earlier Estimates Committee study on transport aircraft. Indeed, by examining the various reports on civil aerospace and aviation between 1958 and 1967, it is possible to see just how much officials could conceal, or rather fail to reveal, about current policy.

The real need is both to deepen Parliament's coverage of specific programmes and to broaden its examination of Government strategy towards public sponsored technology as a whole. This should be done on a regular basis, as much to anticipate future as to analyse existing problems. The new functional committees are a step in the right direction. The Industry Committee's first adventures into civil aerospace cover familiar ground, with two reports on Concorde and one on Rolls-Royce.[40] In its conclusions about Concorde, however, the sense of *deja vu* is striking. The Committee noted, *inter alia*, that the United Kingdom was still paying more than its fair share of support costs, that the ultimate cost of the programme was still unknown, that Departmental forecasts appeared to be over-optimistic, and that the project had 'acquired a life of its own and was out of control'.[41] The fact that so little had changed does not say very much for the past efforts to bring Concorde within the scope of effective accountability. The Government's rather dismissive response to these latest reports suggests that little might change in the future.

The Committee's Report on Rolls-Royce was more low key. It noted with satisfaction that although Rolls faced a number of difficulties in the short term, it had learnt the lessons of the 1970s.[42] The most significant part of this Report was in the Committee's recommendations about the role of Parliament in the future control of civil and military technology. It took note of the 'uneasiness which the House sometimes feels about the control of major projects' and suggested that Parliament should consider 'whether parliamentary approval should be specifically sought at the outset for individual projects for which substantial sums of public money will be required, perhaps spread over many years to come'.[43] If this were to occur, it would represent a marked, even a radical advance in the provision of public accountability. It is, however, difficult to conceive of Whitehall rushing to concede such a role to Parliament.

In any event, Parliament would require a massive improvement in its capacity to research and evaluate projects. Changes of this sort would also have to be linked with reforms in the status and compass of the Comptroller and Auditor General's Office. Moreover, as many of the questions of accountability in long term projects stem from incremental decisions and consequential expenditure, Parliament would still have to improve its ability to monitor programmes once they had been authorised, and it would also have to come to terms with the international dimension of many projects. Its response to general EEC legislation and policy has been reasonably satisfactory, but to secure accountability over transnational programmes, even in Europe, will be more difficult. Indeed, now that collaboration outside Europe is becoming as important as cooperation within the Community Parliament will face even more complex problems of accountability. These are not insurmountable but their solutions will require a consistent and persistent commitment to Parliamentary reform, and a constant willingness to confront Government on the central right of Parliament to be informed about, and involved in the policy process.

There can be little doubt that there is a need for a more open and wider scrutiny of civil aerospace and other technological decisions. Choices are rarely based upon wholly objective values, and a narrow, perhaps self-serving range of judgements is less likely to prove an accurate guide to action than one open to broader and more independent assessment. There is, of course, no monopoly of error; an independent viewpoint is not bound to be sound just because it is independent. However, the experience of civil aerospace suggests that a closed policy system is not conducive to good decision-making. There must be some opportunity to test policy assumptions, to query the range of the accepted uncertainty, and to point the gaps in analysis perhaps deliberately omitted for political or bureaucratic reasons.

An open and more accountable approach to policy-making might also help to resolve the dilemma of control and autonomy in the relationship between Government and industry. On balance, industry is best placed to take the greater responsibility for technical and commercial decisions. The preliminary assessment of projects requiring, directly or indirectly, public expenditure should still be a partnership between Government and industry, and a basic account of industrial efficiency in implementing decisions should still be rendered. But in general, the contractor should be given the benefit of autonomy, particularly as the time-scale for development will transcend the political lifetime of any one administration. The corollary is, however, that not only should that preliminary assessment be based upon the principles of broad accountability, but that any later review should be open to similar scrutiny and assessment. Accountability in this sense is not interference but an adjunct to managerial judgement which, justifiably, is bound to be devoted to the interests narrowly defined of an individual programme and one technology. We are not alone in advocating what essentially amounts to a change of attitude on the part of industry as much as of Government. As a journal usually sympathetic towards the aircraft industry, *Flight International* has long preached the need for industry to take a lead in these matters. Secrecy and ignorance of how and why public money is being spent on civil projects, can only harm the public's confidence in the industry and may in the end lead to demands for tighter and more restrictive controls.

We are left with what amounts to a plea for an attitudinal change because, ultimately, there is no simple institutional or procedural reform which will be entirely satisfactory without a substantial reorientation of political, official and industrial views about public accountability. A more open and comprehensive public scrutiny of technology policy should not, and must not, be regarded as a panacea – more accountability does not reduce technical complexity or limit the effects of external uncertainty – but it does allow the possibility of improving the range of options which might be considered by Government, and increases the scope of advice available to decision makers. As Williams observes, 'so long as it is considered enough to rely on the amateurs which Ministers and MPs – and in this type of case, officials too – must be, on journalistic investigation which, however good, is necessarily intermittent, and on academics and private individuals, then so long will policy continue to be essentially unaccountable, and because unaccountable, inadequate more often than it need be'.[40] Increasing public accountability, is not itself a complete answer. It may, however, provide a better approach and one more likely to succeed in improving the quality of technology policy-making than the application of simplistic, ideological nostrums.

After nearly four decades of this particular Government–industry partnership, it is difficult to avoid the view that British civil aerospace and the public financing of civil aircraft and engines is still on trial. Despite some real technological achievements, there are legitimate doubts about the value of civil aerospace to the United Kingdom. Admittedly, we are necessarily dealing with a large number of subjective factors, and there have surely been more wasteful areas of public expenditure. As ever, the crux of the matter is the question of future expectations. So often in the past, failure or only limited success has been covered by promises of a better return 'the next time'. The British civil aerospace industry is again poised to share in what could be a very large market for aircraft and engines. The need is, of course, to turn promises into confirmed orders, and to obtain a steady commercial return from investment in civil projects.

Rolls has survived its past crises to remain one of only three design and production centres for large civil engines. BAe, as a member of Airbus Industrie, and now that Lockheed has again left the civil arena, is also one of a limited number of airframe manufacturers likely to be building large airliners into the 1990s. Both companies will need large sums for developing the next generation of aircraft and engines. Airbus Industrie has launched, subject to Governmental approval, the 150 seat A320 and are considering other versions of the A300 and A310. Rolls has also been working on the RJ500 engine which is designed for use in European and American 150 seat airliners. The company is already collaborating with the Japanese, and has re-opened negotiations with Pratt and Whitney to join them on the RJ500. Rolls, and possibly BAe would hope to attract some private capital, but both will be dependent upon Government to provide, or to guarantee a large part of their financial requirements.

The consensus is that the 150 seat airliner and its engine will sell in large numbers, and both the A320 and the RJ500 are ahead of the likely competition. The short term outlook, however, is very bleak indeed. Owing to the world economic recession and the chaotic state of the airline industry, the demand for new civil aircraft is currently at its lowest since the war. Airlines have rapidly reduced their fleets of older types, and have sought to cut their orders for newer designs just coming into production. Rolls has been particularly hard hit by Lockheed's cancellation of the L1011, a decision brought on by the slump in demand for airliners. As a result, Rolls expect to lose between £250 and £300 million of turnover in the 1980s, equal to between £50 and £70 million off profits.[45] British Airways would also like to limit or to delay its initial purchase of Rolls engined Boeing 757s, and there are some fears that Boeing would like to curtail 757 production. Clearly, any threat to the 757 would have serious consequences for Rolls. Although the expectation is of an inevitable and substantial upturn as traffic recovers and airlines have to buy quieter and fuel efficient equipment, its timing is very uncertain. In the meantime, manufacturers must support current production and finance new development, a nerve-racking and expensive business with demand so slack.

The British Government, then, faces another set of important decisions affecting civil aerospace. They are perhaps not as vital as those taken in 1978, when BAe was officially confirmed as a 'European' manufacturer, but they will certainly have long-term consequences for both sectors of the aircraft industry. From the industry's perspective, the best outcome would be a firm commitment to both the RJ500 and the A320, with the former established as a launch engine on the European airframe. The French Government has no doubts about the significance of the A320 and its associated engine, having already agreed to finance Aerospatiale and SNECMA. The French are determined to hold and to expand their place as a leading aeronautical power. The British Government, preoccupied with limiting public spending, has yet to commit itself.

It could be tempting to support the RJ500, but not BAe's share of the A320. Rolls' links with Japan, and probably Pratt and Whitney, presents a very attractive technical and commercial option. The RJ500 would not be limited to the A320, but would be targeted at any prospective 150-seat design. The Government might also contend that the French would not be able to resist pressure from customers specifying the Rolls engine for the A320. BAe would naturally contest these arguments. Although it has a large part of the A300 and A310 programmes, the A320 is needed to maintain its civil design and production capabilities into the next decade. Similarly, the French might try very hard to protect their interests, especially if BAe was not a main partner in the A320, and seek at all cost to maintain the dominance of Franco-American engines in Airbus

Industries output.

On balance, it would seem prudent to support both projects and continue to maintain a comprehensive civil aerospace capability. There is no direct interdependence between Rolls and BAe in civil technology. However, this could be a rare opportunity to take a clear lead in shaping the direction of European civil aerospace, and one which would benefit all sectors of the British aircraft industry. In this respect, the advantages to the British equipment and avionic industries should not be ignored. There is certainly merit in trying to attract private capital from those who might stand to benefit from British civil development, but it should not be the decisive factor in any decision. As ever, given the long term nature of the business, it must remain a matter of fine calculation to weigh the large cost of supporting all aspects of British civil aerospace against the uncertain expectations of commercial success and the value of unquantifiable externalities.

It is hard to challenge the constraints imposed by important technological and industrial commitments built up over the decades, and reinforced by institutional links between a Government and its major contractors. It is essential, however, that the British Government should be a critical partner, and to do this it must put some distance between itself and the technology it supports. Government must be vigilant against the over-optimism of technological enthusiasts, and to be aware of the dangers of over-commitment and unnecessary risks taken by its agents. Similarly, while it is difficult to avoid following well established patterns of technological investment, Government must also be conscious of the needs of other, newer technology-based industries. Officials and politicians must accept that rather than being a threat to their power and authority, public accountability in its widest sense will help them make the best use of scarce national resources, and will assist them in the struggle to win control over the momentum generated by any large-scale technology.

Notes

Abbreviations used in the Notes

AWST Aviation Week and Space Technology
HC   House of Commons (Papers)
HCD House of Commons Debates
HL   House of Lords (Papers)
HLD House of Lords Debates

Introduction

1 For perhaps the best technical and commercial analysis of the evolution of the modern airliner, see R. Millar and D. Sawyer, *The Technical Development of Modern Aviation*, London, 1968.
2 See G. Eades, 'US Government support for civilian technology: economic theory versus political practice', *Research Policy*, III, 1974, pp. 9–11.
3 Figures derived from Commission of the European Communities, *The Aeronautical and Space Industries of the Community Compared with those of the United Kingdom and United States*, 'Competition Industry' – 1971–4, Brussels 1971 (The SORRIS Report), I, pp. 59–61, 149 and 153. HC347 (1971–2), p. 376.
4 Ibid. See also *Flight*, 29 Oct. 1977; *AWST*, 13 March 1978, pp. 145–9.
5 See Chapter 5.
6 *Report of the Committee of Inquiry into the Aircraft Industry*, Cmnd 2538, London, 1965, para. 128.
7 A. Reed, *Britain's Aircraft Industry*, London, 1973, p. 1.
8 HCD 454, 27 July 1948, col. 1237.
9 Cmnd 2538, para. 469.
10 See Chapter 7.
11 See HC 347 (1971–2), paras 27–8, 47.
12 See HC34 (1956–7), paras 125–8. Cmnd 2538, Chapters 9 and 10, provides a broad summary of why the British industry has failed to reach an adequate level of profitability.
13 See N. K. A. Gardner, 'The economics of launch aid', in A. Whiting (ed.), *The Economics of Industrial Subsidies*, London, 1976.
14 *Flight*, 15 Jan. 1960, p. 66.
15 HC 347 (1971–2), Q. 1022.
16 L. R. Smith, 'Accountability and independence in the contract state', in L. R. Smith and D. C. Hague, *The Dilemma of Accountability in Modern Government*, London, 1971, p. 4.

17 HC 347 (1971–2), Q. 1060.
18 A. J. Pierre, *Nuclear Politics*, Oxford, 1972, p. 4.

1 Establishing the Partnership, 1945–59

1 For a history of British air policy between 1918 and 1939 see H. Montgomery Hyde, *British Air Policy Between the Wars, 1918–1939*, London, 1976, esp. ch. 9.
2 See Appendix I for a list of the Brabazon Types and see Appendix II for the 'interim designs'.
3 Cmnd 2538, para. 88, HC 34 (1956–7), paras 23–4.
4 The De Haviland Dove, for example, was a private venture.
5 HC 34 (1956–7), para. 15; Gardner, 'Economics of launch aid', p. 153.
6 See HCD 454, 27 July 1948, col. 1237.
7 HCD 424, 26 June 1946, col. 1428.
8 HCD 418, 24 Jan. 1946, cols 322–5, HCD 424, 26 June 1946, cols 1407–9.
9 HCD 447, 26 Feb. 1948, col. 2152–3.
10 E. Devons, 'The aircraft industry', in D. Burns (ed.), *The Structure of British Industry*, Cambridge, 1958, II, pp. 69–70.
11 See Sir George Edwards, *Aeronautical Journal*, April 1964, p. 138; Sir Peter Masefield, cited in Reed, *Britain: Aircraft Industry*, pp. 24–5.
12 P. Dempster, *The Tale of the Comet*, London, 1958, p. 65.
13 Millar and Sawyer, *Technical Development*, pp. 179–80.
14 There was, in fact, a proposal put before the United States Congress to authorise Federal money to finance the development of a comparable jet aircraft.
15 Reed, *Britain's Aircraft Industry*, pp. 17–19.
16 One of the most significant of these was the possibility of Bristol Aeroplanes building the Lockheed Constellation under licence.
17 Millar and Sawyer, *Technical Development*, ch. 6.
18 C. D. Bright, *The Jet Makers*, Kansas, 1978, pp. 87–8.
19 Cited in Dempster, *Tale of the Comet*, p. 94.
20 Ibid., pp. 100–99; Reed, *Britain's Aircraft Industry*, ch. 3.
21 HC 42 (1963–4), Qs 19 and 193; HC 240 (1963–4), Q. 1616.
22 HC 348 (1955–6), paras 54–6; Dempster, *Tale of the Comet*, pp. 188–96.
23 Millar and Sawyer, *Technical Development*, pp. 187–8.
24 Ibid., pp. 188–9.
25 J. B. Rae, *Climb to Greatness: The American Aircraft Industry 1920–1960*, Cambridge, Mass., (1968), ch. 10. Bright, *Jet Makers*, pp. 90–3. R. E. G. Davies, *A History of the World's Airlines*, Oxford, 1964, p. 480.
26 The Rolls-Royce Avon, and the first section of the Comet fuselage under licence from De Haviland.
27 For the debate about medium-range turbo-props and jets, see Lord Douglas of Kirtleside, *Journal of the Institute of Transport*, May 1957, and references in BEA Annual Report of 1957, Cmnd 251. See also HC673 (1966–7), Q. 322.
28 D. Wood, *Project Cancelled*, London, 1975, pp. 89–94. See also HC34 (1955–6), paras. 28–31.
29 Wood, *Project Cancelled*, pp. 94–7.

30 HCD 546, 28 Nov. 1955, cols 1921–4 and 1927; HCD 547, 8 Dec. 1955, cols 665–7 and 676–81.
31 HC 213 (1958–9), Q. 239.
32 HCD 558, 2 Nov. 1956, cols 1777–81.
33 HC 240 (1963–4), Qs 1545 and 1546.
34 HCD 558, 2 Nov. 1956, cols 1777–81.
35 HCD 560, 19 Nov. 1956, cols 1431–2.
36 HC 240 (1963–4), Q. 1589.
37 HC 240 (1963–4), para. 38; HC 213 (1958–9), Q. 820.
38 HC 42 (1963–4), Q. 431.
39 Sir Basil Smallpiece, later Managing Director of BOAC: HC 240 (1963–4), Q. 1200; see also BOAC Annual Report for 1962, Cmnd 255, p. 14.
40 Viscount Watkinson, *Blue Print for Survival*, London, 1976, p. 48.
41 HC 240 (1963–4), para. 40, Q. 1472.
42 Ibid., Q. 1547.
43 Ibid., para. 48.
44 Ibid., paras 50–2; *The Times*, 15 Jan. 1958.
45 HC 240 (1963–4), Q. 1548.
46 HC 42 (1963–4), Q. 1557.
47 Millar and Sawyer, *Technical Development*, pp. 194–5.
48 Both cited by Reed, *Britain's Aircraft Industry*, pp. 4 and 8.
49 Millar and Sawyer, *Technical Development*, p. 195.
50 HC 213 (1958–9), Q. 119.
51 Lord Hives of Rolls-Royce for instance. HC 34 (1955–6), paras 109–10. See also Devons, 'Aircraft industry', pp. 47–50.
52 The SBAC still thought the contrary; see HC 34 (1955–6), paras 109–10.
53 Ibid., para. 111.
54 HCD 567 (written answers), 25 Mar. 1957, cols 90–1.
55 See HC 34 (1955–6), para. 115; HCD 579, 9 Dec. 1957, cols 870–1.
56 For details of the TSR-2 programme and the Government's manipulation of the contract mechanism, see J. Simpson, F. Gregory and G. Williams: *Crisis in Procurement -- A Case Study of the TSR-2*, London, 1969.
57 HCD 581, 27 Jan. 1958, col. 45.
58 HC 213 (1958–9), Qs 199–200, 362 and 385; *The Times*, 28 Dec. 1957, 1, 4 and 17 Jan. 1958.
59 *The Times*, 1 Feb. 1958.
60 HC 42 (1963–4), Q. 367.
61 *Flight*, 17 Jan. 1958, p. 69; *The Times*, 9 Jan. 1958.
62 HC 42 (1963–4), Q. 365; HC 213 (1958–9), Q. 92; *The Times*, 31 Jan. 1958; HC 673 (1966–7), Qs 816, 694, 111 and 113.
63 HCD 588, 22 May 1958, col. 1531.
64 Ibid., col. 229.
65 Ibid., col. 1525.
66 Ibid., see also, chapter 2.
67 Ibid., col. 1531.
68 Ibid., col. 1523.
69 HC 213 (1957–8), Qs 5 and 22.
70 HC 42 (1963–4), Qs 1527, 1530.
71 BEA annual report for 1964, Cmnd 348, p. 12.

72 Cited in HC 240 (1963–4), Q. 1173.
73 HC 213 (1957–8), Qs 350, 432, 1760–2, 2364, 2722; Appendix 8, p. 311; HC 42 (1963–4), Q. 438; BOAC annual report for 1959, Cmnd 259, p. 2–3.
74 HC 213 (1957–8), para. 68.
75 Cmnd 2853, para. 356; HC 213 (1957–8), Qs 427 and 435.
76 HC673 (1966–7), Q. 429.
77 HC 240 (1963–4), para. 48.
78 Millar and Sawyer, *Technical Development*, p. 201.
79 *Flight*, 15 May 1959, p. 856; HC 42 (1963–4), Q. 726; HC 673 (1966–7), Q. 820.
80 HC 42 (1963–4), Q. 341.
81 HC42 (1963–4), Q. 726; HC 673 (1966–7), Q. 820.
82 At BEA's suggestion, Boeing and De Haviland discussed the possibility of a joint project. Nothing transpired, but those involved with the Trident programme are convinced De Haviland's research showed Boeing the way in which to point 727 development.
83 See ch. 4.
84 C. Harlow, *Innovation and Productivity under Nationalisation*, London, 1977, p. 50.
85 See, HC 673 (1966–7), para. 26, Qs 821 and 877–7; Cmnd 2853, para. 334; *Productivity of the National Aircraft Effort* (Report of the Elstub Committee), London, 1969, paras 174–7.
86 Harlow, *Innovation*.
87 HC 213 (1958–9), paras 55–60, HC 42 (1963–4), paras 12–34.
88 HC 213 (1958–9), paras 65–7; HC 42 (1963–4), paras 28–32.
89 Ibid., paras 28–32.
90 HCD 588, 22 May 1958, cols 1607–11.
91 *The Times*, 24 April 1957; see also, *The Banker*, 8 Nov. 1957, pp. 721–6.
92 Derek Wood, *Interavia*, Sept. 1958, pp. 903–4.

2 Confirming the Partnership, 1960–4

1 H. Evans, *Vickers Against the Odds*, Sevenoaks, 1978, pp. 39, 58–9. K. Hartley, 'The mergers in the UK aircraft industry', *Journal of the Royal Aeronautical Society*, LXIX, Dec. 1965, p. 850; HC 240 (1963–4), Q. 1565.
2 Evans, *Vickers*, p. 60.
3 *The Times*, 15 Sept. 1959.
4 *Sunday Times*, 8 Feb. 1976.
5 HC 42 (1963–4) Qs 1467–8.
6 For a more complete history of the mergers see: Hartley, 'Mergers', passim; also J. Costello and T. Hughes, *Concorde*, London, 1976, pp. 39–41.
7 Of the more famous names in British aviation, Handley Page, still led by its founder, resisted, and drifted into insolvency and eventual bankruptcy. For a more favourable insider's view of rationalisation, see Sir Reginald Verdon Smith, 'The British Aircraft Corporation: the first twelve years', *Aeronautical Journal*, Jan. 1974.
8 HCD 617, 15 Feb. 1960, cols 957–60; see also *The Times*, 13 Jan. 1960.
9 *Rolls-Royce Limited*, Cmnd 4860 (1971), Appendix A; see also Gardner, 'Economic of launch aid', passim.

10 Cmnd 4860 (1971), Appendix A.
11 HC42 (1963–4), Qs 163 and 956–60.
12 Ibid., Qs 320 and 967–70.
13 See Sir Kenneth Keith, Chairman of Rolls-Royce, HL 305 (1975–6), Q. 550.
14 HC 42 (1963–4), Q. 176.
15 Ibid., Qs 948 and 973–88.
16 Ibid., Q. 320.
17 Ibid., Q. 952; Cmnd 4860 (1971), Appendix A.
18 HC 42 (1963–4), Qs 1210 and 1221–2.
19 HC 537 (1970–1), Qs 3277 and 3279.
20 See K. Hartley, *A Market for Aircraft*, Hobart Paper, No. 57, London, 1974, and Gardner, 'Economics of launch aid', and see Chapter 8.
21 See pp. 71–80.
22 HC 42 (1963–4), Q. 176.
23 HC 347 (1971–2), Q. 2495; HC 42 (1963–4), Q. 158; HC 537 (1970–1), Q. 2789.
24 BAC 1-11, the HS748, the Rolls-Royce Spey engine, all eventually produced some profit. The Spey and HS748, in fact, are still earning money.
25 HC 42 (1963–4), Q. 395.
26 *BOAC annual report for 1961*, Cmnd 258, pp. 99. HCD 685, 2 Dec. 1963, col. 798; *The Financial Problems of the British Overseas Airways Corporation*, cmnd 5, passim. HC 42 (1963–4), Q. 1542.
27 HC 42 (1963–4), Q. 1528; HC 240 (1963–4), para. 55.
28 HC 42 (1963–4), Q. 1538.
29 HC 240 (1963–4), para. 56.
30 *Flight*, 8 Mar. 1962, p. 348.
31 HC 240 (1963–4), Q. 1173.
32 Ibid., Appendix 19.
33 Ibid., See also Q. 1173.
34 *Financial Problems of BOAC*.
35 *Flight*, 17 Sept. 1964, p. 500; 5 Dec. 1963, p. 915.
36 HCD 699, 22 July 1964, cols 531–2.
37 Ibid., col. 500.
38 HC 42 (1963–4), paras 57–8.
39 HC 240 (1963–4), Q. 1485.
40 HC 213 (1958–9), Q, 76.
41 W. A. Robson, *Nationalised Industry and Public Ownership*, London, 1962, p. 157.
42 D. Corbett, *Politics and the Airlines*, London, 1967, p. 261.
43 *Flight*, 23 July 1964, p. 124.
44 BOAC annual report for 1964, Cmnd 349, pp. 47–9; *Flight*, 1 Oct. 1964, pp. 564–5.
45 *The Times*, 4 May and 17 July 1964; *Flight*, 18 Jan. 1965. p. 841; HCD 685, 2 Dec. 1963, cols 877 and 900–1.
46 HCD 699, 20 July 1964, cols 40–5.
47 Ibid., col. 619.
48 *Flight*, 23 July 1964, p. 124.
49 HC 240 (1963–4), Q. 283; HCD 699, 20 July 1964, col. 495.
50 S. Wheatcroft, *Air Transport Policy*, London, 1964, p. 220. As a senior

BEA executive, Wheatcroft may be inclined towards an airline-orientated view of procurement policy.

51 Costello and Hughes, *Concorde*. J. Davies, *The Concorde Affair*, (London, 1969). For an insider's view, G. Knight, *Concorde*, London, 1967. For details of the decision-making process, see especially J. Bruce-Gardyne and N. Lawson, *The Power Game*, London, 1976, and two *Sunday Times* articles, 13 and 20 Feb. 1976. Both of these sources have been confirmed in interview as being very accurate accounts of the manoevring behind the SST programme.

52 See Sir George Edwards, *Flight*, 20 Feb. 1964, pp. 285–7.

53 Sir Morian Morgan, 'A new shape in the sky', *Aeronautical Journal*, Jan. 1972, p. 2.

54 Ibid., pp. 2–3.

55 HC 42 (1963–4), Q. 821.

56 See above p. 00.

57 Morgan, 'New shape', pp. 3–4; Knight, *Concorde*, p. 15.

58 *Sunday Times*, 8 Feb. 1976; *Economist*, 3 Sept. 1960, pp. 918–19.

59 Cited in *Sunday Times*, 8 Feb. 1976.

60 Ibid. See also Bruce-Gardyne and Lawson, *Power Game*, pp. 18–20.

61 *Sunday Times*, 8 Feb. 1976.

62 D. Henderson, 'The calculus of Concorde', *Listener*, 3 Nov. 1977, p. 580.

63 HC 42 (1963–4), Qs 882 and 1392–3.

64 Ibid., Qs 117–28, 1137, 1141–2 and 1163.

65 Henderson, 'Calculus of Concorde'.

66 For a more detailed analysis of European collaboration, see R. Williams, *European Technology*, London, 1973.

67 *Flight*, 15 Nov 1962, pp. 771–2.

68 Rippon was, in fact, accused of 'leaking' RAE data to the French to encourage their research and to indicate the desirability of cooperation. *Sunday Times*, 15 Feb. 1976; Bruce-Gardyne and Lawson, *Power Game*, p. 17.

69 Ibid., *Sunday Times*.

70 These events coincided with the Skybolt affair, where Britain's dependence on the US for nuclear weapons technology was fully exposed.

71 Rolls proposed a brand new turbo-fan engine. This promised to be quieter and more efficient than the Olympus, but a good deal more expensive. Rolls believed that it was involved in SST negotiations simply to force better contract conditions from BSE. See *Sunday Times*, 15 Feb. 1976; Bruce-Gardyne and Lawson, *Power Game*, pp. 15–16; Knight, *Concorde*, p. 22.

72 Costello and Hughes, *Concorde*, pp. 42–7; Knight, *Concorde*, p. 22.

73 *Flight*, 6 Jan. 1961, p. 7. See also, Sir Aubrey Burke, Chairman of De Haviland (HSA), *Flight*, 23 Sept. 1962, p. 272.

74 *Sunday Times*, 15 Feb. 1976; Bruce-Gardyne and Lawson, *Power Game*, pp. 25–8.

75 According to Perry's table of technological advance ratings of mainly post-war military projects, Concorde ranks as the most ambitious of all aircraft developed since 1945. (See M. Kaldor, 'Technical change in the defence industry', in K. Pavitt, *Technological Innovation and British Economic Performance*, London, 1980, pp. 110–111.)

76 In the event, some disparity in the share of costs has emerged and to the detriment of the United Kingdom. See Chapter 5.
77 On the other hand, significant delays occurred *after* the dual programme was eventually abandoned. Similarly, airlines were sceptical about the SST long before the energy crisis of 1973.
78 M. S. Hochmuth, *Organising the Transnational*, Leiden, 1974, pp. 137—8.
79 Knight, *Concorde*, ch. 4; Costello and Hughes, *Concorde*, ch. 8.
80 See HC 647 (1966—7), Qs 1356—64, 1370—2, 1492 and 1513; HC 314 (1967—8), Q. 1460—8; HC 335/353 (1972—3), Q. 1607; HC 531 (1976—7), Q. 1541. The UK continues to pay more than the French to support Concorde operations. See HC 265 (1980—1).
81 HC 335/353 (1972—3), para. 12.
82 Davies, *Concorde Affair*, p. 84; G. Joucla, *La Cooperation dans les Industries Aeronautiques Européenes*, Paris, 1971, pp. 88—9.
83 *Flight*, 6 Dec. 1962, p. 895.
84 See Chapter 3.
85 *Economist*, 1 Sept. 1962, p. 828.

3 Subsonic Politics, 1964—70

1 For a review of Labour technology policies see N. Vig, 'Policies for science and technology in Great Britain', in T. Dixon Long and C. Wright, *Science Policies of Industrial Nations*, New York, 1976.
2 The Ministry of Aviation was merged with the Ministry of Technology in 1966.
3 HCD 7.03, 9 Dec. 1964, cols 1528 and 1550—1; *The Times*, 28 Oct. 1964; *Flight*, 11 Mar. 1965, p. 356.
4 HCD 706, 9 Feb. 1965, cols 213, 226, 228—9, 234—9, 240—1 and 251; HCD 710, 13 Apr. 1965, cols 190—5, 1173—88 and 1217; HCD 722, 13 Dec. 1965, col. 1035.
5 See Ministry of Defence Statement, *Flight*, 15 Mar. 1965, p. 551; *The Times*, 18 May 1965; *Flight*, 27 May 1965, p. 815.
6 *Flight*, 6 July 1967, p. 17.
7 John Stonehouse, HCD 740, 1 Feb. 1967, col. 421.
8 See Vig, 'Policies for science', pp. 70—4.
9 Cmnd 2853, ch. 38.
10 *New Technology*, Jan. 1967.
11 Ibid., Jan. 1968.
12 See F. Broadway, *State Intervention in British Industry, 1964—8*, London, 1969; Williams, *European Technology*, pp. 5—20; H. Rose and S. Rose, *Science and Society*, Harmondsworth, 1970, ch. 6.
13 Cmnd 2853, paras 325—6.
14 Ibid., section IX.
15 Ibid.
16 Ibid., ch. 22.
17 Ibid., chs. 26, 34, 36 and 37.
18 HCD 723, 1 Feb. 1966, cols 893—6.
19 Ibid.
20 *Flight*, 21 July 1966, pp. 87—8.

21 Speech to RAe Society Centenary Congress, Sept. 1966, *Aircraft Engineering*, Nov. 1960, p. 10.
22 HCD 723, 1 Feb. 1966, cols 908–10.
23 *Economist*, 2 Sept. 1966, pp. 391–4.
24 *Flight*, 3 June 1965, p. 869; HCD 717 (written answers), 28 July 1965, col. 127.
25 HCD 728, 11 May 1966, cols 373–4.
26 HCD 725, 9 Mar. 1966, col. 2110.
27 *The Times*, 2 May 1966; HCD 728, 11 May 1966, col. 260.
28 HCD 733, 2 Aug. 1966, cols 260–1.
29 See pp. 000–00.
30 Significantly, the 111 was not launched on the basis of a BEA specification.
31 *New Scientist*, 7 Jan. 1965, pp. 35–6.
32 'The A300B', *Air Enthusiast*, Aug. 1972; *Flight*, 27 Oct. 1976, p. 695; 3 Apr. 1966, p. 337; *Interavia*, July 1966, p. 1016.
33 HCD 717 (written answers), 28 July 1965, col. 127; see also interview with Jenkins in *Flight*, 3 June 1965, p. 869; see also, 22 Apr. 1966, p. 621, and 22 May 1965, p. 819.
34 'The A300B'; HCD 740, 1 Feb. 1967, cols 487–8; *The Times*, 4 July 1966.
35 K. Hayward, 'Politics and European Aerospace Cooperation: The A300 Airbus', *Journal of Common Market Studies*, June 1976, pp. 364–5.
36 *Cmnd 2853*, para. 84; *Rolls-Royce Limited:* Investigation under Section 1965(*a*)(*i*) of the Companies Act 1948. Report by R. A. MacCrindle, Q.C. and P. Godfrey, F.C.A., London, 1973, paras 25–7 (referred to in future as *Rolls-Royce Ltd*).
37 *Rolls-Royce Ltd*, paras 25–7.
38 M. Edmonds, 'The Self-nationalisation of Rolls-Royce', in D. C. Hague, W. J. M. Mackenzie and A. Barker, *Public Policy and Private Interests*, London, 1975, pp. 66–7.
39 Geoffrey Knight, Managing Director of BAC, *Flight*, 18 June 1970, p. 1009; Sir George Edwards, Chairman of BAC, *Flight*, 6 Feb. 1969, p. 206; and Sir Ian Orr-Ewing, MP, letter to *The Times*, 17 Aug. 1969.
40 Edmonds, 'Self-nationalisation', passim.
41 *Rolls-Royce Ltd*, paras 196, 201.
42 *AWST*, 29 May 1967, p. 273.
43 *Rolls-Royce Ltd*, para. 34.
44 *Fortune*, Mar. 1969.
45 Fred Mulley, Minister of Aviation, *Flight*, 1 Sept. 1966, p. 320; see also 8 Sept. 1966, p. 408.
46 *The Times*, 15 June 1966, 21 June 1967, 16 Dec. 1967; HCD 736, 21 Nov. 1966, cols 911–17; HCD 740 (written answers), 3 Feb. 1967, col. 178; *Flight*, 1 Sept. 1966, 2 Nov. 1967, pp. 319–20; see also Evans, *Vickers*, pp. 123–4.
47 *Flight*, 9 Nov. 1972, pp. 649–52.
48 B. Blackwell, *Flight*, 24 Jan. 1973, p. 17.
49 *AWST*, 29 May 1967, p. 95.
50 *Flight*, 8 May 1967, p. 777; 'The A300B'.
51 HCD 747, 6 June 1967, cols 768–9, HCD 751, 26 July 1967, cols 740–2; *Flight*, 5 Oct. 1967, p. 550; see also Ministry of Technology evidence to HC

673 (1966–7), QS 1501, 1503.
52 HC 213 (1968–9), Appendix 58.
53 HCD 751, 26 July 1967, col. 741–2; HC 673 (1966–7), Qs 1504, 1509 and 1512.
54 John Stonehouse, *AWST*, 31 July 1967, p. 25.
55 Robert Carr, Conservative spokesman on Aviation, *Flight*, 17 Aug. 1967, p. 251.
56 *Flight* (ed), 1 June 1967.
57 *AWST*, 2 Oct. 1967, p. 30.
58 BEA annual report for 1966, Cmnd 134; HCD 733, 2 Aug. 1966, cols 260–1; HCD 782, 24 Apr. 1969, col. 684; HCD 721, 22 Nov. 1965, cols 32–46; HVD 736, 21 Nov. 1966, col. 1974; HC 673 (1966–7), Qs 1249, 1464, 1467 and 1492–3; *Flight*, 16 March 1967, pp. 391–4.
59 HCD 743, 15 Mar. 1967, col. 492.
60 HCD 756, 15 Dec. 1967, cols 779–83; HCD 762, 4 Apr. 1968, cols 632–7; *The Times*, 15 Sept. 1967.
61 HC 673 (1966–7), Q. 1494.
62 *The Times*, 16 Dec. 1967.
63 HCD 756, 15 Dec. 1967, cols 779–83.
64 Memorandum by Sir David Hudie and Sir Denning Pearson, published in HC 347 (1971–2), p. 471.
65 *Rolls-Royce Ltd*, paras 207–9.
66 Ibid., para. 210.
67 Ibid., see also HCD 751 (written answers), 28 July 1967, col. 293.
68 Sir Denning Pearson, HC347 (1971–2), Q. 2035.
69 Cited in R. Gray, *Rolls on the Rocks*, Salisbury, 1971, pp. 75–6.
70 HC 347 (1971–2), Q. 3092.
71 Ibid., Qs 2 and 273–4.
72 HCD 811, 8 Feb. 1971, col. 13.
73 Edmonds, 'Self-nationalisation', p. 70.
74 *Rolls-Royce Ltd*, para. 243.
75 J. E. B. Perkins, Commercial Director, Derby Division, ibid., para. 273.
76 Ibid.
77 See Chapter 4.
78 HCD 762, 1 Apr. 1968, col. 44.
79 *Flight*, 21 Sept. 1967, p. 433.
80 Cited in Reed, *Britain's Aircraft Industry*, p. 129–30.
81 *Flight*, 21 Sept. 1967, p. 433; July 18 1968, p. 87.
82 HCD 762, 1 Apr. 1968, cols 45–6.
83 *Flight*, 4 Apr. 1968, p. 481; 9 May 1968, p. 2.
84 'The A300B'.
85 *Flight*, 13 June 1965, p. 830.
86 HCD 758, 12 Feb. 1968, cols 922–4.
87 Ibid., HCD 767, 2 Apr. 1968, cols 1–3.
88 R. H. S. Crossman, *The Diaries of a Cabinet Minister*, London, 1977, III, p. 152.
89 *Flight*, 18 July 1968, p. 86–7, 19 Sept. 1968, p. 7; 24 Oct. 1968, p. 40; *The Times*, 31 Oct. 1968.
90 *Financial Times*, 13 Nov. 1968.

91 *Rolls-Royce Ltd*, paras 335–7 and 340–4.
92 *Flight*, 21 Nov. (ed) and p. 808; 28 Nov. 1968, pp. 882–3; 5 Dec. 1968;
    AWST, 18 Nov. 1968, p. 35.
93 'The A300B', *Flight*, 19 Dec. 1968.
94 HCD 775 (written answers), 12 Dec. 1968, cols 203–4; *The Times*, 13 Dec.
    1968.
95 HCD 770, 14 Oct. 1968, col. 8, HCD 779, Jan. 1969, col. 1304.
96 *Flight*, 23 Jan. 1969, p. 119; *The Times*, 9 Jan. 1969; *Financial Times*, 10
    Jan. 1969, 14 Feb. 1969; *Frankfurter Allgemeine Zeitung*, 25 Jan. 1969.
97 HCD 781, 16 Apr. 1969, col. 127; *Flight*, 27 Mar. 1969, p. 462.
98 Cited in Reed, *Britain's Aircraft Industry*, p. 121.
99 Elstub, *Productivity*, paras 183–92.
100 *Flight*, 3 July 1969, p. 2.
101 *The Times*, 11 Apr. 1969.
102 HCD 794 (written answers), 26 Jan. 1970, cols 8 and 973–4; HCD 796, 23
    Feb. 1970, cols 794–6; *Flight*, 23 Oct. 1969, p. 626; *The Times*, 16 Dec.
    1969.
103 See Chapter 4.
104 *Action Programme for the European Aeronautical Sector*, EEC
    Commission, EEC Bulletin, Nov. 1975, p. 14.
105 HC 673 (1966–7), paras 63–6.

4 Government, Rolls-Royce and the RB211, 1962–71

1   HCD 811, 8 Feb. 1971, col. 72.
2   HC 447 (1971–2), Q. 1410.
3   Ibid., Qs 1476–86; see also HCD 809, 20 Jan. 1971.
4   HC 447 (1971–2), Qs 1399, 1400 and 1447.
5   *Sunday Times*, 7 Feb. 1971.
6   This was certainly the view of Sir Kenneth Keith, later Chairman of Rolls-
    Royce (1971) Ltd. See HC 347 (1971–2), Q. 1967.
7   See Edmonds, 'Self-nationalisation', passim.
8   See Sir Denning Pearson's evidence to HC 347 (1971–2), Q. 2057.
9   HCD 810, 23 Nov. 1970, col. 41.
10 HCD 811, 8 Feb. 1971, col. 64.
11 *Rolls-Royce Ltd*, para. 270.
12 HC 447 (1971–2), Q. 1443.
13 Ibid. Qs 1506 and 1510.
14 The Conservative Government, for example, had given Vickers launch aid
    for the Super VC10 in order to help their cash-flow problems in 1960.
    Similarly, BAC and HSA were given 100 per cent aid for the BAC 111-500
    and Trident 3B in order to facilitate a 'buy British' policy for BEA. Perhaps
    not directly relevant to the Rolls case, but sufficient to indicate the flexibility
    political interest could bring to launch aid 'disciplines'.
15 Ian Morrow, later Chief Executive of Rolls, HC 347 (1971–2), Q. 2702; see
    also, Q. 2042.
16 Lord Beeching, member of Rolls Board from 1969, ibid, Qs 1900 and 1935.
17 HCD 811, 11 Feb. 1971, col. 852.
18 See *Rolls-Royce Ltd*, para. 298; *The Observer*, 7 Apr. 1971.

19 HCD 807, 23 Nov. 1970, col. 40.
20 *Rolls-Royce Ltd*, paras 184–5, 192–3.
21 HC 347 (1971–2), Qs 1900–1.
22 *Rolls-Royce Ltd*, para. 170.
23 Ibid., paras 202 and 374; HC 347 (1971–2), Q. 2035; HC 447 (1971–2), Qs 1391–4.
24 Edmonds, 'Self-nationalisation', p. 79.
25 *Rolls-Royce Ltd*, paras 207 and 374–5; HC 347 (1971–2), Q. 2035; HC 447 (1971–2), Qs 1391–4.
26 Cited in Gray, *Rolls on the Rocks*, p. 75.
27 HC 447 (1971–2), Qs 1391 and 1452.
28 Ibid., Qs 1407 and 1410.
29 Evidence cited in *Rolls Royce Ltd*, para. 268.
30 Ibid., paras 357, 367 and 360–2.
31 For a detailed analysis of the IRC and its procedures, see S. Young and D. Lowe, *Intervention in the Mixed Economy*, London, 1974.
32 IRC Report, published as Annex B to *Rolls Royce Limited and the RB211 Aero-engine*, London, 1972; Cmnd 4800, pp. 6 and 11.
33 HC 347 (1971–2), Q. 1204.
34 HCD 811, 8 Feb. 1971, col. 67.
35 HC 447 (1971–2), Qs 1937–40 and 1980.
36 Edmonds, 'Self-nationalisation', p. 87.
37 HC 347 (1971–2), Q. 1704 and 1741.
38 *Rolls-Royce Ltd*, para. 382.
39 HC 447 (1971–2), Q. 1879; Cmnd 4860, para. 3.
40 *Rolls-Royce Ltd*, paras 399–402.
41 Ibid., para 406; Reed, *Britain's Aircraft Industry*, p. 131; *Flight*, 30 July 1970, p. 148.
42 *Rolls-Royce Ltd*, paras 406–10.
43 Sir Keith Joseph, cited in Young and Lowe, *Intervention*, p. 128.
44 The Ministry of Technology was dissolved in the autumn of 1970. Pending a White Paper on the reorganisation of central government and an investigation of the machinery for aerospace policy conducted by Sir Derek Rayner, all aerospace matters were made the responsibility of a Ministry of Aviation Supply. See Chapter 7, pp. 000–00.
45 *Rolls-Royce Ltd*, paras 410; Cmnd 4860, para. 5.
46 HCD 811, 8 Feb. 1971, col. 53.
47 *Rolls-Royce Ltd*, paras 417–18.
48 Ibid., para. 427.
49 Ibid.
50 HCD 807, 30 Nov. 1970, col. 899.
51 Ibid., HCD 806, 11 Nov. 1970, cols 399–402; HCD 807, 23 Nov. 1970, cols 54–5.
52 *Sunday Times*, 7 Feb. 1971.
53 HCD 811, 11 Feb. 1971, col. 927.
54 *Rolls-Royce Ltd*, paras 455 and 460.
55 *Sunday Times*, 6 Dec. 1970; *The Times*, 29 Sept. 1970; *Flight*, 17 Sept. 1970, p. 401.
56 *Flight* (ed.), 23 July 1970.

57 *Observer*, 25 Oct. 1970.
58 *AWST* (ed.), 14 Sept. 1970.
59 *The Times*, 27 Oct. 1970; *Financial Times*, 24 Nov. 1970.
60 Evans, *Vickers*, p. 185.
61 HCD 807, 2 Dec. 1970, cols 1293 and 1286.
62 *The Times*, 3 Dec. 1970; *Financial Times*, 4 Dec. 1970.
63 *Rolls-Royce Ltd*, paras 468–73 and 476.
64 HC 447 (1971–2), Qs 1407, 1407, 1450(a), 1453, 1882, 1884 and 1887.
65 *Rolls-Royce Ltd*, para. 481.
66 BBC Radio 4, *Analysis: The Crash of Rolls Royce*, 20 Jan. 1981.
67 Cmnd 4860, para. 28; see also HCD 812, 26 Feb. 1971, col. 1094.
68 Cmnd 4860, para. 30–1; HCD 811, 8 Feb. 1971, col. 103.
69 Cmnd 4860, paras 30–1; *Rolls-Royce Ltd*, para. 497; *Sunday Times*, 7 Feb.
   1976; *Observer*, 2 Feb. 1971.
70 BBC Radio 4, *Analysis*.
71 *Flight*, 11 Feb. 1971, p. 182.
72 *Sunday Times*, 7 Feb. 1971.
73 *Flight*, 11 Feb. 1971.
74 BBC Radio 4, *Analysis*.
75 HCD 810, 4 Feb. 1971, col. 1922.
76 HCD 811, 8 Feb. 1971, col. 103.
77 Ibid., cols 59 and 822.
78 Ibid., col. 99.
79 HCD 813, 11 Mar. 1971, col. 657.
80 HCD 811, 8 Feb. 1971, col. 41.
81 HCD 856, 15 May 1973, col. 1253.
82 BBC Radio 4, *Analysis*.
83 *Flight*, 5 July 1973.
84 See Young and Lowe, *Intervention*.
85 HCD 817, 10 May 1971, cols 32–5.
86 Cmnd 4860, paras 51–2.
87 Ibid., para. 56.
88 BBC Radio 4, *Analysis*.
89 HC 447 (1971–2), Qs 1914 and 1475.
90 Ibid., Q. 1510.
91 Chapter 7, pp. 000–00.
92 HC 537 (1970–1), Q. 2819.
93 Ibid., Q. 2797.
94 Ibid., Q. 2823. The aircraft concerned were the Brittan-Norman Nymph
   and Trilander.
95 Ibid., Qs 2808–9 and 2812.
96 *Rolls-Royce Ltd*, para. 553.
97 Dell, *Political Responsibility*, pp. 161–6.

5 Controlling Concorde, 1962–81

1 See Chapter 2, note 51. For an analysis of the trans-national aspects of
   programme management, see Hochmuth, *Organising the Transnational*.
2 See table 6.1, cited by M. Kaldor, 'Technical Change'.

3 The Lockheed SR71 Blackbird reconnaissance aircraft is another. The Soviet SST, the Tu 144 might have been a third.
4 HC 362 (1968–9), Q. 4438.
5 HC 265 (1964–5), Q. 635; see also Q. 653.
6 HC 42 (1963–4), para. 78.
7 Costello and Hughes, *Concorde*, pp. 84–5.
8 It has been suggested that the US Government applied pressure through the IMF to have Concorde cancelled as a condition for an IMF loan. The reasoning being that the Americans wanted a clear run for their SST. See Knight, *Concorde*, p. 48. This was hotly denied by George Brown, a senior member of the Wilson Government, in a letter to *The Times*, 7 May 1976.
9 HCD 701, 5 Nov. 1964, cols 503–14.
10 HCD 705, 20 Jan. 1965, cols 197–202.
11 See A. Wilson, *The Concorde Fiasco*, Harmondsworth, 1973, pp. 48–9.
12 Costello and Hughes, *Concorde*, pp. 135–41.
13 See Chapter 2 for an analysis of the Treaty. See also HC 335/353 (1972–3), para. 64.
14 HC 362 (1968–9), Qs 4457, 4460, 4592, 4602, 4687 and 4773.
15 Knight, *Concorde*, pp. 52–3.
16 HC 335/353 (1972–3), Q. 1479.
17 See HC 347 (1971–2), Q. 674, for an official view on Concorde spin-off.
18 HC 362 (1968–9), Qs 308, 332 and 4556; HC 335/353 (1972–3), Qs 1608–18.
19 HC 42 (1963–4), Qs 851–2.
20 See Costello and Hughes, *Concorde*, chs 19–20.
21 *Flight*, 8 Mar. 1973, p. 327.
22 Ibid., 21 Mar. 1974, p. 356.
23 Ibid.
24 Ibid., 30 May 1974, p. 684.
25 HC 531 (1976–7), para. 25.
26 *Flight*, 3 Mar. 1979, p. 609.
27 HC 265 (1980–1), paras 17–27, Qs 206–7, 217 and 281.
28 Ibid., paras 55–6, Q. 297, Conclusions (iii).
29 Ibid., para. 42.
30 HC 647 (1966–7), Q. 1543.
31 HC 347 (1971–2), Qs 2432, HC 531 (1976–7), Q. 1521.
32 CAG Report, 1964–5, paras 9–11, HC 265 (1964–5), Q. 168.
33 Cited by Williams, *European Technology*, p. 122.
34 HC 335/353 (1972–3), Q. 1900 and 1926. See Hochmuth, *Organising the Transnational*, pp. 150–1; Knight, *Concorde*, ch. 8.
35 HC 362 (1968–9), Q. 4439.
36 Ibid., Qs 4569, 4583–8.
37 HC 531 (1976–7), Q. 1524; HC 362 (1968–9), Qs 4644 and 4570; HC 297 (1969–70), Q. 2327.
38 HC 362 (1968–9), Qs 4439, 4614, 4617–22, 4681, 4702–6 and 4740.
39 According to one analysis of the origins of PERT in the US Polaris missile submarine programme, the use of these techniques was largely designed to convince potential critics of the programme that it was being managed effectively and efficiently. See H. M. Sapolsky, *The Polaris System*

Development, Cambridge, Mass., 1972, ch. 4.

40 HC 531 (1976–7), Qs 1524; HC 362 (1968–9), Qs 4644 and 4570; HC 297 (1969–70), Q. 2327.
41 Hochmuth, *Organising the Transnational*, pp. 151–3; Knight, *Concorde*, ch. 8.
42 Ibid., Hochmuth.
43 Knight, *Concorde*, pp. 81–2; see also HC 335/353 (1972–3), Q. 1926.
44 HC 647 (1966–7), p. 1569; HC 362 (1968–9), Qs 4751, 4776–8 and 5355; HC 297 (1969–70), Q. 2327.
45 HC 335/353 (1972–3), Q. 1946.
46 Ibid.
47 Knight, *Concorde*, pp. 57–62.
48 HC 347 (1971–2), Q. 743.
49 Cited by Williams, *European Technology*, p. 120.
50 HC 647 (1966–7), Qs 1528, 1531–5, 1600–2.
51 Ibid., Q. 1535–8.
52 Ibid., Q. 1525–7.
53 HC 362 (1968–9), Q. 4634.
54 HC 297 (1969–70), Qs 2025–6, 3029, 3034 and 3091; HC 314 (1967–8), Qs 1760, 1788 and 1795.
55 HC 335/353 (1972–3), Qs 1946, 1957–9, 2031–3.
56 Ibid., Qs 1805–10; HC 502 (1974–5), Q. 2063.
57 HC 347 (1971–3), para. 81.
58 Ibid., Q. 1688; HC 335/353 (1972–3), Qs 2002 and 2011; see also Williams, *European Technology*, p. 121.
59 HC 531 (1976–7), paras 16 and 25, Qs 1522, 1526, 1531 and 1540.
60 Ibid., Qs 1547, 1572–3.
61 HC 502 (1974–5), Q. 2063.
62 HC 347 (1971–2), para. 2063.
63 HC 362 (1968–9), Qs 4633, 4651 and 4683.
64 HC 347 (1971–2), Q. 773.
65 Knight, *Concorde*, pp. 81–2.
66 HC 335/353 (1972–3), Q. 2134.
67 Ibid., Q. 1866.
68 HC 362 (1968–9), Q. 4438.
69 P. D. Henderson, 'Two British errors: their probable size and some possible lessons', in C. Pollitt, *et al.*, *Public Policy in Theory and Practice*, London, 1979. Henderson's analysis is based upon estimates of Concorde's known costs and estimated future costs. He also provides an estimate of future returns based upon British Airways net outgoings, Concorde production costs and, optimistically, the sale of the five outstanding aircraft. The data relating to intangible gains and losses he admits to being subjective and difficult to estimate with confidence, but he does try to use the most optimistic assumptions. Figures are rendered constant to 1976 prices and his calculations are derived from the Government's own Test Rate of Discount and a lower factor provided by another cost-benefit analyst, and regarded by Henderson as being a fairer test of real expenditure.
70 Ibid., pp. 236–7.
71 See Sir Arnold Hall, HC 347 (1971–2), Q. 1074.

72 Williams, *European Technology*, pp. 130–4.
73 HC 347 (1971–2), paras 84–6.
74 Ibid.
75 Ibid., Q. 2602.
76 Ibid., para. 91.
77 *Flight* (ed.), 11 Apr. 1974.
78 *Flight*, cited by Williams, *European Technology*, p. 135.
79 D. Henderson, 'Under the Whitehall Blanket', *Listener*, 17 Nov. 1977, p. 636.
80 See Edmonds, 'Self-nationalisation', passim.

6 Government and Civil Aerospace in the 1970s

1 HC 203 (1974), paras 17–19.
2 HC 347 (1971–2), Q. 669.
3 Ibid., Q. 1041.
4 Ibid., Q. 872.
5 Ibid., Q. 588.
6 HC 537 (1970–1), Q. 2779.
7 HC 347 (1971–2), Q. 615.
8 HC 537 (1970–1), para. 67.
9 Ibid., Qs 2828–30.
10 HC 347 (1971–2), Q. 364.
11 See Chapter 7.
12 See HCD 807, 2 Dec. 1970, cols 1286–93.
13 HCD 828, 15 Dec. 1971, cols 641–2.
14 See *Flight*, 18 May 1972, p. 725; 14 Dec. 1972, p. 802; 5 July 1974, p. 14.
15 HCD 852, 5 Mar. 1973, cols 7–8.
16 HCD 828, 15 Dec. 1971, cols 634–5; HCD 901, 2 Dec. 1975, cols 1467; HCD 916, 29 July 1976, cols 992; HCD 812, 3 Mar. 1971, col. 1702; *Flight*, 19 Jan. 1973, pp. 886–7.
17 *Flight*, 7 Sept. 1972, p. 316; 31 May 1973, p. 823.
18 Ibid., 7 June 1973, p. 876; *Financial Times*, 31 May 1973.
19 HCD 811, 11 Feb. 1971, cols 99 and 820.
20 *Financial Times*, 7 Feb. 1972.
21 *AWST*, 31 May 1971, p. 92; *Interavia*, Feb. 1972, p. 108; *Flight* (ed.), 2 Mar. 1971. See especially J. Isnard of *Le Monde*, in *The Times*, 6 Nov. 1972.
22 HL 305 (1975–6), Qs 560, 528 and 535.
23 Williams, *European Technology*, p. 66.
24 Ibid.
25 *Flight* (ed.), 6 Sept. 1973, p. 395.
26 HCD 861, 22 Oct. 1973, cols 687–8.
27 D. L. B. Jones, Under Secretary of State, DTI, *Interavia*, Jan. 1974, p. 64.
28 Data derived from *The European Aerospace Industry: Position and Figures*, Commission of the EEC, Brussels, May 1976, SEC(76) 2657.
29 See Chapter 7.
30 *Flight* (Commercial Aircraft Surveys), 24 Oct. 1974; 23 Oct. 1975; 9 Oct. 1976; 11 Nov. 1978.

31 Ibid., 12 Sept. 1974, p. 296; 29 May, 1975, p. 863.
32 *The Times*, 11 Dec. 1975.
33 See *Flight*, 17 Jan. 1972, pp. 53–4; 29 Aug. 1974, p. 18; 12 June 1976, p. 1550; *AWST*, 31 May 1971, p. 58.
34 *Financial Times*, 31 May 1973.
35 EEC Commission, R2462/75.
36 Ibid., p. 13.
37 HL 305 (1975–6), Q. 476.
38 Ibid., Qs 563 and 593.
39 HLD 398, 8 Dec. 1976, cols 1137 and 1164.
40 HL 305 (1975–6), Q. 439.
41 For a critical analysis of Spinelli, see R. Williams, M. Edmonds, with M. Dillon and K. Hayward, 'Air policy', in G. Ionescu (ed.), *The European Alternatives* (Leiden, 1980).
42 HL 305 (1975–6), Q. 593.
43 *Flight*, 19 June 1975, p. 960.
44 *AWST*, 19 Apr. 1976, p. 24–5; *Interavia*, July 1976, pp. 609–11; *The Times*, 26 Apr. and 21 May 1976.
45 HL 305 (1975–6), Q. 598.
46 HCD 914, 29 June 1976, cols 236–7.
47 *The Times*, 10 and 20 May 1976; *AWST*, 24 May 1976, p. 24; *Flight*, 15 May 1976, p. 1282; 19 June 1976, p. 1598; 24 July 1970, p. 211; 4 Sept. 1976, p. 326; *Sunday Times*, 13 June 1976.
48 HL 305 (1975–6), paras 412–14, 416–17 and 634; *Flight*, 10 July 1976, p. 69.
49 *AWST*, 6 Sept. 1976, pp. 76–7.
50 *Flight*, 12 June 1976, pp. 1551–2; *AWST*, 13 Sept. 1976, pp. 20–1.
51 Ibid. *Flight*.
52 HL 305 (1975–6), Q. 528; *Economist*, 2 Sept. 1972, pp. 51–2; *The Times*, 4 Sept. 1972.
53 HL 305 (1974–5), Q. 535; *Flight*, 26 June 1973, p. 938; 11 Oct. 1973, p. 589; 13 Dec. 1975, p. 710; 24 Jan. 1976, p. 143; 6 Mar. 1976, p. 514; 24 May 1976, p. 13; 17 July 1976, p. 127; 26 Nov. 1976, p. 1; *AWST*, 31 Aug. 1972, p. 12; 11 Sept. 1972, p. 23; 8 Nov. 1976, p. 34–5; 6 Sept. 1976, pp. 108–9; 8 Nov. 1976, pp. 34–5.
54 HC 502 (1974–5), Q. 2118; *Flight*, 26 June 1976; 24 July 1976, p. 210; 14 Aug, 1976, p. 336; *The Times*, 19 Aug. 1976.
55 *Flight*, 26 June 1976; *Sunday Times*, 9 Apr. 1978.
56 *Flight*, 16 Oct. 1976, p. 1176.
57 HCD 916, 2 July 1976, col. 1203; *Flight*, 18 Sept. 1976, p. 873; *The Times*, 7 Sept. 1976.
58 *Flight*, 3 Dec. 1977, p. 1648; 11 Dec. 1977, p. 1406; *AWST*, 3 Dec. 1977, p. 1148.
59 HCD 921, 1 Dec. 1976, col. 1015.
60 *Flight*, 27 Nov. 1976, pp. 1577–80; 7 May 1977; 18/25 June 1977; *AWST*, 29 Nov. 1976, pp. 12–13; 13 June 1976, p. 33; 20 June 1976, p. 16; 7 Nov. 1977, pp. 59–63.
61 *Flight*, 2 July 1977, pp. 7–8; *AWST*, 6 June 1977, pp. 217–19.
62 HCD 942, 23 Jan. 1978, col. 1112.

63 Ibid., cols 1113–14.
64 *Flight*, 3 Dec. 1977, p. 1048; 11 Dec. 1977, p. 1406; *AWST*, 3 Dec. 1977, p. 1648.
65 *Flight*, 17 Dec. 1977, p. 1783; *AWST*, 7 Nov. 1977, pp. 65–7; 21 Nov. 1977, p. 35; 19 Dec. 1977, pp. 23–5.
66 *Flight*, 24 Dec. 1977, pp. 1844 and 1848.
67 *AWST*, 7 Nov. 1977, pp. 65–7.
68 *AWST*, 7 Nov. 1977, p.65; *Flight*, 18 Feb. 1978; 29 Apr. 1978, p. 1246.
69 *Sunday Times*, 8 May 1980; 16 Nov. 1980; *Flight*, 30 Aug. 1980; *AWST*, 16 May 1977, p. 17.
70 HC 781 (1980–1), Appendix III.
71 Ibid., Q. 5201; *AWST*, 29 May 1978, pp. 31–2.
72 HC 621 (1977–8), Q. 2661; *Guardian*, 5 May 1978.
73 *Sunday Times*, 7 May 1978. C. F. Wilde, a Boeing Vice-President, stated that there was 'no real compelling pressure to launch the 757'. *AWST*, 13 Mar. 1978, p. 159. In the summer of 1982, Beswick's warnings about Boeing's priorities were looking remarkably prescient amidst reports that Boeing was considering abandoning the 757 in favour of the 737-300 (*Guardian*, 28 Aug. 1982).
74 *Flight*, 29 Apr. 1978, pp. 1245–6; *AWST*, 24 Apr. 1978, pp. 28–30.
75 *Guardian*, 14 Apr. 1978; *Flight*, 22 Apr. 1978, pp. 1085–6; 29 Apr. 1978, pp. 28–30; *AWST*, 24 Apr. 1978, pp. 28–30. Boeing's offer to increase BAe's share was not entirely altruistic; Boeing was expecting problems accommodating production demands if all three of its proposals were launched.
76 *AWST*, 24 Apr. 1978, pp. 28–30.
77 *Flight*, 22 Apr. 1978, p. 1087; 29 Apr. 1978, pp. 1242–3; *AWST*, 1 May 1978, pp. 24–8; 24 Nov. 1977; 3 Dec. 1977, p. 1047.
78 *Flight*, 22 Apr. 1978, p. 1087.
79 HCD 948, 24 Apr. 1978, cols 978–90 (written answers), cols 453–4.
80 HCD 950, 26 May 1978, cols 1920–4.
81 *AWST*, 22 May 1978, p. 33; *Flight*, 3 June 1978, p. 1634. *Guardian*, 29 June 1978; 8 July 1978; *Sunday Times*, 1 July 1978; 8 July 1978.
82 *Guardian*, 13 July 1978; *Flight*, 22 July 1978, pp. 255; *AWST*, 17 July 1978, p. 24; 24 July 1978, p. 18.
83 HCD 953, 10 July 1978, cols 1101–4.
84 Later, SAAB also accepted a risk-sharing subcontract, leaving BAe to carry 60 per cent of the development risk.
85 *Guardian*, 1 Sept. 1979.
86 *The Times*, 1 Sept. 1979.
87 *AWST*, 25 Sept. 1978, p. 39; *Flight*, 23 Sept. 1978, p. 1146.
88 *Guardian*, 1 Sept. 1978.
89 *AWST*, 4 Sept. 1978, pp. 20–3; 11 Sept. 1978, p. 17.
90 *AWST*, 11 Sept. 1978, p. 17.
91 *AWST*, 23 Oct. 1978, pp. 58–61; 9 Oct. 1978, p. 26; *Flight*, 7 Oct. 1978, p. 1294; 14 Oct. 1978, p. 1378.
92 HCD 957 (written answers), 6 Nov. 1978, cols 19–20.
93 *Flight* (ed.), 11 Nov. 1978.
94 *Sunday Times*, 22 Oct. 1978.

95 *Flight*, 4 Nov. 1978, pp. 1622–3.
96 *Flight* (ed.), 11 Nov. 1978.
97 See British Aerospace (Flotation prospectus), Feb. 1981, p. 25.
98 *Flight*, 15 Dec. 1980, p. 1842; 6 Dec. 190, p. 2078; 27 Dec. 1980, p. 2302; 7 Feb. 1981, p. 829.

7 From Private to Public Enterprise, the Monitoring and Control of Civil Aerospace, 1970–81

1 *Government Organisation for Defence Procurement and Civil Aerospace*, Cmnd 4641, London, 1971.
2 Ibid., Section A, especially paras 2–4.
3 Ibid., paras 7–8, 123; see also, HC 347 (1971–2), Qs 2434 and 2444.
4 Cmnd 4641, para. 122.
5 HC 347 (1971–2), Qs 2437 and 2435.
6 Cmnd 4641, para. 122.
7 Ibid., Section A, paras 115–18.
8 HCD 850, 12 Feb. 1973, cols 1244–5.
9 Ibid., col. 1247.
10 HC 347 (1971–2), Q. 2488.
11 HCD 861, 22 Oct. 1973, cols 687–8; *Flight*, 6 Sept. 1973, pp. 395–6.
12 HC 347 (1971–2), Q. 2490.
13 *Flight*, 15 Aug. 1974, p. 152.
14 Cited in *Flight*, 19 Dec. 1974, p. 863.
15 Reprinted in *Flight*, 14 Nov. 1974, p. 665.
16 Ibid., 24 Oct. 1974; 19 Dec. 1974, p. 862.
17 Ibid., 19 Dec. 1974, pp. 862–3; 20 Feb. 1975, p. 281. The £4 million in launch aid was subsequently written off by BAe.
18 Short Bros of Northern Ireland had long been in public hands.
19 The Health government did encourage such a merger, but the terms and the form of the proposed amalgamation were not acceptable to the two companies.
20 HCD 884, 15 Jan. 1975, cols 454–5; *Flight*, 23 Jan. 1975, pp. 83–4.
21 HCD 901, 2 Dec. 1975, col. 1451.
22 Ibid., cols 1445–6.
23 *Flight*, 23 Jan. 1975, p. 84.
24 HCD 901, 2 Dec. 1975, col. 1464; HCD 888, 17 Mar. 1975, cols 1146–51; *Flight*, 17 Apr. 1975, pp. 625–6; 20 Jan. 1975, p. 123; 20 July 1975, p. 2778. Mr Heseltine in office proved to be quite as ruthless a controller of public expenditure, albeit in respect of the local authorities.
25 *Flight*, 11 Dec. 1975, p. 875.
26 *The Aircraft and Shipbuilding Industries Act, 1977:* Sections 7, 10 and 45. See also Lord Beswick's evidence to HC 88 (1977–8), Qs 4–5, 14–17 and 22.
27 Speech to the Royal Aeronautical Society, *Flight*, 5 Feb. 1977, p. 268.
28 HC 303 (1974), para. 23.
29 Ibid., and Q. 3303.
30 Ibid., paras 23–4, Qs 1300–12; HC 502 (1974–5), Qs 2103–4.
31 HC 303 (1974), paras 28 and 31.

32 HC 334 (1975–6), Qs 958–9.
33 Ibid., Qs 959–66.
34 Ibid., para. 56, Qs 996, 997 and 1000.
35 Ibid., para. 58.
36 Ibid., Q. 1612. The French had fewer qualms about leaving the project, which they later abandoned to the British. *The Times*, 25 Mar. 1976.
37 *Sunday Times*, 25 Nov. 1979; *Observer*, 11 Nov. 1979.
38 *Flight*, 14 Feb. 1976, p. 332.
39 HC, 334 (1975–6), paras 54–6.
40 Ibid., Q. 737 and Appendix V.
41 Ibid., Qs 721, 735 and 754.
42 HC 531 (1976–7), Qs 2183 and 2184.
43 The Comptroller and Auditor General's Report (CAG), in HC 446 (1979–80), para. 15.
44 Rolls later raised private loans of £140 million to cover civil development. See *Flight*, 2 Feb. 1980, p. 292.
45 HC 446 (1979–80), para. 17, Qs 1429, 1438–9 and 1456.
46 Ibid., Qs 1465, 1494–5; HC 779 (1980–1), Qs 5165, 5167 and 5174.
47 HC 779 (1980–1), para. 20 and Q. 5124.
48 HC 621 (1977–8), Q. 2639.
49 HC 779 (1980–1), Qs 5146, 5667, 5442, 5702 and Appendix IV, para. 24.
50 Ibid., Q. 5149.
51 HC 779 (1980–1), para. 32.
52 Ibid., Q. 5651.
53 Ibid., para. 20, Qs 5650 and 5672.
54 Ibid., Qs 5179, 5656–62.
55 Ibid., Qs 5179, 5181 and 5184.
56 Ibid., Qs 5169 and 5179.
57 Ibid., Qs 5190–1.
58 Ibid., Q. 5179.
59 Ibid., Qs 5191 and 5711.
60 See Sir Leslie's evidence to HC 621 (1977–8), Q. 2643. Paradoxically, in May 1978 Sir Leslie told the Public Accounts Committee that he felt the NEB was 'completely involved' in major decisions made by Rolls. Moreover, Dr Robert Lickley, the head of the NEB's Rolls-Royce Support Staff, was well respected by Rolls, and consulted by its management. He spent his 'full time in making himself familiar with Rolls-Royces policies and problems'. Sir Leslie was then of the opinion that overall the NEB and Rolls had an 'excellent' relationship, which worked out 'extremely well, and just as I would want it to'. So the relationship between Murphy and Keith had either gone downhill very rapidly indeed, or Sir Leslie's evidence tended to hid a growing disquiet about the way Rolls was approaching its business. See HC 621 (1977–8), Q. 2647.
61 *Flight*, 3 Nov. 1979, p. 1403; *Sunday Times*, 25 Nov. 1975; *Observer*, 11 Nov. 1979.
62 *Flight*, 17 Nov. 1979.
63 HC 446 (1979–80), Q. 1488; HC 779 (1980–1), Q. 5677.
64 HC 446 (1979–80), Qs 1489–91 and 1498.
65 HC 779 (1980–1), Qs 5690 and 5683.

66 Ibid., Q. 5179.
67 Ibid., Q. 5692.
68 Ibid., Q. 5718.
69 *Guardian*, 1 May 1981.
70 HC 779 (1980–1), para. 32. Rolls now routinely cover forward all contracts vulnerable to exchange rate fluctuations. See HC 389 (1981–2), Q. 274.
71 Ibid., HC 779 (1980–1).

8 Conclusions

1 Sir Robert Marshall, DTI, HC 347 (1971–2), Q. 2495.
2 Ibid.; see also J. Hamilton, DTI, Q. 673.
3 See SBAC evidence to HC 347, Appendix 6, and DTI memorandum, pp. 378–9.
4 Ibid., Q. 618.
5 See Gardner, 'Economics of launch aid', p. 147.
6 See, for example, Appendix K to Cmnd 2843, The Plowden Report, 1965.
7 Ibid., para. 521.
8 K. Hartley, *A Market for Aircraft*, Hobart Paper No. 57, London, 1974, p. 52.
9 Ibid., pp. 60–7.
10 Gardner, 'Economics of launch aid', p. 149.
11 Ibid., p. 152.
12 Eades, 'US Government support', p. 149.
13 See M. J. Peck, 'Science and technology', in R. E. Caves and L. B. Krause (eds.), *Britain's Economic Prospects*, Washington, DC, 1961; Sir Ieuan Maddock, 'End of the glamorous adventure', *New Scientist*, 13 Feb. 1975; C. Freeman, 'Technological innovation and British trade policy', in F. Blackaby (ed.), *De-industrialisation*, London, 1979.
14 K. Pavitt, 'The choices and targets and instruments for Government support of scientific research', in Whiting, *Economics of Industrial Subsidies*, p. 117.
15 See, for example, C. Bore, 'An aerospace reply to Sir Ieuan', *Guardian*, 14 Feb. 1978.
16 *Guardian*, 28 Feb. 1979.
17 Dell, *Political Responsibility*, p. 30.
18 HC 347 (1971–2), Q. 1934.
19 J. Jewkes, 'Government and high technology', in G. Boyle, D. Elliot and R. Roy, *The Politics of Technology*, London, 1977, p. 93.
20 HC 347 (1971–2), Q. 1915.
21 See Chapter 5, note 69.
22 The Spinelli Report, p. 3.
23 *New Scientist*, 14 Oct. 1976, p. 81.
24 Ibid.
25 See HC 347 (1971–2), Qs 644 and 664.
26 R. Williams, *The Nuclear Power Decisions*, London, 1980, p. 320.
27 D. Zysman, 'Between the market and the state', *Research Policy*, III, 1975, p. 314.
28 See Williams, *Nuclear Power Decision*; D. Burn, *Nuclear Power and the*

Energy Crisis, London, 1978; E. F. Wonder, 'Decision-making and the reorganisation of the British nuclear industry', *Research Policy*, V, 1977.
29 See Dell, *Political Responsibility*, p. 24; H. Rose and S. Rose, *Science and Society*, Harmondsworth, 1969, p. 78.
30 See P. S. Johnson, *The Economics of Innovation*, Oxford, 1975. Johnson attributes the failure of the Hovercraft to attract early attention from the Ministries of Supply and Aviation to the dominance of conventional aircraft interests.
31 For a discussion of the nature of uncertainty in technological development see M. J. Peck and F. M. Scherer, *The Weapons Acquisition Process*, Cambridge, Mass., 1962, ch. 2.
32 HC 347 (1971–2), Q. 1060.
33 The Elstub Report, para. 205.
34 N. Abraham, *Big Business and Government; the New Disorder*, London, 1974, p. 8.
35 B. L. Smith, *The New Political Economy*, London, 1975, p. ix.
36 The other appellations are to be found respectively in M. Weidenbaum, *The Modern Public Sector*, BAsic Books, New York, 1969, and D. K. Price, *Government and Science*, New York, 1954.
37 HC 779 (1980–1), Appendix 3.
38 HCD 740, 1 Feb. 1967, col. 436.
39 E. L. Normanton, *The Accountability and Audit of Government*, Manchester, 1966, p. 330.
40 HC 265 (1980–1); HC 193 (1981–2); HC 389 (1981–2).
41 HC 265 (1980–1), Conclusions.
42 For example, Rolls now routinely cover forward all contracts vulnerable to exchange rate fluctuations.
43 HC 389 (1981–2), para. 26.
44 R. Williams, *Nuclear Power Decisions*, p. 330.
45 HC 389 (1981–2), para. 14.

Appendix I

THE BRABAZON TYPES

Type No.	Designation	Comments
1A	Bristol Brabazon	Long-range, piston-engined; first flight 4 Sept. 1949; cancelled 1952.
11A	Airspeed Ambassador	Short-range, piston-engined; first flight 10 July 1947; 20 built for BEA.
11B	Vickers Viscount	Short-range, turbo-prop; most successful post-war British airliner.
11B	Armstrong Whitworth Apollo	Short-range, turbo-prop; insurance for Viscount; only 2 aircraft built.
111A	Avro 693	Medium-range, turbo-prop/jet, cancelled 1947 in design stage.
111B	Avro Tudor II	Developed from interim type; unsuccessful.
IV	Comet 1	World's first jet airliner; fatal crashes 1953.
VA	Miles Marathon	Piston-engined feederliner; first flight 19 May 1947; small batch sold to RAF.
VB	De Haviland Dove	Charter/executive type, twin piston engines; first flight 25 Sept. 1945; 500 sold; evolved into equally successful Heron.

Source   P. Brooks, *The Modern Airliner*, New York, 1961.

Appendix II

THE 'INTERIM DESIGNS'

Type	Comments
Vickers Viking	Wellington derivative; 600 built.
Avro Tudor	Britain's first pressurised airliner.
Handley Page Hermes	Halifax derivative.
Bristol 170	Civil and military freight aircraft.

Note also, Britain's first post-war airliner was the Avro York, a conversion of the Lancaster bomber, first produced in limited numbers in 1943.

Source   P. Brooks, *The Modern Airliner*, New York, 1961.

Appendix III

CIVIL AIRCRAFT (1948–81)
REFERRED TO IN TEXT

Type		Comments
British		
British Aerospace (ex HSA)	146	Short-range jet feederliner; first flight 1981.
British Aerospace (ex HSA)	748	Short-range turbo prop; first flight 1960.
British Aerospace (ex BAC)	1-11 series	Short-range jet; launched 1961.
BAC	Superb	Larger super VC10 derivative; cancelled 1966.
BAC	2-11	Larger 1-11 derivative; cancelled 1967.
BAC	3-11	Short/medium-range wide-bodied jet; cancelled 1970.
Bristol Britannia		Long-range turbo-prop; launched 1947; first flight 1952; in service 1957.
De Haviland	Comet 4 series	Short/medium-range jet; first flight 1958.
HSA (ex De Haviland)	Trident series	Short/medium-range jet; first flight 1962.
Vickers	Vanguard	Short/medium-range turbo-prop; first flight 1956.
Vickers	V1000/VC7	Long-range jet; cancelled 1955.
Vickers	VC10/Super VC10	Long-range jets; first flights 1962/4.
French		
Sud Aviation	Caravelle	Short-range jet; first flight 1955.
Dassault	Mercure	Short-range jet; first flight 1972.
European Joint Programmes		
HSA, Sud Aviation DA Gmbh.	A300	Launched 1967; short/medium-range wide-bodied jet; superseded by A300B.
Airbus Industrie	A300B	Launched 1970; short/medium-range, wide-bodied jet.
Airbus Industrie	A310	Smaller A300B derivative.
Airbus Industrie	A320	Proposed narrow-bodied 150-seat jet.

Type		Comments
Aerospatiale (Sud Aviation) – British Aerospace (BAC)	Concorde	Long-range, supersonic airliner; first flight 1972.
VFW-Fokker	614	Short-range jet feederliner; production ceased 1977.
JET, 1, 2 & 3		Various design proposals considered from mid-1970s; superseded by Airbus derivatives.
USA		
Boeing 707 series		Long-range jet; first flight of prototype 1954; in service 1959.
Boeing 720		Short/medium-range jet; first flight 1959.
Boeing 727 series		Short/medium-range jet; first flight 1963.
Boeing 737 series		Short-range jet; launched 1965.
Boeing 747 series		Long-range wide-bodied; first flight 1969.
Boeing 757		Short/medium-range jet; development of 7N7 proposal; launched 1978.
Boeing 767		Medium-range, wide-bodied jet; development of 7X7 proposal; launched 1977.
Convair 880/990		Short/medium-range jets; first flights 1959/1961.
Douglas (later McDonnell-Douglas	DC8 series	Long-range jet; first flight 1958; in service 1959.
McDonnell-Douglas	DC10 series	Long-range, wide-bodied jet; first flight 1969.
McDonnell-Douglas	ATMR	Medium-range jet; design proposal, mid-1970s onward.
Lockheed	L1011 (Tristar)	Long-range, wide-bodied jet; first flight 1970.

Appendix IV

MAIN STRUCTURAL CHANGES IN THE BRITISH AIRCRAFT INDUSTRY, 1957–77

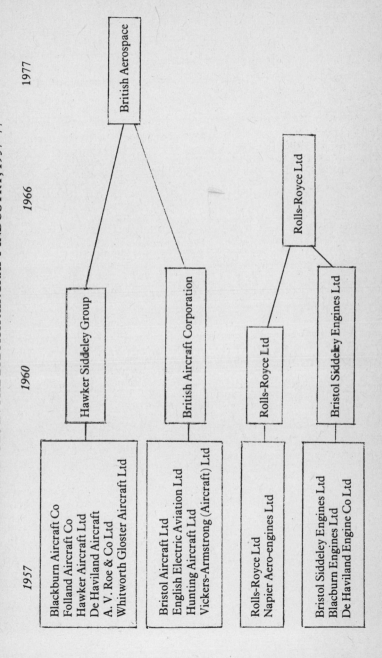

1957	1960	1966	1977

1977: British Aerospace

1960: Hawker Siddeley Group

1957:
Blackburn Aircraft Co
Folland Aircraft Co
Hawker Aircraft Ltd
De Haviland Aircraft
A. V. Roe & Co Ltd
Whitworth Gloster Aircraft Ltd

1966: British Aircraft Corporation

1957:
Bristol Aircraft Ltd
English Electric Aviation Ltd
Hunting Aircraft Ltd
Vickers-Armstrong (Aircraft) Ltd

1966: Rolls-Royce Ltd

1960: Rolls-Royce Ltd

1957:
Rolls-Royce Ltd
Napier Aero-engines Ltd

1960: Bristol Siddeley Engines Ltd

1957:
Bristol Siddeley Engines Ltd
Blacburn Engines Ltd
De Haviland Engine Co Ltd

Index

A200, 172
A300, *see* Airbus
A300B, *see* Airbus
A310, 166, 179, 182–4, 233,
A320, 223, 233, 234
Abraham, Norman, 226
accountability, 44, 106, 227, 232;
  Concorde and, 143, 146–50;
  nationalisation and, 193–4;
  Parliament and, 170–73, 230–31
*Action Programme for European
  Aerospace, see* Spinelli Report
Advanced Gas Cooled Reactor (AGR),
  148
Aerospatiale (*see also* Sud
  Aviation), 97, 161, 165, 168,
  172–3, 234
AFVG, 80, 84
Airbus, 119, 145, 150, 161, 163, 166,
  183, 196–7, 233; A300B, 93, 95–7,
  111–12; British Airways and, 167,
  179; BAC and, 79, 91, 110–11;
  BAC 2–11 and, 85–6; BAC 3–11
  and, 91–3, 95–7; 111–12; BEA
  and, 77, 84–86, 90, 92; Benn, Tony
  and, 93, 95; CF6 and, 95;
  collaboration and, 75, 85–6, 91,
  94–5, 111; costs of 83, 90–91, 93,
  167, 183; EEC and, 84, 91, 95, 111;
  French Government and, 78, 83–4,
  92–3, 97; German Government
  and, 73, 83, 93, 97; Hawker
  Siddeley and, 77–9, 81, 86, 91, 95,
  111, 166; Lufthansa and, 79, 84,
  92; Memorandum of
  Understanding and, 83–4, 93–4;
  origins of, 75, 77–8; RB207 and,
  83, 85, 90, 92–3; RB211 and, 90,
  92–3, 95, 112; Rolls Royce and,
79–81, 90, 92, 95–6, 112;
  Stonehouse, John and, 83, 85, 91,
  93, 94
Airbus Industrie, 161, 174, 181, 218,
  233; British Airways and, 167, 179,
  183–4; British Aerospace and, 146,
  173–4, 180–8; French Government
  and, 165–6, 172, 183; formation of,
  95; Hawker Siddeley and, 95–7,
  166–7, 196; structure of, 196–7
Aircraft and Shipbuilding Industries
  Act, 184, 196
Aircraft and Shipbuilding Industries
  Bill, *see* House of Commons
Airco, 30, 33, 38
Air France, 79, 84, 130
Air Holdings, 89
Air Transport, 13–14
Ambassador, 16
American Airlines, 185
Amery, Sir Julian, 59, 63–4, 66, 70,
  125; Concorde and, 63–4, 66, 125;
  VC10 and, 48, 49, 51, 52
Armstrong Siddeley, 36
*Aviation Week and Space Technology
  (AWST)*, 111
Avro, 16

BAC 1–11, 46, 76–7, 79, 85, 91, 122,
  178
BAC 2–11, 76, 85–6, 122
BAC 223, *see* Concorde
BAC 3–11, 91–2, 93, 95–7, 108,
  110–12, 122, 222
BAC X–11, 170, 172–3
Bank of England, 108–9
Barnett, Joel, 154
Beeching, Lord, 107, 115, 219
Benn, Tony, 71, 72, 93, 95, 131, 147,

191–2; RB211 and, 88, 89, 99, 101, 104, 107, 117, 120, 122
Benson, Sir Henry, 110, 112, 114
Berril, Sir Frank, 181
Beswick, Lord, 37, 161, 167, 176, 180, 183, 195
Board of Trade, 71, 85
Boeing, 21, 26, 39, 160; Aerospatiale and, 165; British Aerospace and, 167–8, 170, 174, 176–7; Rolls Royce and, 174, 179, 202–3, 234
Boeing 367–80, 21, 22
Boeing 707, 20, 21, 23–4, 25, 26, 27, 36, 51
Boeing 720, 26, 39
Boeing 727, 33, 34, 76, 239 n82
Boeing 737, 76, 177, 178–9, 182
Boeing 747, 75–6, 169
Boeing 757, 161, 174, 175, 176–7, 179, 234
Boeing 767, 160
Brabazon, 17
Brabazon, Lord, 13
Brabazon Committee, 13–14, 16
Brabazon Programme, 13, 15–16, 19
Breguet, 78
Bristol 200, 29, 33
Bristol Aircraft, 29, 38, 42
Bristol Siddeley, 41, 80–83, 128
Britannia, 19, 21, 23, 32
British Aerospace (BAe) 160, 170, 176, 180–81, 233–4; Airbus Industrie and, 166–7, 170, 174, 179, 183–5, 196–7, 223, 233–4; Boeing and, 167–8, 170, 172, 174, 176–8; formation of, 193–5
British Aircraft Corporation (BAC), 44, 76, 153, 156, 161–2, 170; Airbus and, 78–9, 85, 91–2; Concorde and, 61–2, 135–7, 140, 142–3; formation of, 41–2; Hawker Siddeley and, 82, 156; VC10 and, 48, 51, 52
British Airways (BA), 98, 131, 132, 167–9, 170, 178–9, 182
British European Airways (BEA), 15, 16, 21–2, 96, 98; Airbus and, 77–8, 84, 85–6, 90–92; 'buy British' and, 15, 31–2, 47; Trident, 29–30, 33–5, 86

British Leyland (BLMC), 70
British Overseas Airways Corporation (BOAC), 15, 16, 17, 19, 20, 22–3, 32, 46, 75–6; 'buy British' and, 15, 31, 47–53; Concorde and, 196; Empire specification of, 20, 23–5, 32–3; Ministry of Aviation and, 47–52; VC10 and, 24–5, 46–52, 75
'buy British' policy, 2, 15, 18–19, 24, 26–7, 31–3, 46–52, 98, 178, 227

Cabinet, British, 56–7, 63–4, 111, 114, 180, 227
Cadman Committee, 12
Callaghan, James, 173–4, 180, 181
Canadian Pacific (CP), 23
Canberra replacement, see TSR2
cancellations (defence projects), 9, 70–71
Caravelle, 21, 34, 60, 97
Carey, Sir Peter, 205
Carr, Lord, 164, 229
Carrington, Lord, 120
CASA, 156
CAST, 156
Central Policy Review Staff (CPRS), 129, 180
CF6, 95, 157
CFM6, 157, 168, 179
Chamont, Jean, 93
Chirac, Jacques, 165
civil aircraft design, 1, 12, 160
Civil Aviation Act, 18, 31, 42
Cole, Lord, 108–9, 113
collaboration (European) (*see also* Airbus, Airbus Industrie, Concorde), 10, 53, 58–9, 91; EEC and, 60–61, 63, 84, 163–4; Plowden Report and, 73–5, 84; Marshall Report and, 155–6; project control and, 196–7, 199–200, 221–2; Rolls Royce and, 83, 106, 117, 156–7, 185
collaboration (USA), 61, 160–63, 168–70
Comet, 15, 16–17, 19–22, 32, 54, 223,
Companies Act, 114
Comptroller and Auditor General, 135, 146, 231
Concorde, 3, 122, 153, 221, 222;

accountability and, 146–50; BAC and, 57, 62, 132, 135–6, 138–40, 142, 149; BAC 223, 62; BOAC and, 130; Bristol Siddeley and, 62, 80; British Airways and, 132; Committee of Directors, 65; Committee of Officials, 65, 134; Concorde Directing Committee, 138, 141; Concorde Division; 134–7; Concorde Executive Committee, 138; Concorde Management Board, 138; contracts and, 140–45; costs of, 55, 67, 125, 127–8, 131–3, 142, 145–7; Department of Trade and Industry and, 142, 146, 147, 188; design problems, 124–5, 128; environment and, 131; European collaboration and, 58–63, 66, 138, European Economic Community and, 60–61, 63, 67; Expenditure Committee and, 149, 230; Industry Committee and, 231; intramural costs, 65–6, 133; management procedures, 64–5, 134–45, 148; market for, 55, 130–31, 142; Ministry of Aviation and, 55–7, 62, 65, 125; Ministry of Technology and, 135–7, 139–41; monitoring, 135–7, 138–9, 150, 228; Olympus and, 62, 80, 128, PERT and, 136–7; Public Accounts Committee and, 143, 146, 230; Rolls Royce and, 62, 80, 139, 142, 149; RAE and, 54, 57, SNECMA and, 62; Sud Aviation (Aerospatiale) and, 62–3, 138–9; Supersonic Transport Aircraft Committee (STAC), 54–5; Technical Committee, 65; Treasury and, 54, 55, 56, 64; Treaty (Anglo-French), 64–6, 126–7, 129, 132–3, 148–9; USA and, 61–2, 130–31
Conservative Party, 2, 4–5, 16, 18, 107, 110, 153, 164, 195
Convair, 26, 39
Convair 880/990, 26, 39
Conway, 22, 81, 103
Cooper Bros, 110
Corbett, David, 50
Corbett Report, 49

Corfield, Sir Frederick, 109, 110, 112, 116–17, 118
Court of Inquiry, 16
Cronin, John, 49
Crossman, Richard, 91, 95

Dart, 103, 210
Dassault, 78, 161, 165, 167–8, 172
Davies, Handel, 163–4
Davis, Sir John, 109
DC-8, 21, 23, 24
DC-10, 102
defence contracts, 2, 21, 36–7, 103
Defence Review, 28, 35, 38
De Haviland, 15, 16, 20–21, 24, 29, 33, 39, 41
Dell, Edmond, 123, 179, 180, 218
Delta Airlines, 185
DH 188, 24
DH 121, *see* Trident
Department of Industry (DoI), 180; Airbus Industrie and, 166–7; Boeing and, 167, 205; British Aerospace and, 196; monitoring and, 196, 200, 204–6, 207–9; NEB and, 200–207; Rolls Royce and, 175, 200–208
Department of Trade, 180
Department of Trade and Industry (DTI), 187; Concorde and, 135–42, 146–7; launch aid, and, 190; HS146 and 190–92; Ministry of Defence (PE) and, 188, 190, 199–200; monitoring and, 191–2, 198–200; Rolls Royce and, 120–21, 197–200
d'Elanger, Sir Gerald, 24, 25, 31, 48, 50
Dornier, 156, 161
Douglas, 1, 26, 39
Douglas of Kirtleside, Lord, 29, 31, 47, 50
Dove, 16
Downey Committee, 103
Dowty, Sir George, 63

Eades, G, 217
Economist, 75
Edmonds, Martin, 80, 89
Edwards, Sir George, 27, 39, 57, 62,

86
Elstub Report, 94–5, 225
embodiment loan, 14
employment, 13, 40, 88, 175, 192, 212–13, 218
English Electric, 41, 42
environment, the, 130–31, 159
equipment industry, 95
Estimates Committee, *see* House of Commons
EURAC, *see* Group of Six
European Economic Community (EEC), 163–4, 220, 231–2; Airbus and, 84–5, 94–5, 97; Britain and, 70; Concorde and, 60–61, 63–4, 67, 125–6, 134; Rolls Royce and, 117
European Technological Community, 94
Europlane, 156
exchange rate, 203–5, 208–9
Expenditure Committee, *see* House of Commons
exports, 3, 13, 46, 154, 210–11
Export Credits Guarantee Department (ECGD), 169
externalities, 145, 210–12, 215, 220

Fairey, 30
Federal Aviation Authority (FAA), 61, 127
Fiat, 196
Fletcher, Sir Peter, 164, 165
Flight (later *Flight International*), 48, 85, 116, 118, 148, 232
Foreign Office, 63, 112, 118, 126, 180, 201
Fortune, 82, 89
France, Government of, 21, 74, 234; Airbus and, 78–9, 83–4, 86, 93–4, 179; Airbus Industrie and, 166–7, 173, 183; Concorde and, 61–3, 67, 125–6, 132; Rolls Royce and, 83, 119; USA and, 172
fuel crisis (1973), 159, 191, 223

Gardner, N. K. A., 216–17
General Electric (USA), 88, 95, 100, 157, 162, 169
General Electric Corporation (GEC), 111, 112

German Federal Republic, Government of, 78, 93, 179, 181, 183
General Elections (UK), 40, 51, 97, 107, 125, 192, 206
Giscard, Valéry d'Estang, 132, 173
Greenwood, Alan, 161, 164
'Group of Six', 161
'Group of Seven', 161
Guardian, 218
guided weapons, 28
Guthrie, Sir Giles, 51, 75

Hall, Sir Arnold, 6, 9, 55, 153, 190, 192
Hamilton, Sir James, 134, 154
Hanbury-Williams Committee, 16, 18
Handley Page, 40, 239/n7
Handley Page, Sir Frederick, 6
Harlow, Christopher, 34
harmonisation (of civil and military design), 35, 36
Hartley, Keith, 215–16
Hawker Siddeley (HSA), 29, 30, 156, 161–2; Airbus and, 77–8, 86, 91, 153; Airbus Industrie and, 95, 111, 166–7; BAC and, 82, 91, 111, 156; rationalisation and, 40, 41
Healey, Denis, 180
Heath, Edward, 109, 115, 128
Henderson, P. D, 58, 145, 219, 249/n69
Heseltine, Michael, 131, 156, 158
Hives, Lord, 28
Houghton, Dan, 101, 110, 114, 115, 116
House of Commons, 23, 42, 111, 146, 175, 179, 182, 230–31; Aircraft and Shipbuilding Industries Bill, 167, 171, 193–6; Estimates Committee, 28; Expenditure Committee, 9, 146, 147, 149, 154, 230; Industry Committee, 133, 231; Nationalised Industries Committee, 32, 48, 49, 230; Public Accounts Committee, 66, 141, 143, 146, 154, 176, 199, 205, 230
House of Lords, 164
HS146, 170, 194, 218; launch of, 157–8; monitoring of, 159–60,

191–3; relaunch of, 182;
  suspension of, 159–60, 191–3
Huckfield, Leslie, 179
Hudie, Sir David, 89, 90, 103, 105,
  107
Hunting, 30, 41
Hyfil, 88, 104, 107

incentive contracts, 140–43
Industrial Development Unit, 207
Industrial Reorganisation
  Corporation (IRC), 88, 104–7, 119,
  267
Industry Committee, *see* House of
  Commons
Industry Expansion Act, 142
inflation, 100, 159, 191, 192, 199, 204
International Civil Aviation
  Organisation (ICAO), 55
International Computers (ICL), 70
International Court of Justice (ICJ),
  126
'interim designs', 13, 15

Japan, 233–4
Jenkins, Roy, 70, 78, 125, 126
JET, 172–3, 180
jet engine, impact of, 1, 13, 19, 21, 22
Jewkes, J, 219
Jones, Aubrey, 29, 30, 31, 39, 40, 54,
  55, 60
Jones, Barry, 205
JT9D, 79, 81–2
JT10, 169, 174–5, 185
Jugoslavia, 110

Kaufman, Gerald, 170, 173
KC-135, 21, 36
Kiesinger, Kurt, 93
Kissinger, Henry, 115
Keith, Sir Kenneth, 157, 169, 175,
  198, 200, 201–2, 206
Knight, Sir Arthur, 175, 228
Knight, G. E, 139, 140, 144, 153
Knollys, Lord, 39
Korean War, 36

L1011, 87–8, 92, 118, 119–20, 169,
  234
Labour Party, 2, 4, 5, 12, 37, 51,

69–70, 117, 125, 150, 193
launch aid, 2, 17, 42–3, 75, 86, 121,
  197; BAC 3–11 and, 96–7, 111–12,
  122; BAe and, 196; Brabazon
  programme and, 13–14, 17;
  changes to, 15–16, 43, 121–2, 189;
  commercial assessment and, 43,
  44–5, 96, 101, 104, 121–2, 189;
  cost estimating and, 43, 86, 103;
  criticisms of, 44, 46, 121–3,
  215–19; HS146 and, 158, 190–92;
  expenditure on, 2–3, 46, 76, 80, 87,
  210–13, goals of, 6, 46, 153–5,
  192–3, 210–14, 220; levy on, 14,
  42–3, 44, 88, 146–7, 203;
  monitoring of, 13, 16, 44–5, 103,
  108, 113–14, 121–2, 189–200,
  227–9; Plowden and, 73–4, 123;
  rationalisation and, 41–3; RB211
  and, 47, 87, 89, 101–4, 121–3,
  198–9, 201–2; re-introduction of,
  38–46; risk discipline and, 42–5,
  101–2, 121, 123, 189, 196;
  technical assessment and, 43, 103,
  104, 121
Layton, Christopher, 111
Lighthall Committee, 77
Lloyds Bank, 109
lobbies, technological, 9, 53, 56, 64,
  224
Lockheed, 21, 91, 118, 153, 160, 267;
  financial problems of, 110, 120;
  L1011 and, 234; RB211 and, 89,
  95, 100–101, 104–5, 106, 108, 113,
  115; Rolls Royce and, 86–9, 95,
  100–101, 104–5, 106, 108, 113,
  115
Lockwood, Sir Joseph, 106, 108, 118
Lombard, Adrian, 81, 103
Lufthansa, 79, 84, 90, 92
Lycoming, 158, 182

M45H, 158, 199–200
McDonnell Douglas, 86, 160, 165, 180
MacFadzean, Sir Frank, 182, 204,
  206, 207
MacMillan, Sir Harold, 40, 55, 60
'magic circle', 4
market estimating, 13, 29, 34, 36, 41,
  43

Marking, Sir Henry, 168
Marshall Report, 155
Marshall, Sir Robert, 121, 147, 188
Maudling, Sir Reginald, 23
Medway, 33
Melville, Sir Richard, 124, 154
Memoranda of Understanding, 84
Mercure, 165
Messerschmitt–Bölkow–Blohm (MBB), 156, 161
Midland Bank, 109
Millar, R and Sawyer, D, 27, 33
Mills, Lord, 88–9
Millward, Sir Anthony, 33, 76, 86, 90–2
Ministry of Aircraft Production (MAP), 13, 14
Ministry of Aviation (MoA), 35, 82; Airbus and, 79; Air Corporations and, 47, 50–51; BOAC and, 47–8, 50; Concorde and, 56–7, 63–4, 125, 134, 140; dissolution of, 70–71; formation of, 40–41; launch aid and, 43, 45; Rolls Royce and, 80–81
Ministry of Civil Aviation, 15, 26, 29, 35, 40, 54
Ministry of Defence, 180, 188
Ministry of Defence (Procurement Executive) (MoD (PE)), 187, 201, 207; Concorde and, 135; HS146 and, 122, 196; M45II and, 199–200; monitoring and, 188, 196, 198–200; Rolls Royce and, 198–9
Ministry of Supply (MoS), 35–6, 38, 40–41; Brabazon Programme and, 13–18; Concorde and, 54, 56, 60–61; rationalisation and, 29–30; Trident and, 29–30, 33–5, 227; V1000 and, 22; VC10 and, 26
Ministry of Technology (Mintech), 85, 96; Concorde and, 134–7, 139, 141–2; formation of, 71–2; IRC and, 105–6, launch aid and, 99–101, 122; monitoring and, 101–2, 103–4, 108, 121–2, 136–9, RB211 and, 87, 103–4, 113–14; Rolls Royce and, 87, 88, 100–101, 108, 121–2, 139
Mitterand, General Jacques, 166, 167

monitoring, 5, 8, 14, 36, 43–5, 97, 145, 226, 288; Concorde and, 134–46, 150; HS146 and, 189–91; RB211 and, 103–4, 108, 114, 121–2, 198–9, 201–2, 205–6, 207, 208
Morgan, Sir Morian, 54, 56
Morrow, Ian, 88, 103, 107, 108, 114, 118, 121
MTU, 169
Mulley, Fred, 74, 76
Murphy, Sir Leslie, 175–6, 206, 254 n60

National Enterprise Board (NEB), 175, 200–204, 206–9, 254 n60
National Gas Turbine Establishment, 2
nationalisation, 4, 5, 161, 228, 229–30; airframe industry and, 82, 166, 167, 171, 193–5; Rolls Royce and, 115–17, 197–209
Nationalised Industries Committee, *see* House of Commons
National Loan Fund, 182
Nicholson, Rupert, 115, 116
Nimrod, 20
Nixon, Richard, 115
Normanton, E.L, 229
nuclear engineering, 217, 221

Olympus, 62, 128, 139, 141–2
Onslow, Sir Cranley, 189
OR339, *see* TSR-2

PanAm, 19, 21, 131, 169
Panavia, 157
Pearson, Sir Denning, 80, 81, 89–90, 101, 103, 106–8
PERT, 135–7
Pierre, Andrew, 10
Pratt and Whitney (P&W), 88, 100, 157, 162, 169–70, 174–5
Price, David, 155
Plowden Report, 3, 4, 70, 74–5, 82, 87, 94, 98, 123, 215
private capitalisation, limits of, 6–7, 72
private venture policy, 18–19, 23, 24, 26, 27–8, 30, 34–6, 39–40, 80, 168

private ventures 16, 18–19, 22, 27, 28, 38, 80
'privatisation', 4, 197, 228
profitability (of aircraft industry), 6–9, 36–8, 53, 72, 202–3
Public Accounts Committee, *see* House of Commons
public ownership, *see* nationalisation

R100/101 Airships, 4
rationalisation (of aircraft industry), 4, 28–30, 35, 37, 39–42, 73, 194
Rayner, Sir Dereck, 155, 187
Rayner Report, 187–8
RB141, *see* Medway
RB163, *see* Spey
RB178, 81
RB199, 154
RB207, 83, 84, 87, 88, 90, 92–3, 102
RB211, 3, 85–6, 91–3, 95, 100, 112–15, 118–19, 121–2, 150, 222; costs of, 104–5, cost escalation and, 102–3, 106, 107, 109, 141; DoI and, 202; DTI and, 198; MoD(PE) and, 198; Mintech and, 100, 103, 105, 108, 121–2
RB211–524, 156, 202–3
RB211–535, 168–9, 174–5, 182, 202, 218
Reed, Arthur, 4, 182
Rippon, Sir Geofrey, 61
RJ500, 233–4
Rogers, William, 147
Rolls Royce (*see also*, M45H, RB series, and RJ500), 38, 41, 62, 70, 77, 152–3, 222, 231, 233–4; Airbus and, 80–81, 90, 92, 94–6, 112; BAC 2–11 and, 87; BAC 3–11 and, 91, 110–12; bankruptcy of, 113–123; Boeing and, 202–5, 207–8; Boeing 747 and, 169; Boeing 757 and, 174–6, 185, BSE and, 81 –2; collaboration (European) and, 83, 117, 156–7, 185; Concorde and, 139, 141–2; exchange rate policy of, 203–5, 207–8; IRC and, 104–7; launch aid and, 80, 86–7, 99–101, 104–5, 107, 109, 120–3, 189; Lockheed and, 87–8, 92, 99–100, 102, 108, 113,

114, 115, 120, 234; management systems of, 101, 103, 106, 152, 197–9; nationalisation and, 116–17; NEB and, 200–202, 205–7, 254 n60; Plowden and, 82; Pratt and Whitney and, 157, 168, 169, 174–5, 233–4; profitability of, 104, 152, 202, 208; rescue package and, 107–10; UK Government and, 80, 82, 87–9, 91, 95–6, 107, 109–110, 227; US strategy of, 81, 86–8, 170, 179, 185
Romania, 110
Rothschild, Lord, 130
Royal Aircraft Establishment (RAE), 54, 57, 88, 140
Royal Air Force (RAF), 20, 22, 36, 51
'rush to jets', 21, 23–4
Russell, Sir Archibald, 62, 138
Ryder, Lord, 200, 201

safety standards, 20
Sandys, Duncan, 41–2, 48, 49, 56, 61
Schmidt, Helmut, 181–2, 183
Select Committees, *see* House of Commons
Short Bros, 158
Slattery, Sir Mathew, 25, 48, 49
Smallpiece, Sir Bazil, 48, 49
Smith, Bruce, 226
SNECMA, 62, 79, 81, 95, 128, 142, 156–7, 234
Society of British Aircraft (later Aerospace) Constructors (SBAC), 39, 71
Spey, 34, 80, 103
Spinelli Report, 163–4
spin-off, 8, 210
Stonehouse, John, 83, 85, 91, 93, 94, 102
Stainton, Ross, 178, 179
Stewart, Michael, 126
strategic reserve, 13, 28, 215
Strauss, George, 16
Sud Aviation (*see also* Aerospatiale), 62, 78, 83, 138, 139
Superb, 75–6, 77
Supersonic Transport (SST), 30, 40, 53
Supersonic Transport Aircraft

Committee, *see* Concorde
Super VC10, *see* VC10
Swinton, Lord, 19

'tailoring', 25, 32–4, 80
technological momentum, 9–10,
 221–2
Thatcher, Margaret, 207, 222
Thorpe, Jeremy, 117
trade unions, 126, 192
Transport Aircraft Requirements
 Committee (TARC), 35, 41, 43, 98,
 227
Trans-World Airlines (TWA), 116
Treasury, 19, 31, 155, 173, 218; BAe
 and, 180, 182, 195; Concorde and,
 54, 56–7, 67, 129, 135, 146; De
 Haviland and, 20; launch aid and,
 45; MoA and, 40–41, 71; Rolls
 Royce and, 169, 204, 205, 207;
 V1000 and, 22–3
Trident, 29–30, 33–5, 36, 38, 46, 78,
 86, 154
Tristar, *see* L1011
TSR-2, 28–29, 39, 41
Tudor, 16
turboprops, 20–23, 37, 223
Tyne, 103

Upper Clyde Shipbuilders, 119

United States of America; aircraft
 industry, 12, 13, 17, 21, 36, 58–9,
 73, 86–7, 108, 160–61, 164;
 Congress of, 120, 237 n14;
 Government of, 115, 120, 131, 217;
 SST, 130–31, 217

V1000, 22–4, 25, 27, 35–6
Vanguard, 21, 28, 38
Varley, Eric, 171, 180, 194
VC7, *see* V1000
VC10, 25–7, 32–3, 36, 39, 47–52, 72,
 75–6
VFW 614, 158
VFW-Fokker, 161, 183
Vickers, 15, 21, 22, 23, 24, 26, 28,
 38–9, 41, 46–7, 51
Viking, 15
Viscount, 15, 16, 19, 28, 210

Wass, Sir Douglas, 219
Watkinson, Sir Harold, 23, 25, 29
Way, Sir Richard, 125
Weinstock, Sir Arnold, 112
Williams, Roger, 146, 221, 223
Wilson, Sir Harold, 84, 93, 94, 118,
 132

Ziegler, Henri, 93, 156
Zysman, D, 223